MIGRATION AND THE MAKING Oⅎ

Migration and the Making of Ireland

BRYAN FANNING

UNIVERSITY COLLEGE DUBLIN PRESS

PREAS CHOLÁISTE OLLSCOILE
BHAILE ÁTHA CLIATH

First published 2018
by University College Dublin Press
UCD Humanities Institute
Belfield
Dublin 4
Ireland

www.ucdpress.ie

ISBN 978-1-910820-25-4 pb

Cataloguing in Publication data available from the British Library

Typeset in Scotland in Plantin and Fournier by Ryan Shiels
Text design by Lyn Davies
Printed and bound by CPI Group (UK) Ltd, Croydon, CR0 4YY

Contents

Acknowledgements

This book follows a number of monographs on racism in Irish society, on Irish responses to immigration and on the integration of migrants. My own contributions to this literature include *Racism and Social Change in the Republic of Ireland* (2002*)*, *New Guests of the Irish Nation* (2009) and *Immigration and Social Cohesion in the Republic of Ireland* (2011). Such books focused more on analysing responses by the state and mainstream society to immigration, than on documenting how immigrants have fared. Much of the focus of *Migration and the Making of Ireland* is about the experiences of those who have settled in Ireland.

I am grateful to many groups and organisations including the Irish Refugee Council, the Africa Centre, the Immigrant Council of Ireland, Holocaust Education Trust Ireland and Forum Polonia. The research I undertook over the years includes many interviews with migrants who remained anonymous in the policy reports and academic publications that followed, in keeping with standard ethics protocols in the social sciences. I owe a huge debt to many people who gave me their time and told me about their lives. Many people helped, educated, advised or assisted me whilst I was writing this book. In particular, I wish to thank Rosemary Adaser, Shaykh Dr Umar Al Quadri, Dr Gerry Boucher, Bruce Bradley SJ, Conrad Bryan, Teresa Buczkowska, Dr James Carr, Declan Downey, Dr Denis Dillon, Mary Dillon, Maurice Earl, Professor Tony Fahey, Mary Fanning, Professor Tom Garvin, Piotr Gawlik, Elizabeth Hassell, Lynn Jackson, Dr Ebun Joseph, Reverend John McNeill Scott, Dr Lucy Michael, Dr Fidèle Mutwarasibo, Professor Willie Nolan, Dr Neil O'Boyle, Professor Philip O'Connell, Professor Tadhg O'Keefe, Jim O'Brien and John O'Dowd. Many of the case studies in this book are about families. This book is dedicated in gratitude to my immediate one – to Joan, Caitriona, Eilis and Ellie.

BRYAN FANNING
University College Dublin
January 2018

ONE

INTRODUCTION

Conversations about immigration in Ireland tend to turn to the experiences of Irish emigrants and of the communities these left behind. Emigration, in the Irish imagination, is associated with the Great Famine and the subsequent hollowing out of rural society due to the exit of millions of people in the decades that followed. Emigration drove down the population of post-independence Ireland and there have been resurgences of emigration during the 1980s and during the last decade. It has been recorded in folk culture and ballads as a great trauma, and has been addressed by playwrights, painters and historians. A considerable body of academic scholarship and literature has sought to grapple with these cultural legacies. By comparison, the lives and travails of recent and past immigrants have yet to become part of the mainstream Irish story.

The number of migrants who have settled in Ireland is small compared to the several million who emigrated during the same period. Yet emigration has also shaped Ireland, mostly through the impact of incomers and their descendants upon Irish society, Ireland's economy and Irish culture. Emigration has affected Ireland mostly through processes of subtraction, with some additions in the form of monetary, cultural and political remittances. The map sketched out in *Migration and the Making of Ireland* places a particular small island at the centre of the world. It explores commonalities and differences between the experiences of incoming and outgoing migrants with a strong emphasis on the recent waves of immigration that are re-shaping twenty-first-century Ireland.

Migration and the Making of Ireland is not the first book of its kind. It follows a decade on from Patrick Fitzgerald and Brian Lambkin's *Migration in Irish History 1607–2007*, which appeared a few years into the period of large-scale immigration considered at length in this book.[1] Fitzgerald and Lambkin's book was mostly focused on the Irish diaspora and on earlier periods of colonial settlement, and was more preoccupied with theories of migration and diaspora, whereas this volume foregrounds the experiences of migrants to Ireland. The literature on Ireland's new immigrant communities is an emerging one: chapters on Poles, Africans and Muslims in this book would have been impossible to write even a few years ago. The research on which these are based is mostly very recent. What both books do share, notwithstanding different methods and approaches, is the same chronological starting place. Following the Flight of Ulster's Gaelic Earls, the seventeenth century witnessed colonial settlement and immigration on an unprecedented scale as well as large-scale emigration. By 1600, migration to and from Ireland was hardly novel, but what was new, as Enda Delaney states, 'were the scale, context and consequences of population movements.'[2]

The perspectives on migration that have intrigued me the most are those of migrants themselves. Most immigrants and emigrants who left or came to Ireland journeyed to improve their circumstances. They often migrated under circumstances that were not of their choosing. However, they generally made the best use they could have of the resources at their disposal. Often these came from family members who had already come to or left Ireland. Processes of chain migration have been common through history whereby migrants remitted resources to their kin that either supported communities at home or helped family members to follow in their wake. Women, like men, emigrated to find better life opportunities and to support their families in Ireland or elsewhere but also to find freedoms denied them at home.[3]

The challenge has been to find similar ways of addressing the experiences of emigrants and immigrants across space and time for all that different political, economic, cultural and religious contexts need to be understood. The basic similarities between what has motivated many migrant journeys make it possible to fruitfully examine both immigration and emigration in the same breath. The kinds of wider circumstances that push and pull migrants from one place to another also recur again and again. Emigration push factors have often much to do with social, economic and political processes that, in effect, squeeze people out. Immigration pull factors include the draw of freedoms and economic opportunities that exceed those in places of origin. The ebb and flow of human beings across the planet occurs within wider economic, legal and political systems that influence migration choices at an individual or family level. For example, economic factors have included systems of indenture that made migration affordable to poorer individuals and schemes of assisted migration operated by governments and private companies. The transportation of migrants has been at times big business for merchants, traffickers and middlemen.

Migration and the Making of Ireland draws on accounts of migrant journeys by historians and sociologists and from memoirs and newspapers mostly since the beginning of the seventeenth century, although the next chapter gives an overview of migration to Ireland during earlier periods. It considers the political, economic and legal circumstances that made immigration and emigration possible or necessary, and provides illustrative examples of the experiences of migrants and their families, while highlighting the differences between the migration experiences of women and men. It draws on biographies, letters, newspaper accounts, recent social research, case studies produced by organisations advocating on behalf of migrants, interviews and the work of historians and social scientists.

At an early stage in the writing of this book I had an exchange with an irate academic friend abou the proper use of terminology. I used the term 'migrant' in Chapter 3 (Plantations) to refer to settlers from Scotland who were part of the early-seventeenth-century plantation of Ulster. 'If the notion of migration is to have any meaning,' he replied, 'it cannot cover just any old movement of people or animals, that's what the word "movement" is for, with all its ambiguities and indeterminacies. And that means there has to be a point where the concept just doesn't apply, as with the Plantation (colonisation), the Vikings (colonisation) and St Patrick (slavery).' Yet the Plantation of Ulster included waves of settlement by ordinary labourers, artisans and by people whose descendants migrated onwards to North American as indentured servants. Some of those who settled in or were planted in Ireland had migrated in order to flee persecution elsewhere.

Many of the Catholic Irish who emigrated were no less part of colonisation projects than those who came to Ulster from Scotland and England. Emigration from Ireland mostly occurred to places that were or had been part of the British Empire. Some Irish migrants who arrived in the Caribbean as indentured servants and some of their descendants became slave-owners. Throughout the British Empire, Irish emigrants became part of colonial systems as soldiers, policemen, administrators and as missionaries.

Not one of the terms generally used to distinguish between migrants – immigrant, emigrant, economic migrant, forced migrant, indentured servant, undocumented person, guest worker, refugee, asylum seeker – is adequate to describe the complexities of specific cases, but the choice of terms tells us a lot about how migrants have been treated or legally defined in specific situations. For example, the legal systems of nation states have come to distinguish between citizens and non-citizens, between guest workers requiring visas and labour migrants from countries where reciprocal agreements permit the free movement of people. Within the administrative logic of such systems human beings become defined by the categories in which they have been placed. Gradations of rights between citizens and non-citizens, immigrant 'guest' workers, undocumented workers, refugees and asylum seekers have emerged in a number of western countries that as recently as a century ago operated few restrictions on immigration.[4]

As well as setting out a broadly chronological account of migration to and from Ireland, the structure of the book is designed to explore and tease out a number of different kinds of category used to classify human migrants in the Irish context. Some chapters explore the experiences of particular groups or categories of immigrants. Others present overviews of larger waves of immigration and emigration whilst providing examples of the experiences of various kinds of migrant journeys. These include two chapters on the seventeenth century. Chapter 3 is mostly focused on English and Scottish migration to Ireland in the wake of the Plantation of Ulster. Chapter 4 examines a complex system of migration to and from Ireland within which there were military migrations in both directions. Catholic Irish exiles served in Spain, Flanders and elsewhere whilst Cromwellian soldiers and later Huguenots who served William of Orange were settled in Ireland. The same conflicts also resulted in the transportation of Catholics to the West Indies, and the movement of Catholic clergy to the Continent. Seventeenth-century conflicts in Ireland had European as well as Atlantic dimensions, and both emigration from Ireland and waves of colonial settlement need to be understood in these wider contexts.[5]

Consideration of emigration from Ireland is divided into chapters that address the experiences of those who left before independence (Chapter 6) and after independence (Chapter 8). It was not until around 1820 that Catholics comprised the majority of migrants from Ireland to North America. Many Protestant emigrants were what came to be called Ulster Scots in Ireland, or Scots Irish in the United States.[6] After the 1820s, lower shipping costs made it easier for Ireland's mostly poorer Catholic majority to cross the Atlantic. Before independence, some emigration was a form of internal migration within the then-United Kingdom of Great Britain and Ireland. After independence, the twenty-six-county Irish state could, in theory, have discouraged emigration or done more to provide alternatives to emigration.

Two chapters examine in detail the experiences over several generations of small immigrant communities in Ireland, and the challenges they faced in maintaining their distinct cultural and religious identities. Chapter 5 examines the experiences of Palatines as German-speaking-refugees-turned-colonial-settlers, and of their descendants who remained in Ireland or immigrated to North America. Chapter 7 examines the experiences of Litvaks, Jews and earlier Jewish migrants to Ireland who settled there in small numbers and had to contend with distinct forms of discrimination. Anti-Semitic immigration laws barred Jews from settling in Britain and Ireland for centuries until these were repealed by Oliver Cromwell. Nineteenth-century Jewish settlers and their descendants had to negotiate anti-Semitism. Yet, Ireland's Jewish communities made a considerable contribution to the political, economic and literary life of Irish society. Their memoirs and family histories are drawn on here.

Chapters addressing the period since the partition of Ireland a century ago have focused on the experiences of migrants on both sides of the border. In some cases there has been much less research on migrant communities in Northern Ireland than in the Republic, sometimes reflecting the smaller size of these communities. Chapter 9 examines the experiences of refugees who arrived in Ireland from several different countries during the twentieth century. These included Jews, Hungarians, Vietnamese and Bosnians. Chapter 10 addresses those of black African immigrants from a number of sub-Saharan countries (but mostly from Nigeria) who were united in their experiences of racism and marginalisation. Many of these arrived as asylum seekers, an administrative category which denied some of the rights granted to those given refugee status by the Irish state, including the right to work. For all that the Irish often remember past waves of emigration as a trauma many of those who left Ireland did so without having to overcome the kinds of barriers and restrictions encountered by some recent migrants who have made Ireland their home.

Chapter 11 compares and contrasts the experiences of immigrants from both European Union member states and non-EU countries who do not have an automatic right to live and work in Ireland. What comes to the fore is how different levels of rights and entitlements affect the experiences of immigrants. The chapter touches on the experiences of people from a number of different countries who have settled in the Republic and in Northern Ireland in significant numbers including Filipinos, Chinese, Lithuanians and Latvians. Chapter 12 examines the specific experiences of recent immigrants from Poland who after 2004, when the European Union was enlarged, became the largest immigrant community in both the Republic and in Northern Ireland. More people in the Republic now speak Polish on a daily basis than speak Gaelic. Chapter 13 is focused on the experiences of Muslim immigrants again on both sides of the border. Whilst Ireland has had a small, predominantly Sunni, Muslim community for decades (mostly comprised of students and medical professionals) this has grown rapidly in recent years making Islam the Republic of Ireland's fastest growing religion. Muslim immigrants have come from several different countries and regions including from North Africa, the Middle East, Sub-Saharan Africa and Pakistan, and Britain. The chapter explores some of the complexity of Islam in Ireland at a time in the West when Islamophobia is rife and Muslims tend to be viewed with suspicion.

A conclusion chapter addresses some key recurring themes: how governments came to regulate migration; the impact of immigration controls on the lives of migrants to and from Ireland; and the influence of economic pressures on decisions to migrate in both directions. It also considers the ways in which migrants to and from Ireland variously came to adapt, assimilate and integrate.

Migration and the Making of Ireland was written at a time when immigration has become a major political issue in many countries. Much of the academic literature about this and most political debates appear to be focused on the perspectives and attitudes of host communities rather than, as here, on the lives and experiences of immigrants. In addition, integration debates as these have played out in a number of European countries have been mostly ones about national identity and about the anxieties of host communities. Whilst these are important issues, responses to immigration that do not also focus on how migrants are faring are at best abstract. One of the key aims of this book is to help make Irish debates about immigration more tangible and more focused on the experiences of immigrants perspectives.

TWO

INVASIONS

Annals dating back to the seventh century posited one of two commonplace Irish theories of migration. This was the presumption that Ireland had experienced several waves of immigration over thousands of years. The centuries-old annals of monks that were compiled into the twelfth-century *Leabhar Gabhála Éireann* (trans. *Book of Invasions*) dated the first settlement of Ireland to some 2,242 years after the creation of the world, as calculated by biblical scholars.[1] Irish myths were shoe-horned into a creationist chronology derived from the Old Testament by clerics who calculated that the world was created several thousand years earlier. These were cited in other early histories transcribed by monks elsewhere, such as the *Historica Brittonum*, which was composed around 830 AD.[2] Myths about Ireland's early inhabitants from the *Book of Invasions* were taken at face value in popular histories of Ireland until the early twentieth century. The second commonplace theory – illustrated by post-fourteenth-century claims that the descendants of Anglo-Norman settlers had become 'more Irish than the Irish themselves' – posited that there were ongoing processes of cultural assimilation through which even invaders were absorbed over time.

The myths which posited the prehistoric making and re-making of Ireland through immigration have been challenged by evidence collected by archaeologists, geneticists and linguistic scholars. Archaeological evidence suggests that a succession of hunter-gatherers settled Ireland when it was still connected by a land bridge to Britain. An ice age curbed populations of flora and fauna until around 10,000 years ago. As the glaciers smothering Ireland and Northern Europe retreated, plants and animals from the warmer climes of Southern Europe made inroads. The first wave of humans seems to have reached Britain 270,000 years ago, during the Pleistocene, or 'First Stone Age' long before this ice age. Around 15,000 years ago, when ice was in retreat, humans returned to Britain.[3] It is likely that people reached Ireland during this period.

A bear bone found in a cave in County Clare, showing signs of cuts made by stone tools, has been dated as around 12,500 years old. The earliest evidence of a human settlement in Ireland is around 8,000 years old, from the Mesolithic or 'Middle Stone Age'.[4] A Mesolithic encampment on Mount Sandel in County Derry was excavated during the 1970s, where the remains of circular huts about six metres across were found along with evidence of hunting, fishing and a diet that may have included apples and hazelnuts. Evidence of similar communities has been found in Scotland and on the Scottish isles suggesting that people crossed over, perhaps, to Antrim. A curious hunter-gatherer looking across the sea at the Mull of Kintyre would have been able to see the Antrim coast on a clear day. Flint, the primary raw material for tools at the time, was abundant in east Antrim whereas it was much harder to find in Scotland.

Early migrants who reached Ireland may also have come from the Isle of Man or Wales, or even from France, where evidence of similar kinds of tools has been found. Definitive proof of where the first settlements were located has, most likely, been washed away by rising sea levels.[5] For 4,000 years the inhabitants of Ireland were hunter-gatherers, and these probably only ever numbered a few thousand. There may have been a second wave of hunter-gatherer settlements 1,000-1,500 years after the first.[6] Another theory is that the Isle of Man experienced an environmental disaster such as extreme land-loss due to rising sea levels, which, like the nineteenth-century Irish Famine, provided the impetus for emigration.[7]

Neolithic peoples developed agriculture around 8000 BC in what is now Syria, Eastern Turkey and Kurdistan. Their techniques seem to have reached Ireland sometime between 5000 and 4000 BC. How this came to pass and where the first farmers in Ireland came from is not clear. Nor is it clear how many Neolithic migrants in total arrived. The techniques that distinguished these newcomers from the resident hunter-gatherers may have been copied or adopted from a small number of actual new arrivals. Maybe (possibly, perhaps) a small number of farmer migrants had many descendants compared to the hunter gatherers who thinly populated continental Europe, Britain and Ireland before the onset of farming. Or it could have been that the farmers who spread westwards century after century were like the European settlers who spread west in North America albeit at a much slower pace. To what extent these colonisers obliterated Mesolithic hunter-gathers as they moved across Europe and into Britain and Ireland or to what extent the descendants of hunter-gathers became farmers is simply not known.

The introduction of farming raised the population of the island considerably. By around 3800 BC, farming had replaced hunter-gathering as the main way of life. Neolithic farmers and perhaps the descendants of Mesolithic people herded livestock, grew wheat and barley and built houses in isolated farmsteads, creating a pattern of land use that persisted in Ireland for millennia. Many artefacts of the Neolithic era, such as flint tools, ceramic pots and megalithic tombs, appear to be nearly identical in both Ireland and Britain, which suggests either a common origin or ongoing contact between the Stone Age farming societies on both islands. Archaeological finds also suggest that Neolithic people and techniques arrived in Ireland from southern Brittany and that there must have been some degree of ocean trading between both places. However, contacts with and connections to Britain seem to have been much stronger.[8]

Traces of Neolithic societies found in Ireland include passage tombs, stone tools, arrowheads, evidence that forests were cleared for agriculture and, at Ballynagilly in County Tyrone, sophisticated farmhouses made of split oak planks. It seems that many of Ireland's Stone Age farmers lived in dwellings that were more sophisticated than those inhabited by much of the island's population during the eighteenth and early nineteenth centuries.[9] Some time before 3000 BC large mounds containing tombs were constructed in the Boyne Valley. Evidence of increasingly sophisticated agriculture can be dated from around 2,500 BC around when the use of bronze tools arrived in Ireland. It has been estimated that Ireland's population by then was somewhere between 50,000 and 100,000.[10] Peter Woodman, the archaeologist who discovered the oldest settlement found to date at Mount Sandel, has argued that Ireland's genetic heritage was most probably fixed by the end of the Stone Age, by which time Ireland had been inhabited for thousands of years:

> The gene pool of the Irish was probably set by the end of the Stone Age when there were very substantial numbers of people present and the landscape had already been frequently altered. The Irish are essentially Pre-Indo-European, they are not physically Celtic. No invasion since could have been sufficiently large to alter that fact completely. Celtic speakers, Vikings and Normans may have made small alterations but it was not until the Plantation period that this gene pool was to be added to significantly.[11]

Woodman wrote this in his contribution to *The People of Ireland*, a book that accompanied a 1988 BBC Northern Ireland television series, and one of a long line of books of invasions to which *Migration and the Making of Ireland* also belongs. More recent surveys of Ireland's genetic profile have not found any significant evidence of large-scale immigration after the Neolithic period, but also conclude that an absence of genetic evidence is not a sound basis for believing that there have been no significant migrant incursions since then.[12]

The evidence of ongoing cultural diffusion – the spread of religions, languages and technologies – is compelling but precisely how and when this occurred before the advent of recorded history is unclear. Efforts to explain successive shifts in how people lived in Ireland – from hunter-gathering to farming, from using stone tools, to working with bronze and iron – tend to emphasize immigration or trade or a mixture of both. There is evidence of trade in copper, tin, gold and in finished goods made from these during the late Bronze age circa 1200–1000BC. Compared to other areas in Europe, a large number of Bronze Age swords have been unearthed in Ireland.[13] Such finds, alongside the remains of hill forts, suggest that Ireland was dominated by a warrior elite but it does not prove that these warriors were descended from a particular wave of Bronze Age invaders.

Cultural diffusion is not of itself evidence of large-scale migration and it is often difficult to glean the causes of cultural changes from artefacts. However, it is possible to identify cultural similarities between similar artefacts found in different places. Similar metal-working techniques were used in both Britain and Ireland during the early Iron Age, which suggest a degree of population movement between the two islands. The evidence for this includes finds of jewellery, horse bridles and other kinds of metalwork, with similar Celtic ornamentation on excavations from both La Tène in Switzerland, where a major trove was unearthed, Britain and Ireland. By the third century BC, the elite in Ireland began, as the archaeologist J. P. Mallory put it, 'to kit themselves out in La Tène equipment.'[14] La Tène finds in Ireland include gold torcs, armlets, brooches, rings, tankards and sword hilts, some of which appear to have been imported into Ireland during the first century AD.

The Celts were Ireland's first identifiable ethnic group, that is, identifiable by traces of a specific language rather than merely by artefacts and biological remains. One of the puzzles is that neither archaeologists nor geneticists have found evidence of significant movements of people or any other major cultural intrusions during the period when Celtic influences must have reached Ireland.[15] However, linguistic scholars suggest that a Celtic language came to Ireland sometime during the late Bronze Age or early during the Iron Age. At that time Indo-European Celtic societies inhabited much of Europe and although Celtic languages have since died out in most places these have survived in Cornwall, Brittany, the Isle of Man, Wales, Scotland and in Ireland. The Celts, which means something like 'stranger' (*keltoi*) in classical Greek, came to be known as 'Gaels.' Related terms include Gaul (an old name for France), Gallic (French), Galicia (an area in Northern Spain) and *Gaeilge* (the Irish language); those labelled 'Celts' by scholars in recent times were a conglomeration of peoples who spoke several related languages.[16] It has been argued that Celtic people moved into Ireland in two waves: from western France or northern Spain into the western seaboard, and another from Britain, which was settled earlier by Celtic tribes.[17] Celts remained the dominant group in Ireland for centuries after they were superseded by the Romans in Gaul, and by the Romans and Germanic peoples in Britain. As a result, Ireland experienced a long period of cultural continuity stretching perhaps from several hundred years BC to the arrival of Christianity in the fifth century AD, by which time the Roman influence in Britain was in decline.[18]

In 431 AD (the first authentically recorded date in Irish history) Pope Celestine I sent Palladius as a missionary to Ireland. Palladius was over-shadowed by Patrick, a Briton, who possibly arrived the following year. Patrick was the son of a minor Roman official who seems to have lived near present-day Carlisle on the Anglo–Scottish border, where he was captured by Irish raiders and sold as a slave. After six years, Patrick managed to make his way back to Britain, returning to Ireland some years later as a missionary. Ships plied trade routes between both islands bearing thousands of slaves, according to Patrick's writings, and missionaries to Ireland.[19]

Ideas, customs and religious practices flowed from Britain to Ireland and then, subsequently from Ireland to Britain. Pre-Christian Ireland had colonies on the Western shores of Britannica, on the Isle of Man and in what is now Wales that lasted for a time after Christianity took root in Ireland.[20] Migrants from Ireland to Britain and Europe in subsequent centuries included Christian missionaries who founded monasteries from the sixth century onwards in several different countries. Migrants moved between a network of monasteries spread across Ireland, the Hebrides, mainland Scotland, England and continental Europe at a time when these were often the closest equivalent to metropolitan centres. Some of this traffic to continental Europe from the eighth century included monks seeking refuge from Norse raiders.[21]

The central puzzle of early Scandinavia is why, after an age of passive isolation, Norse communities 'suddenly exploded' during the eight century, sending wave after wave of fleets, warriors, and colonists into every corner of Northern Europe including Ireland. Theories about why these did so variously refer to 'a serious ecological imbalance between demographic levels and available resources' at the end of a mild climate period that may have encouraged unsustainable growth in population density.[22] Most Norse had lived in coastal farming communities where short summers demanded a period of intense labour. During the spring and autumn, when the fjords were free from ice, fishing and raiding expeditions seem to have been part of the annual cycle and constituted a form of seasonal migration. Over time, this turned into large-scale emigration. Advanced shipbuilding techniques put the islands to the south, including Ireland, in range.

The Northmen who reached Ireland came mostly from what is now Norway. Like the pre-Christian Irish, they took, ransomed and sold slaves. Raids from the end of the eighth century were followed by the establishment of a number of coastal bases by the 830s that connected these with Viking settlements elsewhere, and provided staging posts for raids inland using rivers. Settlements developed where the main rivers reached the coast, most notably Hlymrekr (Limerick), Ventrafjorth (Waterford), Veigsfjorth (Wexford) and at Vikingalo (Wicklow).[23] These traded with and had political links to settlements in Scandinavia, Britain and what came to be known as Normandy in western France. The Vikings dominated some towns – never large swathes of territory as they did in England – and appear never to have constituted more than a small proportion of the population. Research by geneticists suggests that these Norse colonial settlements were largely composed of indigenous Irish and that the actual numbers of immigrant settlers living in these could have been quite low.[24]

Vikings based in Irish settlements took part in raids in France which led to the ceding of Normandy to Norsemen. For example, Nantes was raided in 843 AD by a fleet of 67 Viking ships that most likely came from an Irish *longphort* ('ship port'). The attackers drew on their experience of raiding in Ireland where they had learned that Church festivals were the most profitable time to attack and gather spoils from churches and slaves.[25] Vikings returned from Brittany to Ireland around 914 AD. After seizing control of both Waterford and Dublin, they crossed over to England, where a few years later (in 919 AD) they conquered York.[26] Vikings had vested interests, formed alliances and took opposite sides in conflicts in Ireland, Britain and Normandy. For example, soldiers from Normandy fought beside the Dublin king Sitric Silkbeard at the Battle of Clontarf in 1014 some 52 years before the Norman invasion of England and some 163 years before the Anglo-Normans formally arrived in Ireland in 1177.[27]

A slave market was established in Viking Dublin where until the eleventh century Irish kings also sold captives who were shipped abroad. It was only when Dublin came under Norman control that slave trading was made illegal.[28] Raids inland for slaves and booty overlapped with commerce. Dublin, Waterford and Limerick each had distinct trading hinterlands but also an economic rivalry in competing for opportunities to trade with prosperous areas of Munster and Leinster, which also resulted in warfare between all three. For example, in 927 AD, Viking Waterford defeated Viking Limerick in battle. Ten years later, Viking Dublin captured the ruler of Limerick and broke up his fleet. In 953 AD, Dublin Vikings attacked Waterford harbour. In the 990s Vikings from Waterford briefly ruled Dublin. Viking settlements feuded with one another, traded with their hinterlands and continued to raid inland.[29] Unsurprisingly, the clergy whose annals comprised the first drafts of Irish history had little positive to say about the Vikings. Yet, during the ninth and tenth centuries, raids on Irish monasteries for plunder and hostages by indigenous Christian raiders far exceeded those attributed to Vikings. Monasteries even went to war with one another; in 807 AD a battle between monasteries in Cork and Clonfert and 817 AD another between monasteries in Taghamon and Ferns in Wexford each resulted in the deaths of several hundred.[30] Excavations of Viking settlements in Dublin revealed drainage systems, house structures, boat-building and much evidence of trading. Irish goods found by archaeologists in Norway seem to be more often the products of trade than plunder.[31]

After generations of raids, Normandy was settled by some 5,000 Norsemen who were allocated lands, took Frankish wives and were baptised as Christians. These became the ruling class of a feudal system.[32] The Normans who invaded England were descended from Scandinavians, and the Anglo-Normans who invaded Ireland a century later belonged to the same castle-building feudal social order that had supplanted Britain's Anglo-Saxon ruling class.[33] In 1165 Diarmait Mac Murchuadha, king of Leinster, sailed to Bristol and travelled to the court of Henry II in Aquitaine to obtain military assistance against other Irish kings. Henry allowed Diarmait to recruit mercenaries from within his kingdom. Dairmait came to an arrangement with Richard Fitzgilbert, Earl of Pembroke, who was known as Strongbow, which included the hand of his daughter in marriage and the promise of lands for Strongbow and his allies. In May 1169 the first few hundred Anglo-Normans landed in Wexford, followed by the arrival of Strongbow at the head of a larger force a year later. Wexford, Waterford and Dublin were captured by August 1170. Strongbow married Aoife and her father died soon after in May 1171. Henry became alarmed that one of his earls had carved out what was potentially a rival kingdom. He and landed in Waterford in October 1171 with a large expeditionary force and remained in Ireland for six months, during which time many of the native Irish kings pledged homage to him.

The Anglo-Normans were not the only newcomers to Ireland during the twelfth century. More than 30 years before the first of these arrived the bishop of Down had encouraged Cistercian monks from France to establish abbeys in Ireland and help reform the Church in Ireland. In 1140 Malachy visited Clairvaux and left a few of his clergy to be trained as Cistercians. These with some French monks established the first Cistercian abbey at Mellifont in County Louth in 1142. By 1169 when the Anglo-Normans formally arrived there were fourteen Cistercian foundations in Ireland. The Anglo-Normans established a further ten Cistercian monasteries in the 50 years after 1169, including Tintern de Voto in Wexford around 1,200 AD. The monastery was established by monks from Tintern Abbey in Wales, and endowed lands in the Wexford barony of Bargy.[34]

Decades before the arrival of the Anglo-Normans, the Church in Ireland had already come within England's orbit as far a Rome was concerned. In 1155 Pope Adrian II, following a petition from his countryman, the Archbishop of Canterbury, granted Ireland to Henry II.[35] The influence of Canterbury was felt in Dublin when, in 1174, Archbishop Lanfranc was asked by clergy there to consecrate their bishop-elect. No Dublin diocese was recognised by the Irish episcopate at the time, nor were other Norse towns represented within its Episcopal structures. Bishops appointed in Waterford and Limerick were also consecrated by Archbishops of Canterbury. The Norse-Irish bishops swore canonical submission to Canterbury and acknowledged Canterbury's primacy over Ireland.[36]

Anglo-Norman secular connections to Ireland also preceded Diarmait's approach to Henry for permission to recruit mercenaries. Some introduction of feudal patterns of land-holding in some Irish kingdoms also preceded the arrival of the Anglo-Normans in the manner in which the hierarchy of tenancies, junior lordships and ruling families were organised.[37] The Ireland that Anglo-Normans arrived into was 'swordland', where possession by right of conquest was an accepted practice, and therefore not unlike what they were well used to.[38] As Robert Frame put it, the Anglo-Normans did not arrive in an exotic backwater of which they knew little. Rather, they entered south-east Ireland along well-established lines of commercial, cultural and military communication.[39]

Henry II gained control of Dublin, Waterford and Wexford, keeping the towns and their hinterlands as royal possessions. Through a series of royal charters, he and his descendants encouraged immigration by making them attractive to traders and craftsmen who from abroad.[40] One of his charters granted Dublin to the men of Bristol – a place with which Dublin already had many links – to colonize and run.[41] Control of trade was similarly exercised in both cities through a merchant guild system as established by royal charters. The first membership roll of the Dublin Merchant Guild from 1190 or earlier, was a list of those permitted to conduct business that contained some 3,000 names. Some had names which indicated that they were descended from Norse settlers. Some were from what is now the Netherlands, and some were from northern and western France. Most were apparently from south Wales, the west midlands of England, especially from Bristol. Clearly Dublin attracted immigrants from a number of countries.

A surviving roll of around 500 men admitted as freemen of Dublin between 1230 and 1249 included bakers, cooks, spicers, taverners, millers, brewers and fishermen, tailors, dyers, fullers, weavers, furriers, goldsmiths, armourers, carpenters, and masons, amongst many other trades. Some of these were immigrants, but many were former inhabitants of other Irish towns and from Dublin's immediate hinterland. By the end of the thirteenth century, the main ocean trading towns – Dublin, Waterford, Cork, Limerick and Drogheda – had all acquired municipal independence from the Crown, and thus could elect a mayor and set their own local taxes. In Dublin's case, freedom from control by Bristol was granted in lieu of repayment of a loan to the Crown made in 1229.[42]

By the beginning of King John's reign in 1199, Anglo-Norman bishops had been appointed to seven dioceses that included the main Norse-founded ports (Waterford, Limerick and Dublin) and places in the east of Ireland which were being colonised (Carlow, Kilkenny, Meath and Down).[43] All the Archbishops of Dublin consecrated between 1181 and 1306 were English born: John Cumin (1191–1212), Henry of London (1181–1212), Luke (1228–55), Fulk of Sandford (1256–71), William of Hotham (1296–8) and Richard of Ferings (1299–1306). English bishops who settled or held appointments in Ireland (these could be absentees) seem to have accommodated a flock of relatives and clients with positions in the country.[44] Churchmen from Britain as well as knights promoted the colonisation of Ireland.

Beyond the towns, Ireland was partly colonised by an international upper class, ecclesial as well as secular, which had, over the previous hundred years conquered England and advanced into Wales, and which was still engaged in infiltrating Scotland. The phenomenon was connected to a wider scattering that had deposited nobles, knights and clergy from Normandy and other parts of northern France in Sicily, Antioch and Palatine.

Anglo-Normans who seized or were granted lands in Ireland were accompanied, chiefly in the south-east, by what has been described as 'a widespread, though patchy settlement by peasants and artisans from England and Wales.'[45] The population of Ireland just before the arrival of the Normans has been estimated at less than 500,000, based on what the then-prevalent pastoral and agricultural economy might support.[46] The Anglo-Normans introduced an arable farming economy in some parts of the country. It is difficult to estimate the numbers of settlers who migrated to Ireland but the number could have been (perhaps) a very small percentage of the overall population.

Wexford acquired the infrastructure of Anglo-Norman settlement including motte and stone castles, abbeys, manorial villages and boroughs.[47] An unknown number of Welsh, English and Flemish settlers were introduced to the area as tenants by Norman barons. It is likely that most of the pre-existing local population remained in the area. This is suggested by the persistence of Gaelic and Norse-Irish family names and the Gaelic names of parishes, townlands and topographical features. However, a distinct dialect, a form of early English with elements of Norman French and Flemish known as Yola, survived as a spoken language in the baronies of Forth and Bargy until the mid-nineteenth century.[48] Forth and Bargy, which contained Wexford town, has the highest concentration of Old English surnames in Ireland.[49] To this day the area continues to have been visibly shaped by its Anglo-Norman heritage.

An area encompassing what is now County Meath and lands that stretched from Castleknock on the outskirts of Dublin to Longford was granted to Walter de Lacy, who also held lands in Hertfordshire, Shropshire, Wales and Normandy. The county was organised into 17 boroughs of which five – Trim, Kells, Navan, Athboy and Drogheda – became walled towns. Colonisation occurred through a process of subinfeudation, whereby tenant retainers provided rents and the services of knights to their lord and in turn sub-let lands they held, mostly to Irish tenants.[50] In Meath a small number of Anglo-Normans relied mostly on native tenants who came to be regarded as hereditarily bound to their lords.[51] de Lacy, like Strongbow and other knights who served them, married the daughters of Irish lords.[52]

Uladh, a territory that includes the present-day east Ulster counties of Down and Antrim was seized by John de Courcy who also held lands in the north-west of England, where many of those he settled in Ulster came from. He was the patron of religious houses in the north of England, the south-west of Scotland and on the Isle of Man, all places from which Down and Antrim could be reached without difficulty. He established Benedictines from Chester and Augustinians from Carlisle at Downpatrick, where he settled. Benedictines from Furness in Lancashire arrived at in County Down.[53] de Courcy married Affreca Godredsdatter, whose father was the Norse king of the Isle of Man. This was in keeping with the sphere of influence he developed on both sides of the Irish Sea.[54] Many colonising lords of this periods and equivalents granted lands in Ireland in subsequent centuries already owned estates in Britain from which settler tenants relocated to Ireland. The east of Ulster came under his control partly because of a local power vacuum. No local lord or alliance of local landowners was strong enough to retain control of the area. However, the territory to the west, which became the O'Neill kingdom of Tyrone, never became part of Anglo-Norman Ireland.[55]

Over time the descendants of the Anglo-Normans came see themselves as the English of Ireland.[56] They also did what the Scandinavians did in Normandy, and the Normans did in England; they married in, came to speak the local language and adopt many local customs. In many respects their descendants became cut off from English politics and society. No English king visited Ireland after John until Richard II in 1399 and none again until 1649–50 when both claimants to the throne, James II and William of Orange, arrived to fight each other. Anglo-Norman power in Ireland declined during the fourteenth century. England was preoccupied by what came to be called the Hundred Years' War. In 1315 Edward Bruce invaded the north of Ireland from Scotland, and the following year declared himself King of Ireland. A cataclysmic war devastated the country as far south as Tipperary and the walls of Dublin. From 1348 the Black Death devastated the Anglo-Norman towns, hitting Drogheda first. One estimate put the number of immediate deaths in Dublin at 14,000.[57] Population decline in England meant that there was no prospect of support let alone any possibility of enticing further settlers to Ireland.[58] Areas that had not been heavily settled by Anglo-Normans came under the control of Gaelic dynasties. English-controlled Ireland shrunk mostly to the Pale, an area that included Dublin and coastal territories to the north and south of the city.[59] An assessment of the Gaelic resurgence was set out in the preamble of the Statutes of Kilkenny, a set of laws passed in 1366 aimed at curbing the decline of Anglo-Norman Lordship in Ireland:

> now many English of the said land, forsaking the English language, fashion, mode of riding, laws and customs, live and comport themselves according to the customs, fashion and language of the Irish enemies; whereby the said land and its liege people, the English language, the allegiance due to our Lord the King, and the English laws there, are subordinated and diminished, and the Irish enemies exalted and raised up, contrary to right.[60]

These concerns about protecting the English language were expressed in French. During the fourteenth century French was still the spoken language of the Anglo-Normans in Ireland and of Lionel Duke of Clarence, third son of Edward III, who presided over the Irish parliament that passed the Statutes of Kilkenny. What we think of as English – the language of William Shakespeare – was imported to Ireland by later waves of colonists.

The prohibitions on Gaelic culture and intermarriage in the Statues of Kilkenny were aimed at lords and clergy – the governing elites –rather than at commoners and 'mere Irish'. There was never much of a concern about what language ordinary people spoke. A kind of English was spoken by at least some of the descendants of the peasants and artisans who were planted by Anglo-Norman lords or who migrated from cities like Bristol to Dublin. Yola, the Forth and Bargy dialect that was spoken until the nineteenth century, differed considerably from the English that was introduced by subsequent colonial planters who arrived in William Shakespeare's lifetime. The Gaelicised descendants of the Anglo-Normans who called themselves English came to be called the Old English following the arrival of new English colonists during the reigns of Elizabeth I and James I.

From the perspective of these New English the Anglo-Norman conquest of Ireland looked more like a failure than a success. Sir John Davies in 1612 in his *Discovery of the true causes why Ireland was never entirely subdued* described the Anglo-Norman conquest as ultimately superficial; Ireland had never been properly conquered to begin with. English laws had not, even after 350 years, been extended to cover the entire population. This particularly mattered because Irish inheritance customs differed from those enshrined in common law: 'For who would plant or improve or build upon this land which a stranger whom he knew not should possess after his death?' Davies maintained that the lands given to Anglo-Norman adventurers were too large to have been colonised properly. They built castles and assigned free-holders to their estates, but these leases 'were not tied to any form of plantation.' Some introduced tenants from abroad, but they were not obliged by law to do so. The result was that many presided over lands that never ceased to be Gaelic. According to Davies, they had been allowed too much independence; they and their descendants never became proper subjects of the Crown.[61]

By the beginning of the seventeenth century Ireland had only been partially colonised and the descendants of settlers who arrived in the wake of various conquerors had become, for the most part, assimilated. Here and there, such as in parts of Wexford and in the vicinity of Dublin, cultural differences from the still-predominantly Gaelic culture of ordinary Irish people had gained some traction. British cultural influences remained strongest in the vicinity of ports through which goods and people moved back and forth. Outside these enclaves Ireland was still very much a Gaelic country.

THREE

PLANTATIONS

The main focus of this chapter is on the plantation of Ulster following the Nine Years' War (1594–1603) that saw the defeat of Gaelic Ulster, the destruction of much of its population and, in 1607, the Flight of the Earls of Tyrone and Tyrconnell. The post-1608 plantation directed by the Crown is examined as a scheme to settle Scottish and English migrants in these counties. Here I mostly focus on Tyrone, using a case study of the plantation of Dunnalong near Strabane. The chapter also examines the separate informal plantation of Antrim and Down in east Ulster and the earlier plantation of Munster. Whilst there were subsequent waves of migration to Ulster, especially from Scotland, this initial period of settlement did much to shape the contours of Ulster's subsequent demography. Plantations were exercises in social engineering designed to promote, amongst other aims, the settlement of migrants from England and Scotland in Ireland.

The plantation of colonists in Ireland occurred in several phases with various degrees of failure and success during Elizabeth's reign and that of her successor, James VI of Scotland, who was crowned James the First in 1603. In the century after 1580 perhaps (maybe, possibly) 100,000 settlers migrated to Ireland from Scotland, England, and Wales.[1] This estimate includes several generations of migrants and most were not part of some specific plantation scheme. Some made their own way over to join second-, third- and fourth- generation descendants of settlers. The plantations were most successful in Ulster which, until the beginning of the seventeenth century, had been the most Gaelic part of Ireland. Ulster, except for its east Coast, was, as Roy Foster put it, 'intractably Gaelic'. Ulster's Gaelic leader Hugh O'Neill, the Earl of Tyrone, was viewed by London as 'a renegade Elizabethan', having been reared as the ward of Sir Henry Sidney, the Queen's chief official in Ireland, from the age of seven until he was seventeen.[2] Compared to a few elite connections with England relationships with Scotland were considerably stronger. There had been many marriages between members of Ulster's and Scotland's ruling families. Tyrone and the Earl of Tyrconnell hired mercenaries from the Highlands and Scottish islands whilst the English army that fought them was supplied by Scottish merchants.[3] To some extent at least, according to Nicholas Canny, Ulster and Scotland were part of the same polity and economy.[4]

After the Flight of the Earls the Crown moved quickly to settle English and Scottish landowners and tenants on confiscated lands in six counties: Donegal, Londonderry, Tyrone, Fermanagh, Armagh and Cavan. This scheme of plantation excluded Antrim and Down on Ulster's east coast where informal schemes of plantation were already underway. It followed centuries after earlier Anglo-Norman attempts to settle parts of Ulster. During the early twelfth century King John had authorised the Norman settlement of the North Antrim coast. The Normans who took possession crossed over from Scotland. Throughout the medieval period Highland clans vied with Ulster Gaels for control of Antrim. Just twelve miles of water separated Antrim from the Scottish highlands and within this 'archipelago' East Ulster, West Scotland and the Scottish isles were more connected geographically, linguistically, culturally and economically than the former was with much of Ireland.[5]

And now a note of caution: we should be careful, some historians advise, about concentrating too much on plantations in seeking to understand social change in seventeenth century Ireland. We focus on plantations and their owners because we have considerable documentary records of these (though far less on how the ordinary migrants who settled on these lived their day-to-day lives). But, as put by Raymond Gillespie, plantations were far from typical places and the arrival of people and new economic systems did not always formally map on to specific plantation arrangements.[6] The challenge, he argues, is not to let the sheer weight of documentation and political discussion that plantations generated, and the focus on land confiscation that has characterised much of historical writing, get in the way of trying to understand wider social and economic changes.[7] The problem is not that different, in a way, from the challenge described in the previous chapter of trying to understand the lives of earlier settlers in Ireland. We have far more information than we do about earlier waves of settlers such as the Celts or Vikings but for the most part, especially for the earlier periods considered in this chapter, ordinary migrants remain invisible. We know perhaps where they came from and their range of occupations but not their particular stories.

Conscious efforts were made to learn from the failures of earlier plantations in Laois, Offaly and in Munster to settle sufficient Scottish and English or British tenants, as these were referred to in early seventeenth century documents, on confiscated lands. The essential lesson was that without a critical mass of settlers no plantation could succeed.[8] However those seeking to profit from schemes of plantation were not necessarily preoccupied with colonisation as an end in itself. According to Thomas Bartlett, during the last decades of the sixteenth century:

> Ireland was a magnet for those down in their luck, younger sons without a fortune, soldiers without a war or for those who had long-term ambitions further afield. Plantations in Ireland could be a stepping stone to similar endeavours in the New World, a career trajectory, so to speak, attested by the (bloody) presence in Ireland from the 1570s of those later New World celebrity colonisers, Francis Drake, Humphrey Gilbert and Walter Raleigh.[9]

The Tudor plantations of the sixteenth century during the reigns of Henry VIII and Elizabeth I, like the later more-successful plantation of Ulster, were preceded by the confiscation of lands held by Hiberno-Norman dynasties (in Munster) and Gaelic clans (in Leinster). Typically, lands were escheated (confiscated by the Crown) after failed rebellions that had been triggered by Tudor expansionism which had managed to exploit divisions between existing Irish landowners. This pattern of exploiting Irish conflicts in order to acquire lands dated back to Strongbow.

The Plantation of King's County (Offaly) and Queen's County (Laois) were officially inaugurated in 1556 when the O'Moore and O'Connor clans were dispossessed.[10] Many of those who undertook the plantation of Laois and Offaly, the 'undertakers', and most of the inadequate numbers of tenants that these recruited, were from the Pale. Few came from England. The 1580s witnessed the more extensive plantation of Munster following the confiscation of lands from Gerald Fitzgerald (Earl of Desmond) and their allocation by the Crown to English-born undertakers.

Ambitions for the expropriation, colonization and resettlement of Munster's Gaelic Irish population had been in the air since the 1560s, but 'the great irony was that a Munster planation, when it finally came in the 1580s was constructed on the ashes of the Geraldine lordship, the relic of the Norman Conquest four centuries earlier'.[11] The scheme was designed so that only those already with large landholdings could qualify to receive 'seignories' of 12,000 acres on which they were typically expected to settle ninety-one families. Each full seignory was to be divided into six freeholds with each freeholder farming 300 acres. Below this a tier six of farmers would each hold 400 acres. 42 copyholders with 100 acres each and 36 lesser tenants would be granted smaller holdings or, if they were tradesmen, live in a village. Each village was to construct a vicarage for a minister and a water mill. Villages, it was envisaged, would be settled with one mason, one carpenter, two gardeners, one wheelwright, one blacksmith, one butcher, one miller, one tailor, a shoemaker and a parish clerk. The entire Munster plantation was to consist of 25 such seignories which meant that its architects envisaged some 2,275 English households.[12]

This corresponded to an envisaged newcomer population of more than 11,375 people, including dependants, being settled on escheated Munster lands.[13] This model was imitated by British settlers in colonies on the far side of the Atlantic ocean during the eighteenth century. In Munster it was aimed, as Nicholas Canny put it, at constituting an English world in an Irish environment.[14] It worked better in theory than in practice.

Estimates suggest that just 4,000 settlers had arrived by 1598 when rebellion broke out again at the beginning of what came to be called the nine year war. By 1598 many of the settlers were clustered in a small number of areas rather than equally dispersed across Munster's confiscated lands.[15] One of the more successful enterprises was the 12,000 acre estate at Cappoquin in County Waterford that came to be owed by Christopher Hatton. By 1598 there were twenty-two English men (some had Welsh surnames) and eight English women on the estate as tenants together with 53 'Irish people descended from the Irish race' with, presumably, all their dependants. The settlers claimed ownership of 300 cattle and 400 sheep, two teams of English horses and sixty cows. The Irish inhabitants between them had eighteen ploughs, 167 cows and 1,000 sheep. Some pre-1598 undertakers apparently preferred Irish tenants who were willing to pay higher rents.[16]

By 1611 the settler population in Munster Plantation counties reached 5,000. By 1622 this had risen to 14,000 and the number of settlers in Munster reached some 22,000 by 1641.[17] About 80 percent of these lived in south Munster forming about seven or eight percent of a regional population of perhaps a quarter of a million. About a third lived in towns and the rest were mostly spread out near rivers and along the coast. The 'colonial showpiece' was the new town of Bandon which had an almost-exclusively English, population. By 1641 almost one in eight of Munster's English settler population lived there.[18]

In assessing the impact of the plantation of Munster there is some disagreement amongst historians about the extent to which new settlers fundamentally changed the region. Early-seventeenth century Munster was already very much a money economy rather than dominated by Gaelic barter customs.[19] Except for a few enclaves like Bandon the population remained for the most part unchanged. Trade came in and out of Cork, as it had done before the plantation. The circulation of coin expanded and there was a proliferation of money-lending tied into rural commercial transactions.[20] As David Dickson put it, 'It was clear that the elites, old and new, were heavily involved in money-lending arrangements and that both landowners and merchants (notably the Old English in Cork city) acted as creditors'.[21]

What did change was the ownership of land. The early seventeenth century also witnessed the transfer of huge concentrations of wealth into the hands of a few. By far the most successful of the New English adventurers was Richard Boyle who in 1602 purchased lands in east Cork (previously owned by Sir Walter Raleigh) and in west Waterford. One of the ways he expanded his Cork holdings was by lending to other landowners and then foreclosing on their debts. By 1636 he owned land in at least seventeen counties but mostly in Munster. He rented out his Munster properties through more than 1,200 individual lease agreements.[22] By 1641 just eight of the original 35 estates were owned by Catholics and another 15 by descendants of the original undertakers.[23]

Not all plantation schemes sought to introduce colonists. In 1590, after the senior Gaelic lord in County Monaghan, Hugh Roe MacMahon, was executed his lands were split into five separate holdings rather than confiscated like Desmond's lands in Munster. These were granted to various MacMahons with other modest parcels distributed amongst other prominent native families. In essence Monaghan was to be pacified rather than colonised, brought under English control but not settled. Similar schemes of native plantation followed the breakup of East Bréifne, which became County Cavan, and West Bréifne, which became County Leitrim.[24]

James, for his own part, had some experience of failed plantations in Scotland. In June 1598 he had, for instance, directed adventurers from Fife (at their own expense) 'to plant policy and civilisation in the hithero most barbarous Isle of Lewis.'[25] He had come to realise that changing the ownership of lands of itself was insufficient. Without also introducing settlers, plantations did not succeed. Scottish involvement in the plantation of Ulster was in some respects an extension of centuries of effort by the lowland Scots to extend their authority over the Gaelic population of the Highlands and islands, a task that acquired a new impetus when the Reformation hit Scotland. James had even described this civilizing mission as one to be realised by 'planting colonies amongst them' and 'planting civility in their roomes' by 'rooting out or transporting the barborous or stubborne sort'.[26]

James' style of rule was very different from that of the Tudors who preceded him. In his first four years as the first British king he adopted something of a Scottish solution to an Irish problem, whilst encouraging Scottish settlement in Antrim and Down on Ulster's Scotland-facing coast.[27]The terms imposed by James in 1603 on the defeated Gaelic earls left these *in situ*. From the perspective of anti-Catholic English officials in Ireland the decision was perverse. But religious motives for the plantation of Ulster should not be overestimated for all that religion became central to conflicts between settlers and natives in subsequent generations. If anything, James sought to avoid transplanting the kinds of religious conflicts that had begun to emerge in Scotland. He was hardly likely to have favoured transferring 'what he regarded as extreme Presbyterians to Ireland as an intelligent way forward, except perhaps as a convenient way of getting them out of Scotland, which might have been understandable'.[28] Moreover, it has been estimated that 20 per cent of seventeenth century Scottish settlers planted in Ulster were Catholic.[29]

ANTRIM AND DOWN

From earliest times there had been travel, trade and the movement back and forth of people in Antrim and Down and Gaelic-speaking Scotland, including Galloway, Strathclyde, Kintyre and the Southern Hebrides.[30] Around 500 AD, settlers from Antrim had crossed to the Mull of Kintyre and taken possession of Argyllshire. During the High Middle Ages, Gaelic language and culture dominated south-western Scotland. Scotland, like Ireland had been invaded and settled by Norsemen but these became, as in the Irish case, linguistically assimilated. For example, Norse-Gaelic speakers from Galloway in Scotland settled in the Lake District after 1100.

In 1177 the Norman Lord John de Courcy seized the east coast, built castles at Dundrum in south-east Down and Carrickfergus in south-east Antrim. His successor Hugh de Lacy became the first earl of Ulster in 1205. The Norman conquest never extended through the entire province. A heartland of Gaelic power in north-west and central Ulster remained virtually intact throughout the medieval period. The Norman colony, for its part, was almost swept away during the early fourteenth century when it came under pressure from an Ulster-Gaelic resurgence in alliance with the Scottish King Robert Bruce who in 1315 invaded Norman Ulster.[31]

At the time of the Norman invasion of Britain northwestern England was under the control of Gaelic-speaking Scottish monarchs.[32] The movement of Gaelic Scots to Ireland included *gallóglaigh* (gallowglass) mercenaries during the thirteenth and fourteenth centuries. During this period a branch of the O'Neills, who came to be known as the Clandeboye O'Neills, took control of south Antrim and north Down. This extension of Gaelic influence effectively split the Norman earldom in two. Carrickfergus was captured in 1384 and thereafter paid a 'black rent' tribute to the Gaelic chiefs. The north east of Antrim fell under the control of highlanders from Argyll across the straits. What Michael Hill calls a 'Scottish Pale' might be identified in Antrim and Down, within which over time Norman influences were supplanted by Scottish ones.[33]

English efforts to establish plantations in East Ulster during Elizabeth's reign were unsuccessful. Sir Thomas Smith obtained a grant from Elizabeth of the entire territory of the Clandeboye O'Neills who by then been established there for three centuries. It was to be his if only he could take and hold it, which he failed to do. After a second ill-conceived effort to settle the Ards peninsula failed in 1573 Smith was obliged to relinquish his claim to Clandeboye. An attempt by the Earl of Essex to colonise parts of Antrim that was jointly funded by the Crown also failed. Essex had mobilised some 400 adventurers protected by around 1,000 soldiers. However, within a few years those who remained were huddled for security around Carrickfergus and along a strip of the Antrim coast near what would become Belfast. Over the next few decades the number settled in the vicinity of Carrickfergus rose. Forty parcels of land were allocated to new settlers in 1595. These were a mixture of New English, Old English and Gaelic. When subsequent parcels were allocated in 1601 and 1603 these went mostly to English settlers.[34]

The plantation of North Down and the Ards peninsula resulted from the machinations of two Scots, James Hamilton and Hugh Montgomery. Montgomery had served as a captain in a Scottish regiment in the Netherlands and was a member of James' court. Both came from families that had been neighbours to the south of Glasgow. At least one of Montgomery's relatives from Ayr in Scotland was already involved in trade with East Ulster and in a position to represent him in his plans to obtain lands there.[35] Hamilton was the son of a Presbyterian minister from Dunlop. In 1587 he took up a position as a schoolmaster in Dublin. When Trinity College was founded in 1592 he became one of its first fellows. Hamilton became bursar of Trinity in 1598. He also acted as an agent for the King of Scotland from 1600 in negotiations in London for the royal succession. The plantation of the Ards was led by a close-knit group who were loyal to James and came to have influence in his court.

Following a 'rebellion' after the seizure of his castle in 1601 the Gaelic lord of Upper Clandeboye, Conn O'Neill was imprisoned in Carrickfergus. From then on his tenure must have been precarious. According to the late-seventeenth century Montgomery papers, which have been frequently cited in histories of the plantation of Down, he was freed from imprisonment with Montgomery's help after he agreed to hand over half of the lands under his control. In Montgomery's account O'Neill had been jailed after some of his men were involved in a brawl in Belfast during which they killed an English soldier. O'Neill supposedly had sent his men there to bring back casks of wine for a feast. Montgomery broke him out of prison in 1604 in return for some of O'Neill's lands. The story is improbable, not least because Belfast was barely a hamlet at the time and would have been an unlikely place to purchase casks of wine.[36] This account seems to have collapsed a number of transactions whereby O'Neill sold off some of his lands over time to Montgomery and others.[37] The essence of the deal was that Montgomery agreed to use his influence with the King to secure O'Neill a royal pardon in return for half of O'Neill's lands. Hamilton used his influence to muscle in on Montgomery's land-grab. The king was convinced that so large a portion of Clandeboye was too large to be successfully planted by any one under-taker and, in any case, was under some pressure to reward a number of his other favourites. In November 1605 Hamilton was formally granted the lordship of Upper Clandeboye and the Great Ards in County Down.

Lower Clandeboye was granted to Arthur Chichester, the military com-mander of the war against the Gaelic earls. In 1601 Chichester had seized Castlereagh, O'Neill's castle, and set in train the events that led to his imprisonment.[38] Chichester was granted the governorship of Carrickfergus and was put in charge of other forts in its vicinity. In November 1603 he was granted Belfast castle and a large surrounding estate which commanded the northern coastline of Belfast Lough and included the site of the future city.[39] Chichester became Lord Deputy of Ireland in 1605. By the time his ten-year term of office was over he had become the largest plantation landowner in Ulster. Due to his position he too was able to obtain some of O'Neill's lands.

Belfast was one of 40 towns to receive charters in 1613. It barely existed until the 1630s but grew to displace Carrickfergus as East Ulster's main port. The earliest documented settlers in Belfast were English. These included a few merchant families who came to own property in the town and land in its vicinity. It is likely that these were amongst families from England's West Country encouraged to settle there by Chichester, who was from Devonshire. From the 1630s Belfast attracted Presbyterian settlers from Scotland. Many of these appear to have belonged to merchant families from the south west of Scotland, particularly from Ayr and Irvine. By the 1640s a number of Carrickfergus merchants transferred their undertakings to Belfast.[40]

Montgomery and Hamilton's success as planters was unprecedented. By 1630 the Hamilton estates contained 928 settlers (and their families) and those of Montgomery contained a further 1,012.[41] Hamilton and Montgomery both recruited tenants from the Scottish Lowlands to migrate to Ulster to farm their newly acquired lands for low rents. They persuaded members of their extended families to come and in May 1606 the first group of farmers, artisans, merchants and chaplains arrived, four years before the main planta-tion of Ulster in 1610. Not unusually, Hamilton employed relatives as agents to manage his estates.[42] He was knighted by James on 14 November 1609.

By 1611 a new town of eighty houses had been established at Bangor where Hamilton lived. His brother John acquired lands in County Armagh and founded the towns of Markethill, Hamiltonsbawn and Newtownhamilton.[43] Montgomery parcelled his lands into sub-units and leased these to Scottish men of property such as John Shaw of Greenock and William Edmonston from Stirling.[44]

The territory of Iveagh to the south of Clandeboye remained in the hands of the Magennis family, but following the Flight of the Earls this was broken into several freeholds. Like Con O'Neill, Art Roe Magennis avoided being pulled down by the Nine Years' War and the Flight of the Earls. By cooperating with Chichester, Magennis secured a title to Iveagh but the deal reduced other branches of his clan to the status of leaseholders on his estate in accordance with English law. A scheme for the freeholding of Iveagh in January 1608 transferred ownership to fifteen individuals including thirteen Magennises. About 85 per cent of the old lordship remained in the hands of Gaelic Catholic tenants. Over time some of these sold up to settlers who had the money to invest in land. Although by 1641 only 48 per cent of the old Magennis lordship remained in the hands of natives, this was considerably more than elsewhere in Ulster.[45] For example, North Antrim remained under the control of the Catholic Scottish Highlander Randal McDonnell. In essence McDonnell had retreated to Ulster, where he held some 300,000 acres, after he lost his Scottish territories to the Campbell clan of Argyll. He encouraged Scottish settlers to join him. Many of these were Catholics. The plantation of the Ards was viewed as successful insofar as it stabilised the area by bringing in significant numbers of settlers.

THE PLANTATION OF ULSTER AFTER 1608

The Flight of the Earls in 1607 created a power vacuum that made a more ambitious scheme of plantation possible than any previously attempted in Ireland. This encompassed what the present-day the counties of Donegal, Londonderry (then named Coleraine County), Tyrone, Fermanagh, Armagh and Cavan where native Catholics granted titles during the 1590s were replaced by Scottish and English undertakers. By 1618 some of these had sold off their lands to settlers in Down. Successful undertakers such as Hamilton and his brothers William and John acquired lands in Cavan and relocated some of their Scottish tenants there.

The plantation was organised through the work of three commissions which sat between 1608 and 1610. Their duties were to escheat lands and try rebels at assizes.[46] Articles of plantation were drawn up and published in May 1609: *A Collection of Such Orders and Conditions as are to be Observed by the Undertakers upon the Distribution and Plantation of Escheated Lands in Ulster.* These allowed for three categories of settler. The first of these were Scots or English undertakers of high rank, who were to receive estates of between 1,000 and 2,000 acres at a rent of £5 6s. 8d per thousand acres. Undertakers were required to build a castle, stone house or a bawn and they could only take English or Scottish tenants. These were required to take the Oath of Supremacy and reside on their estates for at least five years. For every thousand acres the undertaker could reserve 300 acres for himself. The remaining 700 acres was supposed to be divided in the following way: 120 acres each for two freeholders, three leaseholders of 100 acres each and at least four families of husbandmen, artificers or cottagers on the remaining 160 acres.[47]

Clearly, in parcelling out these smaller estates to the Ulster undertakers, efforts had been made to learn from the mistakes of the Munster plantation, where blocks of 12,000 acres had been allocated.[48] It was argued when plans for the more successful Ulster plantations were being drawn up, that the Elizabethan plantations had failed to live up to expectations, partly because financial inducements to attract the right sorts of tenants had not been put in place and partly because they had been too large.[49] The second category, 'servitors', were mainly former army officers who were granted estates of similar size at a rent of £8 per 1,000 acres. Again, these were required to build a stone house or bawn. They were trusted to take on Irish tenants. But undertakers and servitors receiving 2,000 acres were also required to settle a minimum of forty-eight Scots or English tenants on their estates. The native Irish who were deemed to have been loyal during the Nine Years' War constituted a third category. These were granted estates of between 100 and 300 acres, and paid £10 13s. 4.d per thousand acres, which was double the rents of English and Scottish settlers, and were allowed Irish tenants.

An August 1610 proclamation declared that the law required that natives inhabiting lands allocated to British undertakers transfer to lands controlled by servitors or native freeholders. In practice, it seems that British under-takers sought to retain native tenants who were needed to make their estates viable as rent-payers, labourers and food producers, as they found it unprofitable to import settlers in sufficient numbers to occupy more than a fraction of their estates. For this reason, the deadline for removing native tenants was delayed and delayed again with the support of Chichester, who was himself a prominent planter. Catholic tenants were fined – in essence required to pay an extra tax – and this was often paid on their behalf by the undertakers, who needed them. Once the deadline passed undertakers with Catholic tenants were deemed to have broken their contracts and to be liable to forfeiture. However, they were allowed to procure new titles at higher rents to the crown if they paid fines. By 1618 it was clear that the segregation would not be enforced; a new notional 1628 deadline was declared, but there is no evidence that any native tenants were moved once this had elapsed, although some undertakers with Catholic tenants were indeed fined.[50]

All in all much more was done to pressure undertakers to introduce settlers than had been the case of earlier attempts at plantation. Even though undertakers and prominent figures like Chichester were mostly focused on securing personal wealth, settlers were introduced in unprecedented numbers. For example, estimates for 1618 put the total number of Scots (tenants and their families) who had by then migrated to Ulster at about 40,000.[51]

A somewhat different scheme of plantation operated in and around Londonderry. Derry, to give it the name still used by Northern Catholics, was a port in Lough Foyle. It had been strategically important during the war with Tyrconnell and Tyrone. In 1600 it was taken over and fortified by Sir Henry Docwra. In 1604 James issued a charter creating Londonderry as a city with its own corporation. A failed uprising in 1608 by Sir Cahir O'Doherty, one of the Gaelic lords who stayed behind when others fled in 1607, cleared the ground in the usual way for forfeiture of his lands and for plantation. The 1608 rising was put down by Chichester who acquired a substantial portion of O'Doherty's escheated lands. Chichester's holdings included most of the Inishowen peninsula, some offshore islands and extensive fishing rights.[52]

The 1604 royal charter made trade and migration from Britain feasible in much the same way as had occurred centuries earlier through charters which granted Dublin to the city of Bristol (see Chapter 2). Rather than introduce undertakers in the vicinity of Londonderry James put pressure on London merchants and financiers to invest in the construction of and settlement of the then-county Coleraine and a small portion of Tyrone (Limavaddy). What came to be called County Londonderry was divided amongst the twelve London guilds: the Cloth-workers, the Drapers, the Fishmongers, the Goldsmiths, the Grocers, the Haberdashers, the Ironmongers, the Mercers, the Merchant Tailors, the Salters, the Skinners and the Vintners. Collectively these formed what came to be called the Honourable Irish Society, in essence, a joint stock company like the East India Company or the Virginia Company.[53] Each guild received just over 3,000 acres of cultivated land, but when bogs and woods were added the landholdings of each amounted to about 40,000 acres. Some of the London guilds had previous contracts to supply provisions to Docwra's troops in 1600.

In January 1610 articles of agreement were signed requiring an initial investment of £20,000 to construct, amongst other things, 200 houses in Londonderry as the initial phase of what was the first major piece of urban planning in Ireland.[54] Several villages were built, such as Draperstown, though in one documented case near Coleraine, English-style thatched and slate-roofed houses were found to be less able for Ulster's winds than the humble Irish hovels, which were built low to the ground.[55] In 1613 Derry was renamed Londonderry. The London companies rented much of the land under their control to native Irish tenants.[56]

Londonderry became an established entry point for migrants. For centuries most incomers had made the short crossing from Western Scotland and settled mostly in the East of Ulster. With the establishment of a trade route to Londonderry it became easier for migrants to reach other parts of Ulster. For example, settlers from the south-east of England, the other main point of origin other than Scotland, predominantly travelled to Londonderry and to English-owned estates. English settlers predominated amongst those initially planted in County Londonderry during the early seventeenth century. These either lived in the city or on lands owned by Englishmen in the vicinity. However, the city's port was also a convenient entry point for Scottish settlers. Londonderry's hinterland included South Tyrone where the settlers mostly came from Scotland.[57]

So far little can be said about the ordinary people who migrated to Ulster during the early seventeenth century. An early reference to the kinds of settlers sought was contained in a pamphlet published in 1610 by Thomas Blennerhasset, an undertaker with 2,000 acres in Fermanagh. Blennerhasset exhorted his fellow Englishmen to settle in Ulster, but only if they had the necessary skills and character. Tradesmen, smiths, weavers, masons, carpenters and husbandmen were needed and would succeed in Ulster. Ministers of God's word were also needed. Poor indigent fellows were advised to stay where they were; they would starve in Ulster.[58] Histories of the Ulster plantations give considerable details of the landholdings, the successes and failures of undertakers and servitors, and the lives of clergy, but when it came to ordinary settlers, there was markedly less information. As summarised by Jonathan Bardon:

> The great migration began, drawn from every class of British society: the families of servitors who had long sought to share in the province they conquered, younger sons of gentlemen eager for lands to call their won; Scottish nobles like the Earl of Abercorn, 'induced' to plant Tyrone 'for a countenance and strength to the rest'; equerries, park-keepers, spies and other servants of the King's household; men accepting estates in lieu of arrears in pay from the Crown; London merchants and 'indwellers' of Edinburgh; sea captains who had fought the Spanish at Cádiz and in the Carribean; Protestant clergy seeking harvests of corn from glebe lands and harvests of the natives' souls; English and Scottish veterans who had served in the armies of Henry of Navarre of France and Maurice of Nassau, Stadholder of

Holland; relatives, neighbours, artisans and dependents of undertakers; 'artificers', both journeymen and apprentices, who had learnt their crafts with the London Companies; rack-rented and evicted Lowland Scots farmers; and horse thieves and other fugitives from justice.[59]

When it comes to the last groups on this list, the majority of ordinary settlers forgotten by history, we are left with little more than a few crude stereotypes. These recall Tom Bartlett's synthesis of accounts of the previous generation of settlers who migrated to Ireland in the years leading up to 1598:

> Skilled tradesmen and husbandmen were what was needed: those who actually arrived were the flotsam and jetsam of late Elizabethan England. Some had fled England to escape authority, others were, as a contemporary observer put it, 'traitors, murderers, thieves, coseners, cony catchers, shifting mates, runners away with other men's wives', and so on.[60]

The stereotypes applied to subsequent generations of Ulster Presbyterians did not necessarily apply to their first generation settler ancestors. Take, for example, the testimony of Andrew Stewart who was the son of a Presbyterian minister who settled in Six Mile Water Valley in South Antrim during the 1620s:

> From Scotland came many, and from England not a few, yet all of them generally the scum of both nations, who for debt, or breaking and fleeing from justice, came hither, hoping to be without fear of man's justice in a land where there was nothing, or but little, as yet, of the fear of God.[61]

Many of the Presbyterian ministers who went to Ulster prior to 1625 were disappointed to find many settlers fairly indifferent to religion.[62] Presbyterianism did not flourish until a few decades after James' plantation. In *The Ulster Scot: His Religion* (1914) the Reverend James Barkley Woodburn sought to explain this early ambivalence by likening early Scottish settlements to mining camps: 'the first to emigrate to a mining camp are generally those who have not succeeded at home, or who have been in debt, or who are dissatisfied with their present condition'.[63]

It is impossible to know what the population of Tyrone was at the end of the Nine Years' War (1594–1603) but it was certainly the case that population density was low.[64] By 1600 it perhaps stood at 20,000, almost all of these Gaelic Irish. One report referred to 3,000 deaths within a few months due to starvation in Tyrone towards the end of the war.[65] There is evidence that some of O'Neill's Gaelic underlings moved between Tyrone and the Pale (to Meath and Louth) as migrant farmworkers.[66]

Both English and lowland Scottish settlers were introduced by under-takers from both countries to Tyrone. Initially 15 of these undertakers were Scottish and 13 were from England. Seven servitors were also allocated lands in Tyrone. Collectively these planted between 232 and 266 adult tenants by 1611 (with their families), rising to around 600 settler tenants by 1613, 1,492 settler tenants by 1619 and 1,991 settler tenants by 1622.[67]

Scottish undertakers were quicker off the mark and more successful in attracting settler tenants. By 1613 some 483 of an estimated 624 male adult tenants (77 per cent) were those of Scottish undertakers. Just 119 were the tenants of English undertakers and the rest were tenants of servitors. By 1613 five of the seven servitors granted lands in Tyrone had no Scottish or English tenants. One of the seven was Arthur Chichester who had a finger in most pies. He granted himself 1,100 acres at Dungannon. By 1618 he had introduced about 70 settlers there, significantly more than any of the other Tyrone servitors.[68]

Scottish settlement in Ulster became consolidated during the period 1613 to 1619 with the disappearance of some unsuccessful planters and their replacement by other more capable ones. Some lands were sold perhaps the same reasons as in Munster, to pay off debts. The most successful Tyrone undertaker was the first Earl of Abercorn, James Hamilton. Like his name-sake, who was involved in the plantation of Down, he was one of James' men and benefited from this. He became a Scottish privy councillor when he was 23 years old and served in 1603 on the Commission on Union between England and Scotland. Abercorn was one of a number of Scottish nobles picked by James to anchor the post-1607 plantation. He was granted 3,000 fertile acres at Strabane and Dunnalong close to the sea and the use of 25 soldiers to help with the initial clearance. Abercorn managed to settle 240 tenants on his estate by 1613, far more than any other undertaker in Tyrone.[69] Many of the tenants planted on the most successful plantation in Ulster were Scottish Catholics,[70] while more generally about twenty percent of Scottish settler tenants by 1622 were Catholic.[71]

Not all plantation landowners, it will be seen, were Protestant. Hamilton's brother Claude received 2,000 adjacent acres at Eden-Killeny, and after a slow start managed to plant 50 tenants on his estate by 1618.[72] Abercorn's brother-in-law Sir Thomas Boyd received 1,500 acres at Shean upon which he had planted 100 adult males by 1619.[73] Another relative, also called George Hamilton, a Catholic who had served in the Swedish army, got 1,000 acres.

The first Earl of Abercorn was succeeded by his son, yet another George Hamilton, who had converted to Catholicism. As a result, his title came under scrutiny but he was granted a new patent at higher rents in 1639. The new patent also set aside some lands that could be leased to Catholics. This second Earl of Abercorn served on the royalist side during the Civil War. He was at various stages a captain of horse, a colonel of foot, governor of Nenagh Castle and he followed Prince Charles into exile and lived for a time in France. Following the restoration of the monarchy his lands were restored to him. He also gained title to lands in Cork, Clare, Tipperary, Limerick, Kilkenny and Longford.[74] William, the eldest son of Sir Claude also converted to Catholicism.[75] Robert Algeo, Sir Claude's agent, was a Catholic who is recorded as having had good relationships with the native Irish. He flouted the terms of undertaking to lease land to the natives.[76] However so did many other undertakers out of financial necessity. From 1628 it was determined that one-quarter of each of the undertaker's estates could be set apart for Irish tenants. In 1631 William was fined for exceeding this quota. He too was a royalist during the Civil War and his lands were confiscated. After the restoration of the monarchy these were returned to him as a loyal Catholic.[77]

From 1619 to 1625 the overall numbers of settlers declined. Yet, there was a new wave of immigration during the 1630s. The push factor was intolerance towards Presbyterianism in Scotland.[78] Between 1628 and 1632 repeated crop failures in Ulster drove setters back to Scotland where they were turned away because of similar bad harvests. In 1638 tenants from north Antrim fled to Kyntyre because of crop failure and cattle disease.[79] At Dunnalong in Tyrone there appears to have been an almost complete turnover of settler tenants between 1630 and 1660. Just one of the leaseholders recorded in 1622 showed up on the 1630 muster roll. Analyses of such settlement patterns suggest experiences of rapid social mobility amongst Scottish settlers during this period whereby they relocated elsewhere in Ulster, including to the new towns.[80] It is also clear that whilst various Hamiltons successfully introduced settlers, many of their tenants were natives and some of their settler tenants were Catholics.[81]

In the baronies of Tyrone granted to Scottish undertakers Scottish surnames predominate in records of tenancies collected in 1622 and 1630. The distribution of settlers in 1622 still mostly reflected patterns of direct plantation. However, by then, there were four estates in south-east Tyrone owned by undertakers from Devon, one of whom was Sir Arthur Chichester. Records of surnames suggest that the tenants on these four estates were predominantly English.[82]

THE PATCHWORK QUILT

The post-1608 plantation turned Ulster's Gaelic heartland into what Marcus Tanner refers to an 'an ethnic and religious patchwork quilt' of mostly Scottish and English settlers living in areas alongside each other.[83]

Each patch of this quilt also retained a Catholic population. This was fundamentally different than the settlement pattern that emerged as a result of the earlier Munster Plantation where many areas remained entirely Catholic. English settlers were most prominent in Derry, Coleraine and its southern and western environs and in areas to the south and west of Lough Neagh. In a 1610 letter Chichester commented that Scottish settlers came better prepared, if with less money in their purses, for conditions in Ulster.[84] It has been argued that the Ulster plantation, by and large, failed to flourish in the two decades after 1609 except in areas settled by Scottish undertakers and their tenants.[85] First-generation Scottish undertakers and settlers were arguably more successful in Ulster than English ones 'because they found an area that was culturally and physically similar to that which they had left behind'.[86] These were also more willing to ignore settlement guidelines.[87] As A. T. Q Stewart wrote, 'When the response of English settlers fell short of the original intention, and progress was slow, the Scots everywhere took up the slack. Not content with their own portions, they moved into most of the others, including those of the Londonderry plantation.'[88]

By 1622 one estimate put the number of adult male British settlers in Ulster, excluding Antrim and Down, at 6,402. The term was used to denote both Scottish and English in various surveys at the time. There were perhaps another 500 settler men on Church-owned lands. The best estimate is that 3,740 of this total were Scots and 3,162 were English. Records from the time estimate that there were three women for every four men suggesting a total settler of 12,079 adults by 1622. The same information suggests a settler population in Antrim and Down of 4,000 adult males and a total of 7,000 adult settlers in all.[89] There were about 30,000 Scottish and English settlers in Ulster by 1630s. By 1659, citing figures that exclude Tyrone, non-Catholic settlers constituted 26,081 or 37 per cent of Ulster's population of 70,890. In no county did English and Scots outnumber Catholics. They came closest in Londonderry (45%), Antrim (45%) and Down (43%).[90] The settlement of Ulster became an ongoing process which resulted in significant Protestant populations in most places.

When the distribution of surnames in Ulster in 1730 is compared to areas allocated to English and Scottish landowners it appears that Scottish settlement in North West Donegal spread beyond the areas initially allocated to Scottish undertakers in 1610. The 1730 distribution of surnames also suggests that Scottish settlers came to predominate in parts of South Tyrone initially allocated to English undertakers. However, with the exception of North West Donegal and South Tyrone, the breakdown between areas of Scottish and English settlement can be mostly explained by initial patterns of direct plantation of settlers by landowners or on the colonial spread of settlers from convenient points of entry. Direct plantation placed some

Scots in inland counties but Scottish settlers also predominated on Ulster's east coast. Just as migrants from south-west Scotland found their own way to Down and Antrim it was also the case that some settlers in other Ulster counties had not been brought their by plantation undertakers.[91]

By 1630 according to such estimates there were perhaps 30,000 settlers in Ulster as a whole with about three of four thousand of these in Tyrone. By 1666 the population of Tyrone had risen to about 37,000. About one-third of these would have been colonial settlers.[92] Much of Ulster remained populated by Irish Gaels. In parts of Antrim and Down Scottish Gaelic enclaves persisted. Hardly anything is recorded of the lives of the settler tenants who populated the estates of undertakers and servitors. As put by Audrey Horning, in an account of the excavation of archaeological remains of a seventeenth-century Scottish Highlander settlement of more than 100 houses at Goodland on the Antrim coast: 'We know a great deal about conflicted and complicated politicians like the Earls of Antrim, but very little about those who carefully cut and stacked turfs to wall their homes'.[93] Until recently these remains had been understood to have been typical basic Gaelic structures of the kind used for centuries. Like most Irish dwellings of the time these huts had no windows or chimneys. However, according to Horning, similar building techniques were brought over by Scottish settlers. The arrival of these settlers, she argued, was marked by continuities as well as rupture, in Antrim at least, because some Scottish settlers and the host Gaelic population shared a common culture and way of life.[94] Scots Gaelic remained the most common language in some parts of Antrim and Down as late as 1800.[95]

Intolerance of Presbyterians in Scotland triggered a further wave of Scottish settlement in Ulster between 1621 and 1632. In 1621 the Scottish parliament ratified articles that had been carried by the General Assembly of the Church of Scotland in 1618. These included the observation of Easter and Christmas, the administration of communion to the dying in their houses and rules governing baptism. Forty-five ministers dissented from these articles and some of these and some of their supporters moved to Ulster and joined the more evangelical Irish Church where they had more room to manoeuvre in the practice of their faith. The Irish Church at the time was more Calvinistic in doctrine. For example, it avoided some distinctions between bishops and presbyters which were much opposed by the Scottish non-conformists. This latitudinarianism was encouraged by James who was anxious to encourage the Scottish settlement in Ulster. The bishops he appointed to Ulster were Scottish conformists, but they were not too strict in enforcing conformity on their fellow countrymen. In some cases conflict was avoided by a 'don't ask, don't tell' approach to Church governance.[96] For two decades after the plantation of Ulster Presbyterian ministers remained part of the Church of Ireland and the kinds of conflicts within Protestantism that pushed some Presbyterians out of Scotland were held in check.

Scottish Presbyterian clergy were encouraged by James Hamilton to settle and minister to his tenants in Clandeboye. These included Robert Cunningham who came to Holywood in 1615 and Robert Blair who settled in Bangor in 1623. Blair had been Professor of Philosophy and Greek at Glasgow College. With Blair's encouragement, James Hamilton, a nephew of Lord Clandeboye, become a minister. James Livingstone, another high-profile opponent of Episcopalianism in Scotland was invited in 1630 by Lord Clandeboye. Other early prominent Presbyterian ministers included John Welsh of Ayr, a relative of John Knox and like Blair a former Professor in Glasgow who settled in Templepatrick in County Antrim. These and other ministers spearheaded the spread of Presbyterianism in Ulster both before and after the 1641 rebellion – though not without setbacks. During the 1630s, during the reign of Charles I, bishops in Ulster sympathetic to Presbyterianism were purged. In response to the imposition of Episcopalianism some Presbyterian ministers including Blair and some members of their congregations took refuge in Scotland.[97]

From October 1641 several thousand settlers were killed in an opportunistic rebellion triggered by the escalation of conflicts in Scotland and England that preceded the English Civil Wars. In the spiral of 'ethnic violence' settlers were, according to William J. Smyth, killed 'in their homes, in the fields, in streets, on bridges, in woods, as prisoners, as well as in convoys trying to escape. Elsewhere, refugee men, women and children were hanged, drowned, starved or otherwise so badly used by stripping and expulsions as to result in their death. Some died of exposure to the winter cold, others of hunger, thirst and exhaustion'[98]. In Ulster this violence was concentrated in a number of places: north Antrim, north-east Londonderry along the Bann, the countryside of both Antrim and Tyrone flanking Lough Neagh, and in Cavan. However, in significant parts of Down, mid-Antrim and in much of Donegal, Londonderry and Tyrone, the available evidence suggests more organised settler resistance and fewer killings of settlers as a result. Based on a correlation between estimated fatalities and the ratio of settlers to natives in particular areas, it seems that killings were most prevalent in areas where settlers were most outnumbered.[99] It is often assumed that the planters remained undisturbed until the rebellion of 1641. This was far from the case. As A. T. Q. Stewart notes the castles, bawns and fortified houses that undertakers and servitors were expected to build were not built for ornament.[100]

In February 1642 the arrival of the Scottish Covenanter Army under General Munroe secured East Ulster and cleared spaces for further

Presbyterian colonisation. The Covenanter Army bought with it a number of Presbyterian ministers as army chaplains. It nurtured a Presbyterian revival in Antrim and Down involving such Ulster-based ministers but also visiting preachers from Scotland.[101] The emergence of Ulster's distinctive Presbyterian movement in effect dated from a period of the intense proselytization during the 1640s. Ulster's Protestant zones underwent what one account describes as a 'Puritan revolution', which also put its stamp on subsequent waves of Scottish settlers.[102]

Following the defeat of the rebels another massive transfer of lands took place. These confiscations paved the way for further settlement after which, when the dust had settled after the restoration of the monarchy and after some forfeited lands were restored to Catholic 'innocents' such as Abercorn, some 78 per cent of land under cultivation in Ireland was owned by Protestants. After the Battle of the Boyne in 1690 yet another settlement was imposed upon Ireland. By 1702, when William of Orange died, the Catholic share had fallen to perhaps 14 per cent because of further forfeitures. The introduction of a number of penal laws in Ireland from 1695, that prevented Catholics from inheriting property, worked to further reduce this proportion over time. Ireland's penal laws were aimed at securing the Protestant interest in the aftermath of the Williamite war.[103] These followed the introduction of some equivalent earlier legislation in England. Some of these laws placed restrictions on Protestant non-conformists. As applied to Irish Catholics, 'scarcely any human relationship or field of human activity escaped regulation'.[104]

Estimates of Ulster's seventeenth-century settler population were just that. By 1630 according to William J. Smyth the probable settler population in Ulster was about 72,000 and by 1641 there may have been as many as 130,000 persons of Scottish and English descent living in Ulster.[105] An 1880s history of the Scottish plantation of Ulster claimed that the North of Ireland was very much what the early seventeenth century had made it:

North Down and Antrim, with the great town of Belfast, are English and Scottish now as they then became, and desire to remain united with the countries from whom their people spring. South Down, on the other hand, was not 'planted', and is Roman Catholic and Nationalist. Londonderry County too is loyalist, for emigrants poured into it through Coleraine and Londonderry city. Northern Armagh was peopled with English and Scottish emigrants, who crowded into it from Antrim and Down, and it desires union with the other island. Tyrone county is all strongly Unionist, but it is the country round Strabane, which the Hamiltons and Stewarts of Garlies so thoroughly colonised, and the eastern portion, on the borders of Lough Neagh, round the colonies founded by Lord Ochiltree that give the Unionists a majority.[106]

Census records told a slightly different story. These distinguished the population of Ulster on the basis of religion rather than on the basis of settler or pre-plantation native ancestry. The 1861 census found a Protestant majority in counties Antrim (75.2 per cent), Down (67.5 per cent), Londonderry (54.7 per cent) and Armagh (51.2 per cent). Protestants descended from plantation settlers and subsequent immigrants were in an overall minority in both Fermanagh (43.5 per cent) and Tyrone (43.5 per cent). By 1901 Protestants in Tyrone constituted 38.7 per cent. Protestants were by then also in the minority in Londonderry (43.4 per cent) and Armagh (44.4 per cent) as well as Fermanagh (43.3 per cent). Scottish Catholic settlers in Tyrone and elsewhere were written out of such Unionist histories of the plantation. Whilst during the seventeenth century some of the Tyrone Hamilton Abercorn family were Catholics their descendants became part of the Protestant Ascendency. By the 1830s, following the repeal of the penal laws, the Abercorn gentry were hardliner opponents of concessions to Catholics who constituted a majority of Tyrone's population.[107]

FOUR

TRANSPLANTATIONS

In 1600, according to one estimate, about two per cent of Ireland's population was of Scottish or English origin or descent. By 1700 this had risen to more than 27 per cent.[1] Thereafter immigration levels remained mostly very low until the economic boom at the end of the twentieth century.[2] Population estimates for the early seventeenth century are just that; sufficient basic data – drawn from, for example, registers of births and deaths or tax records – is not available. Guestimates of Ireland's population in 1600 have been extrapolated from late-seventeenth-century estimates and from subsequent revisions of these. The earliest systematic attempts to measure Ireland's population were by William Petty, who concluded that the island had a population of 1.1 million in 1672, 1.2 million in 1676 and 1.3 million in 1687.[3] Demographers have since revised these estimates upwards to almost double the figures proposed by Petty.[4] Seventeenth-century Ireland experienced two major war-induced famines in 1602 and 1652 and, possibly, another in 1674, without which the increase in population could have been significantly higher.[5] Emigration also diminished what would have been otherwise a larger population.

Some of these emigrants were similar to those who flooded into England during the nineteenth century. There were, for example, reports that the western counties of England suffered a large influx of Irish vagrants fleeing crop failure and hunger in 1628, noting that ship owners made considerable profit by transporting them at three shillings apiece.[6] There are, again, no reliable figures on seventeenth-century migration to England. The flow of migrants out of Ireland would have included Protestant settlers seeking places of greater safety during times of conflict.

A very large proportion were Catholic soldiers who were shipped to the Continent in several waves throughout the century. Between 1605 and 1640 some 24,500 are estimated to have emigrated of which about 13,000 enlisted in Spanish Flanders, about 7000 in France with others scattered to Sweden and elsewhere.[7] Between 1642 and 1655 up to 35,000 more Irishmen were shipped to the Continent and then following the Treaty of Limerick in 1691 a further 14,000 defeated Irish soldiers went into exile. Some military migration to Europe also occurred during the intervals between these three main waves. Some women and dependants travelled with their menfolk but these seem to have been a small percentage overall and were mostly related to officers rather than to ordinary soldiers.[8] Most of the rank and file were forced migrants, compelled to leave or commanded to do so. They were unwillingly separated from their families like millions of migrants around the world since then. Many died of disease or were demobilised in far-away countries after years of service, often without pay. Most are as invisible to history as the migrant tenants brought over by undertakers and servitors from Scotland and England. As in the case of such landowners, emigrant Old English and Gaelic officers left considerable traces in various records through which it is possible to understand the Continental networks that bound them to their kin and compatriots. Many of the Irish regiments were bands of actual brothers, fathers, sons, uncles and cousins.

During the seventeenth century much of the ownership of land in Ireland changed hands. In 1600 nearly all land was controlled by Catholics. By 1641 the share of Catholic-held land had fallen to 59 per cent, by 1688 to 22 per cent and by 1703 to about 14 per cent.[9] Waves of confiscations followed by colonial plantations occurred in the aftermaths of three wars. Large numbers of people died during these conflagrations and afterwards from hunger. Ireland's Catholic elites were displaced, again in three waves, by mostly English and Scottish landowners. Following the Flight of the Earls, English and Scottish undertakers and servitors granted their confiscated lands were required plant immigrant tenants. As in the case of the Elizabethan plantations of Munster beforehand, the aim of the post-1607 plantation of Ulster was to ensure that new landowners were accompanied by English or Scottish settlers. There was no such requirement in the case of the post-1653 Cromwellian plantation. Landowners who were deemed disloyal to the Commonwealth were to be sent 'to Hell or to Connaught'. Their lands in ten counties were parcelled out to investors who had adventured capital to fund the re-conquest of Ireland. Lands in a number of other counties were allocated to Cromwell's officers and soldiers in lieu of several years' wages, but only some of these men settled in Ireland. No provision was made for importing tenants as in the case of the Ulster plantation.

A third wave of land confiscations was triggered by the defeat of James II by William of Orange in 1691. The terms of the surrender that followed the siege of Limerick led to further large-scale exodus of Irish soldiers to the Continent. There were echoes of earlier patterns of plantation on newly confiscated lands. William rewarded some of his supporters with Irish estates.

Catholic Irish soldiers who had fought against William of Orange subsequently served in the French army during the Nine Years' War (1688–1697) in which the French fought an alliance that included England, Spain, the Holy Roman Empire and the Dutch Republic. Huguenot regiments that had fought for William in Ireland were redeployed against the French and their Irish 'Wild Geese' regiments until, following the Treaty of Ryswick (1697), they were demobilised in Ireland, where some settled.

The decision by Parliament to pension off Huguenot regiments in Ireland echoed what occurred during the Cromwellian plantation, but differed in that most Huguenots settled in towns and cities. Though on a smaller scale, efforts to encourage Huguenot soldiers to settle were more successful insofar as demobilised soldiers who settled in Ireland were accompanied by family members, and Huguenot civilians engaged in trade and in the manufacture of linen. To some extent the experiences of these French Protestants who came to be transplanted to Ireland via England and Holland mirrored those of the Irish emigrant soldiers who were transported to Spanish Flanders, Spain and France. All had been displaced as part of Europe-wide conflicts between Catholics and Protestants, which followed the Reformation.

MILITARY AND CLERICAL MIGRATIONS

The seventeenth century witnessed a sustained process of large-scale military migration to mainland Europe which carried on into the eighteenth century, but this was part of a longstanding tradition of military employment on the Continent. Irish soldiers had fought in Calais and Agincourt during the fourteenth century and with the collapse of the Gaelic order many sought employment abroad. Soldiers were not the sole migrants during this period but they were the most significant group 'in terms of numbers and repute'.[10] This military diaspora consisted predominantly of Catholic gentry and the men who served under them on the losing sides of conflicts from the late Tudor period onwards. After the Desmond rebellion was crushed in 1563 some Irish soldiers moved to Spain and at least 200 were part of the Spanish Armada. The year 1587 saw the first large group of Irish enter Spanish military service in Flanders;[11] they had been part of an English expedition sent by Elizabeth to support a Protestant rebellion in the Low Countries against Spain, led by Sir William Stanley. About 1,100 troops were raised by Stanley in Ireland, including around 500 kerne (Gaelic light infantry). The rest had previously served as part of the Queen's army in Ireland.

Stanley was a Catholic. Two of his brothers were Jesuit priests. Yet he had become one of Elizabeth's most successful and most trusted commanders. In her service in Ireland he played a key role in suppressing a number of rebellions, including the second Desmond rebellion in 1583 that preceded the Munster plantation. In 1584, during his three-month stint as acting governor of Munster he executed 300 suspected rebels. Yet in Flanders, after several months fighting against the Spanish, he defected and brought across about 730 of his men to join the Spainish Army. Stanley was given command of a regiment that included Scottish and English Catholic recruits as well his own Irish troops. Stanley's defection was probably triggered by fears that he would be implicated in a conspiracy by Elizabeth's Catholic enemies in England that he had nothing to do with. His regiment came to be known as the Irish regiment; it was the first of its kind in Spanish Flanders.[12]

The growth and consolidation of an Irish military contingent in Europe from the 1580s and 1590s occurred in parallel with migration by scholars and clerics to European universities and seminaries. The Counter-Reformation placed a strong emphasis on the education of clergy. A system of Irish colleges emerged to support Irish clergy abroad, but this seminary-based instruction was only possible in parts of Europe where the dominant secular power was Catholic, or where tolerance of Catholicism could be counted on. During the course of the seventeenth century, the nature of Irish religious colleges changed from being accommodation for seminarians to institutes commanding significant resources which could offer scholarships and financial support to clerical students from Ireland. This system provided the supressed Church in Ireland with a continuous supply of qualified clerics, trained to provide religious instruction in accordance with rules set down by the Council of Trent.[13]

Irish troops in Spanish Flanders came to be part of a wider Catholic Irish émigré and religious Irish community that aligned itself with Spain. Irish priests and diplomats – groups that often overlapped – and some noble refugees preceded the arrival of soldiers in large numbers on the Continent. With the help of the Franciscan order a number of Irish nobles sought refuge at the Spanish Court in Madrid from the 1560s onwards. In 1598, the year of the death of King Philip II, there were several 'Irish' bishops in Spain. These included the Bishop of Leighlin, Francisco Ribera de Toledo, the Bishop-elect of Dublin, Mateo de Oviedo, as well as Irish-born clerics such as Bonaventure Naughten, who had been appointed Bishop of Ross in 1582 and Cornelius O'Mulrian, the Bishop of Killaloe.[14] The number of Irish at the Spanish Court swelled over time into what one account called a 'troublesome lobby group'. Émigré nobles and officers submitted numerous petitions seeking compensation for their military service after the failed Spanish intervention at Kinsale. Clergy and seminarians also sought financial support.[15] By July 1604 some 1,700 Irish refugees had arrived at the Spanish court.[16]

The most significant Irish point of entry was at the port of A Coruña in Galicia in the north-west of Spain. Hugh O'Donnell landed there in 1602 with a retinue of 25 and he was followed soon after by several other Irish lords, their families and retainers. The Irish community in the town grew, and special measures were put in place to deal with the Irish refugee problem and to prevent further refugees from attempting to join the Spanish court. An Irish Franciscan, Flory Conry, who had travelled with O'Donnell, was appointed liaison to the office of Protector of the Irish set up by Philip III to deal with the immigrants. From September 1604 the Crown ordered the governors of Galicia and Portugal to prevent further Irish refugees from coming ashore. Money was even allocated to repatriate newcomers back to Ireland. Deportations of some unwanted Irish were mooted. A December 1605 letter from the governor of Galicia described having to deal with over 800 refugees ranging from those of high rank to the poorest, having to put up with 'the insults of the Irish who out of pure hunger cannot avoid their anger' and having to spend what it would cost to run an entire regiment without solving the problem.[17] The problem for the Spanish was that Irish nobles travelled with retinues of extended family. In February 1606 almost half of those receiving official aid were considered to be 'useless people' or unproductive followers of Gaelic nobles and soldiers.[18] Yet it was the presence of these dependants that made the Irish community in Coruña distinctive. Other seventeenth-century Irish migrations to the Continent were mostly comprised of soldiers with very few dependants, which made the formation of lasting Irish communities impossible.

In November 1605, when the repatriation of many of the Irish women and children was being considered, the Crown was careful to solicit the approval of Irish nobles and clergy in Galicia. Spain's image as the great Catholic power might well have been tarnished if there had been criticism of its plans to deport Catholic refugees to Protestant-dominated Ireland. No doubt under pressure to do so, and mindful of their own need for Spanish patronage, the leaders of the Irish agreed to what was being proposed, but no one was deported in the end.[19] The number of Irish in Galicia during the crisis peaked at around 2,700, and somewhere between 3,000 and 4,000 Irish landed there between 1602 and 1606. More arrived subsequently, but because they were no longer entitled to financial assistance, they do not appear in the records.

Between 1608 and 1640 this mostly Gaelic community comprised between 70 and 90 families totalling between 500 and 600 persons.[20] Others who sought refuge in Galicia moved on, whether to Flanders, elsewhere in Spain or back to Ireland. What distinguished Galicia from other seventeenth-century Continental destinations was the inter-generational persistence of functioning Gaelic kinship structures, though these altered somewhat over time in keeping with Spanish customs, law and the constrained financial circumstances of those involved. The main sources of income for these landless households were salaries from the king to the heads of families, so they simply could not afford to fully operate traditional Gaelic kinship systems of patronage.[21]

Irish Colleges offering support to émigrés were established in Salamanca (1592), Valladoid (1592), Santiago de Compostela (1605) and Seville (1612).[22] Many of these were run by the Franciscans, who during the sixteenth century had become the largest religious order in Ireland, with around 60 houses and monasteries. Irish Colleges were also established in Douai (1594) and Leuven (1607) in Spanish Flanders. During the seventeenth century the Irish Franciscans ran five Irish colleges including St Anthony's College in Louvain.[23] Both Douai and Louvain exercised considerable influence on the development of the Catholic Church in Ireland throughout the seventeenth century and subsequently. They also offered refuge to Irish scholars like Mícheál Ó Cléirigh, one of the Four Masters, whose predecessors could have counted on the patronage of Gaelic lords in Ireland. Gaelic poets and historians were drawn from hereditary learned families and some members of this bardic class became seminarians on the Continent.[24] The Irish Franciscans in Louvain acquired a printing press with Gaelic typeface and produced many books in Irish including the *Annals of the Four Masters* and catechisms in Irish for use at home in Ireland.[25]

Priests who founded or studied in these communities were part of networks that represented Catholic Irish interests. For example, Robert Chamberlin, ordained in 1599 in Salamanca, was posted to the diocese of Armagh where he served as a chaplain to Hugh O'Neill. He returned to Spain a few years later and was a mentor to O'Neill's second son, Henry, who had been sent there when he was 13 years of age. Together with Florence Conry, Chamberlin subsequently co-founded St Anthony's, the Franciscan Irish College at Louvain. Conry became professor of philosophy and theology there and served as chief chaplain to the Irish regiment. In 1601 he travelled to Ireland with the Spanish Armada after which he escorted Hugh O'Donnell to Madrid in 1602 to request further military aid from Spain. Conry was appointed Archbishop of Tuam in 1608 but never visited his diocese. He died in Madrid in November 1629.[26]

Henry O'Neill had travelled to Spain in 1600 along with some other Irish youths. They were sent as hostages as part of a deal that included military support from Spain for Tyrone's rebellion which had begun in 1595. Henry was enrolled in the University of Salamanca under the direction of an Irish Franciscan priest, Fr MacCaughwell. After Hugh O'Neill's defeat at the Battle of Kinsale, Henry and his compatriots remained in Spain. He made the case for drawing the disaffected into a regiment under his command. This was initially resisted by the Spanish king who was justifiably concerned that the establishment of such a regiment would be perceived as a provocation by

England and might undermine a recently-agreed truce. At the same time, it might draw many of the unwanted Irish away from Spain. Henry was appointed as its Colonel, and his regiment became part of the Spainish Army under the command of the Archduke Albert of Austria. Exiled Irishmen converged on Flanders to enlist.[27] Following Henry's death in 1610, his brother John O'Neill took command of the regiment until 1621 when he, in turn, was replaced by another O'Neill.

In Spanish Flanders, up to 10,000 Irish soldiers served between 1586 and 1610,[28] and their officers tended to migrate and to enlist alongside their kin. A number of regiments were named for the descendants of Gaelic lords who led them. However, there are striking differences between the Irish communities in Spanish Flanders and Galicia. Those who travelled to Spanish Flanders, whether directly from Ireland or indirectly from Spain bought with them far fewer dependants, and records suggest ongoing affiliations with family or property matters in Ireland; some 130 approvals for leaves of absence between 1597 and 1610 are documented.[29] Fresh waves of migrants followed in one another's footsteps, but, unlike in Galicia, left few intergenerational traces of a distinct ethnic community.

Some Irish officers settled in the vicinity of Brussels, which was a regimental headquarters, and others settled and intermarried in Bruges.[30] Only small numbers of Irish women and children (likely related to officers) were recorded. Some marriages within this Irish community are documented. By December 1605 48 'Irish' baptisms were registered at St Michel et St Gudule, a church in Brussels that served the Irish there. By October 1610 that number had increased to only 86. A number of the children of Irish captains who grew up on the Continent later served in the Army of Flanders. Ordinary soldiers were not, for the most part, accompanied by wives and families. Some Irish women who travelled to Flanders were 'camp followers'. Regimental rules in the Army of Flanders that included O'Neill's Irish regiment allowed for between four and eight prostitutes per company of 200 men. They were expected to work 'under the disguise of being washerwomen'.[31]

By 1628 there were no fewer than 33 Irish chaplains attached to the O'Neill regiment. Between 1590 and 1615 it has been estimated that some 300 priests were educated in Louvain and Douai.[32] Many of these returned to Ireland. According to one estimate during the seventeenth century, about one quarter of diocesan priests in Ireland were educated on the Continent. Out of 1,088 registered parish priests in 1704 just 253 had been educated there.[33] However, not all of the Irish clergy abroad returned to Ireland. Many lived out their lives in Catholic regions on the Continent where they did not have to face persecution.

By 1609, following the beginning of what would be a twelve-year truce between Spanish Flanders and the Protestant-controlled Low Countries, just 700 Irishmen remained employed in the O'Neill regiment. The options available to the former soldiers of the Irish earls were limited and bleak. 1,200 of Hugh O'Neill's men were shipped to serve the King of Sweden against the King of Poland in 1609, where they served for three years before being disbanded, supposedly without pay.[34] Efforts by O'Neill from his refuge in Rome to have these men transferred into the service of the King of Spain in Flanders were unsuccessful. A 1613 letter from the Spanish ambassador in Rome described them as reduced to begging. It was claimed in 1649 that there had been 12,000 deaths in the original O'Neill regiment from the time of its establishment. As always, seventeenth-century estimates need to be treated with caution, and this one was almost certainly too high.[35] Many, including Henry O'Neill, were killed by disease.

COLONIAL PLANTATIONS AND TRANSPLANTATIONS

In response to the 1641 revolt in Ireland King Charles I pledged some 2,500,000 acres of Irish lands to the 1043 investors who adventured money needed to pay an army to put down the rebellion. In return for their capital these expected to be granted lands in Ireland. When the country was retaken a decade later by Oliver Cromwell's New Model Army more than 30,000 soldiers and their officers now also had to be paid off with Irish lands. Many of these sold on their debentures to speculators such as William Petty who have been placed in charge of the 'Down Survey', a land register and mapping exercise that made the administration of such a complex process of reallocation feasible. A third category of creditors rewarded with estates in Ireland included those who had loaned money to the Commonwealth or those like Petty who were owed fees for their services in Ireland.[36] There were significant administrative complexities in disbursing Irish spoils to those who invested in or fought for English victory. By May 1657 the transplantation of Catholics to 'Hell or to Connaught', as it passed into folklore, was deemed to be complete. Yet many former Catholic landowners remained *in situ* as leaseholders and many Catholic tenants merely changed landlords.[37] It is not clear how many of those who were instructed to move to Connaught actually settled there before May 1657 when efforts to enforce this transplantation were abandoned. In 1641, 59 per cent of Irish lands were held by 5,000 or so Catholic proprietors. Of these about 2000 were Old English.[38] About 1,900 mostly Old English landowners were transplanted to smaller landholdings on confiscated lands west of the Shannon. Many of these seemed to have returned to the parts of Ireland they were displaced from when the dust had settled.[39]

On the basis of Petty's work some 8,400,000 acres of forfeited land were allocated to new and mostly Protestant owners.[40] However, these new land-owners were not accompanied by significant numbers of immigrant tenants. Over half of the 1,533 identified adventurers who invested in the re-conquest of Ireland were from London. They came to be represented by a select committee of 20 Londoners from this group. One of these was a Michael Herring, a merchant, who invested £600 and drew 2,000 acres in Tipperary. Two other members of the committee from London, Thomas Foote and John Kendricke, who were Aldermen, invested £700 each. Kendricke drew 1,555 acres in Tipperary. Many members of the committee had been fund-raisers for the Parliamentarians during the Civil War.[41] Several adventurers were also investors in other colonial enterprises. For example, Maurice Thompson traded in slaves and tobacco between the Guinea coast of Africa, the West Indies and Virginia. He acquired a tobacco plantation in St Kitts and a sugar plantation in Barbados.[42] In April 1652, the committee representing the Adventurers petitioned parliament to request, amongst other things, that the lands allocated to them be contiguous. In essence they did not want to have to contend with potentially rebellious neighbours. Parliament then directed the Council of State to come up with a plan for the settlement of Ireland to include 'the transporting out of Ireland into foreign parts such of the Irish as they shall think for the advantage of the commonwealth' and make provision touching the transporting of persons from one part of the nation to another'.[43]

Records for the Barony of Ardee in County Louth on the east coast identify 89 proprietors who had forfeited their lands.[44] Of these it seems that a far smaller number were expected to relocate their families, retainers and livestock to Connaught and County Clare on the far side of the country. Amongst those who lost their lands was Alice, widow of Charles Lord Moore who was killed fighting for the Commonwealth in May 1649. However, her sons Henry and Garrett had defected to Ormond in May 1649 and for this, lands owned by the Moores were sequestered.[45] In July 1653 the Commonwealth Commissioners in Ireland recommended to the English parliament that these lands in Ardee be allocated to disbanded soldiers in lieu of their unpaid wages earned since June 1649. 19,318 acres were set aside to pay £23,132 owed to disbanded officers and soldiers. Other lands in Ardee were allocated to the archbishopric of Armagh and to Christ Church Cathedral in Dublin. The report to parliament argued that these soldiers should be settled in areas in which they had served and with which they were best acquainted. Lands in Louth were allocated to the garrison stationed at Drogheda where Catholics had been massacred in 1649.

Records from 1654 suggest that 21 of the displaced families who made petitions were permitted to delay their departures a number of months. This meant that they could stay in Louth, 'to mingle with the "common sort of persons" (i.e. not landowners) for whom the Commonwealth Settlement meant only a change in landlord.' A number of these families became tenants of the new owners. Some senior officers acquired large estates such as Major Aston, who acquired more than 1,300 acres including 88 acres of bog lands together with a couple of townlands, and later took charge of a further 1,894 acres to be distributed to his troopers. At the lower end of the spectrum, William Halfpenny an ordinary soldier who was owed one pound, seven shillings and four pence, was to receive just over one acre of land.[46] Some soldiers immediately sold on their entitlements to land (debentures) to new landowners including Aston and to investors from Dublin.

In Kerry, another county in which confiscated lands were allocated to soldiers, the purchase of debentures occurred on a much larger scale. Much of south Kerry was earmarked for distribution to the demobilised members of three regiments. William Petty sought to acquire all of this land and succeeded in buying up 164,000 acres for just £3,700. Petty's plan for his Kerry estate was to attract English settlers to replace the soldiers he purchased it from. However, much of this land was unsuited to farming. He founded the town of Kenmare as a Protestant colony. The problems he faced in planting his lands with English settlers recalled those of Elizabethan-era planters in Munster who found it difficult to attract and retain significant numbers of English tenants even though they had been offered preferential rents.[47] Petty hoped to develop an Irish smelting industry, but this plan also collapsed. There is little evidence to suggest that Petty sought to Anglicise the local population.[48] In the end he was stuck with mostly-Irish Catholic tenants. At most 15,000 out of 35,000 or so adventurers and demobilised soldiers who were allocated lands took these up.[49] By 1670 the number of estates in the hands of new settlers was around 8,000. By then, some Royalist Catholics had regained some of their lands after the restoration of the monarchy.[50]

Petty, the administrative architect of the Cromwellian plantation, believed that it had never gone far enough. He presented pamphlets to the King that called for the clearance of Catholics from Ireland. In *The Treatise of Ireland* (1687) he calculated that there were about eight Catholics in Ireland for every one Protestant: 145,000 non-Catholics of all sorts and 1,155,000 Catholics.[51] As far as Petty was concerned this political arithmetic could not but eventually undermine Protestant supremacy in Ireland. He argued that it would take the transplantation of the majority of these Catholics to stabilise Ireland in perpetuity. The resultant land clearance would, he claimed, bring considerable economic benefits; if Ireland was turned into a great ranch it could hold six million cattle to feed England.[52]

Some unwanted Irish were transported to England's colonies but never in sufficient numbers to alter the political arithmetic. Up to 10,000 mostly-Catholic Irishmen and women were shipped against their will to the West Indies during the Cromwellian period to work on farms and plantations. Most of these would have been indentured for a period of around seven years but most would have become 'free' after the Restoration in 1660.[53] Some Irish migrants voluntarily signed contracts of indenture. During the 1630s a number of ship-loads of Irish men and women embarked from Kinsale to the West Indies and to other colonies. According to records left by one ship captain, Thomas Anthony, who transported a cargo of Irishmen and Irishwomen to the West Indies, he had initially had planned to sail to Virginia but his prospective passengers wished to go to the West Indies. Seemingly, those being transported had some degree of autonomy. They seemed to have considerable knowledge of what they might expect in various colonies. They knew, for example, that wage rates were higher in the West Indies than in Virginia. Anthony carried 61 passengers to St Christopher where the contracts of the 53 who survived the journey were sold for between 450 and 500 pounds of tobacco apiece.[54]

Wherever Irish Catholics went, their clergy followed. In 1637 two priests from the Diocese of Tuam embarked with a shipload of emigrants to the West Indies where they ministered to Catholics on a number of islands. The penal laws were applied there no less than to Ireland at the time. The Church was inhibited but not prohibited as long as it did not become too assertive, for instance, by building actual churches.[55] In 1641, fearing reprisals in response to reports of massacres of Protestants in Ulster, some Irish Catholics fled from English-controlled settlements. Spanish colonial records from the 1640s reported the arrival of Irish refugees from English-controlled islands to places in the Spanish Caribbean including Portabello, Cartagena, Santo Domingo, Margarita, Puerto Rico and Veracruz.[56]

A July 1653 order issued by the Commissioners for the Administration of the Affairs of the Commonwealth of England in Ireland addressed how transplantation might rid Ireland of some of its poorer and most vulnerable inhabitants:

> Upon consideration had of the multitude of persons, especially women and children wandering up and down the country, that daily perish in ditches, and are starved for want of relief: it is thought fit that such women as have able bodies to work with, and such children of about twelve years, whose husbands or parents are dead or gone beyond the seas, or friends to maintain them, or means of their own to preserve them from starving, maybe taken up by the overseer of the poor, and that to prevent such persons from starving, the overseers are hereby authorised to treat with merchants for the transplanting of said persons into some English plantation in America.[57]

Some records of such transplantations survive. In September 1653 David Selleck, a Boston merchant and ship-owner, was given a licence to ship 400 children from Ireland to both New England and Virginia.[58] In October 1654 Selleck and his partner, a Bristol merchant, obtained a further licences to carry 250 Irishwomen aged 15 years and older to New England, and to transport a ship-load of 'rogues and vagabonds to Virginia'.[59] Many Catholic priests were forcibly transplanted, and some were executed for having failed to comply with a January 1653 edict by the Commissioners that Catholic priests had 20 days to leave Ireland before the 27th Act of Elizabeth I (1587) was implemented. This Act declared that any priest who was caught was to be hanged, cut down while still alive, disembowelled and then burnt. In February 1653 the Commission decided that priests held in prisons in Dublin would be shipped with Irish soldiers being transplanted to Spain. It became policy to ship priests under 40 years of age to the West Indies and those older than 40 to the Continent. People suspected of being rebels were also transported.[60]

According to Donald Akenson, there is a tendency, in what he terms 'Catholic martyrology' to describe the Irish who were transported to the West Indies as slaves.[61] Many such migrants were temporarily indentured, but were no longer so by the time black slaves began to arrive from Africa in significant numbers. There is a fundamental difference between temporary indenture and the kinds of chattel slavery experienced by black Africans and their descendants who were enslaved from birth. However, there is still a tendency (on some Irish-American internet sites in particular) to conflate two very different conditions.[62] Though some white migrants considered their period of indenture as a form of enslavement, many who entered contracts of indenture left Ireland by choice:

> One reason that the idea of the Irish-as-slave, or as proto-slaves, or as black men in white skins, must be resisted is that it conjoins with a stream in Irish historical writing that presents Irish settlers in various New Worlds as being passive emigrants, victims and therefore blameless in the furtherance of the several imperialisms in which they participated. The overwhelming majority of Irish indentured servants who went to Montserrat did so by personal choice, with information in hand, and, in fact, made reasonable decisions between two alternatives: remain in Ireland or emigrate. That neither of these alternatives may have been very attractive does not detract either from the self-preserving agency of the individuals involved, nor obfuscate the impact on other cultures which the exercise of that agency involved.[63]

Whilst thousands of Irishmen and women were 'Barbadosed' to toil in tobacco or cane fields, some of these became slave-owners once their period of indenture had come to an end.[64] Records from 1656 note that Cornelius Bryan, an Irishman in Barbados, was sentenced to 21 lashes on his bare back as punishment for 'a mutinous speech'. Thirty years later in his will he bequeathed 'a mansion house', 22 acres and 'eleven negroes and their increase', that is, any descendants of his slaves, to his wife Margaret and their six children.[65] The Irish in the colonies, whether those of England or Spain, came to have more in common with English settlers than with African slaves. Some, who knew how to tap into Spanish patronage networks, sought to benefit from Spanish colonialism and, in one case, even proposed new colonial ventures. For example, during the early 1630s an Irish merchant, Jasper Sheehan, proposed to Spain's Council of the Indies a joint venture that would involve Irish troops from Flanders and Irish Catholic settlers.[66]

Montserrat became the first place in the British Empire where the Irish constituted a majority of white settlers. On arrival many had worked as indentured labourers harvesting tobacco. By the time black slaves began to arrive in large numbers the Irish were no longer indentured and the main crop became the harvesting of sugar. Whilst they may have worked along-side Africans on the plantations many were on their way to become slave-owners. Hence the title of Akenson's study of the settlement of Montserrat, *If Ireland Ruled the World*. According to a 1672 census Montserrat had a white population of 1,171 males of which some 67 per cent were Irish which when women and children were added came to a total of about 2,800. A large proportion of these had arrived from Ireland during the 1650s and 1660s. By 1678 the island had a population of between 1,500 and 2,250 slaves.[67]

By 1729 the Irish were, on average, bigger planters and owned more slaves than other white (mainly British) settlers in Montserrat.[68] Throughout the eighteenth century this white population did not increase by much. The majority were descended from Irish Catholic settlers.[69] However the number of slaves on the island increased considerably, from 6,063 in 1729 to 9,834 by 1775. The Irish on the island were part of a white Ascendency even if the penal laws still applied to them. Viewed as a 'laboratory', Montserrat, where the Irish owned thousands of African slaves, is a particular case, but it should be borne in mind that Irish emigrants came to own slaves elsewhere in the Americas.

MILITARY TRANSPORTATIONS

After the defeat of the Catholic Confederacy of Kilkenny and their royalist allies by Cromwell, some 34,000 men, according to Petty, departed for the Continent between 1651 and 1654. Unlike some of Petty's other estimates, this one is still regarded as accurate.[70] Coincidently, this was about the same as the number of English soldiers who received debentures to lands in Ireland. Whilst Cromwell's victory triggered a new wave of military migration to the Continent, Irish soldiers were already a sought-after commodity in a Europe embroiled since 1618 in what came to be called the Thirty Years' War. This had become more than simply a war between Catholic and Protestant kingdoms. It became a conflict between France and the Habsburgs who dominated Spain for supremacy in Europe. Irish soldiers who arrived in the aftermath of the Thirty Years' War served Spain or France and sometimes even switched their loyalties back and forth.[71]

Seven regiments, comprising 10,000 men, were raised in France during the late 1630s under Colonels O'Reilly, Cullen, Sinnot, Crosbie, Bellings, Wall and Fitzwilliam. Most of these officers came from Old English families.[72] Two Franciscans sought to broker the defection of Irish regiments under Colonels John O'Neill and Hugh Albert O'Donnell from the Spanish to the French side. They were acting for Cardinal Richelieu, the dominant figure in France. O'Neill reported this overture to the Spanish and this may had had an influence on efforts by the Spanish to recruit soldiers directly from Ireland thereafter.

Spain had a desperate need for troops during the 1640s and, by then contained a small assimilated Irish immigrant population dating back to the aftermath of the Battle of Kinsale.[73] Once again Galicia became the main point of entry. Between 1641 and 1654 English contractors received payments on delivery for a total of 22,531 'troops' from Ireland.[74] An Irish priest in Madrid likened those shipped from Ireland to slaves: 'Half the men who arrive desert immediately because of the neglect of the contractors, who in order to do business, purchase most of the men from the heretics as if they were slaves, and put them on board the ships by force.'[75] They may not have been slaves but, according to one analysis, they had had little or no freedom and were treated no better than if they were:

> Although (strictly speaking) the men were not abducted like slaves, or even (technically) pressed into service, they often had as much choice in the matter as the products of slave-hunts or battle-captures in middle Africa. After 1650, many of them were fugitives or prisoners of war in their own land, at best facing intolerable privation, at worse potentially serious charges and rough justice. A large proportion were about to lose their families through disease, or the tenancies of their farms through the operation of the Settlement.[76]

By way of example, some 5,000 were shipped as part of a contract between an English officer, Captain George Walters, and his partner Thomas Skinner, a ship-owner, with the Spanish ambassador in London, Alonso de Cárdenas. These surrendered troops were sent from Waterford to Dover and from there to Spain. In February 1654 an English observer described the circum-stances aboard one the seven ships in the flotilla put together by Skinner and the last one to disembark in Coruna: 'above one half the men died for want of food, and poisoned by the infection of the sick people and dead carcasses among them in so much that the shore was be-spread with them, and the hogs and dogs fed on their bodies.'[77] Many of surviving Irish who were transported to Spain were eventually deployed in Flanders.

The soldiers who were transplanted to Galicia in 1654 do not seem to have benefited from the presence of an Irish community in the region. It does not seem that the Galician Irish kept up strong links with parts of Ireland from which their parents and grandparents had emigrated from. One scheme to recruit Irishmen from Munster to fight for Spain involved Dermot O'Sullivan, the Spanish-born heir of Donal O'Sullivan Beare, a leader of the post-Battle of Kinsale exodus. In essence, O'Sullivan, who had spent much of his life in the Spanish court, acted as a paid consultant in a recruitment drive that saw him visit Ireland for the first time in 1648.[78]

After the signing of the Treaty of Limerick (1691) some 14,000 soldiers and about 2000 women and children followed Patrick Sarsfield to France to serve King James's army in exile. They followed the well-trodden path of previous Irish military emigrants pushed out of Ireland by terms of surrender and pulled to the Continent as grist to the mill of European conflicts. Sarsfield's men joined several thousand Irish soldiers of the Mountcashel Brigade who were already in France. He was fatally wounded in the battle of Landen.

As part of the Treaty of Ryswick that concluded the Nine Years' War, France recognised William III as the rightful king of England. Irishmen who fought in France for James against William had no option but to keep soldiering on the Continent. For example, following the death of the last Habsburg king of Spain Irish soldiers fought on both sides of the War of Spanish Succession (1701-1714).[79] Tantalising glimpses into the lives of ordinary Irishmen who served in French army are to be found in the records of the Hotel Royal des Invalides in Paris. This institution came to accom-modate more than 2,300 Irish veterans of the Wild Geese regiments that had fought in the Rhineland, Flanders, Italy and Spain.[80] Simon Dougan from County Monaghan had been just fourteen when he enlisted. He served a total of 15 years in two different regiments before losing his right arm from a gunshot wound in 1704 at the age of 28.[81] A number had been already quite old when they quit Ireland for France. Sergeant Patrick Fackener (names were recorded phonetically), a carpenter by trade from county Louth, was 72 years old and married in Paris when he unsuccessfully sought admission in 1710. He claimed more than 20 years' service. Fackener's papers were supposedly forged. He had previously been expelled from Hotel Royal des

Invalides in 1701 along with 25 other Irish claimants whose documents also turned out to have been forgeries.[82] Yet his right hand had been crippled from a gunshot wound. Unable to return to Ireland, old soldiers got by as best they could.

HUGUENOTS

Huguenot settlement in Ireland owed its origin to the religious persecution of Protestants in France during the 1680s before and after the revocation of the Edict of Nantes in 1685.[83] The Edict had followed the Saint Bartholomew Day Massacre of French Protestants in Paris in 1572 and the religious tolerance it promised was a compromise aimed at ending a religious civil war. The origin of the word Huguenot is unclear. One theory is that it derives from the combination of two German words, *eid* and *genossen* (*eydgenoss* trans, 'oath participants'). Calvinism spread from Geneva where German was spoken. [84] French Calvinists prospered during the first two thirds of the seventeenth century in agriculture, trade and linen manufacture. Huguenot regiments served in the King's army during the Thirty Years' War. France however remained a Catholic power. From 1681 onwards between 150,000 and 200,000 emigrated from France to Switzerland, England and the Dutch Republic. Secondary migrations resulted in the resettlement of many of these in the Rhineland-Palatinate, Scandinavia, British North America, South Africa and Ireland. About 40,000 Huguenots in all settled in England, and while there are estimates that 10,000 may have settled in Ireland, exact numbers are unclear because records focus on the circumstances of pensioned-off officers and well-to-do merchants rather than on ordinary soldiers and the poorer classes.[85]

The first significant sponsor of Huguenot settlement in Ireland was James Butler, the Duke of Ormond, who was Lord Lieutenant in the post-Restoration period. Ormond's contacts with Huguenots dated from his years in exile in France with the king before 1660. He sought to encourage skilled Huguenot artisans in the woollen and linen trades to settle in Ireland. By 1668 about 200 Huguenots had arrived. Some settled in houses constructed by Ormond in Chapelizod near Dublin.[86] Following the arrival of this initial group there were two main phases of Huguenot migration to Ireland: the first coincided with the rise of religious persecution in France during the 1680s; the second and main phase of settlement occurred when demobilised Huguenot soldiers who had fought for William of Orange in Ireland and Europe were pensioned off in Ireland after Treaty of Ryswick in 1697. This latter group was accompanied by family members and others seeking to establish trade and industry.

In 1665, under Ormond's direction as Lord Lieutenant, the Lady Chapel at St Patrick's Cathedral in Dublin had been designated as a place of worship for French-speaking Protestants, with a stipulation that services be held wholly according to the rites of the Church of Ireland.[87] Simply put, Calvinist Huguenot settlers were expected to conform to the established Church as much as possible. Incentives for them to do so, in the form of support for religious worship in the French language and salaries for Huguenot ministers were offered.[88]

That so many did so or that French-speaking churches adhered to the rites of the established Church might appear puzzling. The Huguenots were, after all, Calvinists, and, as such, shared a religious heritage with dissenting Northern Presbyterians descended from Scottish Calvinists. However, Scottish Calvinists came to view themselves as persecuted by the established Church and this worked to amplify differences between varieties of Protestantism in Scotland and the North of Ireland. By comparison, French Huguenots saw themselves as persecuted by Catholics, and were less preoccupied with distinctions within Protestantism.[89] Scottish and French Calvinists worshipped using the same psalter, and acquired a similar range of emotional responses to the preaching of the gospel. They had similar beliefs about human sinfulness and the possibly of personal redemption. However, the Reformed Dutch and French churches acknowledged holy days, a cultural holdover from Romanism that Scottish Calvinists disapproved of to the extent, in some cases, of considering that Christmas day should not be celebrated.[90] One area where Huguenots from France differed from the established Church was on the matter of language. However, those who wanted to worship in French were facilitated from the outset.

Encouraged by Ormond, Dublin's Huguenot community numbered about 600 by the mid-1680s. In 1681 he recruited a chaplain, Pierre Drelincourt, to minister to newly arrived refugees from France. Drelincourt was also appointed as a private tutor to Ormond's grandson James Butler. In 1688 Drelincourt authored a pamphlet, *De l'état present d'Irlande, et des avantages qu'y peuvent trouver les protestans françois*, which emphasised economic opportunities for Protestant settlers in Ireland, including what came to be called 'ascendency'. He commended Ireland as a Protestant polity protected by Protestant soldiers.[91] However, Huguenot settlers could share this ascendency only as members of the established Church.[92]

The main influx of Huguenots did not occur until the Peace of Ryswick in 1697, after which William's Huguenot regiments were disbanded. As the English parliament was unwilling to provide for them, they were all – both officers and soldiers – placed on the Irish Establishment. Huguenot veterans were required to reside in Ireland in order to receive their pensions, and around 590 officers who demobilised in Ireland appear to have received pensions by 1702. The registers of the French churches in Dublin record some 165 officers who appear to have settled permanently in the city. Many of the officers who were pensioned off in Ireland had passed middle age, having left France many years earlier.[93]

One of William's commanders Henry Massue, Marquis de Ruvigny became Earl of Galway for his part in the battle of Aughrim. Ruvigny was granted an estate in Portarlington that, under his influence, became the most prominent Huguenot settlement outside of Dublin. Deputy-general of the Huguenot churches in France since 1658, he had become a prominent advocate for his coreligionists in the French court. In exile in Holland, where he became a lieutenant general in William's army, he played a similar role and did so again in Ireland as Lord Galway and as Chief Justice for Ireland, a position designed to give him influence on Irish affairs in order to pave the way for Huguenot settlement.[94] Ruvigny was also an advocate of Huguenot settlements in British North America, the most successful of which was founded in Virginia.[95]

Studies of those who settled in Portarlington, Lisburn, Waterford, Youghal and Cork reveal close family ties and mobility between Irish Huguenots and those in France, Britain and the Netherlands. Huguenot involvement in maritime trade had much to do with the decisions of some of their number to settle in Ireland. Huguenot areas in France included parts of the South-West of France which produced wine and brandy,[96] and there existed well-established trade routes from the French ports to Waterford, Youghal and Cork. Many settlers seem to have chosen the line of least resistance in deciding where to live by either remaining in the ports at which they arrived, or in a handful of towns, most notably Portarlington and Lisburn, where some incentives had been made to attract them.[97]

Portarlington became the sole settlement where French settlers out-numbered all other inhabitants.[98] The town was named for its founder, Lord Arlington, who in 1666 acquired lands seized from the O'Dempseys for their involvement in the Kilkenny Confederacy. A map of the town from 1666 shows a small fort, surrounded by earthworks, a moat and the River Barrow with a market square and four streets leading from this with land holdings neatly plotted out. Arlington, a supporter of Charles II, never made a success of the estate because, Arlington claimed, the tenants he attracted 'did not prove their worth'. In 1685 he sold the estate to Sir Patrick Trant, a Jacobite from whom it had been confiscated in 1692.[99]

Ruvigny and other Huguenot regimental leaders settled many of their officers in Portarlington as tenants. However, William's gift of the Portarlington estate to Ruvigny was challenged by Parliament, and his title and the leases of his tenants were not secured until 1702. This left many of these settlers impoverished, initially, and they appealed to the French Church of St Patrick's for seed and cattle to allow them to begin farming, and for the services of a surgeon.[100] A 1701 pamphlet (published at a time when the King's grant of the town to Lord Galway was being challenged) referred to 'the deplorable condition of the poor French Protestants at Portarlington' living in 130 dwellings that had been constructed by Ruvigny.

The Church built by Ruvigny in the town in 1694 was Calvinist in orientation, and the Huguenots in Portarlington came under pressure to conform to the Established Church. Ruvigny and his tenants also found their leases challenged. The deal that was struck in 1702 which finally secured the leases of Huguenots in Portarlington included a requirement to embrace the established Church. When Pasteur Benjamin de Daillon, the Huguenot minister in Portarlington, refused to adopt the required liturgy, a second minister, Pasteur Bonneval was installed. Daillon held out in Portarlington until 1708 when he moved to Carlow.[101]

Portarlington was not an economic success. An overt dependency on military pensions by its somewhat elderly population did not auger well. Portarlington did not draw the kind of Huguenot settlers who set up linen manufacturing as in Lisburn, or engaged in trade with the Continent as did a number of those in coastal towns. However, some sons of demobilised soldiers became Church of Ireland clergy, proof beyond doubt of their assimilation. Others entered 'small trade', and a few set up schools that came to be highly regarded.[102] The birth rate amongst Huguenots declined rapidly after an initial burst of post-war marriages; much of the community had already reached middle age by the time they settled in the town.[103]

Some surviving accounts by refugees from France give a sense of the dynamics of the Huguenot diaspora. During the 1680s, up to 150,000 Huguenots left France. Among them were two female members of the Robillard de Champagné family, who left accounts of their escape from France.[104] Marie de La Rochefoucauld, dame de Champagné, described the journey she made with her eldest son, who would subsequently settle in Ireland in Portarlington. In her account she passes from one Huguenot enclave to another, and is helped at each stage along the way by co-religionists and compatriots. In 1722 she moved to Portarlington to live with her eldest son, Josias de Champagné, until her death in 1730.

Decades later en route to Holland, Marie spent three months in England (from June to September 1687) where she was reunited with her 19-year-old daughter, Suzanne, who had escaped separately out of France with all but one of Marie's six other children. A newborn baby who, it was feared, might not survive the journey, was placed in an orphanage and later taken from France by another relative. In Holland, using her social connections, Marie managed to place her second son as a page in court. In May 1688 she went to live with relatives who were already established in Voorburg. In June 1688 she was reunited with her husband, the Chevalier Josias de Robillard, Seigneur de Champagné. In September 1688, he embarked with William's army to Ireland, and soon after, died in Belfast from an illness. After his death, his eldest son, Josias, who later settled in Portarlington, received a commission as an ensign in William's army.

Suzanne de Robillard de Champagné, who had travelled with six of her younger siblings from Berneré to the port of La Rochelle, sailed from there to Falmouth in England, and then via Dartmouth and Exeter to Rotterdam. In 1692, Suzanne married Baron Tonnay Boutonne de Saint Surin, who came from an aristocratic Huguenot family that had fallen on hard times. They had a son, Henri, Baron de la Motte Fouqué, who served as a general in the army of Fredrick the Great.[105] After her husband's death, Suzanne lived as a genteel companion to a noblewoman in Celle in Germany.

Josias Champagné fought in the Battle of the Boyne and rose to the rank of major. After he settled in Portarlington, he married Jane, the eldest daughter of Arthur Forbes, second Earl of Granard. He became a prominent member of the Portarlington community.[106] He went into business using money borrowed from his brother François Auguste. He acquired and sub-let a number of properties and became a trader of 'turf, sheep, firewood, chickens, ducks and grain'.[107] Josias appears to have been considerably younger than many of the other leading Huguenot settlers in Portarlington, who were contemporaries of his deceased father. While many Huguenot settlers had kept up connections with family and co-religionists on the Continent, some, like Champagné, married English Protestants. Between 1699 and 1718, just 15 out of a total of 95 recorded Huguenot marriages were to non-Huguenots. The numbers of such exogamous unions increased considerably after the 1720s, by which time the first Irish-born generation had become adults,[108] and appear to have been thoroughly assimilated. Josias's son, Arthur Champagné, was educated in Trinity College and took Holy Orders. His wife, Marianne, was the daughter of another Huguenot settler, Major Isaac Hamon.[109] Arthur became Vicar of Mullingar in 1746 and Dean of Clonmacnoise in 1761.

Retired soldiers also settled in Lisburn in County Antrim which had served as the headquarters of William's army including its Huguenot regiments in 1689. These included members of the de la Cherois, or Cheroy family. Many Huguenot surnames referred to a place the family held title to in France, in this case to Cheroy a small town in the province of Champagne. Prior to the revocation of the Treaty of the Nantes members of the de la Cherois family served as officers the French army. Three brothers entered the service of William in Holland. Of these, Bourjouval was killed in a skirmish near Dungannon in 1689. His elder bother Daniel was appointed by William as governor of Ponticherry in the West Indies. He amassed a large fortune as a merchant. Nicholas de la Cherois, who settled in Lisburn, served William of Orange in various European campaigns until about 1694 after the defeat of James II in Ulster.[110]

Whilst retired military were also an important element of the Huguenot community in Lisburn in County Antrim, the dynamics were considerably different because of the role played by the linen industry in attracting settlers. In 1698 Louis Crommelin, a linen manufacturer who had become established in Holland, accompanied by his son, travelled to Ireland and selected Lisburn as a suitable site for his business. In France, Crommelin's ancestors had worked at linen manufacturing for centuries and had owned estates in Picardy. Some members of the family also became merchants and bankers in Holland.[111] By the time of Louis Crommelin's death in 1727, the linen industry had become established in Antrim, Down, Armagh, Tyrone, and Derry.[112]

Crommelin recruited other Huguenots and imported 1,000 looms and spinning wheels, built a church and employed a chaplain who had served with Ruvigny. According to one account, about 75 families were initially settled in Lisburn and these were joined by another 50 in time, bringing the total strength of the Huguenot colony in Ulster to about 500 persons. Two of Crommelin's three siblings who followed him to Lisburn invested £10,000 each, about the same amount that Louis had into Lisburn. To put the scale of this investment in context, Civil List funds, totalling £2,486 were spent on providing assistance to Huguenot refugees of all classes in England in 1696, rising to £12,025 by 1699; by the standards of the time, this was a huge state expenditure.[113]

In addition to the main settlement in Lisburn, some Huguenots settled nearby in Castleblaney, Lambeg, Killeshandra, and Collon in what were effectively offshoots of the main community. But not all efforts to found Huguenot settlements succeeded; for example, attempts to attract Huguenot agricultural tenants to an estate in Castleblaney in County Monaghan failed even though a French minister was promised.[114] Most Huguenot settlement in Ireland was urban, which amplified an already-established demographic trend. In France over 40 per cent of the Huguenot population had lived in towns with more than 2,000 inhabitants compared to 15–19 per cent of the total French population around 1700.[115]

Some Huguenots conformed to the established Church from the outset. To some extent, religious assimilation occurred because many Huguenots settled in towns where the Protestant populations were members of the established Church. Except in Portarlington, and there only for a time, Huguenots constituted a minority of Protestants in such towns. In time they came to be a minority there also. They do not appear to have joined Irish Presbyterian congregations. At its peak, the Huguenot community in Dublin supported four French-speaking Church of Ireland congregations,[116] with the one in St Patrick's Cathedral lasting until 1817. Even in Portarlington, use of the French language declined over time as the Huguenots ceased to be a majority of Protestants in the area.[117] Religious services in French in the Cathedral finally ceased in 1841.[118]

SETTLERS, EMIGRANTS AND EXILES

The early eighteenth century brought the beginning of a long era of Irish emigration, one that has continued in stops and starts since then. It would not be until the 1960s that migration added to Ireland's population, with the return of some who had left to seek employment. It would not be until the end of the twentieth century that other kinds of immigration occurred to any great extent, and some exceptions to this are considered in subsequent chapters. In effect, then, by the end of the seventeenth century, the die was cast, and the composition of Irish society, with its large Catholic majority and a Protestant minority, was fixed. From these ingredients the modern Irish nation was forged.

There were no further schemes to encourage European Protestant settlers in Ireland, with one exception: the Palatines, examined in the next chapter. There was a wave of migration from Scotland to Ulster during the 1690s, but this was not directed by the Crown. By the eighteenth century, North America had become more accessible as a destination for migrants from England and Scotland. Not only did North America attract more immigrants than did Ireland, it also drew Protestant dissenter emigrants from Ulster who sought religious freedom as well as better economic opportunities. England had also become an immigrant destination, and successive monarchs and parliaments encouraged the settlement of European Protestants. Their motives variously included feelings of religious solidarity with European Protestants like the Huguenots, economic reasons, but also a degree of concern about the loss of population to the colonies. The Huguenots were, in a sense, Ireland's last colonists. They were encouraged, facilitated and assisted to settle in Ireland with the aim of shoring up earlier plantations, and were expected to become part of the ruling Protestant elite. Some managed to put down roots in Ireland whilst keeping a sense of their pre-migration identity for a few generations, even though they ultimately became assimilated into the wider Protestant ruling minority.

The huge changes that took place in Ireland during the seventeenth century were partly the product of incoming and outgoing migrations. It is unsurprising that incoming Protestant settlers fared better than the no-less large numbers who emigrated, especially to the Continent. Ireland's seventeenth-century diaspora included Gaels, old English, and even recently arrived New English who ventured across the Atlantic. Irish merchants and landlords collaborated with adventurers from Newfoundland to the Amazon Basin, Virginia, and the West Indies.[119] The indentured Irish who were transplanted to the New World were colonists rather than slaves, for all that many of them may have been sorely exploited. These were followed in subsequent centuries by large numbers of immigrant Irish settlers who, from the vantage point of the native populations, were also colonists.

If soldiers constituted the biggest emigrant group throughout the seventeenth century, they were perhaps the least successful. They served kings and countries that did not want the soldiers' families and dependants as settlers. Soldiering persisted as a way out of poverty into the eighteenth and nineteenth centuries, and for this reason, large numbers of Irishmen took the English King's shilling once it became possible to do so during the eighteenth century.[120] The traces left by Irish emigrants on the Continent were mostly of the Gaelic and Old English elites, and unlike Protestant military settlers in Ireland, these received no offers of land in lieu of wages or other inducements to settle. They were transported but not transplanted.

FIVE

PALATINES

The settlement of Protestants in Ireland included not just immigrants from England and Scotland but, in smaller numbers, the Huguenots described in the last chapter, and, fewer still, German Protestants from the Rhineland, who had been encouraged to settle in England during Queen Anne's reign. Some 13,500 'poor Palatines' arrived in London in 1709, and of these 3,000 were shipped onwards to Dublin with the aim of making them subsidised tenants to Protestant landlords. They formed but a small per cent of plantation settlers, and warranted little more than footnote in Lecky's multivolume history of Ireland's eighteenth century. There was not much to be said, Lecky began, before touching on a hidden history about which a lot might be said. He got some of his facts wrong in even this brief account of the Palatines, which points to how assimilation writes diversity out of history. In Lecky's summary, about 800 families were settled for the most part as tenant families by a small number of large landlords. Unlike the native Irish, they obtained intergenerational leases at low rents and more so than the native Irish, according to Lecky, they improved their lands, bringing distinctive farming techniques. They kept up a German identity for more than three-quarters of a century and even appointed a burgomaster to settle their disputes. They usually adhered to a nonconformist type of Protestantism, but got on well with their Catholic neighbours. They did better than their neighbours because of the exceptional advantages they were granted when they first arrived, and when in the course of time their original three-generation leases ended, they passed into the condition of ordinary Irish tenants and, according to Lecky, their colony effectively disappeared.[1]

An 1861 account of the Palatines in County Limerick described the persistence of their discernible cultural differences from the surrounding population:

> We visited several of their cottages in the neighbourhood of Adare; and the neatness, good order, and quantity and quality of the furniture – useful and ornamental – too surely indicated that we were not in an Irish cabin. Huge flitches

of bacon hung from the rafters; the chairs were in several instances composed of walnut tree and oak; massive and heavy although rudely carved chests contained, we were told, the house linen and woollens, and the wardrobes of the inhabitants. The elders of the family preserve, in a great degree, the language, customs and religion of their old country; but the younger mingle and marry with their Irish neighbours. The men are tall, fine stout fellows, but there is a calm and stern severity and reserve in this respect that is anything but cheering to the traveller to meet, particularly after being accustomed to the brilliant smiles and hearty "God save ye kindly", so perpetually on the Irish peasant's lips and always in his eyes. This characteristic is also remarkable in the cottages – the women are sombre looking, and their large blue eyes are neither bright or expressive; they are slow to bid you welcome; and, if they rise from their seats, resume them quickly and hardly suspend their occupations to talk with you; not that they are uncourteous – they are simply reserved and of that high toned manner which is at ease with or careless in the presence of strangers. In their dealings they are considered upright and honourable, like the Quakers of old; they do not interfere with either politics or religion, are cautious as to land taking; and in troublous times, when the generality of persons were afraid to walk forth, the quiet Palatine pursued his avocations without let or hindrance, being rarely if ever molested.[2]

Perhaps they were rarely molested in 1861, but in the aftermath of the 1798 rebellion and even into the 1850s, Palatines were the objects of violent attacks from Catholic neighbours who resented their preferential tenancies, closer relationships with landlords, membership of Protestant militias and their loyalism. Such tensions across the community played a part in shaping decisions by generations of Palatines in Limerick to migrate once again, mostly to Canada. In County Wexford, the other main site of Palatine settlement in Ireland, there was little impetus for a drip-feed of sectarian conflict after 1798 because the main Palatine 'colony' had been burnt out, its members scattered, and a number of them murdered during the rebellion.[3]

As non-English-speaking Protestants, the first generation of Palatines stood out from other planted colonists. Specifically, as immigrants who spoke neither English nor Irish, some of the challenges they faced – and presented to the host population – resemble those experienced by some immigrants in early-twenty-first-century Ireland. The politics of the Palatines' admission into England and dispersal onwards in many respects anticipated the dynamics of many modern immigration debates. Explanations of why Palatine migration to England was actively encouraged and, within a short time, then perceived as a crisis is echoed in how immigration can become politicised in our own time. There exists a mass of recorded detail of their migration from the Lower Palatinate to holding camps in Rotterdam, from there to refugee camps in south London and onwards from these to Dublin.

In London, the Palatines were initially welcomed by the Crown, which paid for their passage, and by the established Church, which raised funds for their shelter. They arrived in the midst of political conflicts between Whigs and Tories about immigration policy, which by the early eighteenth century had been written into law. Arguments for and against policies of deliberately encouraging immigration of European Protestants and for and against their naturalisation as British subjects played out along party lines. Behind these lay economic policies and more generally, mercantilist ideology, religious affinities shaped by the Reformation, as well as disputes within English Protestantism between what had become the established Church and Protestant dissenters. The welcome extended to European Calvinists and Lutherans by English Protestants depended upon where they stood in such disputes. Then, political pressures mounted as a result of the arrival of immigrants; it was one thing for Queen Anne's Whig government to transport some 13,500 Palatines to London, a city of about 300,000, but it was another thing to feed and accommodate them, pay for it, and then design viable plans to ship them onwards to the colonies (as the Palatines hoped), or to disperse them successfully around Britain.

The Palatines who came to Ireland travelled down the Rhine to Rotterdam, where they found themselves in the first of three transit camps awaiting passage – many believed to North America. A period in what might now be described as a refugee camp in Rotherham was followed for most by a longer stay in another in London. On their arrival in Dublin they found themselves for the third time in makeshift camps and accommodation. Some 3,000 were sent to Ireland, and not for the first or last time in Irish history, many of these were unwilling immigrants.

DEPARTURES AND ARRIVALS

The Lower Palatinate was a region bisected by the Rhine to the north of Alsace that included the towns of Worms and Heidelberg. It was here that Protestantism germinated when Martin Luther first took his stand against the Roman Church, and it later became a centre of Calvinism. The 'poor Palatines' were understood to have suffered from religious persecution, the ravages of the Thirty Years' War and, just before their migration to England in 1709, a particularly cold winter that devastated the vineyards in which many of them worked. For several years prior to this they had been supported in their grievances as a Protestant people in a Catholic principality, and had found support from England's Queen Anne. After winning the 1708 election, the Whigs proposed a bill that allowed for the naturalisation of foreign Protestants for a fee of one shilling. The Tories opposed the bill and then won an amendment that required naturalised foreigners to become members of the established Church. Within weeks of the passing of the Foreign Protestants Naturalisation Act in March 1709, thousands of Palatines began to enter the country.[4]

The sympathy of the English Crown towards European Protestant migrants was hardly surprising. In June 1681, Charles II had issued a proclamation to attract French Huguenots to England, having nine years earlier extended a similar invitation to Dutch artisans. Huguenots had been encouraged to emigrate to England and Ireland since the reign of Elizabeth I and did so, in the case of the former, at those times when the fears of Protestants in Catholic France ran high. They were less attracted to Ireland, not least because its reputation after 1641 as a place where Catholics massacred Protestants. In 1688, William of Orange with his wife, Mary, took the English throne from his father-in-law, James II, to secure England for the Protestant cause. His army, which defeated James in Ireland, contained hundreds of Huguenot officers and soldiers, some of whom settled there (see chapter 4). From her accession in 1701 Queen Anne supported the interests of European Protestants and their settlement in England. Because the Act of Succession (1701) prohibited Catholics from ascending the throne the Crown passed after Anne's death in 1714 to George I, a German unable to speak English. At the time of the Palatine migration to England he was the Prince Elector of Hanover, so Protestant England was open to German migrants at the very apex as well as at the bottom of its social hierarchy.

When Anne's consort, Prince George of Denmark, died on 28 October 1708, the funeral sermon was delivered by the Reverend John Tribbeko, a Lutheran who in May the following year became involved in the settlement of the thousands of Palatines arriving in London. The Queen actively took up the case of the oppressed co-religionists of her departed husband,[5] while the established Church of England, represented by Anglicans in Parliament, viewed European Protestant immigration as a threat to its own status.

Then as now, support and opposition to immigration turned on ideology. The Whigs were proponents of a Mercantilist doctrine which maintained as 'a Fundamental Maxim in Sound Politicks, that the Greatness, Wealth, and Strength of a Country, consist in the Number of its Inhabitants.'[6] Immigration was seen as necessary to counterbalance emigration to the colonies, and the English government under Anne embarked upon a policy of encouraging and subsidising immigration. The preamble to the Foreign Protestants Naturalisation Act (1709) observed that 'the increase of people is a means of advancing the wealth and strength of a nation.'[7] However, the migration of Palatine Germans to England was hardly Anne's idea or that of one of her officials; for two decades, the Palatinate had been bombarded with advertising campaigns offering a promised land to enterprising settlers willing to cross the Atlantic. Colonial speculators including William Penn circulated letters and pamphlets in German advertising free land in North America to home-steaders. A 1709 pamphlet, known as 'The Golden Book', with a picture of Queen Anne on the cover, encouraged Palatines to come to England in order to be sent to Carolina or another of the colonies.[8] But the likes of Penn, who had spent much of 1708 in prison for unpaid debts, were unable to deliver on such promises.[9]

Yet, there existed precedents for government-assisted immigration to England's dominions. For example, in 1679 Charles II sent two ship-loads of Huguenots to South Carolina in order to introduce the cultivation of grapes, olives and the silk-worm. Precedents could also be found, at least in theory, in the case of Irish plantations. In 1694, a Baron de Luttichaw petitioned for funds to import 200 Protestant families, some 1,000 persons, from Silesia in Germany as his tenants. He sought a grant of forfeited lands to him and his heirs, as well as funds to cover the costs of hiring two ships to bring them from Hamburg to Ireland. This particular scheme never came to pass.[10]

In 1709, what could be seen as a chain migration saw thousands of Palatines leave for London. A small group had already become established there, and reports of their positive experiences had filtered home. In January 1708 Joshua von Kocherthal, a Lutheran minister, had led a group of 40 Palatines to London and had secured onward passage to New York and employment for these in the manufacture of naval stores. He had used an English agency in Frankfurt to secure permission and funding for their journey to London. Frankfurt had previously been a staging post for Huguenot emigration following the Edict of Fontainebleau in 1685 which revoked religious tolerance towards them in France.[11] Other such small groups followed and, after the bad winter of 1709 and the passing of naturalisation legislation in England, this trickle became a flood.[12] It is likely that most of the new arrivals expected to be settled in the New World, and many, however unrealistically, expected to be granted lands. Most of the 13,000 or so who abandoned their homes and travelled down the Rhine did not expect to be settled in England and Ireland. Most of the 3,000 Palatines who ended up in Ireland were among the first 11,064 travelling in six or eight parties who embarked from Rotterdam to London between May and July 1709. At the request of the English authorities the names, marital status and occupations of these were recorded, as well as their religion.[13]

By December 1708 Palatine refugees had begun to arrive in Rotterdam to seek passage to England. Within weeks of the Foreign Protestants Naturalisation Act receiving royal assent on 23 March 1709 thousands had embarked.[14] The first contingent arrived in London around 3 May having waited a number of weeks for passage in Rotterdam. Funding for their passage provided by the Crown and their passage to England was overseen by James Dayrolle, England's representative in The Hague. From 29 March onwards, Dayrolle issued travel passes to batches of 60 or 100 families at a time. He requested that the transports bringing troops from England to the Low Countries to fight against the French in the War of the Spanish Succession return to England with the Palatines. Late in April, four such transports carried 852 Palatines to London. Their subsistence on the voyage was funded in part by the burgomasters of Rotterdam who were sympathetic to the Palatines but also anxious that they be moved on. On 17 May Dayrolle received authorisation to organise of the transportation of all Palatine refugees in Rotterdam at government expense. By 8 June, over 6,000 Palatines had been shipped at the expense of the British government.[15]

But on 24 June, in response to reports he submitted to London that the flow of Palatines showed no signs of abating, Dayrolle was instructed to arrange passage only for those who had arrived by Rotterdam by then. Another 1,776 were shipped to London on 29 June, and Dayrolle moved to block further Palatines from making their way down the Rhine. Some were turned back, and notices that more would be accepted were posted in a Cologne gazette. But on 5 July Dayrolle he made the case for 500 more still waiting in Rotterdam to be allowed into England. By the time he got approval to ship these the total in Rotterdam had risen to about 2000. On 18 July Dayrolle dispatched 1,433 of these to London even as orders to stop any more were on their way to him. In August a further 1,000 refugees, paid for by the Dutch and without papers from England, sailed for London. On 15 July another 2,776 sailed from Rotterdam to London followed by a further 1,443 on 28 July. By the end of the summer of 1709, approximately 13,500 Palatines had landed in England.[16]

DISPERSAL

The March 1709 Act prepared England for immigration in theory only; no plans existed to deal with large numbers of real migrants. As has happened many times since, a mood of initial benevolence quickly shifted towards antipathy, hostility and moral panic. Two Lutheran ministers, John Tribbeko and George Andrew Ruperti, took charge of assisting the first batch of arrivals, who supported a royal warrant from Anne that granted £16 a day to help feed and accommodate this group of 852. But by the end of the summer more than 10,000 Palatines with no means of support were accommodated in camps at Greenwich, Blackheath and Camberwell. Unsurprisingly, this presented a crisis for London, which at the time had a population of about 300,000. Whig pamphlets, most notably those of Daniel Defoe, earnestly exalted the contributions the Palatines might make to England, while Tory opponents of immigration whipped up populist hostility to their presence in London. Meanwhile, the equivalents perhaps of modern-day refugee support groups put their shoulders to the wheel and organised practical support.

The refugees – for that was what they were at that stage – apparently destitute, living in camps under considerable privation with many cordoned off from the host population – depended on charitable donations. The Queen issued an appeal to all Churches and congregations to collect alms to pay for food and accommodation, as well as contributing significant amounts herself. Tens of thousands of pounds were collected, with over £20,000 raised in London alone,[17] some organised by Justices of the Peace. Many Anglican congregations contributed generously though support from some established Church leaders outside of London was half-hearted. The Queen appointed commissioners to assess living conditions and distribute donations and to administer the funds collected. Among them was John Tribbeko, the former chaplain of her deceased husband, Prince George of Denmark. From 6 July the commissioners met several times a week to address London's refugee crisis.[18]

About 13,500 Palatines reached London, though this number excluded some who had travelled independently to England at their own expense. Of these, some 2,257 Roman Catholics were sent back late in September, having first being given the choice of converting to Protestantism or returning to their homes on the Rhine. At least one of these, John Adam Jacobi (later anglicised as Jacobs), who subsequently settled in Wexford, seems to have taken up this offer. He was listed in June 1709 as a Catholic who 'will turn Protestant'.[19] In addition to the deported Catholics, about 900 Protestant Palatines declared that they wished to return home. On 3 March 1710 Dayrolle reported that they had safely arrived in Holland; he gave them five gilders each to speed them on their way home.[20]

The Palatines had expected to be dispatched onwards from England, but no such plans had been put in place. As an interim measure, 1,600 tents were issued by the Board of Ordnance and encampments set up at Camberwell and Blackheath on the south side of the Thames, and at Greenwich across the river to the north, to accommodate about 6,500. Others were accommodated in barns and cheap properties around the city. The Palatine encampments were attacked by London mobs, on one occasion by about 2,000 Englishmen armed with axes, scythes, and smith hammers.[21] Correspondence from the time blamed the Palatines for outbreaks of smallpox in the city, and indeed nearly 1,000 died of fevers and plagues. Petitions from London parishes adjacent to Palatine encampments were organised by the Tories who had opposed their admission in the first place. An account survives of the response of some Palatines who overheard three or four

Englishmen, drinking a pot or two of ale, who 'made some Reflections upon the Receiving of these People into the Kingdom'; the Englishmen were beaten 'in a very rude and inhuman manner'.[22]

It was clear that the Palatines could only be briefly accommodated in London, and attention soon focused on how they might be resettled elsewhere. Daniel Defoe published a plan to settle Palatine families in communities small enough to ensure their assimilation over time. In a July 1709 article Defoe proposed:

> That the Palatine Strangers may be planted in small Townships, like little Colonies, in the several Forrests and Wastes of England. . . These little Colonies, I Propose, should consist of about 50 or 100 families each, as the Goodness of the Land, or the Extent of the Forrests or Wastes they are settled in will admit, but none to contain above 100 Families for several Reasons; particularly that the Language and Customs of the People as Foreigners, may not be too long preserv'd, but that they may by Time, and mingling themselves with us become the same People with ourselves, as all other Nations we have entertain'd hitherto have done.[23]

Defoe also published a plan to settle 20 families on a 4,000-acre tract of land in the New Forest with loans of £200 to each family to help them establish farms.[24] After wide-ranging debate, nothing as generous as this was actually attempted in England, nor subsequently in Ireland, where the aim instead was that such 'little colonies' might bolster a minority Protestant presence on estates where most tenants were Catholics.

All such schemes in Ireland depended upon subsidies for landowners willing to take on Palatine tenants. Three main problems arose. First, many of the Palatines wanted to settle in the colonies. Some wanted to be sent to the West Indies, but the view of the Board of Trade was that they would not be able to handle the climate, and that it would be more practical and beneficial to settle many of them in England. The second problem was that the Palatines had emigrated in order to obtain land, not to become the tenants of others. The third problem was the expense of subsidy-based schemes to the crown, and land owners wanted subsidies and grants for taking on Palatine tenants.

In the absence of plans to ship them to the colonies, and in the face of pressure to move them out of London, the government offered three pounds per head to parishes throughout the country which were willing to receive them. In some cases where this offer was taken up, the immigrants, unhappy with their treatment, returned to London again. In one case, 16 families were sent to the town of Sunderland in Durham, where they expected to receive grants of land, but were instead made to work as day labourers.

Liverpool received 130 Palatines, but they drifted away as soon as the government support had been exhausted. A navy captain, Thomas Ekines, proposed that 600 Palatines, about 150 families, should be settled in the Scilly Islands off the southwest coast of England, and so, on 21 September and 2 October, two shiploads of 450 passengers were dispatched from London. The inhabitants of the islands protested. After spending three months confined to the ships, the refugees were returned to Blackheath. The failed effort to settle them on the Scilly Islands cost £1,500. Some of the returned Palatines enlisted in the army, and about 150 were sent to serve in Lord Galloway's regiment, then on duty in Portugal.[25]

Overall, between 2,000 and 3,000 Palatines were settled across England by various such schemes, leaving more than 7,000 still in London at the end of the summer of 1709. Of these, 821 families – 1,898 adults and 1,175 under 14 years of age – were shipped to Dublin from Chester, most of them in September and October 1710, and all by January 1710.[26]

SETTLEMENTS

A panel of Irish Commissioners for Settling the Poor Distressed Palatines in Ireland was appointed. It included a number of Protestant landlords who hoped to profit from taking on Palatine tenants. To finance their settlement, the Crown appropriated £15,000 from Irish revenues. Soon afterwards, a further £9,000 was added to this pot along with £409 in charitable donations.[27] One hand appeared to wash the other in how decisions were made to disperse Palatines and allocate the funds. Nine commissioners were amongst those Protestant landowners selected by lottery to benefit from contracts to settle Palatines as their tenants.[28] One of these landowners, Stephen Sweet, received a contract to settle 18 families on his estate at Coonamuck near Inistioge in County Kilkenny. He drew up maps that specified allotments of just four and a half acres each for each family, well below the size specified by the Commissioners and, incidentally, a fraction of the farm sizes proposed by Defoe. Between 1710 and 1720 all 18 families quit Sweet's estate. When interviewed in London some of these claimed 'hard usage' by Sweet, and that they had not been paid the agreed subsistence allowance.[29]

In all, 533 families, composed of 2,098 men, women and children, were dispersed over the countryside and offered tenancies at rents a third less than offered to other tenants, which nevertheless fell short of the expectations of many that they would get land rent-free. By November 1709, some 232 families had left Ireland and returned to England followed by more in the months that followed. By February 1711, just 188 of the 533 families that had been distributed around Ireland remained on the estates to which they were sent. Over 300 families had stayed in Dublin, where many of the men had found temporary work building a government arsenal. As more and more Palatines returned to England, a revised scheme was mooted that would grant 40 shillings per annum for 21 years to each family. In March 1711, the English government approved such a scheme limited to seven years. By November 1711, the estimated number of Palatines in Ireland had dropped to 979 persons in 263 families. It appeared that about two-thirds had left Ireland and most sought to return to Germany. [30] Of the 43 landlords who had signed up to take on Palatines, only 13 managed to retain their initial complement of tenants.[31]

The most successful landlord was Sir Thomas Southwell from Castle Matrix, also known as Castle Matress (derived from 'Matres', a reference in Latin to the triple mother-goddesses of the pagan Celts) near Rathkeale in County Limerick. Castle Matrix had been built in 1410 by the Fitzgeralds. The area remained under the control of the Fitzgerald dynasty of Desmond until 1583, when Gerald Fitzgerald Earl of Desmond was defeated in a rebellion against Elizabeth I following a long war that is thought killed one-third of the population of Munster. The town of Rathkeale was burned, and the lands of the Munster Geraldines were mostly divided between Walter Raleigh, Edmund Spenser and Edmund Southwell. Raleigh repaired Castle Matrix and introduced potato tubers to the area. Potatoes were initially harvested in the land around Castle Matrix in 1610, by which time it had become the property of Southwell. Castle Matrix had been the location of a meeting between Spenser and Raleigh that is credited with inspiring Spenser's poem *The Faerie Queen*.

Unlike Sweet and many other landlords who fell along the wayside, Thomas Southwell stuck to the terms of settlement, though it took years to recoup funding owed to him from the government. One hundred and thirty Palatine families were eventually settled successfully in Southwell's lands, mostly in three townlands. In both Castle Matrix (which came to be known as Court Village) and Killeheen clusters of 20 to 25 family homesteads were established, and in Ballingrane more than 50 households were settled in small groups of houses. Southwell had been a prominent member of the Commission. His principal motivation was probably to strengthen the Protestant presence on his lands. Each of Southwell's male adult Palatine tenants was issued with an aptly named Queen Anne musket, and this Protestant militia came to be known as the German Fusiliers.[32]

The next-largest lasting settlement of Palatines comprised 35 families on lands owned by Abel Ram in Gorey and in Old Ross in County Wexford. Over time, a further 28 families became his tenants. Ram, like Southwell, was a Commissioner and a keen advocate of Palatine settlement in Ireland.

Another commissioner, Benjamin Burton, who owned lands in north County Carlow, successfully settled 15 of the 20 families he had been allocated in a village known as Palatinestown or Palatine near Burton Hall. In Cork, 29 families settled as tenants of six different landlords. Some others were scattered around Ireland, a family here, a family there.[33]

Between 1747 and 1789, the Palatines (mainly those in Limerick) were repeatedly visited by John Wesley, who successfully converted many of them to Methodism. He recorded his impressions of their communities and how these changed over time in his journal. In 1758, Wesley estimated that 110 Palatine families lived in various communities in County Limerick in the vicinity of Southwell's estate. In addition to the three original settlements, he described a newer, second-generation community of some 20 families in on the Bury estate about four miles away Pallaskenry. One of its founders in 1747 was Jaspar St John from Ballingrane, the largest of the initial three Palatine communities and most of the other Palatine families who moved there also came from Ballingrane.[34] By the 1770s, groups of Irish-born Palatines had moved to form a number of smaller settlements in other parts of County Limerick but also in the adjoining counties of Cork and Kerry, presumably because they were unable to rent lands adjacent to the those leased by their families, or because leases could be had on better terms further afield.

A lot changed in and around 1760. Until then, German had been widely spoken within the Limerick communities, but from then it seems to have rapidly declined. The Limerick Palatines were preached to by Wesley in English. After 1760 Methodism rather than the German language seems to become the main marker of Palatine cultural distinctiveness in Limerick. Children during the early eighteenth century received some primary education in German, but this seems to have come to an end by 1760.

The lands leased from Southwell in three clusters in Limerick were unable to meet the needs of a growing population. The threat of massive rent increases, as initial leaseholds came to an end, pushed Palatines to seek more advantageous tenancies elsewhere, again in groups, and the result was the establishment of a number of new communities elsewhere in Limerick and in the adjoining counties of Tipperary and Kerry. But it was also the case that many Palatines emigrated to the United States and Canada.[35]

Most of their new settlements were far smaller in number than those originally established on the Southwell estate. In some cases, Protestant landlords took an active role nurturing these new settlements. From the late 1750s to the 1780s one such community was established at Kilnaughtin near Tarbert on the Shannon estuary. The largest new settlement sponsored by a landlord was established on the Oliver estate in South County Limerick. Twenty seven families moved there in 1759–60 on attractive terms: their landholdings, ranging from 13 to 30 acres, were larger than those held by earlier generations, but the land itself, in hilly country, was not as good. The Palatines worked it successfully as tillage farmers. They were offered rents at two-thirds the going rate for three lifetimes, and houses were built for them at a total cost of around £500. Within 15 years, three tightly clustered village settlements on Oliver lands at Ballyriggin, Ballyorgan and Glenosheen accommodated at least 60 families. Over time, place names in Ballyriggin came to include a Palatine Hill and a Palatine Rock, and these new communities appointed a burgomaster. Along similar lines, Sir William Barker established his Palatine tenants in the adjoining townlands of Newpark and Bawnlea on Slieve Ardagh in County Tipperary in order to bring marginal hill lands into use.[36]

Considering that they had previously paid one-third the going rate for rents, the prospect of massive rent rises saw many families migrate elsewhere in Limerick, Kerry and Tipperary. However, the problem was that the original Southwell settlements had become overcrowded. Sometimes, like their Catholic neighbours, Palatine tenants subdivided their leases amongst their children which meant they became poorer than their parents. Population pressures were evident in some of the older settlements such as Courtmatrix, leading to an ongoing exodus of young people.[37]

Wesley described the Palatines' 'plain' peasant farmer way of life as similar in many respects to North American Protestant sects such as the Amish in Pennsylvania or the Mennonites in Ontario, who were also descended from German migrants. Court Village had acquired a preaching house that drew its congregation also from Killeheen and Ballingrane. None of these three townlands possessed a tavern, though their inhabitants would not have had to travel far to find one in adjoining Catholic areas. It seems that the Limerick Palatines were without pastors and somewhat lax in their religion before Wesley galvanised them, as they were renowned for their excellent cider, and Wesley described some of them as having been infamous for their drunkenness in their early days in Ireland. He certainly curbed this behaviour, but cider-making persisted as a tradition in the area until the twentieth century.[38] Wesley, by converting many of the second-generation Palatines to Methodism, did much to foster an ongoing sense of cohesion amongst their descendants, but Methodism also worked to smother some of the cultural practices that the Palatines had brought from Germany, including the use of the German language.[39]

During the second half of the eighteenth century, Irish Palatine emigrants to the United States played an important role in the establishment of Methodism there. In June 1760, about 40 people, mostly from Ballingrane and Pallaskenry, embarked from Limerick and settled in Albany in New York state. There is some evidence that Irish Palatine migrants in America intermarried, and began a chain migration whereby later parties of Limerick Palatines joined earlier arrivals. Their social cohesion in North America owed much to their Methodism as well to their kinship and shared Limerick roots. From 1770 the Limerick Palatines settled a 2,557-acre tract of land in the then Charlotte County in the northernmost part of New York state. During the American War of Independence, they moved farther north to Canada, where they settled in number of clusters in Ontario. Switzerville, Ontario took its name from members of the Palatine Switzer family who had migrated via New York from Courtmatrix. Another Switzer left Newpark, one of the Slieve Ardagh settlements, in 1804 to settle in Streetsville, Ontario, and by the 1820s had been joined by several of his brothers and many of his former neighbours.[40]

There are a number of amateur genealogy websites charting the Canadian descendants of Limerick Palatines, of which the genealogy of the Shier (or Shire) family is perhaps representative. Adam Scheier settled in Courtmatrix after travelling from the Palatinate, and his grandson, Henry, born in 1746 into the third generation of Limerick Palatines, emigrated to New York and worked as a customs officer. During the American War of Independence, Henry resettled in Canada. Meanwhile, Henry's siblings and cousins remained in Courtmatrix, but his nephew Richard Shier (born in 1796 into the fourth generation of Limerick Palatines) emigrated to Canada with his wife in 1822. Richard was one of nine siblings. All remained in Ireland except for one sister, but several of Richard's cousins also emigrated to Canada around 1822. A fifth generation member of the Shier family is recorded as having emigrated at the age of twenty with his wife to Canada about 1851. Across these generations emigrant Palatines from Limerick were typically in their early twenties.[41]

Palatines became part of a predominantly-Protestant eighteenth-century wave of migration from Ireland to North America driven by the hope of better economic opportunities. Such migration, as described in the previous chapter included landowners with the resources to ship their families and others who signed contracts of indenture. The Palatines were tenants but were more prosperous than their Catholic neighbours who did not migrate across the Atlantic until the nineteenth century, by which time the cost of the crossing to North America had become cheaper and therefore more generally affordable.

CONFLICTS

Economic necessity does not seem to have been the only driver of emigration. In the early years of the Palatine settlement, though there was some evidence of contention with the local population, in the main it appears to have been relatively non-violent.[42] This ultimately gave way to a few decades of simmering agrarian violence, after which Palatine distinctness in County Wexford was shattered during the 1798 rebellion. An extensive catalogue of attacks on the Palatine communities in Limerick appear in police records, revealing that 'despite the belief that there was little religious conflict between the Palatines and their neighbours, some of the attacks were fuelled or at least excused by their being Protestants.' This history of violence explains at least in part why so many emigrated during the first half of the nineteenth century.

The literature on the 1798 rebellion, which is mainly focused on County Wexford, tends to play up the role of ideology, such as the influence of the United Irishmen, and does not always acknowledge the role that communal animosities played in the killings that took place.[43] In Killanne, County Wexford, a history of violent clashes with Catholic neighbours can be traced to a Whiteboy attack in 1775 on the home of the parish clerk and proctor of Killanne, George Hornick. Some accounts state that Hornick and his brother Philip repelled the attack, killed a leader of the Whiteboys and wounded others. Other accounts claim that Hornick and his brother killed three of their attackers.[44] According to a local historian, the Hornicks of Killanne had during the 1770s disturbances 'become famous as hunters of Whiteboys and were detested by at least some elements in the area ever since for it'.[45] Behind such emphasis on the notoriety of the Hornicks lay a wider animosity towards Palatines in Killanne and in County Wexford more generally.

Killanne was designated a parish of the established Church. It sat on lands that had been confiscated from the Kavanaghs during the late seventeenth century and assigned to new owners. These were 'changes which made little or no difference to the lives of the long established population of either Killanne or Templeudigan parishes since none of the new owners or their representatives had taken up residence there'.[46] The Palatines settled in the midst of mostly indigenous Catholic tenants. During the 1740s much of the parish was sold to the Rev Arthur Jacobs who was entitled to rents as well as tithes. Jacobs replaced some of his Catholic tenants with Protestants, and in addition to being parish clerk, George Hornick also held the position of rent collector.[47]

During the 1798 rebellion, seven members of the same Hornick clan who had been involved in violence in the 1770s were captured and killed by the rebels. According to Kevin Whelan, 'the first target that Fr Father Philip Roche made for in 1798 was Hornick's house: as George was being piked to death, he was asked sarcastically, 'Do you remember 9 July 1775 now?'[48] Hornick's son, Robert, somehow survived the systematic killing of 'unpopular local Protestants' at the rebel camp on Vinegar Hill. Though wounded – an eyewitness described him as a naked man with dark streams of blood running down his sides rushing down the hill past a group of women prisoners – he managed the six-mile journey home only to find that the house was burned and that his family had fled. He was captured again and murdered at a gravel pit in the parish of Rossdriot.[49]

George Hornick's brother Philip was one of a group of 126 men, women and children murdered by rebels at a farm in Scullabogue in south County Wexford, about six miles from New Ross. The victims had been rounded up from a number of Protestant enclaves including the Palatine settlement on the Ram estate. The 103 men included 16 tradesmen, a schoolteacher and an excise officer; the rest were likely farmers. Several were family members of Militiamen. Some of those imprisoned included multiple members of the same families. Fifteen were Catholics, including members of the Ryan family who owned the farm at Scullabogue. One of their daughters supposedly had an affair with a 'gentleman' in Duncannon.[50] Some of the Catholics killed were servants of loyalists. The killings at Scullabogue began with the shooting in batches of four of 37 male captives who had been held in the house. They were made kneel on the lawn, were shot and then finished off with pikes. The other captives, including the women and children, were burned alive in the barn. Pikemen forced those who tried to escape back into the burning barn. In all, about 17 rebels seem to have participated directly in the killings, although a large crowd stood by and watched.[51]

On 31 May 1798 many Protestants, including the entire Palatine community at Old Ross, evacuated their homes and fled to either the town of New Ross or to the fort at Duncannon. [52] All but four of the 100 houses in Old Ross were burned by the rebels as was the Palatines' church, the only church burned during the rebellion. The community never recovered.[53] By 1810, only nine holdings seem to have still been in the hands of tenants with Palatine surnames,[54] and while some Palatine surnames can be traced around the county any distinctive Palatine identity had withered away by the mid-nineteenth century.

In Limerick during the 1798 rebellion a local leader of the United Irishmen, William 'Staker' Wallace was arrested by Captain Oliver and the Kilfinane yeomanry. He was imprisoned for a number of weeks and repeatedly flogged by one of the Palatine militia before being hung without trial – although Captain Oliver was also the local magistrate. In the aftermath of the rebellion, resentment towards the Palatines as loyalist Protestants and as militiamen simmered.

There were many attacks on Palatine homes in the years after 1803 when on the night of 23 October 1803 a group of men who attempted in turn to burn down a number of houses and barns in Pallingarrane.[55] Palatine homes were raided by for guns by Whiteboys and later by Rockites, with incidents recorded in police reports and in other sources during 1813, 1821, 1822, and 1823.[56] Five Palatines were killed in such incidents or murdered between 1818 and 1822. In one such raid near Ballingarry on 6 February 1818, George Switzer was relieved of the pistol he kept in his bedroom, dragged out of the house by a dozen assailants and mortally wounded. According to Vivian Hick, who has catalogued attacks on and killings of Palatines in Limerick, almost every week during the summer and autumn of 1821 saw at least one attack on Palatine homes or persons. John Corneal, who worked as a corn proctor, was murdered that year whilst attempting to collect rent in Killeen, as was a member of the militia from Adare.[57]

The events leading up to the murder of Christopher Sparling in October 1821 recall those of George Hornick from Wexford. Sparling was killed some time after a raid on his home in which one of his servants perished. The purpose of the raid had been to seize guns he kept in his house. He posted a reward for information leading to the capture of these assailants and became identified as a prominent enemy of the Whiteboys. This lead to his murder. Sparling had taken over the tenancy of a farm on the Courtenay estate from which others, presumably Catholics, had been evicted. In January 1821, Sparling also posted some of the reward offered for information leading to the conviction of Whiteboys who had sought unsuccessfully to kill Alexander Hoskins, the rent agent who had replaced the murdered John Corneal. In a separate incident, Hoskins's 16-year-old son was shot 15 times by the same group of assailants and died subsequently from his injuries. There was an attack on Sparling's home in 1817 in which eight armed men broke unto his house and 'carried away two fine muskets', and another in 1818, during which some Whiteboys were injured. In the month after Sparling's death, six other homes were attacked by a group of about 30 men, and Christopher's brother George Sparling was beaten to death during a Whiteboy raid on his house whilst the trial of men accused of the murder of his brother was taking place.[58]

On the basis of testimony at that trial from Christopher Sparling's widow and other members of his household, four men were hanged. These executions seem to have increased resentment towards the Palatines from their Catholic neighbours, and in January 1822, Christopher Sparling's son-in-law, who was English, was murdered in broad daylight and in view of some Catholic houses whose inhabitants reputedly closed their doors as the killing took place. In February 1822, a group of men looking to seize weapons broke into the home of Christopher Sparling's widow. In February 1822, the county was placed under martial law. On the evening of 29 April the village of Glenosheen (near Ballyorgan), where most of the inhabitants were Palatines, was attacked by a group of 100 Rockites. Some houses and a police barracks were burned and inhabitants shot at. Two of the attackers were subsequently tried and executed, and two others were transported to Van Diemen's Land. In 1839 three men attempted to murder Constable Joseph Miller, a Palatine, near Kilfinane. He managed to run away from his attackers but was refused shelter in a nearby house.[59] These were just some of the incidents of violence towards Palatines during this period.

It is not clear how much sectarian conflict influenced the emigration of Palatines. Emigration patterns were well established by the time that this commenced in either Wexford or Limerick. It is not known where those who were driven out of Wexford went, whether they left Ireland or not. In Ireland, as elsewhere, many of those displaced by conflict become lost to history; once out of sight, out of mind. In Limerick, however, where there was a greater number of Palatines from the outset, identifiable Palatine communities prevailed for generations and our knowledge of these draws on family histories of Palatine emigrants as well as from local historical sources.

ASSIMILATION

Because of their cultural heritage, writings about the Palatines were preoccupied with the extent of, or their resistance to, assimilation. Walter Knittle, the American author of a history of Palatine migration to Ireland and to the United States visited County Limerick in 1934. He found that some Palatine descendants had forgotten much about their origins. One interviewee responded to a question about German customs with the query: 'Were the Palatines Germans?' Knittle concluded that they had indeed become assimilated into the same wider modern world that had also changed the ways of life of their Catholic neighbours:

> Of German customs there are none. Sourcrout is unheard of and other Pennsylvania German customs have no foothold in Limerick County. That great quencher of German thirst, beer, is not popular and even the cider for which the district was noted some years ago has lost its popularity. I did notice an old home-made cider press now resting after more than a century of use. John Wesley and his successors have done a thorough job. The Palatines are today a monument to the good influence of a strict but honest discipline. It must also be noted that some of the Palatines have become Catholic, and this is attributed by the Protestant clergy to the influence of the mixed marriages. I sought in vain for the remnant of a German custom. This failure to find one and the assimilation are to be explained largely by the fact that no further immigration of Germans took place . . . . However, it is well to keep in mind that the Irish themselves have been fairly Anglicized too, at least, to adopting the English language.[60]

Under the surface, however, traces of cultural difference were evident in farming practices that were distinct from those of their neighbours, but had since died out:

One custom was still recalled. That was the custom of the Palatines of having their own Burgomaster, who judged their disputes. In later years he was known as 'the King of the Palatines'. The last really to hold that title was James Teskey and that was over 60 years ago. There had been burgomasters in the original colonies, on Slieve Ardagn and amongst the 1770s New York settlement. Several have been referred to since then by that title but apparently only in a facetious manner. Here again is proof that assimilation occurred about the middle of the nineteenth century.[61]

Yet, much of the writings about the Palatines emphasised how they were different from their Catholic neighbours. Visiting travel writers contrasted the virtues of the Palatines – their industry, piety, cleanliness, sobriety – with the vices and failings of their neighbours. For example, Arthur Young depicted the Palatine women he met when he visited County Limerick in October 1777 – 'the goodness and cleanliness of their houses' the capacity for industry they passed onto their children – as in 'perfect contrast to the Irish ladies in the cabins'.[62]

Against this, Catholic novelist Gerald Griffin (1803–1840), who lived near Adare, wrote a number of stories that stereotyped the Palatines as 'wicked, ugly, stupid and ridiculous'.[63] According to Griffin they were industrious tenants: 'attentive, even to a degree of puritanical exactness, to their religious obligations – presenting, in the unremitting acquisition which they employ to the acquisition of money, the caution which they manifest in its distribution'. The response of their neighbours, Griffin suggested, was one of resentment and contempt.[64]

Catholic antipathy towards Palatines also found expression through folk tales and ribald ballads. One folk tale that was recorded in different versions told of a Palatine youth who inserted a consecrated host into the barrel of his rifle, according to different versions of the tale, either 'in the name of the fiend' or in an effort to charm his gun, fired a shot into the wall of a church or discharged it at a barn leaving an indelible bloodstain where it struck.[65] A ballad called 'Orange Kilfinane' told the story of a Protestant celebration on the Oliver estate at which a Palatine leader swore out that he would kill the Pope.[66] In Wexford, the Hornicks were remembered as folk devils: one mid-twentieth-century storyteller recounted how the Hornicks broke all the headstones in Old Cross graveyard during the 1798 rebellion, were notorious priest hunters and how one of them nearly beat a priest to death. The priest, according to this storyteller, prevented his parishioners from killing this

Hornick, but had prophesied that 'they'll have enough murder in their own family yet'.[67]

In Limerick, antagonism festered for decades after 1798, which was either ignored or missed by travel writers and others drawn to the curious case of the Limerick Palatines. An aforementioned 1861 account claimed that they had been 'rarely if ever molested' in times of trouble times, and this was echoed in a 1937 local history: 'Even in the turbulent period of Whiteboyism, when the people in their neighbourhood adopted violent methods to end intolerable evils, they do not seem to have been molested in any way.'[68] Such forgetting or downplaying illustrates how assimilation can be a corollary of amnesia.

SIX

EMIGRATIONS

From the early eighteenth century until the late twentieth century, most of the migration that affected Ireland was emigration. The population of Ireland doubled from 2 million in 1672, to 4 million by 1788, and again to 8 million by 1841, by which time a further million had emigrated to North America. This period of population growth also witnessed ongoing emigration and to a considerable extent emigration patterns were shaped by religiosity with Protestants more likely to be able to afford the passage to North America until ocean travel became significantly cheaper during the nineteenth century. During the eighteenth century between one-fifth and one-quarter of Irish emigrants to the New World were Catholic, between three quarters and four fifths were Protestant.[1] From 1845 to 1855, that is, during and after the Great Famine, Catholics made up 90 per cent of emigrants. During this ten-year period, an estimated 2,100,000 emigrated. Between 1856 and 1921 a further 4,400,000 departed. Of these, 80 per cent were Catholics. In the years between 1815 and 1900 about 7,720,000 in total emigrated from Ireland. The biggest portion, some 4,765,000, migrated to the United States. 1,468,00 went to mainland Britain, 1,057,000 to British North America (what became Canada), 361,000 to Australia and New Zealand, 35,000 to Africa and about 34,000 to other parts of the world including South America.[2]

Post-1700 patterns of emigration reflected religious, cultural, political, and economic divisions in Ireland, and reproduced elements of these in some host countries. Donald Akenson in his introduction to *The Irish Diaspora* made the case for seeing past such divisions in trying to define who was Irish:

The answer is clear: anyone who lived permanently within the social system that was the island of Ireland. This includes Catholics and Protestants, Kerrymen, Ulstermen, descendants of Norman invaders and of Scottish planters as well of earlier Celtic invaders, speakers of English as well as speakers of Irish Gaelic. That there were during the nineteenth and early twentieth centuries complex political arguments about what was the proper definition of Irish nationality is here irrelevant. It matters not if an individual was (for example) a Catholic whose family during the penal times turned Protestant: he or she was Irish. It does not matter if the person was the descendent of some Norman soldier whose family had Hibernicised and become more Irish than the Irish they conquered: he or she was Irish. It matters not if the individual came by descent from one of the Cromwellians or from the Confederacy soldiers whom Cromwell defeated: she or he was Irish. Ireland was a political and social system and Ireland formed everyone who lived in it. They could hate Ireland, love it, hate each other, it mattered not. They were of Ireland: hence Irish.[3]

Against this it has been argued that such an ideal conception of Irishness was never influential in Ireland nor, in particular, amongst the Irish in America or their descendants. As put by Laurence McCarthy in *The Irish Catholic Diaspora in America*, conflicts between Catholics and Protestants in Ireland also emigrated.[4] The first edition of McCarthy's book was called *The Irish Diaspora in America*.[5] Since its publication in 1976 scholarship on Irish emigration has expanded considerably to take account of the realisation, as McCarthy put it, 'that a majority of people who now define themselves as Irish-American are not Catholic'.[6]

The focus of this chapter is on both Protestant and Catholic emigrations from 1700 to the establishment of the Irish Free State and the partition of Ireland in 1922. Many claims were made, particularly during the nineteenth century, that Catholic and Protestant emigrants had different characteristics, which explained how each group tended to fare. The prevailing stereotypes also permeated analyses of the condition of Ireland before, during, and after the Great Famine. These also echoed wider debates about modernity found in analyses of the industrial revolution and the rise of capitalism such as Max Weber's *The Protestant Ethic and the Spirit of Capitalism* (1904). Within the academic literature on Irish emigration there have been somewhat heated debates about stereotypes that contrast supposedly backward Catholic emigrants ill-prepared to venture into the more modern world outside of Ireland with enterprising Protestants. Of interest here is how and why various kinds of Irish emigrants settled in the places they did, as well their experiences of emigration.

At the beginning of the eighteenth century the population of Ulster was, according to some estimates, just in excess of half a million people.[7] Other estimates suggest that it might have been as high as 0.82 million in 1712.[8] By 1841 the population of Ulster had risen to some 2.4 million. Even though Protestants of all denominations constituted less than thirty per cent of Ireland's population by the beginning of the eighteenth century, about three-quarters of all emigrants from Ireland from 1700 to 1819 were Protestant, and of these about 70 per cent were Ulster Presbyterians.[9] Between 1700 and 1776 more than 200,000 Presbyterians quit Ulster, mostly for North America.[10]

For most of the nineteenth century emigration levels were the highest in Europe. In an 1853 article in the *New York Daily Tribune*, Karl Marx described the large-scale emigration from Ireland during and after the famine as 'forced emigration'. Marx's analysis was that most of the 1,200,436 who emigrated from Ireland between the beginning of 1847 and June 1853 had been driven out. The social system founded on smallholdings and potato cultivation had broken down; the pauperised inhabitants of 'Green Erin' were being swept away by agricultural improvements; they had become, from a capitalist perspective, an unwanted surplus population.[11] The Great Famine resulted in the deaths of between 1,000,000 and 1,500,000 people from starvation and disease between 1846 and 1855, out of a population of 8,500,000; a further 2,100,000 emigrated. About 1,500,000 settled in the United States, and a further 300,000 travelled to Canada, although many of these subsequently migrated southward.[12] Of the four main waves of Irish emigration to America – colonial, pre-Famine, Famine, and post-Famine – the last was by far the largest, accounting for almost half of emigrants who left Ireland after 1700. The Irish-born population of the United States reached a peak of 1,871,509 in 1890. There were also 2,924,172 second-generation Irish-Americans, giving a total of 4.8 million.[13]

After the United States, Britain has received the second-largest number of Irish immigrants, and has been the main destination of these since the early twentieth century.[14] Half a million Irish settled in Britain during the 1840s and 1850s, with about half concentrated in and around the cities of London, Manchester, Liverpool, and Glasgow. As many as a million Irish arrived in Liverpool as transients between 1847 and 1853, most seeking transport on to America if they could afford it; those who couldn't settled in Britain.[15]

The main period of Irish emigration to British North America (Canada) was in the three decades after the Napoleonic War, when a period of agricultural prosperity for Ireland came to an end.[16] Around 55 per cent of Irish settlers in Canada were Protestant, and predominantly Anglican rather than Presbyterian, mainly drawn from the northern third of Ireland – the nine counties of pre-1922 Ulster and the adjoining counties of Leinster – and from the significantly Protestant cores in Munster and south Leinster. Of the 45 per cent who were Catholic as many as a third came from Ulster.[17]

The most intensive decades of migration from Ireland to Australia and New Zealand were the 1850s (101,451), the 1860s (82,917), the 1870s (61,946) and the 1880s (55,476). By 1861 the Irish-born population of Australia (177,505) constituted 15.4 per cent of the total population and 24.5 per cent of the foreign-born. The number of Irish-born peaked in 1891 at 229,156 by which time these constituted just 9.5 per cent of the total population and 22.7 of the foreign-born. By 1921 the Irish-born population (106,274) were just 2.0 per cent of the population.[18]

The Irish diaspora was mostly a movement of people who could speak English before they migrated to various corners of the English-speaking world. As English speakers, they had the advantage of what David Fitzpatrick described as 'preliminary acculturation'.[19] The Irish did not go in significant numbers anywhere that the British had not gone first, and wherever Irish Catholics went, the Catholic Church followed. Catholics as well as Protestants helped run the British Empire.

Pre-migratory conflicts and the consequences of religious discrimination in Ireland affected their lives to different extents in different emigrant destinations. The levels of wealth and resources that emigrants could command also affected how immigrant families fared, for even when emigrants travelled as individuals they often depended on the resources of their families in Ireland or on remittances from family members who had already emigrated. Various studies cited in this chapter emphasise how even the apparently least-well-organised emigrants seem to have made decisions about where to go based on the best information they could get their hands on and on the resources at their disposal.

QUAKERS

The initial wave of emigration from Ulster to the American colonies that occurred during the 1680s mostly consisted of Presbyterians, who came to be called Ulster Scots. Also significant were members of the Society of Friends, known as Quakers, who, like the Ulster Scots, were colonial settlers in Ireland or their descendants. Quaker missionaries from England had travelled to North America, the Caribbean and Ireland from the 1650s. Founded by George Fox in 1647, the Society of Friends expanded rapidly across England during the 1650s. One estimate puts the number of Quaker converts in England at between 35,000 and 40,000 by the early 1660s.[20] During 1655 and 1656 the sect attracted converts from Oliver Cromwell's New Model Army in Ireland including Cork, Kinsale, Cashel, Limerick, Bandon, Londonderry, Belturbet, Cavan, Dublin, Galway, Wexford, New Ross, Mountmellick and Kilkenny.[21] These converts were treated as subversives and as a threat to discipline; the ranks of regiments in Ireland and Scotland were purged, and officers who became Quakers were cashiered. Some of these former New Model Army members settled permanently in Ireland. Visiting Quakers responsible for conversions were banished from

Ireland, and 92 missionaries were imprisoned in 1655 and 1656.[22] After the Restoration in 1660, Quaker meetings in Ireland were suppressed, and in some towns, Quakers were banned altogether.[23]

William Edmundson (1627–1712), the first leader of the Quakers in Ireland, came originally from the northwest of England. He had served with the New Model Army from 1650 in both Scotland and England. His brother John was a member of Cromwell's army in Ireland, and persuaded him to settle there, which William did with his wife and servant in 1652. He set up initially as a trader in Antrim town, where his brother lived. On a return visit to England in 1653, he attended a meeting addressed by George Fox, after which he embraced Quakerism along with other members of his family. In spring 1654, he moved to Lurgan in County Antrim, where he rented land to graze cattle as well as keeping a shop. With his brother and wife he founded a small Quaker community there. After a period of imprisonment in Armagh for preaching, Edmundson quit his shop and rented a farm in Cavan 'in order that he might set an example of bearing testimony against tithes,' which he refused to pay. Edmondson was imprisoned again, but made a number of converts.[24] Quakerism was heavily repressed in Ulster yet in some Southern garrison towns like Kinsale and Cork army governors and commanding officers were better disposed towards missionaries and converts.[25]

The most influential Quaker in Ireland was undoubtedly William Penn (1644–1718), the founder of the Pennsylvania colony, who grew up partly in Ireland. There, his father, Sir William Penn, had extensive estates, obtained as part of the Cromwellian settlement for his having served as a navy commander, which he continued to do after the Restoration. In 1657 Penn first encountered a travelling Quaker preacher, Thomas Loe, in Macroom Castle in County Cork, which was part of one of his father's estates. After a period of education in Oxford and France, Penn joined the Society of Friends in 1667 and was imprisoned a number of times, once in the Tower of London and twice in Newgate. Penn preached around Ireland and advocated on behalf of Quakers there, as well becoming involved in the management of his father's estate in Kinsale, which he inherited in 1670. He became the leader of efforts by Quakers in England to establish a colony in North America where religious freedom might be secured.[26]

Pennsylvania was named for Sir William, rather than for his son, the founder of the colony, by Charles II. The grant of lands to William Penn of 40,000 square miles made him the largest proprietor in North America, and was supposedly in lieu of debts of £16,000 owed by the King to Sir William. By convention, such loans would not have been expected ever to have been repaid, nor could the King make any such grant without the support of his Privy Council. Nor would it have been politic of the King to openly favour the Quakers to such an extent, given that they were aligned with Whig opponents of his supporters. The 'repayment' narrative seems to have been a face-saving device proposed by Penn and endorsed by the King as means of getting rid of unwanted Quakers.[27]

Two of the key figures in Penn's colony were Irish Quakers. His agent, James Logan (1674–1751) was from Lurgan. His father, Patrick Logan had been a clergyman from East Lothian in Scotland, who, according to his son's autobiography, 'was obliged to go to Ireland and to teach a Latin School there' in order to support his family when he quit the Established Church to become a Quaker.[28] James Logan had been apprenticed to a linen draper at the age of 14 years, but during the Williamite war was evacuated to Edinburgh with other members of his family. His father secured a teaching position in Bristol for a while, with the help of the Quaker community there, before returning to Ireland in 1693, leaving his son in charge of the school. James Logan had by then taught himself mathematics and studied French, Italian, and some Spanish. He remained a teacher until the Treaty of Ryswick in 1687. After a return visit that year to see his parents he entered the shipping business, organising trade between Bristol and Dublin before taking up an offer of employment from William Penn as his secretary.[29] Logan accompanied Penn on his second voyage to Pennsylvania in 1699. Penn left Logan in temporary charge of the colony when he returned to England in 1701.

Captain Thomas Holme (1624–95) who became the Surveyor-General of Pennsylvania was born in England, possibly in Yorkshire in 1624 and served in the New Model Army in Ireland after which he settled first in Limerick and then in Wexford. By 1655 he had become a Quaker. In 1658 he was one of 59 signatures on a petition to Parliament on 'the Cruel and Unjust Sufferings of the People of God in the Nation of Ireland Called Quakers'. The pamphlet described how Holme and other Quakers had been turned out of Wexford by the mayor of the town. It seems likely that he received his allotment of land in Limerick but moved to Wexford. In 1660 he was arrested along with other Quakers in Dublin and imprisoned in Newgate. In 1672 he co-authored a pamphlet with another Irish Quaker detailing persecutions experienced by members of the Society of Friends. Holme was fined £200 in 1673 for refusing to take an oath in court. In 1676 crops from his farm in Wexford were seized in lieu of tithes that Holme had refused to pay. Notwithstanding such privations, Holme prospered in Ireland; he became a stockholding member of the Free Society of Traders, and was amongst the first to purchase land in Penn's colony. He acquired the title to 5,000 acres and was appointed to the post of Surveyor. Holme sailed with his family to Pennsylvania in April 1682. Within a year, he had designed and had printed in London street plans for the City of Philadelphia.

In 1684 he was one a group of three who drew up a charter for the incorporation of Philadelphia as a borough. In 1685, Holme served as acting governor of the colony in Penn's absence.[30]

Prospective migrants were expected to obtain testimonials from the congregation they were leaving to present to the community they wished to join. Analysis of 'certificates of removal' presented to meetings in Pennsylvania from 1682–1750 identify 172 family groups arriving from Ulster, 183 from Leinster (including 54 from Dublin) and 42 from Munster, from around 29 Quaker congregations across Ireland. The total number of migrants, including family members, has been estimated at between 1,500 and 2,000. One certificate of removal recorded that in January 1682 the Ballyhagen meeting in County Armagh approved the decision of Ann Milicum, a comfortably well-off widow, to emigrate with her daughter because her other daughter's husband and children were also planning to emigrate.[31] Another such testimonial, signed by William Edmundson amongst others, vouched for the characters of Nicholas Newland and his two sons from Mountmellick, who settled in Chester County in Pennsylvania, as did many other rural Quakers from Ireland.[32] Those who had lived in towns settled mostly in Philadelphia.[33]

Thomas Parke, a farmer who owned several tracts of land in County Carlow, emigrated in May 1724 with all of his family excepting two married daughters. Initially he leased land from an Irish Friend, and then purchased 500 acres of land that must have been already cleared from another Irish Quaker family in Chester County. In an October 1725 letter, he urged relatives to follow his family as soon as possible, pointing out that land in the area was becoming more expensive every year. He reported that in his first year he had planted 200 acres of wheat and seven acres of rye and had harvested a crop of oats, barley, Indian corn and buckwheat that had been planted as soon as they had arrived. In the spring of 1728, his sister and her husband presented their certificate of removal to a meeting in Chester County.[34] Whist many of the Quakers who migrated from Ireland to Pennsylvania were prosperous, records also exist of poorer Quakers assisted by co-religionists to emigrate. For example, certificates of removal from 1741 describe how two families from Charlemount in County Armagh received a loan of £15 to help to pay for their passage and other necessities.[35]

ULSTER SCOTS

In 1684 a number of ministers from the suppressed Laggan Presbytery announced their intention to emigrate, citing not only 'persecutions' but also 'the general poverty abounding in these parts'. A report on conditions in

County Tyrone from early 1684, after the introduction of official measures aimed at suppressing Presbyterian worship, noted that some dissenters had been brought to conform, but 'others threaten to go to Carolina'. The assessment was that threats to emigrate were primarily efforts by Presbyterian tenant farmers 'to make their landlords more indulgent to them'. A severe winter was also cited as a cause of disaffection.[36] The accession of a Catholic king, James II, in 1685 could not but have been another cause. Ulster then experienced the ravages of the Williamite war from 1688 to 1691. This was followed by a further wave of migration from Scotland, after which Ulster and Ireland more generally were supplanted by the New World as the main immigrant destination. Emigration to North America was made possible due to the existence of trade routes that included a number of Ulster ports. For example, customs records from the early eighteenth century record regular traffic to the American colonies from Belfast and Londonderry, as well as occasional ventures from other northern ports.[37] Between 1680 and 1716, about 3,000 quit Ulster for the New World; they were followed by between 4,500 and 7,000 others between 1717 and 1719, and during the 1720s a further 15,000 or so emigrants, again mostly Presbyterians.[38] Between 1717 and 1775 according to some historians an estimated 250,000 Ulster Scots left Ireland for the American Colonies, with about 10,000 migrants per annum making the journey during the five years before the American Revolution.[39] Others put the total far lower at around 100,000.[40]

The beginning of this outflow coincided with an Act passed in 1719 that granted religious toleration to Presbyterians. They were clearly better off than the dispossessed Catholic majority even if they were ranked below the landowning Anglican elite. However, most were tenants rather than landowners and because of this they could not be represented in Parliament. They enjoyed better tenancy conditions than elsewhere on the island due to the practice of the 'Ulster Custom', which guaranteed security of tenure as long as rents were paid and compensated tenants for improvements to property. However, this custom did not stop rents from rising rapidly during the early eighteenth century.[41] For example, in 1718 an emigrant family surrendered the lease on the farm in County Monaghan that had seen rent rises of almost 300 per cent during the period they were tenants; in the relatively prosperous area around Lurgan, County Armagh, where tenant farmers also engaged in linen manufacture, rents increased by more than 60 per cent between 1710 and 1719. Nineteen holdings on one estate in south Donegal were re-let in 1720 on seven-year leases with rents more than 75 per cent higher than before.[42] Presbyterian settlers had been enticed to Ireland by favourable leases, and some proved willing to quit the country when such leases came to an end and they became subject to significantly higher rents.

Rural Quakers in Ireland, who were mostly to be found in Ulster, emigrated for similar reasons.[43]

Emigrants, who came mostly came from the counties of Derry, Donegal, Tyrone and Antrim, departed principally from the ports of Londonderry, Belfast, Larne, Portrush and Newry.[44] Nineteen ships alone sailed from Londonderry between 1717 and 1719.[45] One 1719 attempt to explain the acceleration of emigration at the time by an Archbishop of the established Church, argued that this had little to do with religious persecution:

> The truth of the case is this: after the Revolution most of the Kingdom was waste, and abundance of people destroyed by the war. The landlords therefore were glad to get tenants at any rate and set their lands at very easy rents. This invited an abundance of people to come over here, especially from Scotland, and they have lived here very happily ever since, but now their leases are expired and they [are] obliged not only to give what was paid before the Revolution, but in most places double and in many places treble, so that it is impossible for people to live or subsist on their farms.[46]

The 'Revolution' Archbishop King referred to was the 'Glorious Revolution', the ascension of William III following the defeat of James II. King had perhaps a vested interest in deemphasising the influence of religious dissent on decisions to emigrate. That said, the available evidence suggests that economic rather than religious considerations provided the chief motive for Scotch-Irish emigration.[47] The tenants he referred to included recent settlers from Scotland attracted to Ireland in the aftermath of the war. Now these, as well as the descendants of earlier settlers, King argued, were being drawn to America mostly by more favourable economic opportunities. The owners of ships employed agents to recruit passengers at markets and fairs, according to one 1729 account, who promised that in America they could expect good land 'for little or no rents, without either paying tithes or taxes.[48]

By 1725 the main destinations for Ulster emigrants were to Pennsylvania and Delaware, and by the mid-eighteenth century Philadelphia became the main port of entry for ships from Ulster.[49] By the time of the American Revolution, Ulster Irish settlers also had become established in Maryland, and further south in Virginia and the Carolinas. By then the Irish in America numbered somewhere between 350,000 and 450,000. By 1790, the Ulster Scots made up more than 26 per cent of the white population in Georgia, almost 26 per cent in South Carolina and almost 24 per cent in Pennsylvania. In New York, New Jersey, Delaware, Maryland, Virginia and North Carolina they accounted for between 12 and 18 per cent of the white population.[50]

Presbyterians who crossed the Atlantic included the children and grandchildren of settlers who had crossed over from Scotland to Ireland, as well as at least some who had recently arrived from Scotland and decided to relocate from Ulster to North America. To give one example, the Witherspoons, a Presbyterian farming family from near Glasgow, left Scotland sometime between 1690 and 1710 and settled in Drumbo, a predominantly Presbyterian distinct in County Down. The Witherspoons, by then in their 60s, with four of their seven adult children, their wives and some grandchildren, some 33 persons in all, relocated to South Carolina between 1732 and 1736 on three separate voyages from Belfast to Charleston. Their decision as to when and where to emigrate can be traced to a scheme in 1731 to establish eleven new frontier townships on the fringes of the colony, and the offer, widely advertised in Ulster, of assisted passages, grants of land, tools and one year's provisions to settlers. Prospective Ulster settlers were also promised a subsidy to pay the salary of a Presbyterian minister, along with the promise of religious freedom.

These were necessary inducements, given that South Carolina was established as an Anglican Protestant colony. In 1731, a few years before settlers from Ulster began to arrive, the population of the colony was around 30,000, of whom 20,000 were slaves. By 1760 it had a population of 83,000 of whom 52,000 were slaves. Robert Witherspoon's memoir of how his extended family settled in the Williamsburg township recalled that his grandmother died on the second day of the voyage from Belfast and that his sister Sarah died soon after their ship landed in Charlestown. After Christmas, in the depth of winter, members of the family were given an open boat with provisions and tools and journeyed up-river to the lands allocated to them. They cleared and planted the land and raised livestock but, in time, became slave owners. Robert, who emigrated from Ulster as a child, began his working life as a weaver, then became a slave overseer and subsequently worked as manager of his father's plantation.[51]

However, before the American Revolution somewhere between half and two-thirds of emigrants from Ulster arrived as indentured servants. Some better-off emigrants secured servants before departing from Ulster, by in essence agreeing to pay their passage. For example, when Robert Parke, a Quaker who had settled in Pennsylvania, returned from a business trip in Ireland in 1728 he bought six servants back with him. Records suggest that there were 67 other indentured passengers on the same ship.[52] Most of those who signed contracts of indenture worked as agricultural workers, whether on plantations in the southern colonies, cutting lumber and clearing land on the frontier or doing general farm work in longer-settled middle colonies such as Pennsylvania. Those offered for 'sale' according to a 1734 advertisement in Charleston, included servants from Ulster skilled in making

'Irish linen, household furniture, butter, cheese, chinaware and all sorts of dry goods'. Those sought in 1760 by a Belfast agent offering passage to America included skilled craftsmen such as gunsmiths, carpenters, blacksmiths and bricklayers; those seeking to indenture themselves had to sign a contract before a magistrate. A 1749 advertisement offering passage to Virginia declared that no person would be signed up without the consent of their parents, husbands, or wives and without a proper discharge from their employers.[53]

Contracts of indenture promised 'freedom dues' at the end of the period of service. During the seventeenth century these were generally meant to include about 50 acres of land as well as corn, clothing, and a musket, or the equivalent of such land and goods in cash.[54] However, this tended to only apply to those pioneers who settled frontier lands. James Logan argued that Ulster Presbyterians were particularly suited to frontier settlement because they had already proven their bravery by defending their homes during the Williamite war.[55] Some Ulster Presbyterians willing to sign contracts of indenture during the early days of the Pennsylvania colony were offered land, but not necessarily those who arrived later.[56] By the 1740s more than 93 per cent of bonded servants were Irish-born. About a quarter of Irish servants in Pennsylvania were indentured to masters or mistresses who were themselves Irish-born or had Irish parentage. Only a small proportion of these servants ever became landowners in Pennsylvania.[57] Generally it proved hard for former indentured servants to obtain land as part of their freedom dues in well-settled areas whatever they had been promised.

It appears that rural Presbyterians and Protestants in general were more willing to emigrate during the eighteenth century than previously, but it is also likely that they had opportunities to emigrate to North America that were not available to much of the rural Catholic majority. Large-scale emigration became possible because the shipping and trade routes by then were established and travel became cheaper. Arthur Dobbs, who became governor of North Carolina in 1753, came originally from County Antrim. Ports in Northern Ireland developed lucrative trade links with Philadelphia and the Delaware Valley In 1739 some 40,000 bushels of flaxseed were exported from Philadelphia to Ireland, rising to 110,412 bushels by 1771. Irish linen and Irish emigrants travelled in the other direction.[58] From 1731 onwards, South Carolina offered generous schemes of assisted passage, land bounties and other benefits to attract 'poor Protestants' from Ireland. Most of the 33,000 emigrants who left Ulster between 1760 and 1775 came to America through such schemes. Equivalent subsidies were not available for Catholics at that time.

Protestant Irish emigrants were also drawn to British North America especially after the United States became independent from Britain. The main period of emigration from Ireland to what became Canada followed the end of the Napoleonic War.[59] From 1818, for the first time, the numbers of emigrants to British North America from Ireland, England, Scotland and Wales exceeded those travelling to the United States. The first group of 30 families to be assisted by the government was from North Tipperary, led by Richard Talbot, a militia officer and landowner from Cloughjordan. The Protestant community in the county dated from the Cromwellian settlement, insofar as the lands they held were transferred to English settlers at that time. About 60 per cent of the families in the Talbot group had lived in Tipperary since that time.[60]

The Talbot group sailed in June 1818 from Cork to Quebec City, where a total of 4,559 Irish emigrants landed that year. Fifteen families from this first North Tipperary group settled in what came to be called Port Talbot in Ontario.[61] News of their successful settlement led to a process of chain migration that saw hundreds more from Tipperary and elsewhere follow them to Upper Canada. These included some poorer smallholders from Mountshannon in County Galway who were acquainted with some of Talbot's party who joined a group of 256 emigrants that sailed in June 1819 from Limerick. A dozen families from this second group settled near Port Talbot. Smaller numbers followed these two initial groups from North Tipperary to Canada: 74 families between 1820 and 1824, another 51 families during the second half of the decade, and a further 123 families between 1830 and 1834.[62] Similar processes of chain migration would have taken place from other parts of Ireland by rural Protestant emigrants to rural Canada.

Most rural Protestant emigrants did not receive subsidies to cover the costs of their journeys, but they were in a position to sell land at home to fund their resettlement in Canada. Immediate economic distress, resulting from the depression of agricultural markets and trade after the Napoleonic War, provided an impetus for emigration, but was not the substantive reason. Those who left seem to have been mostly drawn to Canada by the prospect of more extensive lands than their families held in Ireland; by the possibility, as one account put it, of a farm for every son at a time when many such families seemed to be more poorer than previous generations.[63]

The Orange Order emerged as a key social institution in areas where Ulster Scots settled in British North America. Orange Lodges established there, as elsewhere, operated as convivial clubs for men, through which members offered mutual aid.[64] The Orange Order offered Protestant newcomers a means of assimilating into the economic and social life of established Protestant settlers. Brotherhood within the Order translated into access to employment, housing and material support.[65] Other immigrants such as Quakers offered similar kinds of mutual support to their co-religionists. The Orange Order professed an explicitly anti-Catholic ethos and practiced a form of sectarian nepotism restricted to fellow Protestants. Overall, this was not much different from how networks formed by Irish Catholic immigrants came to operate, especially in the United States. Rural lodges were comprised of small tenant farmers, agricultural labourers, and linen-workers. By 1835, the Order had 1,500 lodges in Ireland, 259 in England, 154 in British North America.[66] There were about 900 Orange Lodges in Ontario by 1870.[67]

CATHOLICS

From the 1820s, Ireland's Catholic population provided the majority of emigrants. Between 1815 and 1870 somewhere between 4 and 4.5 million people migrated from Ireland. By 1890 there were 3 million Irish-born people living abroad. Up until 1845 Irish emigrants predominantly settled on the British mainland or in what became Canada. After the mid-1840s, that is during and after the Famine, until the First World War, most migrated to the US or to Britain, afterwards most to England.[68]

Much of the writing about the Irish in America has highlighted differences between Catholic and Protestant emigrant stereotypes that, as have been recounted, are also a feature of such writing. Stereotypes associated specifically with Irish Catholics have been invoked to explain why they apparently fared worse that Protestant Irish settlers and seemed less willing to integrate. In *Emigrants and Exiles Ireland and the Irish Exodus to North America* (1985) Kerby Miller argued that the cliché of the self-pitying, homesick, Anglophobic Irish 'exile' needs to be taken seriously precisely because so many Irish emigrants defined themselves in such terms. In Miller's summary of writings about the Catholic Irish in America, many of these remained spiritually and emotionally fixated on Ireland. Rather than focus on adjusting to life in the United States they became preoccupied with dreams to free Ireland from English rule. Nationalists and clergy based in the United States never tired of declaring that the Irish had been driven out of Erin like the children of Israel, that Irish emigration had not been a social necessity but had been artificially induced by political oppression. These arguments and perceptions found expression not just in popular ideology but in emigrants' own letters that expressed longing for home.[69]

Miller saw the Catholic Irish émigré 'culture of exile' as having a number of root causes. A history of political exile and unwilling emigration during the seventeenth century (see Chapter 3) had found cultural expression in Gaelic literature and folk memory. There was also an apparently deep attachment to place and locality amongst the rural Catholic peasantry.[70] Not unreasonably, eighteenth-century Irish Catholics saw themselves as victims of English and Protestant oppression. Catholics endured discrimination due to penal laws for more than a century longer than Protestant dissenters. The dominant political movement of the early nineteenth century was Daniel O'Connell's Catholic party, which campaigned for emancipation from the penal laws. Catholic Emancipation was achieved in 1829, but was followed 16 years later by a famine that was blamed by émigré nationalists like John Mitchel on British colonialism.[71] This argument found an audience amongst the Catholic Irish in America whose numbers were swelled by emigration during and after the Famine.

Miller also emphasised the influence of perceived differences in character between Catholic and Protestant emigrants as these were portrayed by Protestant elites in Ireland, England and the United States:

> In broadest terms, much evidence indicates that, in contrast to the Protestants they encountered in Ireland and North America, the Catholic Irish were more communal than individualistic, more dependent than independent, more fatalistic than optimistic, more prone to accept conditions passively than to take initiatives for change, and more sensitive to the weight of tradition, than to innovative possibilities for the future. Indeed their perspectives seemed so premodern that, to bourgeois observers from business-minded cultures, the native Irish often appeared 'feckless', 'child-like' and 'irresponsible': inclined to behave or justify behaviour in ways which avoided personal initiative and individual responsibility, especially to livelihood.[72]

Miller's analysis of the Catholic Irish in America came in for a lot of criticism from historians sympathetic to Catholic perspectives; as one such historian put it, it was difficult to distinguish Miller's account of the nineteenth-century rural Irish poor from those of hostile British or Protestant contemporaries.[73] English economists during the nineteenth century expressed similar perspectives on the Catholic Irish in Ireland; they variously advocated laissez-faire liberal economics and the value of what Max Weber would later call the Protestant ethic. Within nineteenth-century political economy writings on how the condition of Ireland might be addressed, there was considerable focus on how the Irish themselves might be 'improved'; a focus on the improvement of character was accompanied by a sense that poverty was a moral problem of individual failure or improvidence. For example, as put by Friedrich Engels in an 1843 newspaper article:

> The Irishman is a carefree, cheerful, potato-eating child of nature. From his native heath, where he grew up, under a broken-down roof, on weak tea and meagre food, he is suddenly thrown into our civilisation. Hunger drives him to England. In the mechanical, egoistic, ice-cold hurly-burly of the English factory towns, his passions are aroused. What does this raw young fellow — whose youth was spent

playing on moors and begging at the roadside — know of thrift? He squanders what he earns, then he starves until the next pay-day or until he again finds work. He is accustomed to going hungry. Then he goes back, seeks out the members of his family on the road where they had scattered in order to beg, from time to time assembling again around the teapot, which the mother carries with her.[74]

Most of the writing on the condition of Ireland by visiting writers before and after the Great Famine expressed concern about the apparent inability of Irish peasants to improve themselves, yet acknowledged to some degree the structural conditions that made such improvement difficult. For example, in the second edition of his *Political Economy* (1836) Thomas Malthus blamed the apparent absence of entrepreneurial habits amongst the Catholic peasantry on all-too-justified perceptions of discrimination and exploitation. They had 'not been subjected to the ordinary stimulants which produce industrious habits'.[75] By way of example he described how a small farm in the Kerry mountains might stand to support a large family, including a number of grown sons, but the business to be done upon the farm was a mere trifle. The greatest part of such work fell to the women. The men were underemployed, unskilled, and unable to access resources to improve the lands they rented or their homes. Malthus doubted whether most people living under such circumstances in any country ever acquired industrious habits.[76]

Four decades later, the visiting English sociologist Harriet Martineau emphasised how prevailing environmental conditions had fostered 'habits of slovenly cultivation, of dependence on the potato, and of consequent idleness'.[77] She documented examples of tenants not being permitted to improve lands they rented but was, in the main, critical of the apparent unwillingness of Catholic peasants to adopt new techniques of working.[78] Martineau, like a number of other advocates of laissez-faire policies in the post-Famine era, endorsed emigration and land clearances as a means of improving the efficiency of Irish agriculture.[79] In the same vein, in 1905, following half-a-century of such clearances, in *Ireland in the New Century*, Horace Plunkett, a Protestant Unionist champion of the cooperative movement, argued that Irish Catholics were 'non-economic if not actually anti-economic' in their thinking as a result of the anti-individualism of their religion.[80] The liberal Protestant critique of Irish Catholicism mirrored prevailing claims about the characters and dispositions of Catholic emigrants.

In Donald Akenson's summary, such arguments maintained that Catholicism in general and Irish Catholicism in particular were cultural-social systems that handicapped emigrants coming into contact with the modernising world. Conversely, it is was claimed that that Protestantism in general, and Irish Protestantism in particular, was much better adapted to economic initiative and to entrepreneurship.[81] For example, Kerby Miller argues that Catholics, who reluctantly emigrated, lacked qualities which the Ulster Scots possessed in great quantity: a 'spirit of enterprise', 'thrift and self-reliance which Catholics in Southern Ireland rarely exhibited'.[82] In such accounts, stereotypes of Catholics and Ulster Scots in America seem to be accepted at face value. With an even greater degree of hyperbole, Arthur Herman in *The Scottish Enlightenment: The Scots' Invention of the Modern World*, makes much of the reputation of the Ulster Scots as 'self-made men' whose work ethic and moral discipline were to be regarded as self-evident. With their fellow Scots they were 'the first echelon of skilled immigrant labour to reach America's shores and make it a productive nation', they were 'the shock troops of modernization', who transformed the new republic from an agricultural community into an industrial powerhouse, and so on.[83]

Even scholars as sympathetic to what became Catholic America as Lawrence McCaffrey could not muster corresponding hyperbole about the Catholic Irish who became the majority of emigrants after 1820. According to McCaffrey, Irish Catholics were the probably 'least sophisticated Europeans' to arrive in the United States during the first half of the nineteenth century. They were also, he added, amongst the most inefficient farmers in Europe. Most Catholic tenants in Ireland had access only to the simplest tools and little experience of the kinds of farming techniques that worked best in America. As such they fared better in Australia and New Zealand ranching cattle and sheep than cultivating wheat or corn in America. It has also been argued that 'Irish Catholics were psychologically unsuited to rural America' where farmsteads were isolated from one another, as this was the antithesis of the kind of communal society they were used to, where farms were so close to one another that parishes and townlands functioned as peasant villages, where social interaction with neighbours was constant. According to a prevailing cliché, they were ill-equipped for the rugged individualism of rural life in America. Most settled in the cities in close proximity to one another where they could maintain the kinds of communal bonds they were used to.[84]

A number of studies of Catholic emigrants have picked holes in such stereotypes. One of pre-Famine seasonal migration to Britain concluded that such migrants 'were aware of the range of choices available' and they chose the option that benefited them the most: 'Chief amongst such benefits was the ability to continue to live on the land; to maintain valued ties of kinship and community; and to continue to exercise autonomy about deci-sions affecting their welfare.'[85] At the time when Ulster Scots constituted the majority of Irish emigrants to North America, Catholic tenants engaged in seasonal migration to England and Scotland. For many of the poorest Irish, who rented small parcels of land planted with potatoes and could find labouring work for only a small part of the year at home, seasonal migration across the Irish Sea proved both necessary and viable. Potatoes were planted in February. As described in 1822 in an article in the *Irish Farmer's Gazette*:

> The peasantry are generally employed in the spring abut six weeks, in digging, planting and sowing for the farmers and cutting his turf; after which they commence their own business of potato tillage, and turf cutting which occupies about three or four weeks more. In the autumn they may be employed about the same length of time, which leaves them about thirty-four week of idleness.[86]

Once tenants had fulfilled their contractual obligations to landlords they could get to England in time for the planting or construction seasons there, and then return home for the winter months, as the potatoes did not need to be lifted until as late as November.[87] This was a way of life that allowed, at its best, for some autonomy, as they moved back and forth as work required, they did not seek to become assimilated when abroad. Interestingly, a failed migrant was one who remained abroad, 'even if highly successful by the standards of the new society', because he or she had abandoned their original aim: to earn sufficient money to be able to return home.[88] In an 1831 letter, written shortly before he was appointed Archbishop of Dublin, Richard Whately, then a political economist at Oxford, described the Irish migrants he had seen there: 'a continual ebb-tide of returning Irish, some labourers, and some beggars, but mostly *both* by turns, who seldom go home empty handed'. At the mendacity office in Oxford, they were sometimes found on being searched to have a few sovereigns in their rags. According to Whately, they held onto their money and, if possible, begged their way home.[89]

According to Ruth-Ann Harris in *The Nearest Place that Wasn't Ireland*, many of those who sought such work in England and Scotland prior to the Great Famine did so not necessarily because they were unable to go to North America, but because they did not wish to cut their ties to Ireland. Migrants giving evidence to parliamentary commissions declared that they would consider going to America only if work in England or Scotland paid less.[90] When the numbers going to Britain shot up during the Famine years, it is likely that many of these hoped to return after the crisis had abated. However, the Famine overwhelmed the seasonal migration economy. Post-Famine migration to Britain was often envisaged as a stepping-stone to permanent migration to North America, the hope being to save enough to secure passage onwards. The evidence of such migration patterns suggest 'the need to look again at the picture of the American Irish as arriving with no prior experience of urban industrial life. Seasonal migrants who re-emigrated were no longer the class of peasant portrayed in most studies of the American Irish, but were already familiar with taking risks, and well able to calculate the costs and benefits of emigration.'[91]

The motivations for eighteenth-century migration to Newfoundland by Catholics, mostly from a 30-mile hinterland of the port of Waterford, were perhaps somewhat similar. By the 1770s about 5,000 Irishmen worked in Newfoundland each year. The cod fisheries recruited young Irishmen as indentured labourers but it was possible for these to envisage returning to Ireland. Waterford, New Ross and Youghal were centres of trade with Newfoundland. Merchants from these Irish ports shipped flour, salted beef and pork there and to other New World markets. The chain of migration from Irish ports to Newfoundland lasted 50 years. Between 1770 and the 1830s about 30,000 Irish settled there. During the 1830s the provisions trade collapsed and bought Irish migration to Newfoundland to a halt.[92]

Catholics comprised close to half those who emigrated from Ireland to Canada after 1818. Some of the earliest of this wave were sponsored as part of a scheme instigated by John Beverly Robinson, the Attorney General for Upper Canada and organised on the ground by his brother Peter Robinson. Plans were made to select 600 Catholic farmers under 45 years of age from distressed areas in Cork, Limerick, Tipperary, and Clare and to organise their shipment to Quebec. In June 1823, two navy ships brought Robinson and his party of 568 settlers from Cork to Quebec. Each family was promised the freehold on 70 acres along with the right to purchase an additional reserved 30 acres should they wish to do so, provided that they cleared some of the land and built a house on it. The group was settled in the Bathurst District of the Ottawa valley. Eighty-two families settled in the Ramsey Township. Most of the remainder were settled in adjacent townships, with food supplies and tools. Those unsuited to farming were helped to obtain jobs in the nearest towns.[93] These included Peggy Casey, aged 18 years, who had travelled to Canada without family and was found work as a servant, and Jeremiah Ryan, a shoemaker from Buttevant who found work in his trade.[94]

John Beverly Robinson returned to Ireland in spring 1824 to fetch another group of Catholic settlers. In his absence, sectarian conflicts developed between the newcomers and their established Presbyterian neighbours from Ulster and Scotland. These included exchanges of gunfire, a death and some men being wounded. Of those involved, only the Catholics were jailed and fined on charges of assault; the local magistrates were Presbyterian, and the militiamen sent to arrest the Catholics for unruly behaviour described themselves as Orangemen. As a result of this sectarian conflict, Robinson settled his next group 200 miles to the southwest in the Newcastle District north of Rice Lake, where there were fewer established Presbyterian settlers.

The practice of separating Catholic from Protestant settlers was not uncommon; certain neighbourhoods came to be dominated by Catholics, others were predominantly Protestant.[95]

By 1825, Robinson had received around 50,000 applications for transit to Canada, all recommended by magistrates, clergymen, and priests. Parliament had agreed funding for 1,500 of these. Robinson stretched this number to 2,000 and after that felt there was no need to subsidise Irish emigration to Canada. Robinson's allocation process sought to favour, as he put it, the poor and the deserving, as well as those with relatives already in Canada. By the end of the year 1,900 settlers, mostly from the Blackwater region in County Cork, had been settled on lands called Scots Plains in Upper Ontario. The area was renamed Peterborough after Robinson.[96] By 1870, there were more than 900 active Orange Lodges in Ontario, including in Peterborough where the order became established during the 1830s. Unsurprisingly, Orange Lodges were located in areas where there were concentrations of Protestant settlers, but the presence of Catholic neighbours, such as in Peterborough, also provided an impetus for their establishment. The Orange Order sought to impose residential segregation from Catholics. For example, in the 1830s, Peterborough Orange 'blazers' carried out sporadic attacks aimed at preventing Catholic settlement.[97]

Many, though not all, of these rural Catholic settlers became successful farmers. Poor land accounted for the failure of some, and sectarian conflict caused a few of the Talbot group to leave. Some Protestant settlers also proved unsuccessful at farming. Catholic settlers were invariably poorer than Protestant ones. For example, Catholic emigrants from North Tipperary during the 1830s were drawn mostly drawn from impoverished mountain parishes, whereas Protestant emigrants from the county had mostly been landowners.[98] Bruce Elliot, in his study of post-1818 Protestant emigration from North Tipperary to Canada argues that Protestant landowners who emigrated to Canada misunderstood the role of land ownership in Canada. In Ireland, land was the basis of the political and economic power of the elite; the social dominance of the gentry was based on the renting of land, which was then sub-leased to tenants or worked by labourers. As Francis Evans, a Protestant emigrant from Roscrea in County Tipperary, wrote in his *Emigrant's Directory and Guide to Obtain Lands and Effect a Settlement in the Canadas* (1833):

> When {a settler} becomes the proprietor of a piece of land, all his work is for his own benefit, no rent or taxes being to be paid: he has the full produce of the soil for his support; and the surplus he can sent to market, when and how he pleases, as he is not in dread of the agent coming to distain him for the rent, or the collection of the county cess, or the tithe proctor, with many others who are the daily visitors of

the farmer in England and Ireland. It is this that makes the Canadian farmer feel really independent; - in fact he is lord and master of his own estate, and many that have landed in Quebec without a pound in the world have been able to realize by this course what is here represented.[99]

Simply put, any expectation that ownership of a greater number of acres would confer increased social status, as had been the case in Ireland for centuries, did not hold in rural Canada, because 'settlers of lesser origins' also got the chance to own and work their own land.

The experience of Catholic Irish emigrants in Australia differed considerably from those who settled in North America, as the first wave consisted of transported convicts. The first convict ship arrived in Botany Bay in 1788 and convict transportation continued until 1853. In all, about 40,000 were transported directly from Ireland, and about 8,000 more transported via Britain. By the 1830s about 30 per cent of the colony's population was Irish-born, of whom about 90 per cent had been convicts. Most of these convicts were male.[100] The lives of convicts during the early decades of the colony, in what was effectively a gulag, were brutally harsh, but conditions became less so over time, and by 1828 between 20 and 25 per cent of Irish former convicts came to own land or livestock.[101] The amount of land under cultivation expanded considerably, and the demand for labour increased. The percentage of the population serving sentences diminished, and the conditions under which new convicts worked as labourers for free settlers, under arrangements akin to terms of indenture, also improved over time.[102]

For example, Michael Hogan from County Tipperary, son of the sole well-to-do member of an impoverished rural family (his father was a cooper and a publican), was a first-time offender convicted of violent assault during a faction fight. He was sentenced to seven years' transportation in July 1834 at the age of 27 years, and became a convict servant for an English emigrant family on a farm in New South Wales. A few years later, he moved to Melbourne as a servant to the the Allen household, received his ticket of leave in March 1840, and 1842 married Margaret O'Brien, a bounty emigrant who had left Tipperary in 1839 and they had several children. By 1856 he was listed as the freehold owner of a house in Melbourne, where he lived alongside several relatives and former neighbours from Tipperary. Various census returns listed his occupation as stonemason (1842), labourer (1847), dairyman (1856) and park-keeper (1870). In letters, he described himself as prosperous to his younger brother Matthew, and encouraged him to join him in Australia. In one letter he wrote that a single labourer might earn £60 per annum, but was able to send his brother two bank drafts for £30 each. In 1865, Matthew Hogan emigrated with his family and settled a few doors away from Michael's house.[103]

In 1841 the transportation of convicts to New South Wales came to an end. That same year saw the arrival of 20,103 'assisted' immigrants, their passages paid on arrival from colonial revenues. Three quarters of them were Irish, selected mostly to work in Australia as agricultural labourers and, the women especially, in domestic service. Most male emigrants would have been listed as agricultural labourers, meaning that they were usually the sons of tenant farmers, whereas women were usually listed as 'servants' but might never have undertaken domestic work outside their mother's household.[104]

Contemporary stereotypes emphasised their ignorance, poor character, and skills, yet data on this 1841 cohort collected by colonial authorities' challenges a lot of the prejudices that have influenced historical accounts of such migrants.[105] Literacy levels amongst Irish migrants (69 per cent for males and 39.8 per cent for females) were considerably higher than those found in the 1841 Irish census. The highest literacy rates were recorded in Ulster (40 per cent in 1841) and Connaught (at 35 per cent) was found to have the lowest.[106] Those transported as convicts from Ireland prior to 1841 also had higher-than-average rates of literacy than for their country of origin. Analyses of records from 1838 found that 46.7 per cent of Irish convicts could both read and write.[107] Literacy likely gave those seeking to subscribe to schemes for assisted emigration an advantage, and letters home also proved to be crucial sources of information and assistance.[108] Although the Irish overall made up about 30 per cent of the population of the British Isles, they comprised 52 per cent of the assisted migrants to New South Wales and to Victoria in the period 1837–50. By 1872 some 140,000 Irish migrants had been assisted to the Australian colonies.[109]

The importance of literacy is illustrated by case studies of mostly Catholic emigrants to Australia, based on the letters of migrants included in David Fitzpatrick's *Oceans of Consolation* (1994). For example, Micheal Normile was part of a family from the townland of Derry in north County Clare with a thirty-acre farm of mostly good land, just one acre of which was given over to potatoes. The family came through the Famine in part because the crops they grew were diverse, in part because of a benevolent landlord, and in part because Michael Normile senior was given employment by the Liscannor Relief Committee on public works from January 1847, even though he was not destitute. After the Famine, many of Michael Normile's siblings emigrated to the United States as well as Australia.

The Normiles were atypical, as fewer than 16 per cent of post-Famine emigrants left Ireland in family groups. The great majority were young, single adults; the median age of emigrants between 1852 and 1891 was 22.5 years for males and 21.2 years for females.[110] In 1854, Michael Normile, then aged 22 years, and his 19-year-old sister Bridget emigrated to New South Wales, having received help from a friendly Protestant rector in completing their application for an assisted passage. Michael quickly found work as a storeman and carter, and continued to do this kind of work. Nearly all the families back in Clare had relatives in Australia who were mentioned in Michael's letters, and chain migration bought an ongoing flow of migrants from the townland of Derry. Government migration schemes facilitated family reunification by allowing settlers to nominate further recipients of state assistance.

In 1853 Michael married Bridget Neylon who had been his next-door neighbour in Ireland. His sister Bridget Normile got married in 1861. In all, 27 members of the Normile family circle aged between 16 and 26 years – siblings, cousins, an uncle, an aunt and in-laws – emigrated to Australia between 1851 and 1866. Just nine out the 27 were listed on immigration records as illiterate. In one of his letters Michael Normile thanked his father for ensuring that he received and education and exhorted him to keep his younger brothers in school. In another, he promised that if his younger siblings stayed in school, he would find them a better place in life in Australia than they could ever expect in County Clare.[111]

Many Irish men and women who emigrated after the Famine to Australia had advantages over equivalent nineteenth-century Catholic emigrants to the United States. They were not, as David Fitzpatrick suggested, latecomers competing against those who had arrived earlier for living space and employment.[112] In terms of occupation, Catholic emigrants and their descendants were only marginally distinct from the Australian population as a whole by the time of the 1921 census. 4.72 per cent of Catholic males were enumerated as professionals compared to 4.78 per cent of the total male population, 22.01 per cent of Catholic males were farmers compared to 22.90 per cent of the total male population. 14.38 per cent were in industrial employment compared to 15.82 per cent as a whole. 9.97 per cent were employed in transport and communications, compared to 8.45 per cent as a whole. 6.94 per cent were in commercial occupations compared to 8.45 per cent as a whole.[113]

By 1841 there were some 419,256 Irish-born living on the British mainland and a decade later, as a result of accelerated emigration triggered by the Famine, this number had risen to 727,326. The 1851 census found that 22.3 per cent of the population of Liverpool, 18.9 per cent of the population of Dundee, 18.2 per cent of the population of Glasgow and 13.1 per cent of the population of Manchester and Salford were Irish born. Most Irish emigrants settled in the north of England or Scotland, and by comparison just 4.6 per cent of the population of London was Irish born in 1851, although it must be borne in mind that that London's population far exceeded that of other English and Scottish cities. In the decades that followed Irish emigration to Britain continued to decline. The exception was that during the early 1900s, there was a sharp rise in migration from the north-east of Ireland.[114]

Most of these migrants were from rural Ireland. A small percentage of them were from middle-class urban or artisan backgrounds. There were three main directions of travel: from north Connaught and Ulster to Scotland; from Connaught and the midlands via Dublin to Liverpool; and from south Leinster and Munster to London, often via Bristol. With the exception of some who worked as farm labourers in Scotland, most migrated to urban areas. By 1851 over 80 per cent of Irish-born immigrants living on the British mainland inhabited towns with populations of more than 10,000. Yet between the 1840s and the 1860s there were also somewhere between 60,000 and 100,000 Irish seasonal labourers. In addition to working as farm labourers, Irish migrants worked in construction and building railways. As such, a significant proportion of the Irish-born population did not settle in one place. Most Irish-born men worked as unskilled or semi-skilled labourers of one sort or another. Many women worked in textile factories, laundries and domestic service. Others did rag-picking, sewing and other kinds of piece-work in their own homes.[115]

Engels' accounts of the Irish ghetto in Manchester capture a sense of a perceived immigration crisis as well as of the prevailing anti-Irish stereotypes. In *The Condition of the Working in* England (1845) he described how in almost every great city in Britain 'a fifth or a quarter of the workers were Irish, or the children of Irish parents who had grown up amongst Irish filth'.[116] A lot of what he wrote drew second-hand on what was written by about Irish immigrants by English writers like Thomas Carlyle and by the authors of public health reports, which he supplemented with his own observations of the condition of the Irish in Manchester. He described an area in the city known as 'little Ireland', where some 4,000 mostly-Irish immigrants lived in sickening filth amongst the effluvia of refuse and offal and the smoke from factory chimneys. Ragged women and children swarmed about, 'as filthy as the swine that thrive amongst the garbage heaps and the puddles'. He described conditions of chronic overcrowding where 20 people might live in a house with two rooms, a garret and perhaps a cellar prone to flooding in streets where 120 persons might have to share a single privy, where often whole Irish families crowded into one bed, 'often a heap of filthy straw or quilts of old sacking cover all in an indiscriminate heap'. He described how many families who had but one room to themselves received lodgers and boarders: 'such lodgers of both sexes by no means rarely sleep in the same bed with the married couple'.[117] The Irish as Engels described them in *The Condition of the Working Class* were incurably debased and degraded.[118]

Yet, the condition of many such Irish improved over time from the kinds of circumstances recorded by Engels. Little Ireland had long vanished by the time the first English-language edition of his book was published in England in 1892. The Catholic Church played a crucial role in regulating and educating post-Famine emigrants who settled in England. The arrival of Catholic migrants from Ireland radically changed the composition of and resuscitated the Church in England and Scotland.[119]

During the centuries after the Reformation, English Catholics and priests had declined in numbers. By 1773 there were about 59,500 Catholics and 886 priests in England and Wales, and this number continued to shrink during the last quarter of the eighteenth century. These were concentrated in areas such as Durham, Lancashire, and Shropshire, where some aristocratic families had held out against the Reformation and where, due to their influence, anti-Catholic penal laws were not always fully implemented. Whilst Catholics comprised a small portion of the aristocracy, they were not part of the rising new industrial proprietor class. In Scotland, land clearances as well as the Reformation contributed to the decline in the numbers of Catholics. Just 30,000 Catholics lived in Scotland by the beginning of the nineteenth century.[120] By 1840, there were about 60 Irish priests working in England, most of these in Lancashire and many of these had been trained at the All Hallows College Seminary in Dublin.[121] In 1842 Cardinal Cullen, the Archbishop of Dublin noted that just one in ten of the 100,000 or so Irish Catholics in Liverpool attended Mass regularly. He attributed this to a shortage of priests and of Catholic schools, the numbers of which expanded rapidly in the decades that followed.[122]

From 1847 Catholic Schools in England received some grant aid from the Government, which was administered by the Catholic Poor School Committee (CPSC), later the Catholic Educational Council. Reports published by the CPSC in 1848 and 1849 respectively declared that the purpose of Catholic education was to convert the masses into 'useful citizens', and to enable a Catholic boy to become 'a working man with cottage and a garden, his own freehold property'.[123] The CPSC aspired to turn the children of immigrants from Ireland into respectable working-class Catholics on an equal footing with their Protestant neighbours. And the condition of the Irish working classes in England was to be improved through education; Catholic education in England sought to instil love for the church and loyalty to its clergy, and to foster a Catholic identity – but not necessarily an Irish one.[124]

REMITTANCES

The development of Irish nationalism in Ireland owes much to the ideological identifications with Ireland and support for Irish self-determination amongst Irish emigrants and their descendants in the United States. Irish-American nationalism was incubated in those parts of the United States where the largest number of Catholic emigrants fetched up, but was not necessarily the main preoccupation of Irish-American identity or politics. Identity most consistently centred on Catholicism, and politics mostly focused specifically on the pressing business of how to win acceptance and success in America.[125] Yet, Lawrence McCaffrey wrote:

> Without Irish America, nationalism in Ireland might not have survived. The Irish diaspora in America provided both the physical force and constitutional nationalist movements in Ireland with the essential funds and passion that enabled them to force British governments to make major concessions regarding Irish religious, social and economic grievances. The democratic, egalitarian, and republican contexts of Fenianism were manifestations of the Irish-American spirit and political value system. Irish Americans authored the New Departure strategy that Michael Davitt and Charles Stewart Parnell directed in the Land War, which also produced tenant rights and eventually peasant proprietorship. Dollars from the United States financed the Home Rule Movement and the Irish parliamentary party. Irish-American money and arms supplied the Irish Republican Army (IRA) in the 1919–21 War of Independence, and Irish-American opinion, joined by voices demanding justice from all over the world, persuaded the British government to offer dominion status to a twenty-six-county Free State that evolved into the present Irish Republic.[126]

If McCaffrey overstates the influence of Irish-Americans on events that shaped modern Ireland he hardly does so by much. What has been dismissed by John A. Murphy as the 'vicarious nationalism' of the Catholic Irish in America was anything but:[127] it was integral to the development of nationalism in Ireland and the creation of the Irish nation state. Amongst the Catholic Irish in the United States, nationalist rhetoric helped to construct a community identity and a sense of ethnic allegiance. In the post-Famine period 'nationalists abroad enjoyed greater success than their compatriots at home', eliciting a fervour for the cause in the aftermath of the failed 1848 rebellion that was largely absent in Ireland itself.[128] The influence of the United States on Ireland predated the existence of a large Catholic Irish-American community. The catechism of the United Irishmen acknowledged as much:

Question: What have you got in your hand?
Answer: A green bough.
Question: Where did it first grow?
Answer: In America.

United Irishmen who found refuge in the United States included Matthew Carey (1760–1839), a Catholic Dublin publisher, who had been editor of *The Freeman's Journal* and *The Volunteer's Journal* in Ireland. In 1781 Carey travelled to Paris where he was employed by Benjamin Franklin as a printer of pamphlets on behalf of the newly independent American government. He emigrated to Philadelphia in 1784, and became a successful publisher of newspapers; the influential periodical, *American Museum*; and Catholic books and novels such as those of James Fenimore Cooper. During the 1790s, some 30,000 Irish settled in Philadelphia, many of whom were influenced by the radicalism of the American and French revolutions before their departure from Ireland.[129] In response to the influx, Carey founded The Hibernian Society for the Relief of Emigrants in 1790, which was both a charitable and a political organisation, designed to help and appeal to the politics of the new arrivals. Similar associations such as the Hibernian Provident Society of New York soon emerged other cities.[130]

Carey championed large-scale immigration by Irish Catholics to the US. In an 1829 essay, *Emigration from Ireland, and Immigration into the United States*, he argued that a shortage of labourers was impeding the expansion of the railways and canals and driving up wages. He made the case for an emigration scheme to fund the passages of between 20,000 and 30,000 migrants each year from Ireland and elsewhere, designed to avoid the kinds of exploitation associated with previous contracts of indenture. He calculated that a steerage passage from Ireland cost about $27.00 per head from Ireland at a time when unskilled labourers could earn between $12.00 and $15.00 plus board and lodging per month. Carey proposed a scheme that emigrants who could not afford to pay their passage could agree to be employed by a canal contractor for three months before becoming a free labourer. Any longer period of indenture was unjustified because fares to the United States had become so much cheaper than hitherto.[131] Carey declared in his 1829 essay that there were many examples of Irish labourers working on the digging of canals who had arrived two or three years earlier in extreme poverty, who were now comfortably settled in small houses of their own.[132] In essence, his argument was that emigration to the United States was now viable for large numbers of the poorest Irish and that, with a little help, they would settle successfully.

The reality of such emigration was more complicated as many did not obtain housing or jobs quickly. Descriptions of the slums and poverty experienced by many newly arrived Catholic Irish immigrants by the Philadelphia Sanitary Committee of the Board of Health echoed those described by Engels in Manchester.[133] Carey's enthusiasm for Catholic Irish immigration was not universally shared in Philadelphia, and the growth of the Irish immigrant community and expansion of the Catholic Church in the 1840s and 1850s was countered by an intensification there and elsewhere on the east coast of Protestant American nativism. During 1844 and 1845 there were sectarian riots in Philadelphia, Richmond and Charleston.[134] Famine-era immigration to America caused a political crisis. The 1850s saw the emergence of the 'Know Nothings', a powerful anti-immigrant organisation that briefly held the balance of power in American politics between the collapse of the Whig Party and the emergence of the Republican Party in 1854.[135] From the 1830s, Catholic Irish immigrants in Philadelphia and elsewhere saw themselves in conflict with black freemen as well as with the descendants of Protestant emigrants.

United Irishmen who settled in Philadelphia had been supporters of the earlier Republican Party of Thomas Jefferson, which in turn was dedicated to preserving national unity through conciliation with the slaveholding South.[136] Daniel O'Connell in Ireland supported the abolition of slavery in America, though many of his Irish-American supporters did not. In June 1837, the Repeal Association, an organisation of several thousand O'Connellites in Philadelphia, split after a statement O'Connell made condemning slavery was published. Many Irish-American leaders distanced themselves from criticism of the American status quo.[137] In *How the Irish Became White*, Noel Ignatiev charts how Irish-Americans overcame anti-Catholic nativism partly through such political alignments: 'The Irish had faded from Green to white bleached by, as O'Connell put it, something in the "atmosphere" of America.'[138]

Nine major mob attacks against black people in Philadelphia were recorded between 1834 and 1849. In one such incident in 1834, a crowd of several hundred white men, including many Irish, wrecked the homes of black people in the neighbourhood, two churches, a grog shop and lodging house that accepted black as well as white customers, and. Two black people were killed and others beaten. The main cause of the riot seems to have been the belief that some employers were hiring black workers over whites, and the aim was to drive black residents, especially apparently prosperous ones, out of a racially mixed area.[139] An account of an attack in 1842 on a black temperance parade on the anniversary of the emancipation of the slaves in the West Indies described how nearly every man 'who was guilty of cruelty and violence towards the colored people was an Irishman'.[140]

Some 539 Irish surnames were listed on an 1850 register of slave owners in the United States. The number of slaves owned by those with Irish surnames rose from at least 99,129 in 1850 to 115,894 by 1860. Compensation records from 1834 for slaveowners in the West Indies identified 231 Irish surnames who had owned 37,104 slaves in total. Many of common Irish surnames were excluded from this analysis, including surnames that were also common in England and Scotland as well as Ulster Scot surnames. The list of Irish slave owners in the United States included the names of many Irish Taoisigh (Prime Ministers) – Lynch, Haughey, FitzGerald, Ahern, Cowen, and Kenny. It also included my own surname, Fanning. Some 97 individual absentee slave owners living in Ireland, who between them owned 15,869 slaves in British colonies claimed compensation in 1834 when slavery was abolished.[141]

In 1845, the first year of the Great Famine, almost 75,000 left Ireland for North America. In 'Black '47' the number had risen to about 214,000. About 100,000, mostly likely the poorest, took the less expensive crossing to Canada. About 10 per cent died during the crossing from disease and malnutrition. Many of those who fled to the United States during early years of the Famine-era flight from Ireland remitted money that enabled other members of their families to follow. Between 1850 and 1855 the Irish in the United States remitted an annual average of £1.2 million. Post-1850 remittances were probably enough to fund the entire flow of emigration from Ireland across the Atlantic though remittances were also used to financially assist relatives in Ireland. The cheapest passage across the Atlantic to Canada at the time could be had for under £5 per head. About 50,000 of the poorest Famine emigrants were 'assisted' in return for peacefully abandoning their homesteads; their departure was funded by either landlords or poor law officials.[142]

Most post-Famine Catholic emigrants to the United settled in urban areas in cities such as New York, Boston, and Philadelphia. In many respects rural Catholic Irish immigrants fared better in Philadelphia than in other urban destinations like Boston. In 1850, Boston had 35,000 Irish born out of a total population of 113,000. Philadelphia by then had 75,000 Irish-born out of a population of 220,000. In both cities the Irish-born made up similar portions of the population, but the capacity of Philadelphia, then the leading industrial city in the United States, to absorb newcomers proved to be much greater. The commercial economy of Boston was, in many respects, closed to the Catholic Irish. In Philadelphia, 'there was simply a better chance for Irishmen to compete', even if such competition was fiercely resisted.[143]

Accounts of the American urban slums into which Catholic immigrants landed recall those from Liverpool and Manchester, but with some differences. As in US cities, the poor Irish in urban England were stereotyped as unruly savages living in filth and depravity. Over time many became absorbed into working class, but the Irish in England, unlike those in the United States, did not become a politically influential ethnic group. In slums such as Five

Points in New York, the 'Bloody Sixth Ward', violence between religious factions was harnessed to great effect by the immigrant leaders of factions who took control of the slums and, over time, clawed their way into positions of power in New York politics.[144] This milieu has been the focus of Martin Scorsese's highly-fictionalised 2002 film *The Gangs of New York* and of Herbert Asbury's 1927 non-fiction book of the same name.[145] Communal political violence was by no means restricted to Catholic immigrants. For example, anti-Catholic nativist riots in 1844 in Philadelphia resulted in more than twenty people (none of these Catholics) being killed by soldiers charged with imposing martial law. In one incident, two soldiers were killed by nativists armed with a canon. In the aftermath of such riots, cities like Philadelphia established police forces and other infrastructure controlled by political patronage, all of which came to be dominated by Catholic Irish-Americans. No equivalent Irish political machine emerged in England. Nineteenth-century American politics was wilder and more populist than English politics, and more open to immigrants who could organise themselves along ethnic lines. Once in office, Irish-American politicians gave jobs and contracts to their own.[146] Where they could, Catholic immigrants mirrored the kinds of sectarian nepotism that also came to be practiced by Orangemen in parts of Canada or Australia in the nineteenth century.[147]

The post-Famine Catholic Irish came to establish a flourishing ethnic subculture by constructing a network of schools, churches, and fraternal societies. Philadelphia had 43 Catholic churches by 1882, alongside which a system of Catholic parish schools was established.[148] The number of Catholics in the United States rose from 663,000 in 1840 to 3,103,000 by 1860. There had been just 480 priests in the United States in 1840, but by 1850 there were 1,500, many of whom were Irish. By the end of the nineteenth century, All Hallows seminary in Dublin alone had sent 1,500 priests across the Atlantic.[149] Crucially, many Church leaders such as Francis Patrick Kendrick, the Bishop of Philadelphia, also came from Ireland. By 1900 two-thirds of Catholic Bishops in the United States were Irish-American.[150] The Irish dominated American Catholicism to the extent that it was sometimes referred to as the 'One Holy, *Irish*, and Apostolic' Church.[151] By contrast, most Catholic Bishops in England came from old English Catholic families even though most of their flocks were Irish.[152] In Philadelphia, as elsewhere, the Church engaged in the moral regulation of Catholic immigrants, ensuring, for example, that the 1875 Philadelphia St Patrick's Day parade included 39 Catholic temperance societies.[153]

Irish-American nationalism emerged alongside a Catholic Irish-American ethnic identity. Both were born out of common ghetto experiences, regardless of where the Irish-Americans originally came from in Ireland, and a perceived need to band together and to mobilise politically in response to nativism. A common historical heritage was built upon shared narratives of exile, pre-migratory colonial exploitation, and nationalist takes on the Famine.[154] Émigré 'Young Irelanders' such as John Mitchel played an important role in shaping such narratives.[155] Mitchel's escape from Van Diemen's Land (now Tasmania) to where he had been transported for sedition was funded by Irish emigrant organisations in New York. Mitchel arrived in New York in December 1853 when the city was in the throes of anti-Catholic, anti-immigrant and abolitionist agitation and, within a few weeks, founded *The Citizen*, a newspaper with a circulation of 50,000 aimed at inflaming Irish-American opinion against Britain. In 1857, another newspaper he edited, *The Southern Citizen*, serialised his influential polemic *The Last Conquest of Ireland (Perhaps)*, an account of the Famine and land clearances in Ireland, which blamed the pacifism of Daniel O'Connell as well as Britain for the post-Famine condition of Ireland.[156] Thomas Francis Meagher, who founded *The Irish News* in 1856, was Brigadier General of the Union Army during the American Civil War, in which as many as 170,000 Irishmen may have served.[157]

After the Civil War many joined the Fenian Brotherhood, founded in 1858 in New York by John O'Mahony, a former member of the Young Ireland movement. It was a sister organisation to the Irish Revolutionary Brotherhood (IRB), which had been organised in Dublin by James Stephens. By 1865, the Fenians had attracted 250,000 followers. About 50,000 of these were Union veterans.[158] In 1866 and 1870 several hundred such Fenians engaged in a number of attacks across the border with British North America aimed at undermining relations between the United States and Britain and thus radicalising the wider Irish-American community. The main consequence of these attacks was to hasten the confederation of British North American colonies into the Dominion of Canada. The 1867 Fenian 'uprising' in Ireland collapsed when, following the arrival of mostly Irish-American officers in Cork, the Irish people failed to rise up in sufficiently large numbers. Irish national-ism, at the time, was less radical in Ireland than the Irish-American strain.

By the late 1870s the Fenians were eclipsed by a new body, Clan na Gael, founded in New York by Jerome Collins. It attracted some 10,000 members and had links to the IRB. Clan na Gael played an important role in funding the 1916 Rising. In 1919, some 5,000 delegates participated in the Irish Race Conference in Philadelphia, one of a series of such funding conventions aimed at asserting the case for Irish independence. Friends of Irish Freedom, an Irish-American organisation founded by Clan na Gael in 1916 reached 100,000 members. The group raised more than $5 million to fund the War of Independence.[159] During the same period Irish nationalist figures such as Éamon de Valera and Hanna Sheehy Skeffington engaged in lengthy American speaking tours aimed at levering American opinion in support of Irish independence.

The influence of the Protestant diaspora on Irish affairs was less pronounced. However, at the time when the first Home Rule bill was being considered in 1886, Reverend R. R. Kane engaged in a similar tour to those undertaken by Irish nationalist leaders, his taking him to Orange Lodges in Canada and the United States, where he raised $20,000 on behalf of the Ulster Loyal Anti-Repeal Union. As a form of cultural diffusion, the spread of the Orange Order to Canada and Australia recalled the spread of Presbyterianism in Northern Ireland in the aftermath of Scottish settlement in Ulster. There were also similarities in how, from the mid-nineteenth century, the Catholic Church in Ireland influenced the development of the Church in the United States. However, for all that, the Orange Order fostered a shared British loyalist identity in Canada and for all that Orangemen in Canada identified with their brethren in Ireland, the Canadian Orange Order did not influence greatly the development of loyalism in Ireland.

Loyalism in the broadest sense was by no means confined to Protestant emigrants in Canada, New Zealand, and Australia. For example, many of the Catholic Irish in Australia supported the constitutional status quo, and were indifferent to Australian republicanism.[160] Many viewed economic and other connections with Britain as crucial, and largely supported Home Rule for Ireland within the empire, rather than Irish independence.[161] Contrast, for example, the post-1848 careers of John Mitchel and other Young Irelanders who preached revolutionary nationalism from the United States with that of Charles Gavan Duffy who emigrated to Australia in 1856. Duffy, like Mitchel, had been imprisoned for sedition in 1848 but was released and became an Irish Party Member of Parliament. He subsequently had a successful political career in Australia with the support of the Irish community who regarded him as a patriotic hero. On arrival in Australia he was feted no less than Mitchel had been in New York. In 1871, Duffy was elected Premier of Victoria, and was knighted two years later. In his autobiography, he described how, at the time of his arrival, Irish Catholics in Victoria were underrepresented in the running of the colony. During the 1850s there was just one Irish Catholic magistrate, and not half a dozen Catholics in the civil service.[162] However, he argued, the reformers of Victoria had won for their colony the kind of autonomy that Irish Home Rule nationalists like him had wanted for Ireland. Catholic influence subsequently grew as he and other Catholics were elected to political office.

Those emigrants who left in their millions affected Ireland greatly by their very absence. For example, emigration 'facilitated the elimination of landless labourers, but made practicable the survival of large families on uneconomic holdings by injecting into the farming sector a steady flow of cash remittances from relatives already prospering overseas'.[163] It could not be denied, Mitchel wrote in *The Last Conquest of Ireland (Perhaps)*, that the living conditions of those who had not died or emigrated had improved. There was a smaller supply of labour, but the demand for it had remained the same, therefore wages were higher. There was more cattle and grain for export to England because large numbers of tenants had been driven off the land to the grave or abroad.[164] In the post-Famine area, especially in rural Ireland, the expectation that many would emigrate became hardwired within families and communities. Chain migration reduced the population of Ireland generation on generation. Emigrants encouraged and often paid for relatives to join them.

SEVEN

JEWS

The Foreign Protestants Naturalisation Act of 1709 allowed immigrants to claim British citizenship upon swearing an oath of allegiance, and taking the sacrament in the established Church. By then, a system of penal laws was in place that prevented Catholics from inheriting or purchasing land, that also excluded them from the professions and prevented them from holding public office. A number of these laws also discriminated against Protestant dissenters such as John Toland (1670–1722). In 1714, Toland published a pamphlet entitled *Reasons for Naturalizing the Jews in Great Britain and Ireland*.[1] Toland was born into a Gaelic-speaking Roman Catholic family in Donegal and at the age of sixteen joined the Church of Ireland, which sponsored him to train as a minister in Glasgow. In 1690 he took his Master's degree from the University of Edinburgh 'a day before the battle of the Boyne'.[2] He became a dissenter and was the first theologian to be called a freethinker.[3] In his 1714 pamphlet, Toland argued trenchantly against anti-Semitism, and declared that any perceptible differences between families or nations 'were accidental, not natural', resulting from differences in education and government.[4] However, his pamphlet also argued that the 1709 Act justly excluded disloyal subjects – namely Catholics – who acknowledged a foreign Potentate and did not tolerate any churches save their own.

Toland described how the Jews who first arrived in England with William the Conqueror 'suffered in their goods and persons all the horrible things that priests and politicians could devise'. During the reign of Richard I 'many were piteously murdered, chiefly at the instigation of the clergy'.[5] They had been 'robbed by the barons and murdered in large numbers for crimes that it was improbable they could have committed', and in 1290 the entire Jewish community of 15,511 was exiled after 220 years of settlement in England.[6]

Some Jews continued to live in England clandestinely. During the sixteenth and seventeenth centuries, these included the 'Marranos' – Sephardic Jews who were refugees from the Spanish Inquisition and who were deemed to be

Spanish subjects. As Spain was a Catholic country, they worshipped in secret, and were normally buried with Catholics. In a 1655 petition to Oliver Cromwell, in response to threat of the confiscation of their property, London's Marranos openly declared themselves to be Jewish. England and Spain were at war at the time. The confiscation was quashed and thereafter Jews lived openly as such in England.[7]

In November 1655, Cromwell's Council of State set up a committee to consider the readmission of the exiled Jews to England in response to a petition submitted by Rabbi Menasseh Ben Israel on behalf of the Marranos. The political and intellectual climate of the day, in essence a theological climate, was very open to the idea.[8] English Puritans including Cromwell were strongly 'philo-Semitic': firstly, they enthusiastically identified in their own religion with Jewish notions of being a chosen people and having a covenant with God; and some studied Hebrew to better understand the Old Testament. Some English Puritans wanted to readmit Jews in order to convert them, a desire that owed much to interpretations of the Book of Revelations that claimed that such a conversion would be one of a number of events that preceded Judgement Day.[9] The notion that thousands of Jews might be pretending to be Roman Catholics also concerned some Puritan advocates for readmission.[10] It was also argued that it was better that Jews be allowed to live in Protestant countries rather than in Catholic or heathen ones.[11]

Many of the pamphlets that made theological arguments also alluded to economic ones for readmission. Toland's fitted into this genre, which by then was at least 70 years old.[12] It was novel not just because it made an early case giving citizenship rights to Jewish denizens. It also set out a secular history of English anti-Semitism that explained this in terms of economic factors, demographic pressures, international rivalries, and ideology.[13] Jews would make ideal immigrants, Toland also argued, because they were not involved in the religious conflicts that threatened the state. No established Church clergyman would 'be kept from a fat Bishoprick by a *Rabbi*'. Protestant dissenters in turn had no reason to be alarmed, because the Jews were hardly going to join the established Church and oppress them.[14]

Toland, in keeping with the mercantilist spirit of Queen Anne's reign, emphasised how immigration contributed to the wealth of nations.[15] Permitting Jewish immigration would increase 'the number of hands for labour and defence, of bellies and backs for the consumption of food and raiment, and of brains for invention and contrivance'. Toland's case for deliberately attracting Jewish immigrants from Europe emphasised the economic benefits these would bring:

We deny not that there will thus be more taylors and shoomakers; but there will also be more suits and shoes made than before. If there be more weavers, watchmakers and other artificers, we can for this reason export more cloth, watches, and more of all other commodities than formally and not only have 'em better made than by the emulation of so many workmen, of such different nations; but likewise have them quicker sold off, for being cheaper wrought than those of others, who come to the same market,. This one Rule of MORE, and BETTER, and CHEAPER will ever carry the market against all expedients and devices.[16]

Toland argued that economic growth was best served by individual liberties, which mirrored the case for encouraging European Protestant immigration that was widely made at the time. Toland argued for a policy of deliberately attracting Jewish immigrants from countries where they were oppressed. He described how Jews were locked up at night in their ghettos in cities such as Prague. Spain, he argued, had 'grown prodigiously weak and poor' since the expulsion of the Jews and Moors, whereas Holland, with comparatively few native inhabitants had grown rich and powerful from 'allowing an unlimited Liberty of Conscience, and receiving all nations to the rights of citizens'.[17] He maintained that immigrants were needed to take the place of those who went to the colonies ('who yearly go to the Plantations, and in the service of the East India Company; not to speak of our Armies, Fleets, or Adventurers'). They would improve England just as plantations in Ireland had brought the land into better use and improved all sorts of arts and manufacturing.[18] He cited as an example of such beneficial immigration 'the late colonies from the Palatines'.[19]

More than a decade earlier, in what became one of his best-known works, Toland edited and wrote an admiring biographical introduction to *The Commonwealth of Oceana and Other Works of James Harrington* that was published in 1700.[20] *Oceana* had been first published in 1656, the year after the Whitehall Conference. In it, Harrington proposed that Jews be settled in Ireland and granted perpetual lease to the island for an annual revenue of £2,000,000 per annum. Harrington argued that removal to Ireland would solve the problem of 'parasitic' Jews living in England.[21] By planting Ireland with Jews and allowing them to practice their own rites there, Ireland would become a magnet for Jews from all parts of the world. Having settled there they would, according to Harrington, take again to farming as well as to trade.[22]

Though Harrington's proposal for Jewish settlement in Ireland had no influence, it was part of the broader climate that endorsed Jewish readmission to England (and by implication, Ireland). A case for planting a colony of Portuguese Marranos in Ireland was put forward by Sir Thomas Shirley in 1607 at a time when various plantation schemes were underway or being envisaged (see Chapter 3). Shirley was an unsuccessful adventurer who had been imprisoned in Constantinople and who would, soon after, be jailed for a while in the Tower of London. He argued that Marrano settlers would foster trade by selling Irish commodities such as salted salmons, corn, hides, wool and tallow to Spain, and such trade would yield considerable taxes to the king. He advised that the Jews should be initially 'be tenderly used' but could be in time ('once you have hold of their persons and goods') be milked for huge taxes.[23] This was, of course, half a century before official recognition that the Marranos were in fact Jews, and by then a few such Sephardim had indeed arrived in Ireland.

EARLY JEWISH SETTLEMENT

The earliest record of Jews in Ireland dates back to 1079, almost a century before the arrival of the Normans. A delegation of five Jews from England or Normandy, who were seeking the right of entry for their co-religionists, was rebuffed by Turlough O'Brien, King of Munster. Two Anglo-Norman adventurers who landed in Wexford in May 1169, Robert Fitz Steven and Maurice Fitz Gerald, had been financed by Josce, a Jewish moneylender from Gloucester. A few Jews arrived in the wake of the Normans as merchants, but nothing is known as to who these were or how they fared; their presence was indicated by a document from July 1232 that listed amongst the duties of the then Chancellor of the Irish Exchequer, custody of the king's Judaism in Ireland. Several surviving documents record a prohibition on transferring land in Ireland to Jews, but this restriction was superseded by their expulsion in 1290.[24]

William Annyas (or Anes), a member of an English-based Marrano family, became Mayor of Youghal in 1555. His son Francis, by trade a soldier of fortune, also served three terms as mayor from 1569, 1576 and 1581; meaning that he, like his father before him, was in charge of the English garrison there.[25] Another member of the Annyas family was recorded as a member of the town garrison. William had previously travelled to the Azores to survey the islands in advance of raids by Sir Francis Drake, as Marranos were used as 'intelligencers' by Elizabethan privateers because of their knowledge of Spanish and Portuguese trade.[26] In 1621, another Marrano, Abraham de Lyon from Eindhoven, was given a residency patent that allowed him to operate his businesses in Ireland and in other British colonies.[27] After readmission in 1656, Jews began to settle in the British Isles, and about five or six years later a handful of Marranos had established themselves in

Dublin, where they were probably known as Portuguese merchants. A few non-Marrano Jews also probably arrived with Dutch merchants who traded in Dublin. The first synagogue in Dublin was established in Crane Lane during the 1660s. David Solom (Solome), the first Jew to hold public office in Dublin, was outwardly a Christian. He became a Justice of the Peace in Meath 1671 and later High Sheriff of Meath in 1675.[28]

Jewish immigration to Ireland after readmission was stymied by legislation that restricted trade with England. An Act passed in 1663 prohibited the exportation of live cattle and farm produce, and also outlawed, with few exceptions, the importation of goods from Europe to Ireland. Only goods made from England and borne by English ships could be imported into the colonies. Such barriers made Ireland unattractive to Jews involved in trade.[29]

In autumn 1689, Parliament sought to impose a levy on English Jewish community to help fund William of Orange's military campaign in Ireland. Thirty wealthy Jews were instead required to loan the campaign £45,000 to help to cover costs. Most of this came from Isaac Pereira, who was appointed a commissary to the king's forces. Pereira employed a number of Sephardic Jews to provide supplies to the army.[30] After the Battle of the Boyne, a small number of Sephardim settled in Dublin, an offshoot of the London community. Towards the end of the seventeenth century, a few Ashkenazi from Germany and Poland began to arrive in England, where they worked as pedlars; the more-established Sephardim were merchants. By the beginning of the eighteenth century maybe eight Ashkenazi families living in Dublin. At the time Toland's pamphlet appeared in 1714, no more than 20 Jewish families lived in Dublin, both Sephardim and Ashkenazim.[31] A Jewish cemetery at Ballybough, near an area now known as Fairview, dates from around 1718. The oldest Jewish gravestone that is still standing dates from 1777.[32]

In 1753 the Westminster Parliament considered a bill for the naturalisation of Jews proposed by George Montagu Dunk, the Earl of Halifax. The bill sought to allow Jews to be naturalised by Parliament without receiving the sacrament in accordance with the established Church.[33] The bill failed to pass in the face of widespread opposition from the established Church, from non-Jewish merchants and due to anti-Semitism whipped up by pamphlets, petitions, and caricatures.[34] Jewish mobilisation in support of the bill contributed to the establishment of a Jewish Board of Deputies a few years later in 1760, which thereafter also had a remit for Jews in Ireland.[35]

An Act passed in 1793 by the Irish Parliament allowed for the naturalisation of all foreign settlers – merchants, traders, artificers, seamen, and farmers – except for Jews. Legislation permitting the naturalisation of Jews was not passed in the Westminster parliament until 1816, fifteen years after the Act of Union. Full Jewish emancipation – the complete removal all forms of political and economic discrimination – did not come to pass until 30 years after Catholic emancipation. The Religious Opinions Relief Act of 1846 removed most forms of discrimination against Jews and dissenters, but did not give them the right to be a member of parliament. Benjamin Disraeli became an MP in 1839, but he had been baptised into the Church of England as a child.[36] David Salamons, the first Jewish Lord Mayor of London, was elected in 1855. Only with the Jews Relief Act (1858) did Jews fully achieve the rights that Catholics had won three decades earlier.

Some of the Jews who settled in Dublin during the eighteenth century converted to Protestantism. For example, Moses Moses, an English-born goldsmith who had grown up in Dublin was baptised in February 1775 at the age of twenty-three. Later that year he married Catherine Know, the daughter of a Sligo merchant, in the Church of Ireland. His son Marcus enrolled in Trinity in 1828 and became partner in a music publishing business. Catherine Know's sister married Dr Alexander McCaul, a Hebrew scholar and missionary. The following year, Moses' sister Phoebe became a Protestant. Marcus's son John graduated from Trinity in 1860 became a Church of Ireland curate in Tuam.[37]

The late eighteenth century witnessed, according to Louis Hyman, 'the almost complete disintegration of the Dublin [Jewish] community'.[38] It had been very small to begin with, and many of its members were transitory; there had been a synagogue, most likely in Crane Lane, that was replaced in 1760 by one at Marlborough Green, where Marlborough Street now meets Abbey Street, but this closed a few decades later. Its Scrolls of Law were moved to the home of Abraham Lyons on Fishamble Street where the community kept *shul*. By 1791 this group had become so small that it could not muster the ten males aged over 13 years of age required to run religious services. On 22 November 1791 the London Jewish community wrote to Lyons asking him to return the two Scrolls of Law that it had previously sent to Dublin. By 1818 there were only two identifiable Jewish families in Dublin, the Cohens, who had settled in Dublin around 1770 (from Lissa in the duchy of Posen) and the Phillips, who had been in Dublin for a century and a half.[39]

Some Jews settled in Ireland once naturalisation was allowed in 1816. Some Polish and German Jews arrived in Dublin in 1822. These had relatives who settled in Birmingham. The revitalised Dublin congregation rented premises at 40 Stafford Street in 1829, lead by Myer Nerwich, a watchmaker and Hebrew scholar, who arrived from Posen in 1810. When his wife died in 1856 he resettled in Birmingham where his brother Abraham lived. One of Myer Nerwich's daughters married and settled in Birmingham. Another, Matilda Nerwich, married Isaac Levy in Dublin. After she died in 1833 her husband married Maria Israel a Londoner who had cousins, the Solomons, in Dublin. Joseph Wolfe Cohen also came to Dublin from Posen via Birmingham from where his wife Rebecca Lazarus came. His daughter Abigail married Benjamin Ralph Isaac from Liverpool who was a grand-nephew of Samuel Solomon from Cork. Her sister Esther married Maurice Salam a Dublin jeweller. Their son Semilim Salam was born in Dublin in 1843. He was the first Jew to qualify in medicine from Trinity and he joined the Indian Medical Service. Joseph Wolfe Cohen's brother Solomon Cohen had two sons born in Dublin but when his wife died in 1843 he appears to have left Dublin. By 1851 he was living in New York but returned to Dublin the following year after receiving congregational funds and private donations to cover his fare. Some of his children settled in America.[40] Dublin's small Jewish community was a transnational one. The children of Jews who migrated to Ireland were likely to travel onwards as adults. Yet, a Dublin community did become established, with ongoing ties through business, family and marriage with Jewish communities in a few other places.

Between 1820 and 1875 Jews arrived from England, Holland, France, Germany, Poland, Galicia, Russia, Lithuania, and Morocco. Those who arrived from Britain came in small numbers from Bath, Birmingham, Bristol, Manchester, Plymouth, Portsmouth, Glasgow and Edinburgh. The first census in 1861 that counted Ireland's Jewish population identified 445 in total, with 52 living in Belfast and most of the rest in Dublin.

In 1836, N. L. Benmohel became the first unconverted Jew to graduate from Trinity College, which was the first Anglican university in the British Isles to admit Jewish students. David Rosenthal (1833–1907), the first Irish-born Jewish Trinity graduate, became a lawyer in Dublin and the Dublin Jewish community's representative on the Board of Deputies in London.[41] The president of the Dublin congregation from 1876 to 1901 was Marinus de Groot (1829–1901), who had been born in Rotterdam and had become a successful merchant in Dublin. He became a Justice of the Peace in Dublin and a Town Commissioner in Bray. The first president of the Dublin congregation's Educational Board and the *Hebrath Meshivath Nephesh*, the Hebrew Philanthropic Society of Ireland founded in 1846, was John I. Davies (1803–82), who was a dentist. Davies's parents were English Jews. Lionel H. Rosenthal, born in 1856 in Harcourt Street and a Trinity Graduate, was the first Jew to be granted silk by the Irish Lord Chancellor. In 1909 he was appointed Senior Crown Prosecutor for County Wexford.[42]

Between 1850 and 1870 a small, number of German Jewish merchants and their families, led by Daniel Joseph Jaffé, settled in Belfast. They ran businesses exporting linen to Europe, Russia, South America and to the United States. They opened Belfast's first synagogue in Great Victoria Street in 1871. The most prominent member of this small community,

Jaffé's son Sir Otto Jaffé, served as Mayor of Belfast from 1899 for two successive one-year terms, and for a third term from 1904. Jaffé opened a new synagogue on Annesley Street having funded much of the building costs. He also funded the establishment of a Jewish school nearby on Cliftonville Road. Both the synagogue and school served a community that had expanded to include new arrivals from what is now Lithuania. Jaffé had worked for the family linen firm in the United States for a number of years before returning to Belfast. Gustav Wilhelm Wolff, co-founder of the Harland and Wolff shipyard, which built the *Titanic*, was the son of German Jews who had converted to Christianity. Wolff joined the Church of Ireland and became a Conservative MP. Jaffé was a member of the Unionist Party.[43]

LITVAKS: THE JEWS OF LITHUANIA

The main period of Jewish immigration to Ireland was during the 1880s and 1890s. Most arrivals were Ashkenazi from the Tsarist province of Kovno, which encompassed much of Lithuania, where, by the end of the nineteenth century about 1.5 million Jews lived. Those who came to Ireland came from Yiddish-speaking *shtetls* (Jewish neighbourhoods in towns) in the north of the province. Most of those who came to Ireland came from ten shtetls that between them in 1897 had a Jewish population of 25,225: Akmyan, Klilul, Kurshany, Papiljan, Plungyan, Shavli, Telz, Vexna, Zedick and Zhager. Only in Akmyan, where a significant portion of those who settled in Ireland came from, did the Jews constitute less than 40 per cent of the population.[44] The Jews from Kovno settled in Dublin, Belfast, Cork and Limerick, where, by 1881 there were already Jewish communities that included some Litvaks. Others then followed in what amounted to a classic example of chain migration.[45] Some arrived directly by sea: ships regularly sailed from the Baltic to Cork. Some migrants came via England, and in some cases lived and worked there for a time before continuing their onward journey. Some were sent by the Jewish Board of Deputies to Ireland, presumably because they would be better off with relatives or former neighbours who had settled there.

According to an 1897 Russian census Jews in Kovno accounted for 18.6 per cent of those in employment but totalled 49.9 per cent of those working in crafts and industry, 51.8 per cent of those in the free professions and civil service and 91.2 per cent of those working in trade and credit. They accounted for just 1.5 per cent of the agricultural workforce. Typically they were better off than the non-Jewish peasantry, for although they faced discrimination, they had never been enserfed, and tended to be better educated. Others had become better off and worked as self-employed craftsmen, merchants, and clerks. Litvaks were disproportionately employed in the corn trade, inn-keeping, brewing, and transport.[46]They were found in the 1897 census to have twice the literacy rate of the wider population, to comprise 90 per cent of all pedlars, general merchants, and dealers in agricultural produce, building materials, and fuel. Men in such trades were used to a life on the road; those who emigrated to Ireland in advance of their families were comparatively well educated and enterprising.[47]

What triggered large-scale Jewish emigration from Lithuania from the 1880s was most likely a combination of a number of factors. The decades after the death of Czar Alexander II witnessed periodic outbreaks of persecution, including the expulsion of thousands of Jews from Moscow in the early 1890s. Legislation banned Jews from living outside the shtetls and from buying land, and also placed quotas on their entry into the professions and the universities. For all that, the economic historian Cormac Ó Gráda argues that the Litvaks who emigrated to Ireland and elsewhere after the 1880s were predominantly economic migrants. Those who came to Ireland emigrated from shtetls that had not experienced pogroms.[48] Jewish emigration from the Baltic provinces was higher than from those parts of Russia most affected by pogroms. It was also the case that some Jews migrated internally to places in Russia where pogroms had occurred.[49] There is a striking absence of first-hand accounts of persecution in the memoirs and family histories of Litvaks who settled in Ireland. However, some of these accounts suggest that fear of conscription into the Russian army was one reason why some men emigrated, as the practice of their religion would have been prohibited in the army, and joining would have entailed the long-term rupture of their families. At the same time anti-Semitism in Lithuania was all too real. Most Jews who did not emigrate were killed by the Nazis or by Lithuanian nationalists during the Second World War. To give but one startling example, in 1897 there were 914 Jews living in the village of Zhidik, or 73 per cent of its population. In June 1941 the 150 Jews who still lived in Zhidik were murdered.[50]

Yet, it is clear that many also emigrated for economic reasons. Ó Gráda suggests that the emancipation of the serfs in 1863 gradually eroded some of the economic niches around which the shtetls had developed. Furthermore, he argues, the economy of the shtetl, based upon artisanal production for local markets, was being undermined by the growing availability of mass-produced goods.[51] Ultimately, many Jews found it hard to make a living in Kovno province.

Some accounts claim that some Litvaks arrived in Cork by mistake, having been tricked into disembarking, believing that they had reached the United States. Gerald Goldberg described his father Louis Goldberg, from Ackmehan in Kovno, as arriving unintentionally in Ireland believing that he was on his way to America.[52] Other, more practical reasons were at stake for other travellers: Enid Mescon claimed that her grandfather disembarked at Cork because the ship that was to take him to New York was out of kosher food;[53] Stanley Price recounted how his grandfather embarked with his two brothers from Lithuania to America but disembarked in Cork, supposedly because of seasickness.[54] It may have been the case that some Litvaks viewed Dublin or Cork as halfway houses both literally and geographically, as places to work and save enough for the fare across the Atlantic.[55]

Louis Lentin in his television documentary about his grandfather Solomon Kalman Lentin, *Grandpa. . . Speak to me in Russian*, argued that stories of Jews disembarking in Cork by mistake were myths: 'People swear their ancestors were swindled, sold half-way tickets then put off the boat at Queenstown, now Cobh. Others, that the emigrants heard "Cork! Cork!" called, mistook it for New York and off they got. Why spoil a good story?' The Litvak migrants were, as he put it, pretty savvy folk, and they had gathered information on Ireland before they left:

> The postal system in Lithuania was extremely good. Letters would have been shown to everyone, news spread. Once it became known that Ireland was badly in need of Jewish pedlars, others decided to give it a try. Journeys were extremely well organised, with competition between the various steamship lines fierce. Local agents sold tickets, others saw to arrangements along the routes. There was money to be made packing holds with human cargo. If your destination was America you most likely took one of the larger boats from the German ports.[56]

News that her sister Freda's husband Peisa Harmel was doing well in 'England Ireland', as Dublin was known to some Lithuanian Jews, prompted Etta Berman (née Zlotover) to encourage her husband to migrate there to seek work. He had not been able to make a living in Vechna (Vexna). Etta Berman had received glowing accounts of life in Dublin. When Berman reached Dublin, his brother-in-law set him up with goods and he travelled initially to Limerick and then to Athlone to work as a pedlar. In time he brought his family over to Ireland where they lived for a time in Athlone and Galway before finally settling in the midst of the Dublin Jewish community.[57] When a number of the extended Zlotover family became established in Dublin, some older relatives moved there to live with them.[58]

Kalman Lentin most likely sailed from the Baltic port of Libau and he would have landed either in London, Grimsby or Hull on the east coast of England from where he took a train to Liverpool and then the boat to Dublin. By the time Kalman emigrated in his early teens two older brothers had already left for America. It is likely that many of the Litvak emigrants had been rerouted by the London Jewish Board of Guardians to Ireland. Once some of these were established in Dublin, Belfast or Cork, others followed in a classic pattern of chain migration.

The 1881 census recorded 352 Jews as living in Dublin at a time when the city had a total population of just over 300,000. Ninety-five of these were recorded as born in Russia and were most likely recent immigrants from Lithuania. Eighteen 'Russian-born' had settled in Belfast by 1881 when by then the city had a Jewish population of just 61. Ten years later the Irish census identified 626 Russian-born males over 10 years of age. Of these all but 195 (31 per cent) worked as drapers, shopkeepers, tailors, pedlars and commercial travellers, occupations they had held in Lithuania. Peddling, in particular, offered many Litvaks a foothold in Ireland;[59] with a small amount of borrowed capital, and a small trade vocabulary taught to them by Jews already established in Ireland, they sold various kinds of goods and clothing from door to door for weekly instalment payments.

As described by Louis Lentin, in a television documentary that presented his grandfather from Zedick as the archetypical Litvak, Kalman Lentin was met on the dockside in Dublin by a member of the Jewish community and put on the road to Cork. He made his way on foot through countryside not unlike that which he had left, rented a cheap room with a landsman amongst the 60 or so Jews in the city. Kalman was instructed by a wholesaler he met at the synagogue in the craft of peddling, made to memorise a few words in English, and put on the road with a trading licence and pack of goods for sale: blankets, shawls, petticoats, and – his best seller – holy pictures.[60]

By the turn of the century many of the Litvaks had become established in a continuum of businesses, working variously as moneylenders, insurance agents, furniture dealers, and self-employed tailors and drapers – the common ground between these being weekly repayment systems.[61] Various memoirs and family histories described similar experiences. As recounted in a privately published family history *The Zlotover Story*, Lieb Berman, 'who relied on family connections both for his passage to Ireland and the capital that started him off as a peddler', earned enough after working about 18 months to bring his wife and children to Ireland. *The Zlotover Story* depicted, in the case of some family members, a transition from peddling and money lending and on to more respectable businesses and the professions within a single generation.[62] Similarly, Myer Joel Widoger, who arrived in Dublin in 1890, recalled his life in a poem, 'Thoughts on my Seventy-Fifth Birthday', which recalled initial hardship, experiences of anti-Semitism and later prosperity after arriving 'penniless in a foreign land':

I did not scorn to carry a bag.
And deal in humble wares,

My back bent low I carried on,
Heedless of stones and stares.

In such a way I struggled on,
Scarce knowing what to do,
I changed my trade a score of times.
Ever trying something new.

Still, my spirit was unconquered,
And my confidence survived,
I forgot my previous failures,
And as a shopkeeper thrived.[63]

In his memoir, *Dublin's Little Jerusalem*, Nick Harris describes how his Litvak parents, Bernard and Edith Chachanoff, arrived in Dublin the early 1900s after working for some years in Birmingham and Wolverhampton in England, where he had changed his surname to Harris. He was a tailor by trade. In Dublin he got a position in a small clothing factory in Middle Abbey Street. Once he had saved some money, he rented two rooms in Aungier Street and set up a firm called XL Tailors, where he had one employee.[64]

The percentage of Litvaks who worked as pedlars, drapers, and travellers declined from over 60 per cent during the 1880s to half that by 1910. The percentage working as tailors rose from under five per cent in the 1880s to more than twenty per cent by 1910. Several factors explained why Litvak immigrants became considerably better off over time. The trading skills they had acquired in the shtetls were transferrable to Ireland even though these were becoming outmoded in Lithuania. Peddling required little start-up capital for those interested in becoming self-employed businessmen. It was easier for Jewish emigrants with very little capital to establish themselves in Ireland than, say, in London.[65]

The Litvaks lived and worshipped separately from Dublin's older community of Anglicised Jews. These lived north of the river Liffey and had a synagogue there. Early arrivals from Lithuania were directed to a tenement south of the Liffey in Chancery Lane next to a police station.[66] Many of the Litvaks settled on the south side in the environs of Lower Clanbrassil Street, where during the 1870s they opened their own prayer houses and from 1891 a cluster of Jewish shops.[67] About 25 premises were occupied by kosher butchers, bakeries, and other Jewish businesses, which drew Jewish customers from other parts of the city and added to the distinctly Jewish character of the area.[68] Many of their homes were three- or four-room, mostly newly built houses for rent in an area comprising six streets between the Grand

Canal and the South Circular Road, which came to be known as Little Jerusalem. In an 1893 article, Fr Thomas Finlay, a Jesuit social reformer and promoter of the co-operative movement, described how, in some streets that opened off the South Circular Road, 'one may walk along the pavement from end to end and hear hardly a word of English spoken by the children who are playing on the footpath. We are in a completely Jewish quarter as if we were in some city of Poland or South Russia.'[69] The density of Jewish settlement in Little Jerusalem rose steadily during the 1880s and 1890s, peaking at more than 80 per cent Jewish on some streets during the first few years of the twentieth century.

A large purpose-built synagogue was opened in 1892 nearby on the Adelaide Road, but failed to unite the different strands of Jewish Dublin. For all that it was located close to the main Litvak community it came to be referred to as 'the English *shul*' (synagogue), and it tended to attract the better-educated and less Orthodox part of the Jewish community, which was English-speaking.[70] Another synagogue was constructed at Grenville House in Dolphin's Barn to accommodate four existing congregations that did not want join the one on Adelaide Road. During the first few decades of the twentieth century, all of the six streets had more than 35 per cent Jewish occupants with this gradually declining over the following decades as more and more people moved two miles south to the prosperous suburb of Terenure. Little Jerusalem remained the epicentre of Dublin's Jewish community for more than half a century.[71]

By 1904, the year in which James Joyce's novel *Ulysses* was set, there were more than 2,000 Jews living in Dublin and a few hundred spread between Belfast, Cork and Limerick. Over half of these had arrived since 1891.[72] Limerick's first synagogue was established in the home of Rabbi Elias Levin on Collooney Street. Another was soon after established on the same street in the home of Louis Goldberg. Cork had only 155 Jews by 1891 but these were organised into two separate congregations. Belfast's Jewish community also fractured into different small groups. However, by 1904 a 'semblance of unity' came about when Sir Otto Joffé opened a new synagogue in the city on Annesley Street.[73]

The entry of some Jewish immigrants from pedlars into shop owners became a focus of nationalist hostility and of expressions of anti-Semitism from trade unions and champions of cooperative movements.[74] Jews were depicted as exploiters of the Catholic majority,[75] as in this early expression of such antipathy towards Jewish immigrants, an 1893 article by Fr Finlay in *The Lyceum*:

Our first duty is to ourselves and to our own people and no sympathy with the suffering and persecuted Jews can avail to free us from this obligation. If the influx of the Jews into Ireland constitutes an economic danger to the industry of the wealth producing classes amongst us, then it would be a duty to resist – not out of hatred of the Jews, but out of concern for ourselves.[76]

An editorial in the *United Irishman* in January 1904 by Arthur Griffith, the founder of Sinn Féin, similarly identified the Jews as enemies of the nation:

No thoughtful Irishman or woman can view without apprehension the continuous influx of Jews into Ireland. . . strange people, alien to us in thought, alien to us in sympathy, from Russia, Poland, Germany and Austria – people who come to live amongst us, but who never become of us. . . Our sympathy – insular as it may be – goes wholly to our countryman the artisan whom the Jew deprives of the means of livelihood, to our countryman the trader whom he ruins in business by unscrupulous methods, to our countryman the farmer whom he draws into his usurer's toils and drives to the workhouse across the water.[77]

In another example, a July 1904 advertisement in nationalist newspaper *The Leader* promoted suits of Irish materials at moderate prices made by Irish tailors under trade union conditions. It exhorted Irishmen to 'help us stamp out sweated Jewish Labour, in the Tailoring Trade in Dublin'.[78] By then, most of a small Jewish community consisting of about twenty-five families had been driven out of Limerick city following a campaign led by a Redemptorist priest who depicted them as enemies of the Irish nation. Fr Creagh was the spiritual director of the Arch-Confraternity of the Holy Family, a Catholic organisation that had a membership of about 6,000. Fr Creagh's sermons regurgitated many of the usual justifications for anti-Semitism: that the Jews had, at one time, engaged in the ritual murder of Christian children and that they had killed Christ. Furthermore, he blamed the Jews for anti-Catholicism in France. He depicted the Jews as enslavers of the Irish people worse than Cromwell. He urged his congregation 'not to be false to Ireland, false to your country and false to your religion, by continuing to deal with the Jews'. He instructed customers of Jewish traders like Kalman Lentin, who by then had settled in Limerick, not to pay their debts. Most, but not all, Jews left Limerick due to the loss of trade and fear of violence, Louis Goldberg among them. He was assaulted and was struck on the head by a man shouting 'I'll kill those bloody Jews'.[79] In 1904, he moved for a while to Leeds, where his brother Solomon lived, and subsequently moved with his family to Cork.[80] Kalman Lentin, on the other hand, stayed and prospered. He established a business on Lower Little Gerald Griffin Street, 'buying and selling all kinds of metals, rags, skins', and sent three of his sons to medical school.

IRISH JEWS

Belfast's Jewish community expanded during the first four decades of the twentieth century, and came to include some of the families expelled from Limerick in 1904. In Belfast as in Limerick, the Jewish community had fractured into a number of congregations, each with their own prayer room, though the Annesley Road synagogue and nearby school built by Sir Otto Jaffé provided a unifying focus. During the First World War, some long-established Jewish merchant families, including the Jaffés, left the city due to anti-German prejudice. Non-German Jews also experienced collateral hostility in the xenophobic climate of the time. Otto Jaffé had become a prominent member of the city's establishment. He was knighted in 1900 after serving his first term as Lord Mayor of Belfast, and he remained a member of the city council after his second term ended in 1905. In the face of considerable hostility – including unfounded accusations that he was a German spy – he quit the city in 1916 and lived for the remainder of his life in London.[81]

The first census after independence in 1926 identified 3,686 Jews in the 26-county Free State; at the time there were 1,254 Jews in the North. Almost all those in the Free State (99.35 per cent) worked in non-agricultural occupations, whereas just over half the wider Irish population worked in agriculture. In Lithuania, according to a 1923 census, which enumerated 153,743 Jews, the equivalent was 94 per cent.[82] The 1926 census found more than half (52.7 per cent) of Jewish men (649) working in commerce, finance or insurance, compared to 11.3 per cent of the population as a whole. A further 27.1 per cent (334) came under the category 'other producers, re-pairers'; 11.5 per cent were described as professionals. By 1946 the percentage working the professions had risen to 16.6 per cent.

After independence in 1922, a number of Jews living in the Free State in time became prominent citizens. Michael Noyk, a solicitor in Dublin, was a close advisor to Michael Collins and was heavily involved in the defence of Sinn Féin prisoners during the War of Independence. When he died in 1966 he was given full military honours by the Dublin Brigade of the IRA. [83] Rabbi Isaac Herzog – the leader of Belfast's Jewish community from 1916 and Dublin's from 1919 – was a friend of Éamon de Valera's, and reputedly gave him shelter in his home on a number of occasions during the War of Independence. His Irish-born son, Chaim Herzog, who became the sixth President of Israel, described his father as an 'open partisan of the Irish cause'.[84] Robert Briscoe, also an aide to Collins, was sent in late 1919 to Germany to purchase weapons for the cause; he was later the first Irish Jew to be elected to the Dáil (Parliament). Together with his son, Ben Briscoe, in keeping with Irish political culture, the Briscoes held a family Dáil seat for an unbroken period of 72 years, and both served terms as Lord Mayor of Dublin. Like the Briscoes, Louis Goldberg's son Gerald Goldberg became a member of Fianna Fáil, the nationalist political party founded by de Valera. He served as an alderman on Cork City Council and became Mayor of Cork in 1977. A number of Jews identified with Irish nationalism prior to independence. For example, two of Gerald Goldberg's sisters, Frances-Rebecca and Molly, became members of the Cork branch of Cumann na mBan, the Republican women's movement.[85]

By the early 1930s Nick Harris' father, Bernard Chachanoff, employed more than 50 people in his clothing factory in Smithfield in Dublin. In 1935, he moved to a factory on Capel Street that employed over 100 workers.[86] Some Litvaks prospered in other kinds of business; Maurice Elliman's first business was a greengrocer's shop, but in 1901, within a year of his arrival, he started showing films using a hand-operated projector. He subsequently built a cinema, the Theatre de Luxe on Camden Street, and by the late 1930s, the Ellimans were established in the theatre as well as the in cinema business. Around 1945 their cinema business was bought out by the J. Arthur Rank organisation and became Odeon (Ireland) Limited.[87] Isaac Eppel, who owned the Palace Cinema, wrote and produced *Irish Destiny*, the 1926 film about the War of Independence and the Civil War.

After Independence Jews were, as Dermot Keogh wrote, safe and respectable within the Free State but nevertheless, felt the need to keep their heads down.[88] Jewish memoirs covering this period tended not to emphasise experiences of anti-Semitism. In his autobiographical poem quoted previously, Myer Widoger wrote of being heedless of stones and stares, while in his memoir, Nick Harris recalled experiencing no 'unpleasantness' as a child, neither from his non-Jewish neighbours nor at the Catholic school he attended.[89] However, Jewish adults did encounter social barriers. The Dublin Macabbi Golfing Society was founded in 1933 by the Jewish community because Jews found it 'very difficult' to join existing golf clubs. In 1944, the Society established the Edmondstown Golf Club, which was open to non-Jewish members.[90]

Harris did describe some personal experiences of anti-Semitism from his adulthood. Once in Liverpool he met some Blackshirts who shouted anti-Jewish propaganda at him. He recalled an incident in Dublin in 1936 that he felt was, by comparison, of little consequence. In a bar one night, a drunken man declared that he 'would love to kill a Jewman'. Harris called him over, said he was Jewish and asked the man if he wanted to start on him. The drunk backed down, and other men in the pub offered to buy Nick a drink. Harris wondered what they might have said if he had not spoken up.[91]

Like Harris, Bethel Solomons recalled experiencing no anti-Semitism in his youth. However, when later in life he moved within affluent Dublin society, he observed unpleasant and insidious unwritten rules against Jews becoming members of tennis and golf clubs, and from employment in certain businesses and hospitals.[92] Anti-Semitism in the medical profession and religious discrimination almost certainly blocked some Jewish medical professionals from consultancy positions in the mostly Catholic hospital sector.[93]

In 1937 Rabbi Herzog, the Chief Rabbi of Ireland, emigrated to Palestine to become the Chief Rabbi there, in the same year that the new constitution officially recognised Ireland's Jewish congregations. During the 1930s, Jewish families in Ireland welcomed refugees from Germany in so far as they could. The Irish state operated explicitly anti-Semitic refugee policies before and after the Holocaust (see Chapter 8). Newspapers reported in November 1937 of an anti-Semitic campaign in Dublin in which 'strongly worded pamphlets' had been put through letterboxes on behalf of the Irish Christian Protection Association.[94] There were other sporadic expressions of anti-Semitism during the late 1930s.[95] Nick Harris recalls helping a refugee from Nazi Germany to set up a business manufacturing men's braces in Dublin; once established, the refugee was permitted to bring his wife and children out of Germany. Harris also helped the daughter of a family friend, Sabina Wyshniak, to get a permit to leave Hungary, where she had fled from Germany, by declaring at the Hungarian Embassy that he was engaged to her.[96] Some Jews fleeing Nazi persecution managed to enter Ireland, and some settled there, as did some refugee children after the Holocaust (see Chapter 9).

Over time more Jews prospered in business in Ireland. The percentage of Jewish men who were manufacturers or company directors – that is, self-employed businessmen – remained under 5 per cent until the 1930s, but this rose steadily to more than 45 per cent by the 1950s. Nick Harris went to work for his father, one such businessman, after a few years of secondary school. He learned the various jobs in his father's garment factory – cutting the cloth for suits, learning how to work the various machines used in their manufacture, despatching finished product – and in 1942 went out on his own, repeating what his father had done; opening a small factory, then moving to a series of larger premises; faring well in business until he retired in 1980. Those who worked as lawyers did not surpass one per cent of the Jewish population until the 1950s but exceeded eight per cent by the 1980s. Those in other white-collar occupations remained at under three per cent until the 1950s, rising to twelve per cent by the 1980s.[97]

However, not all Jews were financially secure. In the aftermath of the Second World War, emigration was no less common than for other sectors of the population. Ireland's clothing and textile industry in which many Jews worked went into decline; it employed 35,000 in 1958, but this number had fallen to 12,000 by 1986. Many poor Jewish families received support from the Board of Guardians, a charitable organisation established in 1889.[98] The Dublin Jewish community set up other welfare organisations including a branch of B'nai B'rith in 1953. This provided some scholarships to several fee-paying Catholic schools as well to the sole Jewish secondary school, Stratford College.[99]

After Independence, the population of the Free State continued to decline mostly for economic reasons. From the 1960s, the population rose with the economic growth, which reduced the need for emigration. The situation amongst Jews in the country was almost exactly the inverse: compared to the main population, there was a proportionally greater decline in numbers in the decades after Independence. Jewish Irish people also experienced economic pressures to emigrate. For example, Nick Harris recalls that after the 1922–3 Civil War, unemployment was rife and some Dublin Jews emigrated to the United States. Yet three of a group of six young Jewish men he named as having emigrated returned home to Dublin after a number of years.[100] One difference was that the main population was comparatively rural and migrated to urban areas abroad but also in Ireland. Jews were mostly concentrated in urban areas to begin with.

The Irish Jewish population gradually declined from an all-island peak of 5,381 in 1946. A number of the causes of this decline have been addressed in the writings of David Marcus who, like most of Cork's small Jewish community, moved away when he grew up. The challenges of being Jewish in Cork came to be echoed to a considerable extent in Dublin, even though the community there was much larger and its decline more gradual. Marcus called his first novel *To Next Year in Jerusalem* (1954). His autobiography was sub-titled *Leaves from the Diary of a Hyphenated Jew* (2001).[101] Marcus was Gerald Goldberg's nephew and, while a young man, translated Gaelic poetry. In his career as an editor of Irish short stories and poetry he emulated Cork Catholic intellectuals like Seán Ó Faoláin. His mother and aunt had been a member of Cumann na mBan. In *To Next Year in Jerusalem*, Marcus's protagonist, Jonathan, wants to leave Ireland for Palestine, but is held back by his love for a Catholic girl and by the fact that he is needed to stay to make up a *minyan*, the quorum of ten men over the age of 13 needed for religious rituals. Ultimately, Jonathan chooses Palestine over intermarriage and loyalty to his Irish fellow Jews.[102] Marcus himself chose to stay in Ireland, but left Cork for Dublin. He subsequently lived for a number of years in London, and when he returned to Ireland he settled in Dublin.

A Jewish elementary school, the Zion School, was established in 1934 by Rabbi Herzog, but many Jewish parents chose non-Jewish schools for their children. An analysis of Jewish education in Dublin noted that leading figures in the community tended to send their children to prestigious Christian schools.[103] Irish Jews like David Marcus and Nick Harris were often educated in Catholic schools, but also received a Jewish religious education.[104]

When Gerald Goldberg became Mayor of Cork in 1977, only a handful of Jews remained in the city. The Jews of Cork as depicted fictionally by Marcus were a tight-knit community surrounded by a sea of Catholicism, one that turned inwards for its physical and spiritual survival.[105] However, the Cork community became too small to sustain a Jewish way of life on a day-to-day basis, and as it got smaller, its decline accelerated. Matters were not helped by what Goldberg described as conflicts over the finer points of social and religious practice. From its heyday of a hundred adult males the Cork community became so small that in order to 'form a *minyan* for Rosh Hashana or Yom Kippur, they have to import a half-dozen young males from Dublin, all expense paid'.[106]

In Northern Ireland the Jewish community declined in size due to emigration following the Second World War, but particularly so during the post-1969 Troubles. The Belfast Jewish Institute, a social club with function rooms, a restaurant and tennis courts was established in 1926 following an incident where some Jewish children were refused membership of a local tennis club, and a successful Jewish Dramatic Society was founded in 1940. Under the leadership of Rabbi Alexander Carlebach, a refugee from Nazi Germany, a large new synagogue was completed in 1964. However, after 1969, the Jewish community began to rapidly decline in size as many migrated to English cities, especially to Manchester, which had a large Jewish community. This in turn made Jewish institutions, clubs and kosher shops less viable, which precipitated further emigration. The post-1969 Northern conflict pushed some to leave. The Belfast Jewish Institute was destroyed by an arson attack in 1981. By 2016 the community was almost as small as it had been before the arrival of the Litvaks.[107]

Dublin's Little Jerusalem went into decline partly because many Jews moved out to larger homes in suburbs. Emigration also took its toll. By 2007 Dublin's Jewish population had declined to 1,800 or so.[108]The old synagogues on the South Circular Road and at Dolphin's Barn eventually closed and were replaced by a new Orthodox synagogue in Terenure and a Reform synagogue in Rathfarnham. Jewish shops on Clanbrassil Street were replaced by kosher food sections in just a few supermarkets.[109] In 1993, Simon Harris, the newly arrived Chief Rabbi, unsuccessfully advocated a return to strict Orthodox Judaism. He instigated an audit of religious practice in Ireland. This included an investigation of all foodstuffs labelled as kosher, which concluded that Irish 'ritually slaughtered' meat was unfit for consumption by Jews.[110] Harris left Ireland after a year. His replacement, Rabbi Broder, declared in 1997 that the bread and cakes supplied by Bretzel, Dublin's main Jewish bakery, could not be deemed kosher. Rabbi Broder supposedly encouraged some Orthodox families to emigrate to places with larger Jewish communities where the strict observance of Jewish rituals might be feasible.[111] By the beginning of the twenty-first century the area had become home to a scattering of halal butchers and food-stores and run by recently arrived Muslim immigrants. A mosque now occupies the site of the Adelaide Road synagogue.[112]

By the 1990s, according to Ray Rivlan, strict orthodoxy was unpalatable to some non-conformist members of Orthodox synagogues as well as to non-Orthodox Jews.[113] In a context where 'everyday Jewishness' as expressed through the use of Hebrew and Yiddish and dietary observances has been in long decline, Jewish identity came to be defined to some extent by Zionism. David Landy's study of early twenty-first century Irish Jews found that Israel was identified as a spiritual homeland for a number of interviewees. Much like David Marcus it was 'a signifier of Jewishness in Ireland and a means that allows Irish Jews to express both their Jewish *and* Irish identities'.[114] In the absence of a universal strong religiosity, Zionism became the glue that worked to loosely bind what was, according to Landy, a fractured community with a bitter history of internal divisions. For all that, support of Israel did not necessarily amount to either a desire to live there or an affinity with the place.[115] Gerald Davis, in a 1997 newspaper article on growing up as a Jew in Ireland, recalled having been a zealous youth leader in Bnei Akivah, a Zionist organisation that encouraged emigration to Israel and the kibbutz movement. However, each actual visit he made to Israel made him feel more and more Irish:

> Israel is, I realised, a Levantine country and I could not fit in to its way of life. I am for, for better or worse, a product of Ireland, my mentality and mores conditioned by a mixture of European and Celtic cultures, albeit with an overlay of traditional Judaism. I am content to conduct my love affair from afar.[116]

The fourth-and fifth-generation Irish Jews interviewed by Landy were not, as he put it, preoccupied with articulating what they meant by Zionism, because any such debate was potentially divisive. What it amounted to, according to Landy, was a modern type of symbolic ethnicity based on tenuous links and symbols, a shift from an old-style community identity.[117] Yet, some left Ireland to secure a stronger sense of Jewish identity in more religiously observant communities,[118] particularly to Manchester, as already mentioned. The city with its community of some 30,000 Jews contained in the second decades of the twenty-first century what Dublin had a hundred years earlier, but on a far greater scale: a predominantly Jewish area with kosher food stores and Hebrew signs as well as a yeshiva (training school for rabbis) and mezuzahs (scroll containing verses from the Torah) on the doors of some houses.[119]

EIGHT

EXPATRIATES

The Protestant population of the South fell from 327,000 in 1911 to 221,000 by 1926. At least some of these left as a result of intimidation and harassment during the War of Independence. Southern loyalists lost status and political power. Hundreds of families fled temporarily but returned to their homes, land, and businesses when it seemed safe. Many others emigrated permanently because of the threat of violence, and as a consequence of social and economic changes brought about by the Great War and due to uncertainty about their future within the new state.[1] To some of the loyalists who fled Ireland, England was hardly a foreign country, but one also thought of as home, and indeed it was a place where some had spent large amounts of time. Yet many Anglo-Irish émigrés who wrote letters or memoirs described their nostalgia for Ireland, and their new-found alienation, particularly those who resettled in English cities.[2] Some of those driven out had been deeply committed to Ireland. For example, Horace Plunkett (1854–1932), a founder of the Irish co-operative movement who contributed hugely to development of Irish agriculture and became in 1922 a member of the Seanad (Senate), moved to England after his house in County Dublin was burned down by the IRA during the Civil War. At least 285 country houses owned by Protestant landowners were burned down by the IRA.[3] Some Irish Protestants were no less refugees than some of the Northern Catholics who were subsequently displaced by the post-1969 Northern conflict and fled south (see Chapter 9).

During the 1890s an average of almost 60,000 people had left Ireland each year, but emigration numbers declined thereafter. Between 1911 and 1926 net emigration averaged less than 30,000 per annum and fell substantially during the decade that followed to an average of 16,675 between 1926 and 1936.[4] Emigration persisted after Independence, but the three main waves occurred during the 1950s, 1980s and in the aftermath of the post-2008 economic crisis. Until the 1960s the population of the 26 counties declined decade on decade, continuing the trend since post-1847 Famine; between 1841 and 1961 this population fell from 6,229,000 to 2,828,000.[5]

During the decades leading up to Independence most emigrants (87 per cent between 1880 and 1921) travelled to the United States. During the first 10 years of the twentieth century these totalled 339,065. This number almost halved between 1911 and 1920, partly because the First World War disrupted travel. From 1921, the United States began to restrict immigration. The 1924 Immigration Act imposed a quota of 28,567 migrants per annum from the Irish Free State. This quota was cut to 17,855 in 1929 at the outset of the economic crash, and all prospective immigrants were now required to obtain a visa from the American Consulate in Dublin. The Great Depression and travel restrictions during the Second World War reduced the flow from Ireland to a trickle. According to the United States Immigration and Naturalisation Service (INES) records, just 13,167 Irish immigrants arrived between 1921 and 1940, with a further 26,967 newcomers during the 1940s.[6]

By 1940 the number of Irish-born people in the United States had fallen to 573,031 from a peak 1,615,459 in 1890. The number of second-generation Irish-Americans – that is those with one or more Irish-born parents – had peaked in 1900 at 3,375,546. By 1940, the number of second-generation Irish Americans still alive had fallen to 1,838,920.[7] The Irish had made up 16 per cent of New York's population in 1860. By 1920 there were some 203,450 Irish-born residents in New York or around 4 per cent of the city's population. Similarly, in Chicago some 18 per cent of the population had been Irish-born in 1860 but by 1920 this had fallen to around two per cent.[8]

During the 1950s some 57,332 went to the United States. This number fell to 37,461 for all of the 1960s and to just 4,130 for the 1970s, totals that fell far short of the Irish quota allowed by INES. This quota rose after 1965 from 17,000 to a maximum of 20,000 per annum. The rules of admission favoured those with close family ties to US citizens, or who possessed skills deemed to be needed in the United States. The family ties requirement was hard to fulfil, because while millions of Americans claimed Irish descent, they did so mostly as the descendants of Irish migrants some generations earlier;[9] most did not have close relatives living in Ireland. Many migrants who went from Ireland to the United States during the 1980s economic recession did not have close American relatives who could act as their sponsors. Many travelled on temporary visas and an estimated 50,000 stayed on as undocumented immigrants.

The Irish who emigrated after Independence mostly travelled from rural areas to British cities. Around 80 per cent of all those who emigrated from the Republic between the 1920s and the 1980s went to Britain. During the

1950s the Republic lost almost 15 per cent of its population, mainly young adults, most of whom were poorly educated and many who were unskilled.[10] By 1961 there were more than 1 million Irish-born migrants on the British mainland. By the time of the 2001 census the number of Irish-born stood at just over 750,531. Out of a total of 674,786 Irish-born then living in England 452,662 were born in the Republic and 215,124 were migrants from Northern Ireland. In 2001 there were 55,176 Irish-born living in Scotland with 31,409 of these from Northern Ireland. Some 20,659 Irish-born were identified by the 2001 census as living in Wales. 12,718 of these were born in the Republic and 7,851 were born in Northern Ireland. A total of 256,384 migrants to the British mainland were born in Northern Ireland.[11]

During the 1980s, the proportion of Irish migrants that went to other destinations rose, but most went to the United Kingdom.[12] Many of the 472,300 who emigrated between 1982 and 1989 were better educated. During this period, some 263,500 returned to Ireland suggesting that migration, more so than for the previous generation, was temporary rather than permanent. Most post-2008 emigrants, like those in previous waves, were in their twenties. Most now came from urban areas and they were better educated than those who left as part of previous waves. More than 40 per cent of those who left between 2008 and 2015 had university degrees, and a further 14 per cent had postgraduate qualifications.[13] The UK remained their main destination followed by Australia and Canada, which operated working holiday visa schemes that were open to Irish citizens.[14]

The experiences of Irish emigrants have changed across the century since Independence as education levels rose, travel became cheaper and communications improved. In 'the old days' according to a 2014 report, migration was 'final, brutal and sad'. Now, it was the more skilled and better educated who were leaving, and 'many did so out of a sense of adventure; they migrated not just for jobs but in search of a better quality of life and of new experiences'.[15] It was increasingly the case that the capabilities of emigrants improved as general education levels rose.

Within Irish popular culture, emigration used to be depicted as a tragedy. A nineteenth-century custom of holding wakes for outgoing emigrants reflected the perception that many of those who left would never see Ireland again. Emigrants could earn higher wages than they might ever get at home but were often exploited and encountered discrimination. Novels and research by sociologists described how some labourers who returned home on holiday put on a big show and splashed their money about, only to return broke to their digs in England knowing that they were ever only temporarily welcome in the communities that they left. John McGahern's 2002 novel *That They Might Face the Rising Sun* turns on the return of Johnny, who left a rural community years earlier to work in the

Ford car factory in Dagenham. Whilst he was made welcome in the family home each year on holiday, the prospect of his permanent return, after he loses his job, is met with trepidation. The sociological phenomena that fuelled generation-on-generation mass emigration also fostered antipathy towards prospective returnees who might place demands on their families.

Behind the trauma of post-Independence emigration, according to historian Joe Lee, lay a reverence for the 'the sanctity of property' and 'the unflinching materialism of farmer calculations'. A 'callously efficient socialisation process postponed marriage and effectively denied a right to marry to a higher proportion of the population than in any other European state, by the simple device of parents disinheriting a high proportion of potential brides and grooms amongst their children'. The dispossessed, according to Lee, became reconciled to emigration and emigration served to channel resentment towards the status quo out of the country.[16] The Church, for its part, feared a loss of faith and devotion amongst emigrants and organised missions in emigrant communities aimed at helping emigrants to keep the faith and at helping them in practical ways. Irish politicians from time to time made sympathetic noises but, in effect, emigrants were not seen as a concern of the Irish state except when their return might benefit the economy or when, in the case of Irish-America, some political or economic gain at home might be realised through cultivating diasporic relationships.

IRISH AMERICA

Martin Nolan, my maternal grandfather, was born in 1903, the youngest of 13 children in Rear Cross in County Tipperary. Eleven of the children were boys. One of the two girls died in infancy, and the other died of diphtheria at the age of seven. Martin's father Edward was a small farmer who also ran a wheelwright and carpentry business. Like several of his 10 brothers, Martin became a carpenter. Three became de la Salle Christian Brothers. Like Martin they attended the primary school at Rear Cross, but continued their education at the de la Salle College in Castletown, County Laois, with the expectation that they would follow religious vocations. Patrick, born in 1895, became Brother Malachy, and, after taking Holy Orders, obtained a degree from the Catholic University of Louvain in Belgium and a Masters degree from Fordham University in New York. He spent his life teaching in various de la Salle colleges in the United States, and died at the age of 103. Michael (Brother Cyprian) spent his life teaching in various schools in England and Wales. He was 81 years old when he died. Daniel (Brother Urban) was sent by the de la Salle Order to the United States. He left the Order and became a teacher in St Francisco.

In 1927 Martin emigrated to the United States with financial help from Brother Malachy. James, the eldest of Martin's siblings, was a carpenter by trade. He went to Queensland in Australia where he died at the age of 38. Their brother Edward went to Australia, where he too worked as a carpenter. He returned to Ireland in his 50s, where he married Delia Toohey from Feakle in County Clare, who had been 'his childhood sweetheart' and who had lived for a similar period in the United States. Nicholas, another carpenter, worked for a number of years in the United States, but returned during the Great Depression to Ireland with his wife and daughter.

In New York, Martin worked as a carpenter, attended night school and qualified as a quantity surveyor. In 1930 he married Johanna 'Josie' Ryan, who came from Doon less than eight miles away from Rear Cross, and whom he had known before he emigrated. Josie, in effect, followed him to the United States. Grace Costello, an aunt who had settled in Rhode Island, paid for Josie, her brother Andy, and sister Hannah to travel to the United States. Josie stayed with Grace and got a job in a bakery where she trained as a confectioner. Martin and Josie got married in the St Rose of Lima church in the Bronx.

Like Nicholas, Martin returned to Ireland during the Depression. By then, he and Josie had one child. They intended to return to the United States but eventually settled in Monard in County Tipperary where Martin worked as a building contractor. Martin's brother-in-law Andy worked for a railway company in New York but enlisted in the United States Navy during the Second World War. He piloted a landing craft during the D-Day landings in Normandy. He retired to Ireland with his wife and settled near Martin and Josie in Monard.

Not all of the Nolans emigrated. William became a blacksmith in the area where he grew up, and died in a road accident in his 50s. Thomas worked all his life on the family farm and like his father also worked as a carpenter. He married, had four sons and died when he was 94 years old. John settled on a farm near Nenagh owned by his wife's family and he also lived until he was 94 years old. Roger worked in Ireland all of his life, mostly as a carpenter in a shipyard at Cobh in County Cork. He married, had a daughter and died at the age of 78. Martin and Josie had nine children, of whom one, my uncle Malachy, died at when he was eight years old. My uncles, like Martin, worked as building contractors or as tradesmen in County Tipperary. My aunts mostly married university-educated men who found employment in Ireland. My father, a graduate in agricultural science, briefly considered emigrating to Zimbabwe before obtaining a job in Ireland. Not one of my uncles or aunts emigrated.

Frank McCourt, author of *Angela's Ashes* and two other celebrated memoirs, was born in New York in 1930 to parents who had emigrated from

Ireland some years earlier.[17] His family, like those of Martin and Nicholas Nolan, returned to Ireland during the Depression. His mother had worked variously as a charwoman, a skivvy, and a maid in Limerick before her mother paid her fare to New York, where she met Malachy McCourt who had grown up on a farm in County Antrim. Angela became pregnant and they married. After their fifth and youngest child died as an infant, the McCourts returned to Limerick, their passage paid for by Angela's mother. Malachy McCourt went to England to seek work during the Second World War and never returned. A number of the McCourts' relatives also worked in England. In 1949, aged 19, Frank McCourt returned to the US and subsequently assisted his siblings and mother to move there also. Migration was not always a one-way journey. Sometimes it was a process of leaving and returning.

Amongst those who emigrated to the United States during the 1940s were a community of Irish-speakers from the Great Blasket, an island about a mile off the Kerry Coast that became a magnet for Gaelic scholars. Several islanders wrote celebrated Irish-language memoirs including Peig Sayers (*Peig*), Muris Ó Shúilleabháin (*Fiche Bliain ag Fás,* trans. *Twenty Years A-Growing*) and Tomás O Criomhthain (*An t-Oileánach,* trans. *The Islandman*). Inhabitants of the island and of the Kerry mainland were part of the same Gaelic-speaking culture and society, but there were differences between them. The 1,132-acre island had a school, but no church, public house, shop, church, priest, graveyard or doctor. In 1916 the island had a population of 176, and during the mid-1920s some 47 children lived on Great Blasket. By 1941, when the school closed, just five children were enrolled.[18]

Islanders migrated to the shore and many emigrated to the United States. Since the 1840s most had settled in Springfield, Massachusetts, and some in Hartford, Connecticut. There was a surge in emigration during the 1920s after commercial fishing on the island collapsed.[19] Many island households relied on cash remittances from relatives who had already settled in the United States: 'So many people from the West Kerry Gaeltacht emigrated to Springfield at the beginning of the twentieth century that it was said that more Irish than English was to be heard outside the Catholic church of Our Lady of Hope in the Hungry Hill area of the city.'[20]

Accounts by twentieth-century islanders described how the oldest children in families would emigrate when they were about 18 years of age. If travel to the United States could not be funded by a relative, prospective emigrants worked on the mainland for a time to save up for their passage. In an example given in a memoir by one islander, a young woman might spend a year or two working in Dingle towards the cost of her passage, and once settled in the United States would send back money so that her siblings could follow one at a time.[21] One of Muiris Ó Súilleabháin's sisters kept a diary in which she described in September 1923 how most of the young people were leaving the island:

> This place is like a sinking ship now – everybody attempting to leave it at the first opportunity. Some of them going to America and more of them going here and there looking for a livelihood. I envy them greatly because they don't have to stay on the sinking ship at all and it is not like that for me – I have to stay here for another while as I wouldn't like to leave my father on his own.[22]

Eibhlin Ní Shúilleabháin's diary, like a number of published memoirs of this period, described how many islanders never fully came to terms with life in urban North America. She joined her sister Máire in Springfield at the end of the 1920s and died there when she was in her forties. She wrote that she never felt at home 'anywhere but at home'.[23]

After the Second World War the last wave of Blasket islanders made their way to Springfield. Micheál Ó Cearnaigh, the last surviving islander, emigrated in 1948. He died in 2013. He had lived in Dublin for 11 years but, following the death of one of his younger brothers, made the decision to move to the United States in order to be able help other members of his family settle in Springfield:

> Now that the War was over and America was open again, I had five brothers on Great Blasket Island and they had nothing to do but look out at the sea every day. I had three uncles and five aunts in Springfield Mass. I had more relatives there than I had at home. I used to write to an uncle of mine, in those days you had to have a letter from a near relative in America who would bring you out and take care of you. My uncle sent me the necessary papers.[24]

In Springfield, he stayed with his uncle and found a job in a supermarket chain where he worked for 25 years. He enrolled in night school and became a store manager. Once he became established, he helped all five of his brothers and his girlfriend, who was from Roscommon, to settle in Springfield. There he found himself in a community attending weekly dances with others from the island, and the surrounding mainland towns and villages of Dingle, Ventry, Dunquin and Ballyferriter.[25] The Kerry community started a Gaelic football team in 1949, and won the New England championship. The Irish government evacuated the last 22 inhabitants of the island in 1953, including Peig Sayers.[26]

For many prospective emigrants America was beyond reach. A 1943 essay by socialist and novelist Peadar O'Donnell described how the old Donegal people were not at their ease until they saw their children safely on the American boat. To earn their passage money some migrants from the

Rosses district of Donegal went to Scotland undertake harvesting work but were in danger, according to O'Donnell, of being sucked permanently into a semi-vagrant way of life if they or their families could not raise their fare to the United States. O'Donnell contrasted the high status enjoyed by returning Yanks ('a visit roused his whole family to arrogance') with the lowly one of those who returned from Scotland. Those who had been to the United States became more self-assured and enjoyed a higher status in the community:

> Whatever the devil is in the way of life of America it re-makes men. What it makes them is not always likeable, but they stand on their feet, hit their heels in the ground, pontificate, like a very young curate. In fact to have a son back from America with silk shirts, and all such like gear, came as near as makes no difference to having a priest in the family. But a man back home from Scotland. . . He was a mere nobody, a misfit, a poor excuse for a success.[27]

O'Donnell's 1943 account of the rough-and-tumble lives of seasonal migrants from Donegal drew on what he had witnessed first-hand when he worked alongside them in his teens on his family's five-acre farm in the Rosses, where he was born in 1893. He argued that the lives of many Irish emigrant labourers in Scotland and England had not improved in decades. He called for the establishment of Irish centres in British cities where affordable accommodation and other forms of assistance could be organised as had occurred in some parts of the United States where Irish associations were long established.

THE CATHOLIC IRISH IN ENGLAND

Mostly the Irish emigrants who flocked to English cities in the decades after the Famine assimilated into the British working classes. In an afterward to the 1892 edition of *The Condition of the Working Class in England*, Friedrich Engels remarked that Irishtown, the Manchester slum he wrote about in 1845, no longer existed.[28] Successive waves were folded into urban Britain, generation on generation, without creating the kind of politically influential ethnic identity that emerged in some Eastern cities of the United States.

The Catholic Church preached a quietist doctrine of accommodation to English culture, whilst simultaneously establishing a system of Catholic schools. Religious differences 'translated into social divides, including wide-spread uneasiness with intermarriage and continuing residential segregation in some cities and towns'.[29] But it would be a mistake to equate Catholicism in England solely with Irish emigrants and their descendants. For example, the Church, a community in England of about 2 million by 1920, included a fairly well-off English minority, and most of its hierarchy came from families that had remained Catholic after the Reformation. Some English Catholics were Tories rather than supporters of the Labour Party, which attracted the support of many Irish immigrants. Notwithstanding the presence of many Irish priests within its ranks, the English Church had a somewhat different feel to the highly authoritarian Irish one, whilst the Catholic Church in America was 'virtually an Irish Church, operating under Irish priests and Cardinals', and by 1959,

> All but one of the nine native-born Cardinals of American history have been the sons of Irish immigrant workers. This Irish dominance explains many of the characteristics of American Catholicism. The Irish hierarchy which rules the American Church is a 'becoming' class. It represents the Irish people struggling upwards in a hostile environment, using the Roman system of authoritative power to compensate for an inner sense of insecurity which still seems to survive from the days when the Irish Catholics were a despised immigrant minority. Boston is aggressively Catholic largely because it is aggressively Irish, and it is aggressively Irish because its people have not quite overcome their sense of being strangers in a strange land.[30]

The Church in England struggled to ensure that the emigrants and their descendants kept the faith. In the 1930s, just 20 to 30 per cent of Catholics in Bermondsey in South London attended Mass, and of these nearly 70 per cent were women. Most of the men ceased to practice their religion once they left school, but 'they were members of the Catholic club, drank 'Catholic beer' and used the church when they wanted to celebrate or grieve'.[31]

Large numbers of Irishmen and Irishwomen were encouraged to work in the United Kingdom as migrant 'guest workers' during the Second World War. In June 1940 free movement from Ireland was suspended.[32] A work visa system was introduced, with a permit office in Dublin, aimed at directing migrants towards agricultural and industrial work. In February 1941 the Irish Department of Agriculture was asked by its Scottish equivalent to interview Irish applicants to the Women's Land Army in order to assess their suitability. Irish officials conducted interviews in Dublin and forwarded their reports to officials in Scotland and Northern Ireland.[33] During the War, labour migration did not depend on help from family or contacts with relatives or former neighbours working in England, as it had done previously. The recruitment of industrial as well as agricultural workers, the allocation of visas and provision of accommodation for those who were selected, became as highly organised as the evacuation of children from British cities during the Blitz. One 1944 account described how such migrants were shipped like cattle on the ferry, with their luggage in brown-paper parcels each wearing a label saying 'British factories' pinned to their clothes.[34] Before departure they were inspected by Irish officials for scabies and lice. An account by James Deeny, the Chief Medical Officer, described how outgoing migrants were stripped naked and hosed down with disinfectants. The atmosphere described by Deeny was one of 'shame, fear and outrage'.[35] Those assigned to work in English factories or building airfields and military bases were accommodated in segregated barracks for the duration of their contracts.

One estimate put the numbers of men and women from Ireland and Northern Ireland working in Britain during the war at 120,000. Another by the Northern Ireland government calculated that about 65,000 workers had transferred to England of which an estimated 9,000 were women. Migrants from the 26 counties also worked as farm labourers in Northern Ireland. Peadar O'Donnell, who had been appointed Advisor on Migratory Labour by de Valera's government estimated in 1945 that around 250,000 Irishmen and Irishwomen had worked on war contracts.[36]

Immigration was portrayed by politicians and in public debates as a national crisis and as a moral one. A 1941 article in *The Bell* by Flann O'Brien poked fun at claims by a priest campaigning against the opening of dance-halls in Donegal because such establishments 'set up a restlessness that causes girls to emigrate'. Emigration, a response to the priest by Peadar O'Donnell in *Irish Press* explained, was not caused by dancing: 'Many Donegal girls come to Dublin. Some get good wages. But they don't stay in Dublin though Dublin has dance halls galore. They feel lonely in Dublin, so they go to Glasgow where hundreds of neighbours have made their homes.'[37] A 1942 piece by Seán O'Faolain described nationalist media responses to emigration as 'sentimental sludge', 'full of the old sentimental rhetoric, but too lazy to make one single constructive proposal of any kind – beyond calling on the Clan of Gaels to answer the voice of Éire in her misery with the fiercely national spirit'.[38]

Yet attitudes of senior government officials to emigration were anything but sentimental. In 1942 the Department of Industry and Commerce proposed restricting the exodus of skilled workers to Britain in 1942. The proposal was shot down in a memorandum by F. H. Boland, Assistant Secretary of the Department of External Affairs, which gave several reasons why emigration was in Ireland's national interest. Boland argued the British 'were very anxious to get these workers' and might retaliate against a drop in Irish emigration to Britain by reducing the supply to Ireland of imported raw materials. Boland cited an estimate by the Department of Finance, which put the weekly figure of emigrant remittances as high as £100,000 or

£150,000. Such remittances, a Department of Finance official was quoted as saying, did much to relieve distress as well as saving the Irish exchequer a lot of money.[39]

Boland worried about what would happen, when the War ended, if the British authorities encouraged the Irish to return home: 'when up to as many as a hundred thousand or more unemployed men (who will, no doubt, have imbibed a good deal of 'leftism' in Britain) are dumped back here within the course of a few short weeks. . . to have piled on top of them, in the course of a short time afterwards all the Irish citizens demobilised from the British armed forces'.[40] At least 70,000 men from the Irish Free State enlisted in the British Armed Forces during the Second World War,[41] of whom some 5,000 deserted from the Irish Army to enlist in the British Army during the War. The threat that Boland worried about – of having to deal with large numbers of returning unemployed migrants – did not come to pass, as post-war economic conditions in Ireland were bleak and many who left during the War stayed away.

The pull factor driving post-war emigration was the promise of much higher wages than they could ever have expected in Ireland. The report of the *Commission on Emigration and Other Population Problems* published in 1956 noted that one Leitrim interviewee who worked as a barman for £1 per week plus meals and accommodation had been offered, via a relative, a similar job in Shrewsbury that would pay £3 per week plus meals and accommodation.[42] Beyond the disparity in wages, an additional factor was the belief that there would be few future opportunities for young people who chose to stay. A study which interviewed 556 prospective emigrants between 15 and 18 years of age in County Cavan in 1965 found that most intended to leave because they believed that they would not be satisfied with the kinds of employment and levels of income that they might obtain in the communities in which they lived.[43] A follow-up study in 1968 that interviewed some of the same respondents or their family members found that those with better education were more likely to emigrate, the inference being that these were less likely to fulfil their aspirations at home.[44]

Concern by Irish clerics for the spiritual and material welfare of emigrants led to the establishment of the kinds of support services that Peadar O'Donnell advocated. The Catholic Social Welfare Bureau (CSWB), established by Archbishop of Dublin John Charles McQuaid in 1942, helped migrants find suitable accommodation and employment. Much of its work was done through correspondence with parishes and Catholic organisations in England. Members of the Legion of Mary who worked as volunteers for the CSWB interviewed emigrants at the ports they were embarking from and on the boat trains and gave them advice on how best to safeguard their religion. Young emigrants, particularly women, were met off the train in

London by members of Catholic groups there, in part in response to a trend also picked up by a 1938 report by the Crusade of Rescue, a London body founded in 1859, which identified 365 Irish unmarried mothers, 80 of whom had become pregnant before leaving Ireland, the rest after they arrived in Britain. The CSWB, for its part, lobbied for controls on young women seeking to emigrate to Britain and sought to repatriate unmarried pregnant women. The Catholic diocese of Westminster operated three homes for unmarried mothers.[45]

Many Irish Catholics ceased to practice their religion once they left Ireland. 'Backsliding' amongst emigrants became the subject of a number of articles in *The Furrow*, a Catholic intellectual magazine, during the 1950s. A 1954 article 'The Irish in Britain' noted that some emigrants 'seem to be able to shake off their religion as soon as they shake the dust of Ireland off their shoes'. The Irishman at home, Fr Eamon Gaynor wrote, was treated as a child, constantly under supervision and never encouraged to think for himself. When he leaves home he 'runs amuk', and even if he doesn't, he remains stunted, never maturing into a responsible Christian man.[46] A 1957 article in *The Furrow* by Frank Duff, founder of the Legion of Mary, concluded from an investigation into religious observance amongst Irish emigrants:

> Ten per cent practice worthily, that is, unfailing Mass, frequent Communion. Forty per cent practice unworthily, that is late for Mass, irregular, infrequent Holy Communion. Fifty per cent do not practice and a substantial portion of the latter are alleged to have no faith. At home all these people looked like good Catholic soldiers, yet they were destined to go down in their first encounter with irreligion.[47]

A 1958 article, 'A Worker in Birmingham', was even less certain that many emigrants would hang onto their faith: 'That the Irish lose faith is without doubt, or to say the most for them, the girls drift and hold on a little but the men drift completely. I will put it this way: a boy and girl of twenty-one may hold on to the Faith, but their children have little hope at all.'[48] Another article in the same issue of *The Furrow*, 'A Letter to an English Priest' declared: 'What is happening today in England cries out for us to cast a critical eye upon our traditional form of Catholicism. What looks so fair at home often shows rent and patch away. The Irish Catholic does not always prove himself an export-quality product.'[49]

An official Church research project led by Anthony Spencer, undertaken in advance of the 1960 congress of The International Catholic Migration Commission, amplified such anxieties. Spencer's report, *Arrangements for the Integration of Irish Immigrants in England and Wales,* was suppressed and not made public until 2005. The report concluded that many Irish practicing Catholics were such only because their lives were under such a degree of scrutiny that they saw no possible alternative. The strong social compulsion to attend Mass in Ireland was absent in England and Wales. In the absence of enforced conformity many Catholic emigrants melted into the large non-religious population of Britain.[50] Social pressures in Ireland shored up the appearance of religious devotion but ill-prepared young men and women for a more autonomous kind of life. Having to conform without the opportunity to do otherwise, the report argued, resulted in 'a lack of self-discipline, and self-control, an underdeveloped sense of responsibility towards work-mates, employers and non-Catholics, a social inferiority complex, a lack of articulateness about religion, a sense of ignorance about sex, and a view of clergy–laity relationships that polarises at either complete acceptance of priestly authority in all matters, or equally complete rejection of any priestly authority'.[51]

In essence, Spencer placed much of the blame for the decline in religious observance amongst emigrants on the system that the Irish Church had developed to incubate Catholicism there. Authoritarianism – Spencer's use of the term can hardly have endeared his report to the Hierarchy – ceased to work for some once the strictures were lifted. Irish emigrants therefore required Irish priests, not English ones who confused them with their more liberal tone, to keep them spiritually in line:

> As well as accepting his authority in all matters the Irish, especially then women, have a great love for the priest. He is a father-figure to be obeyed and revered, not a personal friend, well-known and to be consulted as an informed and valued counsellor. So long as he is in Ireland the pressure of group conformity maintains this attitude, but once out of Ireland a significant minority reacts strongly against it. This reaction takes several forms which priests have observed with concern. In extreme cases it leads to violent anti-clericalism, joining the Communists or the Connolly Association and bitter public criticism of the priests. But usually the reaction is milder – attempts to avoid the priests, shyness with priests, and a general lack of co-operation. It also leads to embarrassing compliments about English priests. The majority response to transplantation in England appears to be a carryover of the authoritarian relationship so long as the priest in question has the same Irish ethos.[52]

According to Spencer, some of those who practiced under pressure in Ireland came to the UK with the intention 'of taking a holiday from religion'. Others, he suggested, suffered from a latent anti-clericalism that bursts into flame once they reach England. This suggestion was angrily dismissed by McQuaid's Catholic Social Welfare Bureau as 'unjustified slander'. The group of emigrants that most concerned Spencer were those who had no deliberate intention of lapsing once in England, but then did so because they did not feel compelled to conform.

One missionary priest estimated in 1956 that there were 150,000 Irish workers in construction, and reported problems of 'loneliness and depression, drunkenness, bad company, irresponsibility and spiritual laxity'. He drew attention to the many families living in trailers and caravans who were 'in dire spiritual need and had, invalid marriages, unbaptised children and no religious instruction'.[53] Spencer's report described how poor living conditions of many emigrant workers drove them to drink:

> The new immigrant is often careless about his diet and accommodation. Having not been used in the past to paying for either he grudges expenditure on them. Lack of a regular balanced diet often results in gastric trouble. Economy over lodging frequently leads him to share a room with half-a-dozen other Irishmen in a lodging house run by landlord on the make, often a fellow Irishman. Sometimes beds are occupied in shifts. It is not surprising that such conditions undermine the immigrant's health. But they also lead to other social evils. When lodging house-keepers overcrowd their rooms the immigrant Irish are forced to spend their leisure hours elsewhere, which usually means the pub. They go out together and each stands his round of beer. In these circumstances drunkenness and disorder soon follows.[54]

In 1957 the Westminster diocese allocated six priests to minister to the 'floating population' of Irish, to make contact with them in dance halls, GAA matches and other social events in London, Nottingham, Northampton, and Birmingham. The Irish Emigrant Chaplaincy Scheme came about when in June 1957 the Irish Hierarchy pledged nine of its priests to minister to the needs of Irish workers on large construction sites in remote areas, and to hotel and catering workers in the West End of London.[55]

The most celebrated chaplain to Irish emigrants in England was Fr Eamon Casey who later became Bishop of Kerry and then Bishop of Galway. Casey, now mostly remembered for his public fall from grace in 1992 when it became known that he had fathered a child, had been much respected for his work in England. In 1960, he became a chaplain in Slough where there were about 12,000 Irish Catholics out of a total population of more than 100,000. Before moving to England, he had served in a Limerick parish from which four-fifths of the men had left Ireland to find work, and he knew that many of the children to whom he gave religious instruction would also have to emigrate. He made contact with emigrant Irish chaplains in England, and, with another priest, set up an emigrant centre in Limerick. Using an inheritance he had received, Casey set up a savings scheme to help Irish migrants buy houses. By 1963, 45 families had purchased houses, and eight families were renting flats in a converted house that he had purchased; a portion of their rents were banked in the tenant's name to enable them to save deposits to purchase houses of their own. Other such housing association schemes followed.[56]

In 1963, Casey moved to London as National Director of the Catholic Housing Aid Society (CHAS) and pioneered housing advice services for the homeless that were widely copied. Branches of CHAS were set up around England. He became director of Shelter, which provided services to homeless people, funded housing associations and other social housing projects. By the time Casey left England in 1969 to become Bishop of Kerry, Shelter had 220 branches in England and Wales. The Irish Emigrant Chaplaincy Scheme also became involved in a host of other housing projects and welfare services for emigrants up until the 1990s. Some of the priests involved at its inception were also behind the establishment of the London Irish Centre, which opened in 1955. The community centre still operates today.

Those who settled permanently in England from the 1950s included many who did not expect to do so. Many worked their lives on the building sites, did not have families of their own, lived in poor-quality accommodation, and experienced poverty and loneliness in old age. Census data found that Irish-born people living in England experienced poorer physical and mental health than the population as a whole. Suicide rates amongst the Irish were found to be 53 per cent higher than average during the late 1980s.[57] Most of the research on the Irish in Britain has focused on those who were most marginalised. Yet, the majority settled successfully, more or less, and were absorbed into urban Britain more or less like previous generations of migrants from Ireland.

EMIGRATION GENERATIONS

John Dillon left East Clare for New York in 1956, where he found work as a gravedigger. He was 44 years old and unmarried when he emigrated. He had lived with his parents until they died and he had inherited their small farm. When he left, he rented out his fields to a neighbour. His older brother and two of his sisters had already settled in New York. Another sister had become a nun. He married Catherine Foley who had worked as a maid in Kenmare in County Kerry before travelling to New York where, like many other young Irish women, she worked as a child-minder. They married in 1960 and became the parents of twin boys, Denis and Patrick, in 1961, and a daughter, Mary, in 1963. They moved back to East Clare in 1964 and had four more children. Mary Dillon obtained a degree in Business Studies in

Galway Regional Technical College, and after graduating worked in a shirt factory. Her hours were cut in 1986, and soon after she was made redundant. The only work she could find in Galway was part-time waitressing. She moved to New York in 1987, followed by her brother Patrick the following year.

When she arrived in New York, she shared a house in the Bronx with a friend with whom she had previously rented a house with in Galway. Shortly afterwards she got a job waitressing in a nearby diner, where she stayed for a few years. Patrick moved into the same house and got a construction job with a business owned by their Irish landlord. Before that he had worked on a building site in London and had shared a house with his brother Denis and several other Irish migrants, including myself. Patrick had a diploma in computer engineering and, after qualifying, got a job in a computer assembly plant in West Clare, which he disliked, and quit after a few months. Before coming to London he worked cutting timber for a while in East Clare.

When Mary Dillon's father became ill in 1989 she returned to East Clare for six months. She went back to the same job in the Bronx for a time, and then got a similar one in Manhattan. In 1995 she moved with her boyfriend George to Key West in Florida. When she became pregnant in 1997, she moved back to Ireland and has lived since then in East Clare in a house she built next to the cottage in which she grew up. Her brother Patrick worked on construction sites in New York until returning to East Clare in 1998 to do similar work, which had become plentiful in what had come to be called the 'Celtic Tiger' era.

Except for the advantage of having American citizenship, the experiences of Mary and Patrick Dillon were similar to those of many well-educated or skilled young Irish people who went to the United States during the 1980s recession. A study by Mary Corcoran interviewed 60 young Irish undocumented immigrants living during the mid-1980s in Queens in New York: most of were in their 20s; most of the men worked 'off-the-books' in construction for small firms willing to hire undocumented workers recommended to them by other Irish migrants who had become trusted employees. Some of the men worked in the bar trade, and most of the women worked as waitresses or as nannies.[58] Irish 'illegals' were English-speaking and many were well educated. They were in a position to exploit contacts in the established Irish community there, and, as such, compared to other undocumented immigrants, were privileged within the informal economy. At the same time, their undocumented status prevented them from integrating fully into American society, and enabled exploitation by unscrupulous employers.

Many found jobs through acquaintances from the neighbourhoods they came from in Ireland. Many were initially helped find accommodation by family members already in New York. Those without contacts who might help them find employment gravitated to Irish bars where information about jobs might be found.[59] Construction was a restricted job market. Employment depended on help from contacts who had already become established as trusted employees with contractors willing to take on vouched-for undocumented Irish. Those without such contacts described being shut out from the jobs market. For example, one interviewee described how the Kerry crowd drank in bars owned by Kerrymen; they were friendly to other Irish migrants, 'but if you tried to get information about jobs they all clam up. They might say something like "there are a lot of guys out of work." But when friends came over from Ireland, and came to the bar, they were offered jobs "off the bat".'[60] Yet the contractors who hired Irishmen, and the Irish brokers who recruited on their behalf drove hard bargains on wages. Undocumented Irish were paid less than the going rate for unionised workers, and often worked longer hours than other employees;[61] women who worked as nannies typically did so for 12-hour days at less than the legal minimum wage.[62]

Josephine, living in County Clare, was working part-time in a fast food restaurant, and in a nightclub, and also claimed the dole. She was encouraged to come to New York by her sister who had already emigrated. The sisters were then joined by their father, who had been unemployed.[63] A high proportion of those interviewed by Corcoran came from families like the Dillons, above, who already had a family history of emigration to the United States or elsewhere; a significant number of 1980s emigrants were the children of Irish emigrants who had returned home from either Britain or the United States during the 1970s.[64]

Migrants with professional qualifications and university degrees typically did the same jobs, such as construction and child care, as previous Irish migrants.[65] Some had been employed in Ireland but had become disaffected. Michael had worked for five years as a secondary school teacher on temporary contracts but had been unable to obtain a permanent job. He went to New York to work in construction during the summers, where he earned more doing so than he did as a teacher, and eventually decided not to return to Ireland. Some other migrants interviewed by Corcoran had taken leave of absences from permanent civil service and local government jobs to work in New York, or had left permanent jobs, either because of low pay, boredom, or the lack of prospects.[66] Some, like Patrick Dillon, had worked in construction in Britain for a period before relocating to New York.

In 1985 I completed an undergraduate degree in European Studies and moved to London. I quickly found work alongside some other Irish graduates and university students and other emigrants as a labourer, building the Docklands Light Railway at Canary Wharf. Everybody I worked with was

Irish. Most, including the ganger man who ran the team I worked for, were from County Galway. I came from County Clare and was referred to by him as 'Clare', never by my own name. He deducted £30 per week from my cash wages for 'social insurance', a fee he charged all members of the gang for letting them keep their jobs. On my first night in London I was meant to stay with an acquaintance at a boarding house for Irish labourers in Shepherd's Bush. Several men, mostly older than me, shared the room where the friend of the friend I had travelled over with stayed. Conditions were as bad as those described in Spencer's 1960 report cited earlier.

A few months later, I had quit the job at Canary Wharf and moved into a bedsit near Regent's Park. I got casual labouring work from an Irish contractor who picked out day-workers early each morning from a throng on the side of the Chalk Farm road. A supervisor with a clipboard pointed to each of us in turn saying 'you' or 'not you' with at least one 'I told you never to come back' to one man looking to be hired for the day. Everybody was Irish. Many of these men appeared old and a few seemed to be the worse for wear from drink. We received our day's pay after a few hours so that we could afford to buy breakfast during our mid-morning break. Johnny, the supervisor I worked for, was a kind man, especially so to a few older men who seemed too infirm to do much work. Mostly they leaned on their shovels and kept up a running commentary whilst the younger ones put their backs into it. But the work – cleaning weeds out from under electric pylons – was not especially onerous, and the older men had spent their entire adult lives in England working as labourers. I was a university graduate who had dipped briefly into their world, inspired to do so by an interest in sociology and my reading of George Orwell's *The Road to Wigan Pier*.

By the end of 1985 I had become a barman in a pub in Vauxhall, but decided to leave for worse-paying temporary office work after a few months. After a few more months, I got my first permanent white-collar job working for the Department of Health and Social Security (DHSS), administering unemployment benefits. Many of the claimants I dealt with were Irish (I was responsible for those with surnames beginning with 'Mc' and 'Mac'). These included homeless men with alcohol problems and, in one case that became etched on my memory, a just-arrived family from Dublin with nowhere to stay who needed an emergency payment to pay for a hostel for the weekend. I enrolled on a Master's degree programme as an evening student, and within a few years, after switching public-sector jobs a few times, enrolled on a doctoral programme, again whilst working full-time in paid employment. Initially I shared a rented house with other Irish migrants including Patrick and Denis Dillon. In 1988 I took out a mortgage on a South London apartment with my girlfriend Joan, who had qualified as an industrial designer in

Dublin and was working as one in London for Glaxo, a pharmaceutical company. After 10 years spent mostly in London I returned to Ireland with Joan and our eldest daughter and have lived there since.

During the Celtic Tiger era, between 1995 and 2000, almost one quarter of a million people (248,100) moved to the Republic of Ireland. Most were returning migrants like me. Some 18 per cent (45,600) were British subjects, a category that included children of emigrants like my daughter Caitriona. Many of these were married to Irish citizens. Seven per cent (16,600) came from the United States. Twelve per cent (29,400) came from elsewhere in the world.[67] Only a few of the Irish graduates that I shared houses with in London, including Denis Dillon, remained permanently in England and, unlike equally educated Irish people who went to the United States, those in England transitioned into white-collar careers. Denis Dillon ran education and training programmes for vulnerable young people, became a Labour Party councillor for the London Borough of Haringey and served as Deputy Leader of the Haringey Council. He also completed a doctorate.

In 1986 Denis Dillon and I shared a house with John and Jim O'Brien, two brothers who were born in England but had Irish emigrant parents. Their father, Peter, the son of a County Tyrone farm labourer, arrived in Liverpool in 1948. He worked as a machine driver for the remainder of his working life on building sites around England, settling in Leicester in the early 1960s with his wife, Mary Kneafsey, from Foxford, County Mayo. She was born in 1925 and moved to York in the 1950s to join some of her younger sisters who had settled there. Their father had died in the early 1940s, and Mary, the eldest, remained at home to help her mother take care of her siblings. For a time she worked in the Foxford woollen mills, the main employer in the town. As soon as she was free to do so, she took a job in York working at the Rowntree chocolate factory. Their eldest son John was born in 1960 in Beverly, a town in Yorkshire. The couple bought their first house in Leicester, and then had three more children. John studied accountancy, Jim philosophy, their brother Peter trained as a computer engineer, and their sister Maureen qualified as a nurse. Jim got a job as a building site clerk and progressed to become a project manager on large construction schemes. He moved to Dublin in early 2001 soon after the birth of his son, as his partner Cornelia was Irish, and they wanted to move closer to her family. She had graduated as an industrial designer with my wife, and had worked in London as a designer, and then as a secondary school teacher. When Jim and Cornelia moved to Dublin, he was able to pick and choose between several similar positions to the one he had in London.

A 1991 report by the Irish National Economic and Social Council (NESC) argued that the well-educated Irish who went to England did so 'in search of high-skilled and prestigious work', as distinct from the sometimes well-paid but low-skilled work that previous cohorts of emigrants had found on building sites. The NESC study also found that comparatively poorly educated young adults from urban areas were the least likely to emigrate; unskilled and poorly educated migrants were now a minority. Many of those who went to the United States during the 1980s worked there illegally. They encountered a relatively benign immigration control regime compared to the current one, but their irregular status made it very difficult for them to transition from traditional Irish emigrant jobs (working in construction, in bars, in restaurants or as child-minders) into professional occupations or permanent jobs that they were qualified to do, or to work for large companies that abided by immigration rules, or to become owners of businesses.[68] Unlike those with equivalent levels of education who moved to England, where immigration status was not a problem, those who went to the United States found it much more difficult to break out of the kinds of work that first generation Irish emigrations had been doing for generations.

Post-2008 emigrants were, once again, better educated than previous cohorts and whilst some found themselves doing work that did not draw on their qualifications more were able to find better jobs and better-paid jobs than could be found at home. Although unemployment shot up to more than 14 per cent, many of those who left had been in unsatisfactory employment. Nearly 50 per cent of those who left had full-time jobs, and another 13 per cent had some paid employment. An analysis of emigration during the post-2008 economic crisis observed that proportionally more left Ireland than emigrated from Spain or Greece – European Union countries with higher levels of unemployment.[69] To some extent this was a matter of choice and inclination. Whilst the twenty-first-century Irish were not forced to emigrate more so than other Western Europeans they were more inclined to do so.

Much of Ireland's post-2008 media coverage of emigration focused on Australia, which, unlike most other English-speaking countries, was in the midst of an economic boom. RTÉ (the Irish national broadcaster) screened programmes such as *Gardaí Down Under*, which documented the lives of Irish police who had quit their jobs for better-paid police work in Western Australia. Irish migrants were typically were admitted via Australia's Working Holiday Maker programme. Between 2002 and 2007 somewhere between 11,000 and 15,000 Irish people had used this scheme, meaning that those who went to Australia after the crash were following an established route.[70] In 2012–13, some 5,209 Irish citizens received permanent residency status and a further 11,817 arrived on working holiday visas.[71] Social media for many replaced the need to hang out in Irish pubs where jobs might be found. Employment networking sites such as LinkedIn reduced the need for personal intermediaries.

A 2016 *Irish Times* survey reported that 69 per cent of the 350 emigrants who had left Ireland since 2008 described themselves as happier than when they lived in Ireland. More than 79 per cent of respondents stated that their quality of life was higher than in Ireland and 98 per cent were currently employed. More than 80 per cent described their job satisfaction as greater. Analysis of the interviews depicted those who were interviewed as 'putting down roots overseas: buying homes, getting promoted, starting families – and feeling happier than they did in Ireland'. More than half had emigrated with somebody they knew, rising to three-quarters of those who moved to Australia. Some 70 per cent of those who emigrated to Australia, Canada or New Zealand had a social circle that was predominantly Irish. Sixty per cent of those in Australia or New Zealand had an Irish partner. Most of those who put down roots did so with other Irish emigrants. Many joined GAA clubs. Many were in constant contact with families and friends in Ireland through social media. The percentage believing that they had no choice but to emigrate was highest (38 per cent) amongst those who left Ireland in 2010 but even during the worst years of the economic crisis mostly believed that they emigrated out of choice.[72]

Sarah Flynn bought a one-way ticket to Vancouver in September 2009 after losing her financial services job in Dublin at the age of 24. Her parents had similarly moved to Canada during the 1980s recession but had since moved back to Dublin. She retrained as a therapist and found a job she liked. She married a Canadian, and they had a child and purchased a house in Vancouver. In 2016 she had no plans to return to Ireland and described life in Canada as 'fantastic'. Some 87 per cent of interviewees who went to Canada had left jobs to do so. Overall, half of the 350 interviewees were promoted in their jobs since emigrating. Aisling Kelly qualified as a nurse in 2011 during a hiring freeze in the HSE, the Irish health service. She found a nursing job in Buckinghamshire, and later moved to London, where she trained as and then worked as a midwife. She described career and promotion opportunities as far better in Britain than in Ireland. She became engaged to a Londoner and believed that she would settle permanently in Britain. Respondents who moved to the United Kingdom reported the highest levels of career progression.

Eimear Beattie, a teacher from County Tipperary who moved to Perth in Western Australia with her family in 2011 described how wages for teachers were significantly higher there even when higher living costs were taken into account. Just 5 per cent were undocumented – most of these lived in the United States. 41 per cent held some type of temporary work visa, 43 per cent had permanent residency status in the countries where they lived an 11 per cent had become citizens of these.[73] She founded Irish Families in Perth in 2016, which has 12,000 Facebook members.

Some 78,900 Irish people migrated to Australia between 2008 and 2013, which far exceeded numbers moving to other countries during the same period. From 2013, some of these relocated to Canada where equivalent visas for another two years could be obtained and where a recent construction boom offered more opportunities for work.[74] Some of those who went to Australia were in their 30s and 40s, had mortgages back in Ireland and brought their families with them.[75] Many of the Irish moved to Perth, where some of the men worked in 'fly-in, fly-out' (FIFO) jobs in mining camps many hundreds of miles into the outback for three- or four-week shifts, usually returning to Perth for a week's leave. FIFO contracts typically produced twice the usual wage for similar work, and workers would move from one temporary contract in one mining camp to another in the next. The day-to-day lives of some FIFO workers – living in camps or in temporary accommodation – echoed those of some Irish labourers in England during the 1950s.[76]

In June 2011 Jim O'Brien was headhunted to work on a mining construction project in Western Australia. He was one of a dozen engineers and project managers recruited at the same time by an agency in Dublin. By then, the Irish building industry had collapsed, Jim's partner had lost her job, and he was commuting back and forth to the UK for work while his family remained in Dublin. He recalled that Monday morning flights to London were full of other men doing the same. The family then moved to Perth, where he would fly out for three-week stints in Pilbara, several hundred miles away in the desert, where he worked on the construction of an iron-ore mine. He had a two-year contract, which if extended, would have enabled him to obtain permanent residency and then become eligible to apply for Australian citizenship.

In 2013, Jim was headhunted again by a recruitment agency, this time on behalf of a hospital construction plant in Montreal. He had encountered a lot of casual anti-Irish racism in Western Australia that reminded him of England during the 1970s, so this, combined with the difficult FIFO working conditions, meant that he was not unhappy to leave Australia. So, after a holiday in Ireland, the family moved on to Canada. Jim worked two years in Canada, after which he was approached once again by an agency to work on a project in Dublin. At the time, the family considered remaining permanently in Canada. There were, however, bureaucratic difficulties in settling permanently in Quebec, where French was the official language and obtaining citizenship required proficiency in Quebecois French. Interestingly, among Jim's colleagues in Montreal were people who had previously worked with him in Australia; by the time Jim returned to Dublin in the summer of 2015, all but one of those 12 colleagues had returned to work in Ireland. Once in Dublin, Jim received a steady stream of queries from Irish former colleagues in Canada seeking jobs in Ireland.

Most of Ireland's most recent 'emigration generation' went to countries where they were given the right to work and reside, were treated well, found that they could access employment and progress in their careers without discrimination, and come and go as they please. This is not to say that migration was simply a lifestyle choice, as many of those who left Ireland during the economic crisis may have done so out a 'mix of desire, necessity and desperation'.[77] Yet, compared to many immigrants who came to Ireland, recent Irish emigrants have faced relatively few obstacles.

NINE

REFUGEES

The aftermath of the Second World War saw international legal agreement on definitions of refugees and obligations towards refugees. The United Nations Convention on the Status of Refugees (1951) defined a refugee as someone who is unable or unwilling to return to their country of origin owing to a well-founded fear of being persecuted for reasons of race, religion, nationality, membership of a particular social group, or political opinion. In 1956 Ireland ratified this Convention.

Before this legal definition emerged refugee had a more general common-sense meaning. Huguenots were the first to call themselves refugees; the word entered the English language from the French *réfugié* during the 1680s. The term, as defined by the UN, would have applied better to those who fled France to Holland than to those who arrived in Ireland as part of William of Orange's army and settled on lands that had been confiscated from Catholics.

The flight of Palatines to England, on the other hand, with their initial reception in camps on the outskirts of London, and attempts to disperse them subsequently to various locations including Ireland, had many of the features of a modern refugee crisis. Responses to the Palatines also anticipated more recent political, legislative, and administrative responses to refugees in Ireland and elsewhere, in terms of the challenges of managing the reception and settlement of large numbers of newcomers. Distinctions between deserving Protestant refugees and Catholic Palatines, who were then weeded out and deported, anticipate the divide in recent decades between those admitted as refugees or granted asylum, and those who have been refused entry or deported.

This chapter firstly examines the experiences of Jews and others seeking sanctuary in Ireland, before, during, and after the Second World War. It then considers the experiences of some groups of 'programme refugees' who arrived following Ireland's ratification of the UN Convention in 1956. These were groups admitted at the behest of the United Nations High Commissioner for Refugees (UNHCR). The Hungarians who arrived that year were followed by a group of Chileans in 1973, Vietnamese in 1979, Bosnians in 1991 and Kosovars in 1997. Responses to such groups are compared to those to Catholic refugees from Northern Ireland who came south after being driven from their homes by sectarian violence in 1969.

In recent decades, some other small groups from refugee camps have been joined by asylum seekers who made their own way to Ireland without the help or support of the UN. The numbers of such asylum seekers remained small until the 1990s at which time their arrival in increasing numbers came to be perceived as a crisis. The experiences of African asylum seekers and the response of the Irish state to these are considered in the following chapter.

An overt policy of discrimination against Jews emerged in Ireland in 1938 which lasted throughout the Second World War and the aftermath of the Holocaust. The Department of Justice routinely advised against the admittance of Jews Ireland ratified the UN Convention on the Status of Refugees in 1956. A striking feature of such institutional anti-Semitism was the extent to which this remained unchanged after the Holocaust. Post-1945 obstacles to the admission of Jewish refugees occurred in a context of Europe-wide chaos where millions of people had been displaced, and some had no chance of returning to where they lived before the War. By 1948, many parts of Europe in which Jews had been persecuted and killed were even more *Judenfrei* than in Hitler's time.[1] Beyond the small number of official refugees admitted by Ireland there had always been others who made their way by other means. These have included small numbers of Jews who and others who had the means to make their own way to safety, individuals assisted by Irish citizens, diplomats or politicians and those who arrived, one way or another, on false papers. This included some Nazi collaborators who were assisted by Catholic networks and so-called 'ratlines' to come to Ireland after the Second World War.

More so than other groups, Jewish refugees who came to Ireland have left extensive documentation including memoirs and autobiographies, while government files and some academic research has addressed elements of the experiences of Hungarian, Vietnamese, Bosnian, and Kosovar refugees who arrived in Ireland during the second half of the twentieth century. Because Ireland had ratified the UN Convention on the Rights of Refugees, none of these groups experienced the degree of opposition encountered by pre-Convention Jewish refugees. That said Ireland remained a reluctant and ambivalent host to such refugees. When in 1975, the UNHCR requested that the Irish government admit just three refugee families, the response was to express regret that, due to current economic circumstances, it would not be feasible to do so.[2] Just a few thousand refugees were admitted by the Irish state during the first eight decades after independence.

JEWS, CATHOLICS AND COLLABORATORS

In the run-up to the Second World War responsibility for vetting refugees coming into Ireland was vested in the Department of Justice. However, this was effectively delegated to a voluntary group, the Irish Co-ordinating Committee for the Relief of Christian Refugees,[3] which ultimately resulted in the Irish state being more receptive to requests for visas from Catholic organisations on behalf of Catholics abroad than on behalf of Jews. The Co-ordinating Committee's remit was to assist Christian, that is Catholic refugees from the Third Reich, and its work mostly focused on refugees from Austria, who had converted to Catholicism, but who were nonetheless classified by the Nuremberg Laws as Jewish. A Department of Justice memorandum on 16 November 1938 endorsed the view of the committee that the state should admit Catholic refugees who had converted from Judaism, but not Jewish refugees.[4] Furthermore, the number of refugees the committee could admit was initially capped at 70.[5] Various Department of Justice memoranda from before, during, and after the Holocaust opposed the admission of Jewish refugees. As stated by one such document from 24 September 1945:

> It is the policy of the Department of Justice to restrict the immigration of Jews. The wealth and influence of the Jewish community in this country, and the murmurs against Jewish wealth and influence are frequently heard. As Jews do not become assimilated with the native population, like other immigrants, there is a danger that any big increase in their numbers might create a social problem.[6]

Another from 28 February 1953 argued that Justice's 'policy' of excluding Jews had been supported by other Government departments: 'In the administration of the alien laws it has always been recognised in the Departments of Justice, Industry and Commerce and External Affairs that the question of the admission of aliens of Jewish blood presents a special problem and the alien laws have been administered less liberally in their case'.[7] Efforts by Irish Jews to rescue co-religionists from the Third Reich were opposed in particular by two prominent officials. One of these was Peter Berry, the senior civil servant in the Department of Justice who wrote the above-cited memoranda and others like it between 1938 and 1953. The other was Charles Bewley, Ireland's envoy to Berlin from 1933 to 1939. Bewley was both openly anti-Semitic and an enthusiastic admirer of the Nazis.[8]

Robert Briscoe, a Jewish member of Fianna Fáil and TD for Dublin became involved in efforts to help Jews leave Germany and Poland before the war. Most of his efforts were focused on assisting Jews to reach Palestine rather than Ireland; Briscoe described himself as a Zionist as well as an Irish nationalist.[9] His wife, Lily, wrote to the Minister of Justice in April 1939 seeking temporary visas to enable Jewish relatives of her husband from Czechoslovakia to travel to America via Ireland. She was informed by Berry that no applications would be considered other than those submitted by the Co-ordinating Committee.[10] Berry's role in blocking Jews from coming to Ireland did not become more widely apparent until government files were made public some decades later. As far as the Briscoes were concerned, Peter Berry was a family friend. He was a frequent visitor to their home for many years and used to play cards with Robert Briscoe.[11]

Bewley appears to have gone further than Berry, going out of his way to thwart visas being issued that had already been approved by Dublin.[12] For example, in July 1938 George Klarr (Clare), a Viennese Jewish banker, travelled to Berlin to collect visas for his family that he had been told were awaiting him at the Irish Legation there. The visas had been approved in return for investment by Klarr of £1,000 in a ribbon factory as part of a wider scheme to allow but a handful of Jews who could demonstrate that they were in a position to contribute to the Irish economy to settle in Ireland. Klarr, 'who did not know the difference between warp and woof, between the front of a loom and the back was to be given an Irish work and entry permit as a ribbon-weaver'.[13] He had been helped by Emil Hirsch, who had already been in negotiation with Seán Lemass, the Minister for Industry and Commerce, to relocate a ribbon factory from Austria to Ireland. That scheme was linked in turn to the establishment of a felt hat factory in Galway by a group of Czech Jews. Klarr found his way into this network because he had audited the ribbon factory on behalf of the bank he worked for. Klarr was also supposed to contribute £1,000 capital to the enterprise. He also pursued other options for getting his family to safety, including taking up an offer of employment in a bank in Paris and considering whether to have his son George baptised so that he might be helped by a group of Quakers in Vienna, who were helping 'non-Ayran' Christian refugees to emigrate.[14]

When, in July 1938, Klarr was removed from his post in the bank (as were other Jews working in the professions), he travelled with his family to Berlin, where they had to wait several weeks before obtaining their visas to Ireland. The Irish Legation there consisted of just Bewley and his secretary, Frau Kamberg, a German woman who also served as general administrator. She told Klarr that the visas were being held back pending the arrival of the machinery for the factory in which Klarr was to be employed in Ireland. After these preconditions were met, however, Bewley disobeyed the instruction from Dublin to release the visas. The Klarrs eventually received their visas only because, they believed, of the persistence of Frau Kamberg.[15]

The Klarrs finally left Germany in September 1938 and travelled to Ireland via London. But Klarr was unhappy in provincial Ireland. A year after arriving in Ireland, Klarr moved to Paris with his wife to take up the offer of a banking position there. His son George Clare tried to convince his mother to remain in Ireland but she wished to accompany her husband. George, who was eighteen years old, then enlisted in the British army. On 4 September 1939 they were interned by the French government along with other German nationals, and were then unable to escape when France was occupied by the Nazis. After the occupation, they made their way to Marseilles, which was part of Vichy France. However, they were subsequently deported by the Vichy government and were killed in Auschwitz.[16]

The Kilkenny writer Hubert Butler worked with a group of Quakers in Vienna during 1938 and 1939 to secure exit visas for Austrian Jews – the same organisation that George Klarr considered approaching to help his son. Getting an exit visa was dependent on having a corresponding entrance visa, to be obtained from the destination country. Butler worked with the Irish Co-ordinating Committee for the Relief of Christian Refugees to secure the entry into Ireland of a group of Vienna Jews who had been expelled from their homes, and had been lodged by the Quakers on a farm at Kagran, on the outskirts of Vienna. Butler went on then to smuggle Erwin Struntz, a Catholic who had converted to Judaism, along with his Jewish wife and family, to Ireland via London. Unlike some members of the Kagran group, Struntz did not meet the criteria for admission operated by the Co-ordinating Committee. He was in imminent danger of being sent to a concentration camp at the time. Other members of the Kagran group were admitted to Ireland.[17]

By stark contrast with the experience of Jews who sought refuge in Ireland, the red carpet was extended to Austrian scientist Erwin Schrödinger, which simply showed what could be achieved when there was political will to admit refugees. In April 1938, Éamon de Valera, who was in Geneva as Head of the League of Nations, instructed his officials to offer asylum to Schrödinger, who had just been dismissed from his academic post for criticising Nazism. Through intermediaries, he was offered sanctuary in Dublin. De Valera was, amongst other things, a mathematician, and wanted to establish an Institute of Advanced Studies in Ireland. Schrödinger fled Austria by train with his wife Anny to the Irish Embassy in Rome. From there, equipped with documentation from the embassy, he travelled to meet de Valera in Geneva, where de Valera put the Schrödingers up for three days in his hotel before they left for to Ireland. A visa was also provided for Schrödinger's mistress and their daughter. Schrödinger's unconventional household had previously caused difficulties for him at Oxford and Princeton, but, according to Schrödinger's biographer, it posed no problem for de Valera.[18]

Some Jewish refugees, including *Kindertransport* children under 17 years of age, who were admitted to Britain, travelled on to Northern Ireland. In 1938, the Belfast Jewish community set up a hostel for young Jewish refugees at Cliftonpark Avenue. A number of other hostels were also organised. In

1939, 30 children were relocated to a derelict 70-acre seafront farm near Millisle some 20 miles from Belfast, where they worked the land. Eugene Patiasz, an agronomist from Hungary, was put in charge of the farm, and a number of other refugee adults – including a doctor, two engineers and a gardener – also worked at Millisle. A barn was converted into a bunkhouse but, initially, the first group of children to arrive slept in tents. The children attended a local Presbyterian school where learning English was a priority. Classes were organised so that each Jewish pupil sat next to a local child. By October 1940 the farm was self-sufficient. More than 300 children stayed at the farm during the war. Afterwards some were reunited with family members. The majority were not. Some settled in Northern Ireland and others settled in Britain.[19]

No *Kindertransport* refugees were admitted to the Irish Free State during the war. Efforts to bring over 100 Jewish orphan children from the Bergen-Belsen concentration camp, soon after the end of the Second World War, were opposed by the Department of Justice even though arrangements to provide for their care had been put in place by the Irish and British Jewish communities at no cost to the state. In August 1946 the Minister of Justice refused permission to admit the children on the grounds that it had always been policy to restrict the admission of Jewish aliens. This decision was overturned after the Chief Rabbi approached de Valera and 137 children were admitted on a temporary basis. They spent around a year recuperating in Cloyne Castle in County Westmeath, which was purchased by a Jewish philanthropist and managed by Rabbi Solomon Schonfeld who was from London. They subsequently re-joined surviving members of their families in England, the United States and Israel.[20] The youngest were around six years old. Alfred Leicht, one of the oldest, was nearly 18 years old when he arrived in Ireland. He came from a small Jewish community in Bilke, a town of around 30,000 in Hungary. In 1942 his father had been arrested by the Hungarian secret police and with a group of other Jews was made dig a mass grave before they were shot and buried there. In 1944, Hungarian Arrow Cross Fascist soldiers herded all surviving Jews from Bilke onto a train for shipment to Auschwitz. On arrival, most of the group, including his mother and his three younger brothers, were sent immediately to the gas chamber. In April 1945 he was sent on a forced march to Buchenwald where, at the age of 15, he was liberated by the Americans.

Leicht made his way back to Bilke, where he found that his family home and all of his family's belongings had been taken over by a gentile neighbour. So, Leicht made his way to Bratislava, where he was united with other surviving Jews. He met Rabbi Schonfeld who had travelled there from London to rescue children like him. He went with Schonfeld's mostly-Czech group of children to Ireland. In 1949 he moved to the United States and eventually settled in Atlanta where he married and built a successful business career as a corporate executive. Of his time in Ireland he wrote:

> It is one of history's mocking ironies that inward-looking Ireland offered us, one hundred disposed and displaced orphans from war-torn Europe, only conditional and temporary status in their land. Yet masses of their own poverty-stricken citizens had emigrated to America during the 19th and the 20th centuries to seek a better life. Some of us might have opted to remain there had we been allowed to do so. But their restrictions were sadly emblematic of the antipathy and apathy that have so often spawned ugly misconceptions and inciting myths about Jews. Despite this our time in Ireland was a flare in the night for all of us and dramatic crossroad in our formative years.[21]

A handful of other Jewish children found their way to Ireland by other means. Robert Collis, a wealthy Protestant paediatrician from Dublin, worked for the Red Cross in Belsen where around 500 Jewish children had survived. He brought six unclaimed orphans to Ireland and adopted two of these, Zoltan and Edith Zinn. Zoltan Zinn-Collis was born in Czechoslovakia in 1940. His father Adolf Zinn was Jewish and was forced to go into hiding. After he was captured by Slovak nationalist Nazis collaborators and tortured, the family was sent with other Jews from the village by train to Ravensbrück, a concentration camp for women and children. Zoltan's mother had been pressured to denounce and divorce her Jewish husband by the leader of the Slovak nationalist unit, which she refused to do. Zoltan's baby sister died in the crush in a cattle car during the rail journey. He recalls seeing her body being taken from his mother's arms and flung over a wall by a guard. His father and other men on the train were sent to gas chamber on arrival at Ravensbrück. The rest of the family were sent onwards to Belsen.

They arrived in early January 1945. Belsen was liberated by the British army in April 1945. By then Zoltan had contracted tuberculosis of the spine. His mother died of typhoid on the very day the camp was liberated and his brother Aladar died shortly afterwards from the same disease. Zoltan and his sister Edit survived, and after a period of recuperation in Sweden, during which Robert Collis travelled to Czechoslovakia to locate any surviving family members of the children, they were taken to Ireland. The children's grandmother had survived, but wanted the children to be adopted. The other four children that Collis brought to Ireland were Suszi and Tibor Molnar, Evelyn Schwartz and Frank Berlin. Suszi Molnar was two years old and her brother was five when they arrived with their mother at Ravensbruck in April 1945. Their father was similarly killed before they arrived with their mother at Belsen. She tied of typhoid shortly before the camp was liberated.

In Ireland, Collis arranged for Suszi and Tibor Molnar to be adopted by an Orthodox Jewish couple, Willie and Elsie Samuels, who lived in Dublin. Zoltan Zinn-Collis received treatment for tuberculosis and had surgery throughout his childhood, and was sent to a Quaker boarding school in Waterford from the age of nine. He worked for 40 years as a chef, including at Kilkea Castle in County Kildare, where his long-time employer turned out to be a survivor of Auschwitz. Although both knew of each other's experiences, they never discussed them.[22]

Not all survivors of the Holocaust who settled in Ireland came immediately after the War. Tomi Reichental was born on a farm in Piestany in Slovakia in 1935, where his family were the only Jews in their village (others had converted to Christianity). From 1942, Jews including relatives of the Reichental's were expelled from Slovakia and sent to Germany, never to be seen again. Tomi's grandparents were arrested for deportation in September 1942. In January 1943 a group of Hlinka guards that included 'neighbours-turned tormentors' arrived to deport the family, but were bribed. After many other relatives were deported, the family obtained false identity cards and moved to another village with the help of a Catholic priest, where they took religious instruction to learn how to pass as Catholics. They then moved to Bratislava.

In October 1944, they were eventually arrested in Bratislava along with members of their extended family and sent to a detention camp 55 kilometres away. From there, they were packed into cattle cars for a seven-day rail journey to Belsen. Tomi's father, who had stayed behind to look after the farm, was arrested but managed to escape, and subsequently joined a group of partisans. In November 1944 Tomi was sent from the Slovakian camp to Bergen-Belsen with his mother, brother, sister, grandmother and other relatives, 13 of them in total. Thirty-five members of his extended family died during the Holocaust.

Tomi, his parents, and several other members of his family survived. They returned to Slovakia they were reunited with his father. Tomi was initially enrolled in a school run by the priest who had helped the family, but moved to Bratislava where after a time he moved to a hostel run by a Zionist Youth organisation. In 1949, at 14, he emigrated to Israel with his brother as part of a group of more than 250 Slovak Jewish children. He lived for a time in a kibbutz and then with his parents, who also settled in Israel. He trained as a machinist and served two years in the Israeli army following his eighteenth birthday in 1953. In 1957, he moved to Germany, where he trained and worked as an engineer. He received an offer of employment from a Jewish company seeking to establish a zip factory in Dublin, and he moved to Ireland, where he got married in 1961. The couple spent some time in Israel but moved back to Dublin permanently after the birth of their first child in 1964. In 1977 he became an Irish citizen.[23]

Neither Tomi Reichental nor Zoltan Zinn-Collis discussed their experiences in Belsen until late in life after retirement. Zoltan began to speak in public, mostly to children in schools, about his experiences in Belsen. His autobiography *Final Witness: My Journey from the Holocaust to Ireland* was published in 2006. Tomi did not speak of his experiences of the Holocaust until 2000, 55 years after the fact. Since then he has spoken at hundreds of schools as part of a programme run by the Holocaust Education Trust Ireland (HETI). His autobiography, *I Was a Boy in Belsen* was published in 2011. In 2017 Irish cinemas screened *Condemned to Remember*, a documentary about Nazi-era and more recent genocides, which he narrated.

Helen Lewis was born in 1916 in Trutnov in the Czech Sudetenland. She studied and later taught dance in Prague where she married Paul Hermann. In 1942 the couple were sent to Terezín concentration camp, separated, and in 1944 were transferred to Auschwitz. Paul Hermann died during a forced march the following year. Her mother was killed in another concentration camp. In January 1945, she escaped during a similar forced march and hid until the Russian army liberated the area. After the war, she returned to Prague where she married Harry Lewis, a Czech friend from before the war who had escaped to Northern Ireland and had settled there. She moved to Belfast in October 1947, where, no longer able to dance, she worked as a choreographer.[24]

Following the defeat of Germany, around 40 Nazi collaborators including some fleeing charges of war crimes or prison sentences were admitted to the Irish Free State. Many arrived with the assistance of clandestine networks or 'ratlines' that facilitated their flights from Europe. Many of those who arrived in Ireland did so using false papers, and some were granted visas from Irish embassies. Catholic religious orders with members sympathetic to Catholic Flemish, Breton or Croatian right-wing, anti-communist nationalists sheltered a number of those who fled to neutral Ireland to escape prosecution or to avoid prison. Some had escaped from prison with the complicity of the Allied gaolers.

Nineteen Bretons and 13 Flemish fugitives came to Ireland after the war, many with their families.[25] The former included members of Bezen Perrot, a Breton militia unit that had been incorporated into the SS (they wore SS uniforms). In one incident in July 1944, 34 members of the French Resistance were murdered by Bezen Perrot. Members of Bezen Perrot arrived in Ireland via England and Wales. Célestin Lainé, the leader of Bezen Perrot, lived under an alias in Dublin and Owenmore in County Galway, until his death in 1983.[26] Among the Flemish Catholic separatist nationalists who fled

Belgium to Ireland were [27] collaborators including Albert Folens, a journalist who had been employed by the Sicherheitsdienst or SD, the intelligence service of the SS, and Alex Colen, who had served in a Flemish military unit that became incorporated into the Waffen-SS.[28] Folens arrived in October 1948, having spent about 32 months in prison. He settled permanently in Ireland and became a successful printer and publisher; the company is still running today. A number of Flemish fugitives who made their way to Ireland had been sheltered in Trappist monasteries and were assisted by Catholic priests.

Willem Sassen, a Dutch collaborator who similarly found his way to Ireland, had been a prisoner of war in 1940. He became a member of the SS. He worked as an embedded war correspondent on the Eastern Front and later for a Nazi radio station in Belgium.[29] After the war, Sassen assumed the identity of Albert Desmedt a Belgian Jew who died with his family at Auschwitz. Sassen flew to Ireland using forged papers on a newly established air route from Amsterdam to Dublin. In Dublin, he was helped by Fr Senan Moynihan, a Franciscan priest. Sassen and his family shared a house in Rathgar in Dublin with two Flemish collaborators and their families. The group left Ireland in September 1948 for South America.[30] In Argentina, Sassen continued to profess his loyalty to the Nazis. He befriended Adolf Eichmann. Hundreds of hours of tapes of Sassen's interviews with Eichmann and their conversations have been transcribed.[31]

Andrija Artukovi had been a member of Ustaše, a Catholic nationalist group that came to power in Croatia as a Nazi puppet regime in 1941. As Minister of the Interior he brought in anti-Jewish racial laws. The Ustaše government presided over the murder of hundreds of thousands of Gypsies, Jews and Serbians.[32] Artukovi escaped after the war with the help of a Croatian Franciscan, and travelled through several different countries including Italy, Austria, and Switzerland, before obtaining permission to enter Ireland from the embassy in Berne. In March 1947, under the name Alois Anich, he travelled to Ireland. Attached to his application were letters of recommendation from the General of the Franciscan Order in Switzerland, Dr Seraphim Perchten. These described 'Dr Anich' as an important supporter of the Catholic Church who was on the run from the Communist regime in Yugoslavia. Artukovi and his family were allowed into Ireland in May 1947. The Irish authorities appear not to have known his real identity. Beyond the reference from the Franciscans, what likely worked in his favour in terms of getting into the country was a general sense of Catholic solidarity, combined with an antipathy to communism amongst the Irish decision-makers involved in such cases.[33] In Ireland, Fr Ivanditch, a Croatian Franciscan friar, helped Artukovi find a place to live.[34] Artukovi stayed with his family at 6 Zion Road in Rathgar, where he supposedly attended

Mass every day for more than a year before departing for the United States.[35] He was extradited from the United States to Yugoslavia in 1985, convicted of ordering mass killings and died in prison there in 1988.

Opposition by the Department of Justice to the admission of Jews persisted during this period when Ireland allowed admission to such European Catholic refugees. By 1951 there were at least 846 refugees living in Ireland. Of these, 242 had become Irish citizens. 265 were Polish.[36] Only a small percentage were Jewish. In February 1953, a request by Robert Briscoe to temporarily admit ten families of Czech and Hungarian Jews at no expense to the Irish state – all costs would, according to Briscoe be covered by Ireland's Jewish community – was refused. Once again, the author of an explicitly anti-Semitic internal memorandum opposing Briscoe's request was Peter Berry.[37]

HUNGARIANS

On 13 November 1956, just two weeks before Ireland ratified the UN Convention on the Rights of Refugees (1951) the government agreed to admit up to 250 refugees from Hungary. Soon after, this number was increased to a potential maximum of 1,000. On 30 November 1956, the Irish Minister of Defence, who at the time was responsible for refugees, was reported in the *Irish Independent* as saying that this number could even be further increased if necessary.[38] This positive political rhetoric seems to have had much to do with Ireland's newly minted membership of the United Nations.[39] Widespread apparent support for the admission of Hungarian refugees also owed much to Catholic solidarity. Catholic sermons at the time, often reprinted in local newspapers in Ireland, referred to the plight of anti-Communist Catholic martyrs in Hungary.[40] A ground swell of public support for admitting Hungarian refugees was evident in the success of a church gate collection by the Irish Red Cross, which raised £170,000 for the care of what were presumed to be a group of Catholic Hungarian refugees.[41]

Once they arrived in Ireland, it was envisaged that the care of the refugees could be devolved to the voluntary sector. Their accommodation in an army barracks at Knocknalisheen in County Clare was funded entirely by the Red Cross, and the refugees received meals and a small cash allowance out of voluntary funds. Although Article 17 of the UN Convention (1951), – which Ireland had just ratified – conferred upon the refugees a right to work, considerable efforts were made to prevent the Hungarians seeking employment. In effect, there was a policy of containment from the outset. Refugees were confined to the camp with the use of quarantine periods for disease; when these elapsed, efforts were made to use the Gardaí to illegally restrict their movements.[42] In essence, the refugees were locked up pending various decisions on policy by government officials. They were less than two months in Ireland before petty officiousness and efforts to control and contain them gave way to a resolve to remove them altogether. Commitments to accept more Hungarian refugees were abandoned.[43]

Soon after they arrived, the Hungarians demanded a role in the administration of the camp. They elected a camp committee, which the Red Cross sought to suppress. On 17 January 1957, the Red Cross wrote to the inter-departmental civil service committee on refugees demanding that 12 'agitators' be removed from the camp. This was refused out of concern that doing so might result in 'undesirable press publicity'.[44] The Red Cross tried again, this time requesting that László Pesthy, the elected leader of the Hungarians, be removed from Knocknalisheen. Pesthy, the 35-year-old engineer had been a political prisoner in Siberia for 29 months before being imprisoned for a time in Hungary. He was reported to have taken part in the original demonstrations against the Hungarian Communist regime with students of the Polytechnic University in Budapest and in the fighting that followed.[45] He had escaped, leaving his wife and three-and-a-half-year-old son behind.

The Red Cross blamed Pesthy for being single-handedly to blame for the conflicts at the camp. It accused him of intimidating other refugees, threatening camp staff, and bringing into his hut 'an undesirable woman for the night and refused to have her placed out of bounds'.[46] A report from the local Garda Superintendent ridiculed the accusations. He pointed out that Mr Pesthy had received overwhelming support from other refugees, having been re-elected as their leader by a massive majority in a secret ballot, with 174 out of 193 votes cast. The so-called 'woman of the night' turned out to be a respectable Limerick woman attempting to recruit refugee musicians to play in a band in the city.[47] She had been turned away from the camp but was eventually allowed to collect the musical instruments she had allowed the refugees to borrow. Whilst the accusations against László Pesthy were not taken seriously by government officials, he was nevertheless seen as a troublemaker. It was decided that Department of External Affairs officials in London should help him find a job in England 'as he had previously indicated some interest in moving there'.[48]

The Hungarians put out statements which were reported in the press. An article in the *Irish Independent* on 11 January 1957 reported complaints that the huts in the camp were cold, damp and unhealthy, and that as a result many women and children had become ill'.[49] Although publically denied at the time, the Red Cross had complained about the unsuitability of conditions for expectant mothers and children in a letter to the Minister for Defence.[50] Furthermore, a December 1956 Department of Defence report had likened Knocknalisheen to an internment camp.[51] Yet no changes to how the camp was run were proposed. It had already been decided that the Republic of Ireland's first refugee crisis would be resolved by 'onward migrations' to Canada; though this would not happen until April 1957.[52] However, at the end of April, the Hungarians were still in County Clare. On 29 April 1957, most of the adults in the camp went on hunger strike. They refused food from the authorities and fed their children from a stockpile they had had saved up in advance.[53] The hunger strike was called off following a long-sought visit from senior civil servants to the camp. Subsequently, most the refugees willingly relocated to Canada.[54] By the beginning of 1959, some 438 of a total of 538 had left the country.[55]

In part, the conflicts between Irish officials at the camp and the refugees can be explained by the lack of deference of the Hungarians. Government reports and correspondence of the era depict them as 'vociferous' in demanding their rights, in seeking to participate in decision-making about their fate and in the administration of the camp. Their willingness to assert themselves was countered by an indigenous Irish culture where those in authority expected deference. Unlike the children and vulnerable adults in Irish institutions such as the Church-run mother-and-child homes, which came under the responsibility of the Department of Education, many of the Hungarians had previous experiences of standing up against officials. Why they might want a say in how they were treated was explained in a statement reported by the *Irish Times* on 14 January 1957:

> However great the material generosity of the Irish people may be, a community of 500 people living in partial confinement without information as to their future can be overcome by a sense of frustration, which grows as this time of uncertainty goes on. Under such conditions, nervous tensions arise; smaller frustrations seem larger, major frustrations unbearable.[56]

The *Irish Times* article reflected the stance that it was one thing to admit some hundreds of refugees, but quite another to respond adequately to their presence in such a way that would not make anyone regret the initial generosity.[57] The regrets followed all too quickly. The response of the state was to endeavour to remove the refugees, rather than to address the shortcomings indicated by their complaints. Within one month of the arrival of the first refugees it was decided that they should be removed. A somewhat similarly ambivalent welcome was extended to subsequent groups of programme refugees. With one major exception, considered next, responses to refugees have been characterised by some degree of petty officialdom and by cack-handed efforts to control people, which turned into official resentment when these failed.

NORTHERN IRISH

The eruption of violence in 1969 resulted in the migration of Catholics from Northern Ireland to the Republic. On 13 August 1969 Taoiseach Jack Lynch announced that he Irish Defence Forces would set up field hospitals along the border. Up to 10,000 fled their homes. Most of those who crossed the border were Catholics whilst displaced Protestants mostly fled to East Belfast. These displaced persons were described as refugees in Republic of Ireland media and government reports.

The overwhelming majority of displaced persons who settled in the Republic were Catholic. Protestants who were displaced by sectarian violence tended to relocate to Protestant enclaves such as east Belfast and some migrated to the British mainland. [58] For example, a Belfast Protestant Relief Committee arranged for women and more than 350 children refugees to be shipped from East Belfast to Liverpool where assistance was organised by the Liverpool Orange Order in August 1971.[59]

A 2005 study estimated that out of 22,390 people identified in the 2002 census as born in Northern Ireland living in the Republic's border counties at least half, 11,000 or more, had sought refuge from the Northern Ireland conflict. Most of these lived Donegal, Louth and Monaghan. A pattern of chain migration emerged whereby those displaced from particular Northern areas settled alongside one another in particular Southern towns. For example, as explained by one interviewee in a study published in 2005 many of those from East Tyrone went to Monaghan. Those from Belfast and South Armagh went to Dundalk, those from Derry and Fermanagh went to Buncrana or Bundoran in Donegal. Some 10,265 of the 22,390 born in the North who were living on the other side of the border in 2002 were in Donegal suggesting that the greatest displacement occurred from Derry. [60] Others emigrated from the North to Britain and the United States or were displaced to another part of the six counties.

None of those who moved south of the border had to apply for refugee status. They were however forced migrants and displaced persons, terms that have only come to be widely used in recent decades. Some moved to the Republic as a result of being made homeless due to the conflict or because they felt intimidated. Some had been victims of conflict-related trauma, violence or threats of violence whether in the neighbourhoods they lived on or in their places of employment. Some also feared arrest and imprisonment without trial after the introduction of internment in August 1971.

The first two refugee camps in the Republic were established in Gormanston in County Meath and in Finner in Donegal, the model being the response to Hungarian refugees in 1956. Army camps were designated as refugee centres under the responsibility of the Minister of Defence rather than local government. In the second week of August 1971 some 2,825 northern refugees were processed through the Gormanstown camp. A further 2,714 were accommodated elsewhere. 600 were housed at the Garda training centre at Templemore in County Tipperary. Additional refugee centres were established in army barracks at Kilworth, Coolmoney, Kildare, Kilkenny, Waterford and Tralee. The Archbishop of Dublin, John Charles McQuaid announced that accommodation would be provided for 1,600 refugees in 8 convents and at other Church properties. Numbers peaked in late 1971 and some of those who fled to the Republic returned subsequently to the North. However, many did not.[61] Conditions were often poor. One interviewee in a study of Northerners who settled in Drogheda recalled that the army huts in which families were accommodated were like garden sheds: 'No kitchen, no bathroom, the toilets were public toilets as were the shower faculties on the campsite.'[62]

From 1972 responsibility for the refugees shifted to local government. According to a 1973 government memorandum approximately 9,800 refugees were handled during the months of July and August in 1972. The memo differentiated those who arrived between 1969 and 1971, who came due to fears about their personal safety, from later arrivals, some of whom were viewed as holidaymakers or, less pejoratively, as people seeking temporary respite from the unnerving atmosphere of the North. The memo complained that refugees 'are not always just frightened people who are thankful for the assistance being given to them. Some of them can be very demanding and ungrateful, even obstreperous and fractious.' The memo also noted a policy that all of Northern Irish refugees should be accepted without question.[63]

VIETNAMESE

After the fall of Saigon in 1975, refugees left southern Vietnam in large numbers for the decade ahead. Almost half a million fled in 1979 alone, and many by sea. That year, the Irish government agreed to accept 212 of the so-called Vietnamese 'boat people' who had reached UN refugee camps. A significant majority of those who came to Ireland had little formal education, and in some cases were illiterate in the languages they spoke.[64] One hundred and nine came from camps in Hong Kong, and 103 from ones in Malaysia.

Tuyan Pham, one of the initial group of 212, was 14 years old in 1979. He arrived with two of his uncles, and the family of one of these. They had lived in a village about 100 kilometres from Saigon. During the Vietnam War, a bomb killed about 27 children from his village on their way to school. He had happened to be late for school that morning, and was unharmed. The extended family escaped from Vietnam by boat to Malaysia as part of a large exodus of refugees. One of his uncles organised the boat in which Pham's relatives set out to sea. Their boat was damaged by a storm and was boarded by Thai pirates; the engine failed, and they had to bail water out of the boat by hand to prevent it from sinking. After drifting for three days, they transferred onto an American oil rig, from which they were taken ashore by the Malaysian navy. In Malaysia, they were crowded into in a football stadium with other refugees, where they remained for five months, from May to October 1979. During this time they feared being taken from the camp and being put out to sea again, which they believed happened to some other refugees before the UNHCR took control of the camp.

Quang Nguyen, a former member of the South Vietnamese army, described being imprisoned for two years in a re-education camp where many fellow prisoners were beaten to death. Eighteen members of the Nguyen family left Vietnam. One of his daughters, who missed the rendezvous at a pre-arranged departure spot on the coast, was never heard from again. After four days drifting at sea, the group were picked up by a passing steamer and paid to be taken to Malaysia. After spending three months in a refugee camp, the family was put on a plane to Ireland.[65]

The Department of Defence initially arranged for the refugees to be placed in two reception centres run by the Irish Red Cross, one in Blanchardstown at the James Connolly Memorial Hospital, and the other in Swords. Like the Hungarians, their accommodation and settlement was largely funded by church charities. A Vietnamese Refugee Resettlement Committee was established. The view of representatives of NGOs as well as government officials on the committee was that families should be settled in different places around the country to encourage them to assimilate as quickly as possible.[66]

However, just two out the 212 refugees spoke English with any degree of fluency. The refugees had received some English-language tuition from untrained volunteers at the Blanchardstown and Swords centres. Once they were dispersed, this voluntary tuition stopped. It took until 1982 for the Department of Education to organise a pilot scheme to teach them English as a second language (ESL), and some of the refugees had to wait another six years to gain access to the scheme.[67]

By June 1980 various families had been accommodated around the Dublin area in houses and institutions owned by Catholic religious orders: a family of five was placed in a house owned by the Daughters of Charity in Tallaght; another family of eight were sent to a convent of the same order in Blackrock; two families were placed in Goldenbridge, the site of a former industrial school run by the Sisters of Mercy. Others families were assigned temporary accommodation in Tralee in County Kerry; in Midletown, County Cork; in Cork City; Sligo; and in Drogheda. Again, this was mostly provided by Catholic religious orders. Thereafter, many of the families housed temporarily in the Dublin area were relocated to smaller Irish towns, in the hope of better local integration.[68]

By 1982 the voluntary apparatus that supported the refugees began to fall apart. Many of the problems – a lack of expertise in dealing with refugees, simplistic views about how these might be assimilated, ad hoc arrangements that left the work up to whoever in the voluntary sector came forward – recalled responses to the Hungarians. So too did the shift from an initial enthusiasm to a sense of disappointment amongst officials charged with co-ordinating the settlement process. Something of a mood of indignation or consternation – a sense of being let down by the refugees – found expression in 1982 when the Vietnamese began to move back to Dublin of their own accord. Concerns expressed about the influence 'sinister elders' and family leaders among the Vietnamese also echoed those expressed by volunteers working with the Hungarians. An unpublished Irish Episcopal Commission for Emigrants (IECE) report in September 1982 described how, amongst those who had worked to settle the Vietnamese around the country, 'faces were dyed red with anger and tinged with embarrassment' because the refugees had rejected the arrangements made for them.[69] It seems that from the outset, some of those who worked with the refugees felt threatened whenever their charges exercised a bit of autonomy. Interviews with Vietnamese recorded by Frieda McGovern recalled, for example, an incident when all the refugees at the Blanchardstown were punished by the withdrawal of their 'pocket money' are a result of an incident involving a few in the group. The pocket money they received as their only personal income was just that, money to buy toiletries, stamps and cigarettes and so on. As in the case of the Hungarians, the emergence of 'leaders' amongst the Vietnamese caused consternation amongst those in charge of the reception programme. An Irish Red Cross report cited by McGovern said that these leaders 'tried to exercise a certain control of their own people' and to promote a 'resentment of authority'; the report referred to the 'devious methods' of leaders amongst the refugees.[70]

Many of the Vietnamese in the reception centre had been traumatised. Some of the women had been raped on the escape boats, and a few had witnessed their husbands being killed. Some of the men, according to Quang Nguyen in a 1987 interview, drank heavily in Ireland and gambled all the time. The initial period in the Swords reception centre was remembered by at least some of the refugees as a difficult time during which relationships with their Irish hosts was often poor. It seems that relationships between the refugees and those placed in charge of them had become tense very early on. Many of the refugees became unhappy during the initial reception-centre phase.[71] One Vietnamese recalled that she hated Blanchardstown and felt like she was treated as a prisoner. Various accounts suggest that an authoritarian atmosphere prevailed.[72] The Vietnamese, like the Hungarians before them and many refugees since, disliked being institutionalised.

After six months, Nguyen family was sent to live in Tralee, County Kerry. There was no hope of getting employment there because none of the family spoke English and, in any case, unemployment was high in the area. During the second half of 1982 Vietnamese families residing in Tralee, Tuam and elsewhere left their accommodation and moved to Dublin. By the late 1980s, most of the Vietnamese were living in local authority estates on the outskirts of Dublin City in places like Coolock, Tallaght, and Clondalkin, all of which had high levels of unemployment. In Dublin a number of the Vietnamese set up 'Chinese' takeaway food businesses but, according to Quang Van Vu, the amount of money that could be earned was no more than what the family had received in social welfare payments.[73]

Many were pushed into takeaway work by the absence of other employment opportunities, and some were still unemployed years after coming to Ireland. Many were comparatively poor for a long time. A 1987 feature article in *Magill* that contained some of the interviews drawn on here describes families with few possessions and houses that were barely furnished. Those who set up take-away businesses encountered many obstacles from officials responsible for enforcing planning and health legislation. Some of the Vietnamese set up takeaways in their homes or in vans. They had, in a number of cases, to pay protection money to Irish criminal gangs. In a 1987 interview Quang Van Vu described the experiences of relatives who had settled in the UK and the US as broadly similar. All, he claimed, would return to Vietnam if it were safe to do so.[74]

But this was not to be. Whilst a small number moved on, mostly to the UK or the US, just one of the original 212 refugees had returned to Vietnam by the end of the century. By 2000, due to births and family reunification, the community rose in size to 823 people.[75] Between 1979 and 1987 some 89 children were born. Some were given Western names like Erin, Kim, Tiffany or Vincent, whereas their older Vietnamese-born siblings retained more traditional ones such as Tuyen, Tuyet or Phuong. Some grew up not being able to speak Vietnamese.[76]

Most of the refugees who arrived in 1979 were eventually able to bring some family members to Ireland. For example, a number of family members subsequently joined Tuyan Pham's family in Ireland, including Pham's parents, uncles, aunts and maternal and paternal grandparents. For some, the application process for family reunification took ten years. Pham secured permission to bring his parents over five years after his arrival, by which point he was 19 years of age. When an application was initially submitted on his behalf, the response was that permission could not be granted because he was too young to support them.

In Vietnam, Tuyan Pham had dropped out of school in 1976 because, as the oldest son, he needed to work to help support his family. He returned to school in Ireland only after he arrived in 1979, where he attended a Christian Brothers primary school. There, he was the only Vietnamese and was much older than the other pupils. He received some one-on-one English language tuition in primary school, and subsequently moved on to secondary school, but quit in 1986 without taking his Leaving Certificate exams. He enrolled in a computer course, after which he worked for three years in Dún Laoghaire for an electronics company. In 1990 he joined UNHCR to work as a translator in refugee camps in Hong Kong, and he returned home to Ireland five years later.[77] Other, younger former refugees and second-generation Vietnamese completed secondary level school and attended university with the aim of having professional careers in areas such as science, information technology and accounting, having being encouraged to do so by their parents. Others have continued to have little choice but to work in family-run Chinese food businesses.[78]

BOSNIANS AND KOSOVARS

In July 1992 the Irish State agreed to admit a group of Bosnian programme refugees from former-Yugoslavia where the war had displaced some three million people. The 178 Bosnians who arrived in September 1992 were the first group of refugees to benefit from a reception and resettlement programme organised and funded by the state[79]. Some of the groups involved in the reception of Vietnamese had campaigned for the establishment of a suitable body to coordinate any future groups of refugees.[80] In 1991 a Refugee Agency was established and funded by the government to co-ordinate the admission, reception, and resettlement of any future groups of refugees. Some lessons from the perceived failures of the Hungarian and Vietnamese reception programmes were taken on board. The crude authoritarianism experienced by the Hungarians and Vietnamese was avoided. No forced dispersals of the kind that was rejected by the Vietnamese were proposed. There was no presumption that splitting up refugee groups and scattering them around the country would result in their successful assimilation. Deliberate efforts were made to settle the Bosnians in clusters in the Greater Dublin area. Family reunification issues were addressed without the decade-long-or-more delays experienced by some of the Vietnamese. By 2008 there were around 1,750 Bosnians in the country including 121 Irish-born children.[81]

As in the case of the Vietnamese the Bosnian refugees were initially accommodated in a reception centre, in this case a converted hostel for nurses in Cherry Orchard in West Dublin. Efforts the respond to this group were better organised and more thought-through than previous ones. English language classes were organised, counselling services were provided, a resettlement programme was drawn up aimed at avoiding he mistakes of the past and a Bosnian Community Development Project was set up. Initially this was run by a committee of officials from government departments and the Refugee Agency. What was optimistically described as a 'comprehensive social, cultural and educational programme' was provided to assist the refugees to familiarise themselves with day-to-day life in Ireland and learn how to access banking and social welfare services.[82]

Most of the Bosnians were resettled within the greater Dublin area. Small clusters of families were placed in proximity to one another although, in practice, the refugees did not have a choice as to where they were placed or in which cluster. Almost half (47 per cent) settled permanently in Dublin 15 in areas such as Blanchardstown, Castleknock, Mulhuddart and Ongar. Others settled in Swords (10 per cent) and Tallaght (19 per cent), and a small number came to live in the inner city (16 per cent). Less than ten per cent settled outside of the greater Dublin area. According a 2005 Bosnian Community Development Project report, the Bosnian community in Ireland was a mixed group consisting of Bosnian Muslims (75 per cent), Bosnian Croats (12 per cent), Bosnian Serbs (8 per cent) with the remaining 5 per cent included those in mixed marriages.[83]

Regardless, Bosnian refugees seem to have been treated as a homogenous group and attempts were made to foster community development on this basis. The remit of the Bosnian Community Development Project was to provide a cultural space, promote integration and to help the Bosnians access public services. Yet, according to one Bosnian who did doctoral research on Bosnian refugees in Ireland, these never became a single community as such.[84] Bosnia had already been a very diverse place before the war that split Yugoslavia on the basis of religious and ethnic lines; one-third of the population was Orthodox Christian, one-sixth Catholic, and the largest population at just under half the population was Muslim, and as viewed as being indigenous to Bosnia. Some of the Muslims were secular, while others devout. In addition, there were Jewish, German, Hungarian and Roma minorities amongst the pre-war population. The Bosnians who came to Ireland from 1992 reflected this diversity. According to a 1998 survey by the Refugee Agency, 37 per cent of them identified as Bosnian, 39 per cent as Muslim and 18 per cent as Bosnian Muslims, that is, as secular European Muslims.[85] The remaining 6 per cent identified as members of various other ethnic groups.[86]

The main problem experienced by the Bosnians was difficulty in finding employment. Like the Vietnamese, few of the Bosnians spoke English. Unlike many of the Vietnamese, however, the Bosnians did not pursue self-employment. Despite their differences, both groups did broadly come to resemble in microcosm economically marginal immigrant communities of the kind found in other countries. A 1999 Refugee Agency report described many of the Bosnians as dependent on social welfare payments and rent allowances, as they were only able to access low-paying jobs and were reluctant to do so; taking on such employment meant forfeiting rent allowances and medical cards, which would leave them worse off. This, at least, was the rational for a programme organised by the Refugee Council to move some of the Bosnians out of the private rented sector and into social housing. The other big problem was the persistence of a language barrier to employment.[87]

In 1999 the Irish State agreed to participate in the UNHCR temporary protection programme for Kosovars who had fled to refugee camps in Macedonia. The group admitted to Ireland was larger than any previous group of programme refugees. Even though it was envisaged that most Kosovars would not settle in Ireland, the reception programme put in place by the Refugee Agency was far superior to those for any previous group. Efforts were made to learn from mistakes made with earlier groups. The approach was, in several respects, more like the response to Northern Ireland Catholics who fled south in 1969, than to previous responses to programme refugees.

The Kosovars were granted a 'leave to remain' status, which was accompanied by a right to work and entitlements to training and support. The Refugee Agency executed an effective regional reception programme that would avoid the need to resettle refugees after a period in an initial reception facility. Efforts were made to learn from the shortcomings of the reception centres set up in Dublin for both the Vietnamese and Hungarians. The aim was to encourage self-sufficiency amongst the refugees from the outset. Ten areas in Kerry, Cork, Waterford, Kildare and Wicklow were designated as sites for the settlement of clusters of refugees in an attempt to avoid the failings of the wider Vietnamese dispersal programme. Agency officials visited local communities in advance to pave the way for the refugees, setting up, in effect, structures within host communities to assist integration. They co-ordinated the efforts of local groups, schools and health services. A number of Albanian-speaking asylum seekers who were already in the country were given leave to remain and recruited to work as interpreters.[88] Members of the Bosnian Community Development Project also visited the ten reception centres soon after these were set up and gave advice on how these should be run.

Between May and June 1999, 1,032 Kosovar refugees arrived in Ireland. They were provided with English language classes, given immediate access to social welfare, an immediate right to work and access to employment training. Not everything went smoothly. Some refugees remained in some reception centres for a year or two although none were compelled to do so. Many found it difficult to find employment. The emphasis from the outset was to facilitate the return of the refugees to Kosovo. From September 1999 'look and see' flights were paid for, to enable Kosovars to decide if it was safe for them to return. Those who decided to return received a repatriation grant. In 2000, believing it was safe to return home, most of the refugees accepted repatriation grants of £5,000 per adult and £2,000 per child. Of the 1,032, just 132 decided to remain in Ireland, and they became entitled to apply for Irish citizenship.

Reception centres in Waterford and Tralee stayed open for Kosovars who remained in Ireland. Very few of those who remained in Waterford had managed to find employment. By contrast, those who had been placed in Millstreet, County Cork, had all found work, but all of these had chosen to return to Kosovo. Many of those who remained in Ireland, according to Department of Justice criticisms of the Refugee Agency settlement programme, were the ones who had become the most institutionalised by being allowed to stay in reception centres for longer.[89]

Yet the analysis that keeping refugees in institutional settings for long periods impeded their integration was a lesson that the Department of Justice itself ignored when, soon after, the Refugee Agency was shut down in 2000 and all responsibility for refugees and asylum seekers came under its control. A new system of 'direct provision', introduced in response to a perceived asylum-seeker crisis, required asylum seekers, who by then significantly outnumbered other categories of refugee, to live – often for several years – in privately run centres. These offered few of the supports made available to earlier groups of refugees and repeated many of the mistakes made in how these were run.

Some of the challenges of integrating groups of refugees had come to be reasonably well understood by the Refugee Agency. Housing, education, English-language training and access to employment came to be recognised as integral to the integration process. However, pretty much all of this experience was to be cast aside when, from the late 1990s, the arrival of growing numbers of asylum seekers became politicised. Whilst the Republic became open to large-scale immigration, responses to refugees have remained ungenerous.

TEN

AFRICANS

African immigrants in Ireland have come to constitute more than one per cent of the population of the Republic of Ireland. Since 2011 a large proportion of these have become Irish citizens. Many arrived in Ireland as asylum seekers from the late-1990s onwards with the greatest numbers coming from English-speaking parts of Nigeria. Census data identified 8,969 Nigerians in 2002, 16,300 by 2006, and 17,672 by 2011.[1] By 2005 there were at least 4.6 million recorded Africans living in the European Union, a figure that did not include undocumented persons.[2] The push factors that influenced their migration to Europe include dysfunctional social conditions, political crises, economic crises, cultural conflicts and wars.[3] Many of those who managed to enter Europe have been amongst the comparatively better off. Many millions more have languished as displaced persons in refugee camps in neighbouring African countries. A key pull factor has been the huge gap between European and African wealth. Europe also appeared, to many, to be a place of greater safety.

Often what African migrants sought, beyond earnings to send home as remittances or to secure for themselves a better standard of living, was the right to free movement conferred by secure residency status; one Nigerian mother of an Irish-born child said when interviewed, 'I want my children to have a future, free movement.'[4] Individual migrations, according to the study that interviewed her, were often undertaken on behalf of wider family groups, their trip subsidised by family in the expectation of remittances to be sent back home such that other family members might follow in their footsteps.[5] Such relationships between migrants and their families recall those of Irish women and men who emigrated to United States or Australia. However, many Africans who sought to settle in Ireland and reunify their families there had to contend with greater restrictions than those experienced by Irish emigrants abroad then and now.

Many of those who came to Ireland, whether on student visas, with work permits, or as asylum seekers, were part of a brain-drain of well-educated women and men from their home countries. More than a third of Africans with higher education have emigrated. Those who left Nigeria during the early twenty-first century included some 20,000 doctors.[6] By 2006, the Republic of Ireland had a sub-Saharan African population of 53,318, of which Nigerians were the largest group. 41 per cent of the 16,667 Nigerians living in Ireland in 2006 were educated to degree level or equivalent, making them better educated on average than European immigrants and better educated than the Irish population.[7]

Many European countries acquired immigrant workers from their former colonies. Ireland of course had no empire, but for many decades Irish religious orders ran missions in Nigeria and other parts of Africa. Irish male religious served across Africa as priests and bishops, and nuns ran schools and hospitals, and religious orders such as the Holy Ghost Fathers also trained African clergy in seminaries in Ireland. Some Africans were drawn to Ireland by their experiences of Irish missionaries. Theo Ejorh, a Nigerian asylum seeker, who subsequently completed a doctorate in sociology, recalled the 'mirthful stories' told to him as a child by Father O'Leary, the Irish priest in his village, about the congeniality of the Irish, their kind-heartedness and warmth.'[8]

During the 1960s two of Nigeria's three Catholic archbishops were Irish, as were more than 500 of the 800 priests in that country. Irish clergy ran 2,419 primary schools in Nigeria catering for 561,318 pupils – twice as many as in the rest of Africa combined – and 47 hospitals. Ireland's sole embassy in Africa was in Lagos. Irish missionaries were especially concentrated in predominantly Catholic Igbo areas of Nigeria, and many Irish clergy sided with the Igbo when Biafra seceded from Nigeria in 1967. The refugee crisis and famine resulting from the post-1967 war prompted the foundation of the Irish aid agency Concern. The Catholic Church in Ireland and Irish newspapers ran high-profile fundraising campaigns for famine relief. During the war, Fr Tony Byrne, an Irish Holy Ghost Father, directed an airlift of supplies into Biafra, with up to 50 flights per night that braved anti-aircraft fire and used an improvised runway on a motorway.[9] The Holy Ghost Fathers were accused of shipping weapons by air into Biafra by a Nigerian diplomat, who claimed that the Irish Minister of External Affairs Frank Aiken had confirmed the involvement of Irish priests in gun-running.[10] Aiken denied having done so – Irish foreign policy supported the legitimacy of the Nigerian state and opposed the secession of Biafra – but correspondence from Irish diplomats since made public reported that an aircraft had been chartered for this purpose by Irish clergy.[11]

In response to this diplomatic incident Robert Collis, the paediatrician who had brought some Jewish refugee children to Ireland and subsequently worked as a professor of child health in Lagos, was persuaded by Aiken to write a series of pro-federalist articles for the *Irish Times*.[12] Collis criticised another series of *Irish Times* articles by David Nolan, an Irish doctor who made the case for an independent Biafra.[13] *Realpolitik* aside, Aiken's views on Nigeria were probably influenced by his son, Frank Jr., an engineer who was employed building churches in eastern Nigeria, whom Aiken visited there in 1964.[14] Whilst many Irish missionaries and aid workers sided with the Igbo, the Irish government did not. Ireland had many links to Nigeria during the early 1960s, and the relationship was widely discussed and debated in the Irish media and in the Dáil.[15]

STUDENTS, MIXED-RACE CHILDREN AND EARLY ARRIVALS

On 20 August 1964 the *Irish Times* reported that a Nigerian judge Mr L. Oluodun Fadipe had compiled a list of 25 attacks on 'coloured students' in Dublin, some of which had resulted in serious injury. One of those who were attacked was Fadipe's own son, a fourth-year medical student at the Royal College of Surgeons, who was recovering in a hospital in London. The article stated that there were some 300 Nigerians studying in the city, and that attacks on three of these had been formally reported. The Department of Justice was reported as wishing to 'keep the matter in its proper perspective'. The official view was that any incidents that had occurred 'were the result of hooliganism rather than racial bitterness'.[16] An article published the following day listed 25 alleged incidents presented by Judge Fadipe (compiled by two Trinity College overseas students), ten of which were assaults on Nigerians. These included an attack on 9 November 1963 in which Patrick Udenze, a Nigerian student at University College Dublin (UCD) lost an eye due to his injuries; an attack on an Indian woman doctor; assaults on an 'Indian girl' who was with an 'Irish boy', both of whom were students at Trinity; and several incidents in which Nigerian students were badly beaten outside dancehalls. Fifteen of the 25 incidents took place in the vicinity of Camden Street where, according to the Irish ambassador in Lagos, 'no right-thinking student should be walking late at night'.[17]

The next day the *Irish Times* reported that following a meeting with the Nigerian Ambassador to Ireland, the Minister for External Affairs, Frank Aiken, issued a strongly worded statement expressing grave concern at 'the accusations of racial prejudice against the Irish people and against the Irish police in particular, on the strength of a few isolated attacks on overseas students.' According to the Minister's statement there were some 1,200 foreign students in Ireland, and he wished to assure their parents that they would enjoy the full protection of the authorities from 'any manifestations in Ireland of the wave of youthful rowdyism which had recently become prevalent in the large industrial cities in the world.'[18] The article failed to mention that Dublin was not such an industrial city. The same edition of the *Irish Times* published a piece on how racism affected the self-esteem of black children in the United States and claimed that this explained, in part, their apathy and the inability of American negroes to escape poverty. What such sterotypes to do with the experiences of middle-class black African university students in Ireland was not addressed.[19] Two 19-year-old men were later arrested for the attack on Charles Fadipe, but the Attorney General determined that there was insufficient evidence to proceed with the charges.[20]

An *Irish Times* editorial described the Nigerian press coverage of the assaults as unbalanced, and Ireland as broadly welcoming to African and Asian students. It concluded that little could be done to make awkward landladies (a tacit admission of housing discrimination against such students) or the population in general treat coloured students with respect except through education and Christian charity. The editorial also inferred that the attacks had something to do with 'rows over girls'.[21] Another article published a week later quoted Vincent Browne, the vice-president of UCD's student union, as saying that a large majority of cases had not occurred in dancehalls, and had not involved women.[22]

Christine Buckley was born in Dublin in 1946, the daughter of a 31-year-old married woman and a single, 20-year-old Nigerian medical student. As a three-week old baby she was given up for fostering, and in 1950, at the age of four, she was sent to Goldenbridge, an orphanage run by the Sisters of Mercy. She came to prominence in 1996 when RTÉ broadcast *Dear Daughter,* a television documentary directed by Louis Lentin about the physical and emotional abuse experienced by Christine and other children at the orphanage. Her activism and the attention garnered by *Dear Daughter,* the title taken from the opening words of a letter from her father after she traced him, were seminal in bringing to light the institutional abuse of children in care in Ireland more generally, and of disavowed 'mixed-race Irish' children given up for adoption who experienced institutional abuse in particular.

After she left school, Christine Buckley trained as a nurse, and during the 1980s, traced her biological parents. Her father, William West, visited Ireland in 1992 and they appeared together on *The Late Late Show.* She campaigned for the establishment of the Commission to Inquire into Child Abuse and the Residential Institutions Redress Board. She stood as an independent candidate in the 1997 Dáil elections. In 1999 she founded a support centre for former residents of industrial schools.[23] In her autobiography, she described a regime in which children were dehumanised – they were referred to by a number rather than by their names (her given number was 89) – and received sadistic punishments. On one occasion a nun poured boiling water on her leg; on another, she received a beating so severe she required more than 80 stitches. In addition to the now well-documented abuse suffered by children in such homes, she and others experienced further abuse because of the colour of her skin.

Somewhat similarly, the soccer star Paul McGrath's mother Betty met Paul's father Festis, a Nigerian medical student at a student's dance in Dublin in 1959. Within a month she was pregnant and when she told her boyfriend he broke off his relationship with her. She travelled to London where she worked as a housekeeper. She gave birth to her son in a home run by nuns in Acton, where most of the other 'girls' there were also Irish. The nuns insisted that Paul be put up for adoption. Betty McGrath eventually agreed to place Paul in foster care in Dublin and, unlike most of the parents of such African-Irish babies, was able to remain in contact with him.[24]

Rosemary Adaser was one of at least 70 African-Irish children given up for adoption in Ireland during the 1950s and 1960s. Her mother worked as a telephonist in the Rotunda Maternity Hospital in Dublin, and her father was a Ghanaian doctor who had also worked there. As an infant she was placed in a mother-and-baby home, and like other African Irish babies, she was never offered up for adoption. Like Christine Buckley, she described experiences of racist abuse from those supposed to care for her, and from other children. She recalled pots of urine and excrement being emptied on her by other children, being made unblock toilets with her bare hands because her skin was black already, and being 'always', she recalled, 'the last child to bathe in the same bath water preceded by thirty other girls for fear my black skin would contaminate the white girls'. She was subjected to sexual abuse by other girls and by a nun. Nuns told her that no man would ever want her because she was black. At the age of 16 she became pregnant, and her baby was taken from her soon after he was born. She worked in Dublin as a telephonist for a few years, during which she continued to experience racism. She emigrated to England when she was 20.[25] During the 1980s she traced her mother and found out that she had a twin brother who was also abandoned.[26] Rosemary Adaser subsequently founded an organisation, the Association of Mixed-Race Irish (AMRI), which has campaigned for acknowledgement of the racism that children like her experienced in the Republic of Ireland by the Irish state.[27]

From the 1980s some Nigerians who had British visas travelled to Ireland to obtain visa extensions that allowed them to remain within the United Kingdom and Republic of Ireland common travel area. Some others came to Ireland from Britain and remained after their visas expired. These migrants were mostly of Yoruba origin, with low levels of education, but with enough resources to establish themselves for an initial short stay in Dublin. A small Nigerian business community, involved in exporting fish and other products, was also established,[28] and some Nigerian business owners already legally resident in other European countries joined this community when they moved to Ireland during the Celtic Tiger era. For example, one respondent interviewed by Julius Komolafe was a British citizen who had run a restaurant in south-east London before moving to Ireland. The Nigerian owner of an African shop on Parnell Street in Dublin that opened in 1997 had previously run a similar business in Greece.[29]

By the late-1990s, Africans had become a visible presence in the Parnell Street and Moore Street areas in Dublin's north inner city, which became the most prominent ethnically distinct locality in the city since the decline of Clanbrassil Street where there had been many Jewish shops and businesses. What was briefly referred to by the media as 'little Africa' – the name did not stick – became a focal point for Africans due to its proximity to the hostels in which asylum seekers were mostly placed before 2000; thereafter, they were dispersed by the state to reception centres around the country. A Nigerian businessman purchased several rundown properties and subsequently opened a record shop, a grocery shop that sold African foods, and three hair salons, one of which sold hair extensions. A few shebeens and social clubs catering mostly to Yoruba clientele operated out of the back rooms of African-owned shops, and African street vendors opened stalls alongside those run for generations by Dubliners on Moore Street.[30]

SEEKERS OF ASYLUM, OPPORTUNITY AND SECURITY

Abel Ugba arrived in Ireland in 1998 after having spent six years living in Germany. In Nigeria he had worked as a journalist. In 2000, with Chinedu Onyejelem, he co-founded *Metro Éireann*, a successful weekly newspaper aimed at immigrants. In 1999 Ugba published a novel based closely on the lives of fellow Africans he met in a number of European countries who were classified as asylum seekers or were undocumented. *Dear Mama* describes how Kwame flees the violence of his homeland, following the deaths of his father, his two brothers and his sister. Kwame pays a Nigerian trafficker to organise his journey to France on false papers. He moves on to Italy, then Austria and finally to Germany, where he finds shelter amongst other African migrants living desperate and chaotic lives in a series of extremely over-crowded apartments. Some of those he meets are involved in selling drugs and in prostitution because other forms of economic activity are shut off from them. Others sought to marry European women in the hope of securing their residency status. *Dear Mama* tells the stories of dozens of Africans who want not so much to live in one or another part of Europe but seek the freedom to choose where to live and to reunite with family members they were forced to leave behind.[31]

Some had been naive about the difficulties they would experience as asylum seekers, having being trafficked into Europe on false papers, and equipped with inadequate bogus stories of lives and persecutions in countries some had never visited and knew little about, turning up in court convinced that they would be disbelieved, yet unable to tell their real stories because they knew that revealing the convoluted journeys that got them into or across Europe would be used against them. Many of the men depicted in *Dear Mama* found themselves running to stand still year after year, engaging in scams to get by, existing for years in overcrowded hostels, allowed to work in Germany but unable to find employment.

Respondents interviewed in a study by Julius Komolafe of how and why undocumented Nigerians travelled to and settled in Ireland alluded to similar experiences to those described in *Dear Mama*.[32] Some others who claimed asylum in Ireland travelled there indirectly from West Africa to North African countries before paying traffickers to bring them across the Mediterranean to Spain. Like many other Africans seeking to live in Europe, they had no legal means of seeking residency status. The asylum process in Ireland, as elsewhere, became the focal point of their efforts to become legal denizens, in the absence of any other opportunity.[33] The perilous journeys made by such women and their families to Ireland were also very similar to those undertaken by migrants from Mexico into the United States where, instead of the risk of drowning in the Mediterranean, there was the danger of death in the desert.[34]

Many arrived in Ireland knowing that if they had an Irish-born child they would be granted leave to remain and a degree of security not available elsewhere in the European Union. For example, 'Mrs C' (interviewed by Komolafe in 2001) moved to Ireland from Germany six years after arriving there from Lagos where she lived as an illegal immigrant. She had her baby in Ireland, and because her child was entitled to Irish citizenship, she obtained Irish residency status.[35] Under the Dublin Convention, an agreement between EU member states, asylum seekers were required to claim asylum in the first EU country they entered. The fact that so many moved between European counties in part explains why such high percentages had their applications for asylum turned down in Ireland and elsewhere.

By the middle of 1998, each of the three maternity hospitals in Dublin, the Rotunda, the National Maternity Hospital and the Coombe Women's Hospital, reported dealing with between four and six pregnant refugees each week.[36] Many were Nigerian, and many had arrived in Ireland on their own in the later stages of pregnancy.[37] Amongst such women interviewed in another study undertaken in 1999, some where found to have children that they did not bring to Ireland.[38] Another study, which interviewed 51 African-born women who were pregnant or who had recently given birth to babies in

Dublin found that just over half of these also had children who were born in Africa. For some of these, Ireland was not a first- or even second-choice destination, but as one interviewee said, 'somewhere to go' if the United Kingdom and America refused you a visa. Some came to Ireland on student visas as fee-paying medical students had done for decades. Others joined family members who had come to Ireland on work visas; these family members included doctors, nurses and entrepreneurs. Some also arrived specifically to have their babies in Ireland. Some had paid bribes to corrupt officials in return for papers that allowed them to reach Ireland. Others paid traffickers and travelled to Ireland via a number of European countries. Six of the women had or were working towards a professional degree in areas including as pharmaceutical microbiology, business administration and social work. Nine were graduates with degrees in subjects including economics, microbiology, journalism and anthropology.[39]

A 2001 study of Nigerian immigrants in Ireland that also interviewed students at universities in Lagos, Ibadan, and Abeokuta, identified a pattern of middle-class chain migration. Many of those seeking to move to Celtic Tiger Ireland were young university graduates who had friends or relatives already there. One interview described a man helping his sister come to Ireland, in part to reduce the burden of sending home remittances of £150 per month, which halved on her arrival. As with all chain migrations, such remittances fostered the image of Ireland as a land of opportunity. To give some context, in 2001, Nigeria's GDP per capita stood at $350.30 compared to $28,051.80 in Ireland. According to Nigerian records, most of those who travelled directly to Ireland between 1996 and 2000 were Yoruba (rising from just eight persons in 1996 to 1,934 in 2000) Most of the rest were Igbo (rising from 5 in 1997 to 523 in 2000).[40]

Only a small percentage of applications for asylum in Ireland were granted. Of the 18,198 applications received between 1994 and 1999 only 920, just over five per cent, obtained refugee status. By 2010 Irish acceptance of asylum claims were the lowest in Fortress Europe at 1.3 per cent. This contrasted with 24 per cent for the United Kingdom, 46 per cent for the Netherlands and 70 per cent positive decisions on applications for asylum in Malta.[41] Those with Irish-born children were encouraged to withdraw their claims for asylum, which meant that, in practice, the percentage of asylum seekers allowed to remain in Ireland was much higher than the official figure. Those who took advantage of the right to residency of Irish-born children were merely navigating an immigration system that was otherwise closed to them. In 1996 142 families received leave to remain as the result of having an Irish-born child, as did 107 families the following year. No applications at all were processed in 1998 but in 1999 some 1,227 families with Irish-born children received leave to remain as did 909 families in

2000. 3,500 Nigerians claimed asylum in Ireland in 2001. A further 10,000 claimed asylum between 2001 and 2015.[42] In total the numbers seeking asylum rose from 39 in 1992 to 7,724 in 1999. There were 10,938 applications for asylum in 2000, 10,325 in 2001 and 11,634 in 2002 after which the numbers began to fall off.[43]

Many women with Irish-born children lived in rented, overcrowded accommodation with their babies. For example, maternity care research undertaken in Dublin 1999 found three women and four children sharing a room with a small bathroom attached. One of the women was eight months pregnant and the mother of an 18-month-old. The room contained three beds, but no cots for the children. In another case an African woman with a three-week-old baby and a toddler was found to be sharing a two-bedroom apartment with another couple and their child and frequently present groups of male visitors. She had become pregnant after having being raped in her own country. She was described by the researchers as exhausted and frightened.[44]

From 2000 on, most newly arrived asylum seekers were dispersed to reception centres that were, in essence, hostels and hotels leased for the purpose. Adults living in the direct provision received small cash allowances of €19.90 per week in addition to bed and board. Children received €9.60. Research by Irish Refugee Council documented considerable poverty and severe overcrowding. Most respondents felt it was necessary to buy extra food to supplement what was provided for themselves and their children in the hostels. Families were typically accommodated in just one hotel room with no cooking facilities. Single men often shared rooms. A 2001 study of asylum-seeker children interviewed a family from the Ivory Coast; soon, the family's six-month-old son died in an accident in the overcrowded room where they had been placed. The field notes of the interviewer described the room in the following terms:

> It is not a very big room, the two single beds are pushed together to make a double, I can't really see where a cot would have fit with any ease, but both said that this room was bigger than the one they had been in. Both were sitting on the bed when I entered the room, both the television and their little radio were on. I sat on a chair under the television, facing them, while they came and sat at the end of the bed. There were a number of boxes and suitcases around the walls of the room. The room was quite small. There was just enough space to walk around the beds. I was sitting in front of a dressing table with some food and other items on top. The kettle was on the floor plugged into an extension lead with four sockets on it.[45]

The inquest into the death of Soluman Dembele heard that the room in which the family lived measured just 13ft by 9ft. Soluman's mother had put on a kettle to boil water to prepare food for him. The kettle was placed on the floor in order to reach the only socket that was not blocked off by furniture. Soluman died from the burns he received when the kettle overturned.[46]

Very few of those who lived in 'direct provision' have published accounts of their experiences under their own names. One exception, Nogugo Mafu, fled Zimbabwe in 2002 with her six-year-old son after her husband, a political activist, was killed. She recalled her time as an asylum seeker in Killarney as 'alienating and dehumanising'. The system, as she described it, turned people into 'helpless institutionalised zombies':

> At these centres nearly every decision about their lives is made for them. This includes what they what they will eat and when they will eat it, where they will sleep. . . in short, someone else determines how they will live their lives. Needless to say that this creates in the asylum seeker feelings of helplessness and dependency, robbing them of their dignity which comes with being able to being able to make decisions regarding one's life.[47]

African asylum seekers came to live in the margins of a number of Irish towns in which direct provision centres were established, often remaining in the system for years whilst not being allowed to work. A study of the psychological health of some in Dublin and Ennis described problems of 'learned helplessness', anxiety, mental health problems and relationship breakdown.[48] Such problems came on top of the stresses of being institutionalised, not being allowed to work and prevented from accessing further education or employment training.

Knocknalisheen, the former army camp where the Hungarian refugees were placed in 1956, was re-opened as an asylum seeker reception centre. History repeated itself when in January 2007 more than 200 asylum seekers in the camp went on hunger strike for two days. The complaints that sparked the protest related to diet and poor accommodation, and had escalated because, according to a letter sent to the Department of Justice, management had 'bluntly refused any forum where these complaints could have been discussed and tackled'.[49]

Similar complaints have emerged in virtually all studies of and reports on direct provision in Ireland, including the absence of autonomy, enforced dependency, and the boredom of day-to-day life without permission to work or access to education. Residents of the camp were housed in six blocks with as many as four people, including children, sharing the one room. Generally, asylum seekers lived in partitioned rooms, sharing a toilet and shower cubicle with one other family that is two one-parent families to a room with a partition between them. Two-parent families were allocated a double room only if they had more than two children. In such cases four or more persons shared the one room.[50] In other reception centres, women reported sexual harassment from male fellow-asylum-seekers and employees of the companies running the hostels in which they were put. A 2012 study found that the Department of Justice placed vulnerable women who had been victims of sex trafficking in hostels alongside male asylum seekers. In one case (in 2009) ten women were put alongside one hundred single male residents.[51]

Interviewees in a study of Somali refugees described living in direct provision hostels for periods of several years after making their way to Ireland. Most were Sunni Muslims. Between 1996 and 2007, some 1535 Somalis claimed asylum in Ireland, having arrived without the kind of UN programme (see Chapter 9) that brought the Vietnamese, Bosnians and Kosovars to Ireland. Like many other Africans in Ireland, many were trafficked across Europe and, in many cases, family members remained scattered across Europe and Africa. In Ireland, many spent several years living in direct provision hostels unable to seek employment or training. Between 1996 and 2007 some 698 Somalis were granted refugee status.[52]

Before 2004, asylum seekers who had Irish-born children were encouraged to abandon their claims for asylum in return for leave to remain. Until 2003, those with Irish-born babies typically received leave to remain; that year, a Supreme Court ruling determined that the constitutional right of the Irish-born applicant to the company and care of its parents within the State was not absolute and unqualified.[53] At the time, some 17,500 applications for residence from such parents were pending;[54] they had been granted temporary leave to remain only, and though their children born before 2004 were entitled to Irish citizenship, few had yet applied for this and received Irish passports.

The 2004 Citizenship Referendum was presented by Michael McDowell, the then-Minister Justice, as a response to African women entering Ireland to exploit a 'loophole' in the Irish constitution, the inference being that the right to Irish citizenship had never been intended for the children of asylum seekers. In essence, the Minister claimed that a crisis in maternity hospitals had had been precipitated by the exploitation by 'non-national' mothers of 'loopholes' in the constitution that allowed them to claim citizenship for their Irish-born children.[55] McDowell was widely criticised because he claimed that African women were exploiting the country's hard-pressed health services by coming to Ireland to have their babies. Yet some African migrants did come to Ireland because they hoped to obtain secure residency status through the birth of their children, because residency was being denied them elsewhere in Europe. The Masters of the Rotunda and the Coombe, two maternity hospitals in Dublin, sought to distance themselves from claims repeated on a number of occasions by McDowell 'that they had pleaded with him to deal with the problem' arguing that a lack of funding for maternity services should not be used to introduce a Referendum.[56]

Shortly before the 2004 Referendum the Department of Justice ceased processing applications for residency status from migrants with Irish-born children, which left thousands of families in a precarious position. Between 2003 and 2005, the Minister of Justice was unwilling to give assurances that families with Irish-born children would not be deported when their temporary leave to remain expired. During this period, some 341 persons were deported, including at least 20 children who were Irish citizens who, the Minister claimed, were voluntarily taken out of Ireland by their deported parents.[57]

In 2005, following a campaign by CADIC (Coalition Against the Deportation of Irish Children), temporary permission to remain in Ireland under what was called the Irish Born Child (IBC/05) scheme was granted to this group: 17,917 applications were received. Of these, more than 93 per cent were granted leave to remain. Some 59 per cent of IBC/05 applicants were Nigerian. Renewed permissions to remain were further extended in 2007, and again in 2010. Long-term residents had to reapply for residency again in 2007. With each application, they were required to present themselves with their Irish-born children to an Immigration Office or Garda Station and to provide evidence of continuous residency with their child in Ireland. They were also required to sign a statement agreeing that renewal of permission to remain in the State did not confer any right to family reunification.[58] As result of the IBC schemes, most Africans who had arrived as asylum seekers became eligible over time to apply for Irish citizenship. Anyone with five years' 'reckonable residence' could apply, namely, a period that did not include periods of irregular immigration status or time spent in the asylum process.

However, a high percentage of this group had their citizenship applications refused. The Irish Citizenship Nationality Act (1956) granted the Minister of Justice 'absolute discretion' in determining all applications for Irish citizenship. According to the Immigrant Council of Ireland, some 47 per cent of applications were refused in 2009. By comparison, equivalent refusal rates for citizenship by naturalisation in other countries were less than 9 per cent in the United Kingdom and Australia, and 3 per cent in Canada.[59] It appeared that Ministerial discretion was being exercised to refuse large numbers of citizenship applications at a time when former asylum seekers accounted for most of these and when Nigerian Africans were the largest group. Whilst these discretionary criteria were not formally set down some were alluded to on government websites. Other criteria being used only became evident when some applicants sought judicial reviews of their cases. These included a definition of being 'of good character' that excluded applicants who had ever become known to the Gardaí. Other applicants were turned down because they had, at some stage, claimed unemployment benefits.[60]

From 2011, a change in government and policy proved more willing to support naturalisation of immigrants from non-European countries. The turn-down rate dropped from 47 per cent to less than 3 per cent of applicants. 24,263 (97.6 per cent) out of a total of 29,412 applications for naturalisation considered in 2013 were granted. Alan Shatter, the Minister of Justice, overturning barriers to citizenship received the *Africa World* newspaper's man of the year award for 2012. 63,900 applications for naturalisation were approved between 1 January 2009 and 31 May 2013, most of these following the 2011 change of government.[61] 1,204 Nigerians became Irish citizens in 2011, 5,702 more in 2012 and a further 5,792 in 2013. More than 11,000 Nigerians became Irish citizens between 2013 and 2015.[62]. Naturalisation ceremonies filled with positive rhetoric were introduced, typically presided over by the Taoiseach or a senior government minister, all of which stood in marked contrast to what had gone before.[63] For example, in a 2012 address to some 2,250 new Irish citizens at a ceremony in Dublin, Taoiseach Enda Kenny said, 'Since you arrived on these shores, you have enriched your communities, enhanced your workplaces, bringing new light, new depth, a new sense of imagining, to what it means to be a citizen of Ireland in the 21st century.'[64]

AFRICAN IRISH

Early African settlement in north inner-city Dublin owed much to the location of hostels where asylum seekers were initially placed in the Parnell Street area. From 2000, however, newly arrived asylum seekers were dispersed around the country, and so, African communities came to be established in a number of such towns. Like Irish emigrants in Britain, North America and Australia, wherever Africans settled in Ireland churches became established. Some Igbo joined Catholic congregations wherever they settled. Many other Nigerians were Pentecostal Christians and by 2001, more than 40 Pentecostal congregations were established in the Greater Dublin Area.[65] Outside of Dublin, branches of the Redeemed Christian Church of God, the largest and the most widespread African-led Pentecostal church in Ireland, were set up in Athy, Castlebar, Cavan, Celbridge, Ennis, Kildare, Letterkenny, Leixlip, Limerick, Longford, Mullingar, Naas, Portlaoise, Shannon, Tralee, Tuam and many other places. By 2007 there were about 40 congregations around the country.[66] Other prominent African-led Pentecostal churches include the Mountain of Fire and Miracles Ministry (MFMM), the Christ Apostolic Church (CAC), the Gospel Faith Mission International (GFM), Christ Co-Workers in Mission (CCM), Hope and Glory Ministries (HGM) and Christ Ambassadors Ministries.

In *Shades of Belonging: African Pentecostals in Twenty-First Century Ireland*, Abel Ugba describes how congregations have offered considerable practical as well as spiritual support to members. To some extent, the themes of songs, prayers and sermons within Pentecostal congregations referred to concerns about of diaspora and exile. Pentecostal churches offered some members 'a place of refuge from the problems, hostilities and rejection' encountered in Irish society. Others viewed Pentecostalism more simply as a channel for finding solutions for problems in their day-to-day lives. Pentecostal services also gave particular expression to a 'health and wealth' Gospel focused on material conditions in Ireland with prayer requests and public worship sessions dominated by concerns about work and residence permits, employment and money worries. As put by Ugba, the future that congregations wished for in prayer and songs was a permanent and settled life in Ireland.[67]

Many of those who were members of such congregations had belonged to similar ones in Africa. According to Ugba, such churches were the only places in Irish society where members could experience 'the sense of self-fulfilment, importance and relevance they had experienced in their home countries'.[68] For all that many such African Evangelical Christians were drawn to Ireland to make better lives for themselves and their families, many also appeared to be alienated from the 'permissiveness and immoralities' of secular Irish society, as one of his interviewees Tokunbo Oluwa put it.[69] For parents like Mrs Oluwna, whose husbands had not yet arrived in Ireland, church membership offered practical, emotional and moral support. It exposed their children to conservative Christian values that appeared to be absent in the wider society. In a sense, devout African Pentecostalists in twenty-first century Ireland lived in what Ugba calls 'a parallel moral and social universe'.[70]

Tokunbo Oluwa's story is a variation of several included earlier in this chapter. Like some of those who migrated directly from Nigeria, she was well-educated and comparatively well-off. Before she first came to Ireland she worked as a lawyer and her husband was an architect. She came to Ireland when she became pregnant with her youngest child. After her baby was born she returned to Nigeria with and then subsequently returned to live in Drogheda with all five of her children. Although she was not keen to make this move – she had a successful legal career was on track for an appointment as a magistrate – her husband argued that their children would receive a better education in Ireland. She was financially supported by her husband, who remained in Nigeria. She had been an ordained minister in the Redeemed Christian Church of God, and she received financial help from them. She set up a branch of the Redeem in Drogheda where she became a pastor. Soon her church had a congregation of 160 'close-knit' worshippers. She provided free legal advice to members of her congregation and retook her legal exams in order to be able to practice law in Ireland. When her husband joined her in Ireland, he also took on a role in the church. [71] In some respects the journey taken by the Oluwa family was a lot like those of Quaker families assisted by congregations in Ireland to resettle in Pennsylvania during the later seventeenth century. Almost 80 per cent of Pentecostalists interviewed as part of Ugba's research had a third-level education. [72]

African communities became established in a number of towns like Drogheda where asylum seekers were placed in direct provision accommodation. The birth of Irish-born children, processes of chain migration and family reunification resulted in permanent, established African communities. By 1999 more than 30 babies were born to African mothers living in Ennis County Clare; all were recent arrivals to the town who had settled there shortly before the introduction of direct provision. The presence of an Irish Refugee Council office in the town (to serve nearby Shannon Airport) had drawn some asylum seekers there even before the formal introduction of a dispersal policy in 2000, [73] and from 2000 a direct provision hostel accommodating 67 single men operated. The 2006 census recorded 634 Africans as resident in Ennis. These amounted to 2.7 per cent of a population of 23, 101. Overall, there were about 1,000 Africans in the county. [74]

Research conducted in County Clare in the wake of the 2007 Knocklalisheen hunger strike found that former Somali and Sudanese asylum seekers to be far more marginalised than Nigerians. The latter appeared to be more successful at building connections with Irish neighbours – for example, with their children's school friends' parents – and with each other. The study portrayed Nigerian parents as 'very ambitious for their children'. Nigerians were described as usually fluent English speakers, often well-educated and as regular Church goers. [75]

In the Republic of Ireland voting rights in local government elections depended on residency rather than citizenship so most immigrants, including asylum seekers, were entitled to vote or stand for election. In 2004 Taiwo Matthew, a former asylum seeker, was elected as a Town Councillor in Ennis and served for one term. He had trained as a doctor in Nigeria. In Ennis he was a pastor in the Christ Faith Tabernacle.

In Portlaoise, Rotimi Adebari, another former asylum seeker, was also elected as a town councillor in 2004 and re-elected in 2009. Adebari was born into middle-class Nigerian Muslim family – his father had been an engineer – but converted to Christianity. He attended university and trained as a teacher. He had completed a degree in economics and political science whilst working as a teacher. In Ireland he became a self-employed diversity trainer. He became a member of the Laois Ethnic Minority Support Group and founder of another group, *Voices Across Cultures*. He joined his local residents' association and school management committee. He became a member of the board of the Irish National Organisation of the Unemployed (INOU), the Dublin AIDS Alliance and joined a number of community organisations. He credited his success, as do many public representatives, to community involvement.

Adebari served a term as mayor of Portlaoise from 2007 and was elected for a second term as a town councillor in 2009. Inspired by Matthews and Adebari, around 20 Africans contested the 2009 local elections in towns with African populations including Letterkenny, Drogheda and Dundalk. These candidates were typically members of Irish community groups and organisations as well as immigrant organisations and, in a number of cases, of immigrant churches. A number had family members who had been involved in politics in their countries of origin. Most were Nigerian. They identified racism as an important issue, but played this down during their campaigns in seeking to win votes from the predominantly non-immigrant communities in which they lived. They included Yinka Dixon, a Nigerian community activist who stood as a Green Party candidate in Drogheda. She was also a Pentecostal pastor and ran a business as a professional trainer.[76] Some, like Matthews and Adebari, stood as independent candidates and others as members of Fianna Fáil, Fine Gael and the Green Party. Voting rights in local government elections depended on residency rather than citizenship so most immigrants, including asylum seekers, were entitled to vote or stand for election.

Many such candidates were members of immigrant-led organisations.[77] These include the Africa Solidarity Centre; is aim has been to advance 'attitudes, policies and actions that promote justice, social inclusion and meaningful participation for African communities in Ireland', and it has published research on immigrant political participation and African civic participation.[78] The Africa Centre, as it was renamed, was co-founded by Fidèle Murtwarasibo, who arrived in Ireland as a refugee from Rwanda in 1994 at a time when the number of Africans in Ireland was still small. He had trained as a teacher and been employed as a rural community development worker in Rwanda. During the genocide both his parents were murdered, as was his wife's father. In Ireland he completed a Master's degree and became a community development worker in Dublin. He subsequently became a driving force behind the Immigrant Council of Ireland and of many initiatives aimed at furthering the integration of immigrants. He completed a doctorate in sociology and was appointed a member of the Irish Human Rights and Equality Commission. His doctoral research examined the biographies and experiences of African activists in politics and immigrant-led organisations.[79]

Salome Mbugua, who first came to Ireland from Kenya as a post-graduate student in a college run by the Holy Ghost Fathers, became in 2001 the founding member and director of Akina Dada Wa Africa (AkiDwA, trans. Sisterhood of Africa). After completing her studies she returned to Kenya, where she married an Irishman who had been a fellow student in Dublin. They worked for a time with the Irish Foundation for Cooperative Development in Uganda. In 1997 she helped set up a community-based network to address the social and economic effects of HIV/AIDS and poverty in Uganda. This collective became the template for AkiDwA, which grew into a network of some 2,500 women from 35 countries of origin. In 2010 Salome Mbugua became the vice chair of the National Women's Council of Ireland.[80]

AkiDwA has run campaigns and undertaken research on the needs of victims of female genital mutilation (FGM), domestic violence and so-called honour killings. A number of African women candidates who stood in the 2009 local government elections were members of AkiDwA.[81] It was estimated (in 2008) that at least 2,585 African women living in Ireland may have undergone FGM. According to research undertaken by AkiDwA, violence towards women appears in some cases to have been triggered by overcrowded living conditions in direct provision. Other cases documented by AkiDwA include the rape of women who found sex painful because of FGM. A major problem has been reluctance of women to seek help from family or friends out of fear of being stigmatised and rejected by their communities.[82] This has been the focus of a 2013 novel by Ebun Joseph Akpoveta, a microbiology graduate who in 2015 completed a PhD on the racial stratification of the Irish labour market at UCD. Ola, the protagonist of Akpoveta's novel, comes to Ireland as a postgraduate student and is reunited with her husband eight months after the birth of her son. Her husband becomes abusive, and her subsequent efforts to break away from him are impeded by family in Nigeria as well as by fellow Nigerians in Ireland.[83] Whilst writing her novel and completing her doctorate, Akpoveta, was a columnist with the *Africa Voice* newspaper and worked as a guidance counsellor, a career that grew out of her involvement with her church.[84]

Esther Owuta-Pepple Onolememen, the founder of Sickle Cell Society Ireland, grew up in Nigeria and trained as a social worker at Trinity College Dublin. Sickle cell disease is a genetic blood condition with a mortality rate of 30 per cent within the first five years of life. It affects people of mainly black African descent the world over. Up to two per cent of babies born in parts of Sub-Saharan Africa may be affected by sickle cell disease. Sufferers are vulnerable to infections and episodes of pain and can be affected by serious complications including strokes and organ damage. [85] In all about 400 children of African parents in Ireland have been diagnosed with the condition, about 70 per cent of whom are children of Nigerian parents. Most were born to African parents before 2005; only a small minority of parents in a study undertaken by Onolememen had received their child's diagnosis before coming to Ireland, and most of the children were born in Ireland.[86] The family of one such child, five-year-old Ayodola Adelkunle, appealed successfully against deportation to Nigeria in 2010. Evidence presented in support of the appeal from a specialist in Crumlin Children's Hospital, where Ayodola had her spleen removed, stated that 50 per cent of children in Africa with the condition died before their fifth birthday, adding that those without a spleen had a high risk of dying from malaria.[87]

By 2002 more than one quarter of all asylum seekers in Dublin were clustered into a single electoral district, Mountjoy B, where these made up 12 per cent of the total population.[88] By 2006, more than half (52.33 per cent) of residents in Mountjoy B were non-Irish nationals.[89] Around 2000 the availability of new housing for rent or purchase during the Celtic Tiger era did much to shape immigrant settlement patterns. Much of this housing was located to the north and west of the city. Africans predominantly settled in the West Dublin Blanchardstown area (Dublin 15), and in Swords to the north of the city, which became the Dublin district with the highest percentage of immigrant residents.

The 2006 census recorded 1,822 Nigerians in Dublin 15. More than half of the African population of Blanchardstown lived in three electoral districts: Mullhuddart, Blakestown, and Abbotstown. According to the 2006 census, the percentage of Africans in these areas was about eight times the national average. One district contained almost 13 times the national average of Africans; 12.69 per cent of those living in Mullhuddart were African. [90]

In 2007, over ten per cent of immigrant children at school identified as in need of English Language Support (ELS) in the entire country were found to live in Dublin 15. These 2,084 children constituted 21 per cent of all pupils in Dublin 15 primary schools. 28 per cent of these 2084 pupils in Dublin 15 were Nigerian, and overall around 40 per cent were Africans. Of 1,910 immigrant families in Dublin 15 receiving rent supplement (an indicator of poverty) some 61 per cent were African.[91]

In the 2009 local elections three African candidates stood for election in Mulhuddart: Idowu Olafimiham on behalf of Fianna Fáil, Adeola Ogunsina on behalf of Fine Gael and Ignatius Okafor as an independent candidate. None were elected, but in the subsequent 2014 local government election, Edmond Lukusa, was elected for Sinn Féin. Lukusa had been a member of the Union for Democracy and Social Progress, an opposition party in the Democratic Republic of the Congo. He moved to Ireland in 2001 and became an Irish citizen.

THE BLACK IRISH

Within a decade of establishing a precarious toehold in Ireland, during which African immigrants became the predominant focus of migration control politics in the Republic of Ireland, most are now Irish citizens or have secure residency status. Africans quickly established institutions in Ireland: churches, immigrant-led organisations, shops and businesses serving immigrant communities and newspapers such as *Metro Éireann* and *The African Voice*. *Metro Éireann* was co-founded in 2000 by Chinedu Onyejelem and is edited by him. Onyejelem obtained a Master's degree in Ethnic and Racial Studies from Trinity College Dublin. Before arriving in Ireland, he received a degree and postgraduate qualifications in education and communications from Nigerian universities. He is also the founder of the Metro Éireann Media and Multicultural Awards (MAMA) and the Ethnic Entrepreneur of the Year Awards. *Metro Éireann* is a popular tabloid with news and features of interest to immigrants in general. It has also campaigned on issues such as the rights of Africans to Irish citizenship and the participation of immigrants in politics. African organisations, newspapers, awards, fashion shows, businesses and entrepreneurial networks have emerged as a distinct immigrant civil society.

The percentage of African immigrants who became established in the professions exceeded those from Poland and other new European Union member states during the first decade of the twenty-first century. For example, the 2006 census identified some 15 per cent of Nigerians as either 'employers and managers', whereas just 6 per cent of Poles and 5 per cent of Lithuanians were similarly categorised. On the other hand, the percentage of Nigerians in employment was the lowest of all the large immigrant groups with male employment at just 50 per cent and with 30 per cent of females in paid employment.[92] There were two main reasons for this. Firstly, Africans who became asylum seekers were often prevented from working for years. And secondly, study after study has found that Africans experienced greater discrimination in accessing employment than other groups.

Research by the Economic and Social Research Institute (ESRI) identified an unemployment rate in 2005 that was nine times that of the population as a whole – and this in a context where some 44 per cent of Africans sampled were educated to at least degree level. Disproportionate levels of unemployment persisted in this community years after.[93] For example, while African men who were unable to obtain many other kinds of work to become self-employed taxi drivers in various cities and towns,[94] research undertaken in Galway published in 2010 identified racist protectionism whereby black drivers were refused registration with taxi dispatcher firms.[95] Other practices found around the country included the intimidation of black drivers on taxi ranks and the use of signs and Irish flags on cars driven by white Irish drivers.[96] Abel Ugba has described how in his conversations with African shop owners in Dublin, he formed the impression that setting up their own business was, to some extent, a strategy for sidestepping racism amongst Irish employers. For example, the owner of an Internet shop on Moore Street complained that he was unable to get a job after completing a computer course whereas his white Irish classmates were employed quickly by white Irish employers.[97] Unemployment rates amongst Africans have remained far higher than the national average. In 2015 when the unemployment rate for Irish-born people stood at 9.5 per cent and amongst foreign-born at 11 per cent, the unemployment rate for Africans specifically stood at 19.1 per cent. [98]

Racism in everyday life has also been documented in a number of studies. The 2005 ESRI study found that black Africans were more likely than other non-EU migrants to experience harassment by neighbours or on the street, but least likely to report such an incident to the police.[99] Research from 2009 interviewed Africans in 27 EU countries about their experiences, and Ireland was placed among the worst five countries for racist violence and harassment.[100] This has included experiences of racial harassment that has forced some immigrants (including Africans) from their homes.[101]

By 2015 one quarter of African children in Ireland attended a school that was designated as in a disadvantaged area compared to just 9 per cent of majority-Irish children. Yet analysis by the Economic and Social Research Institute, of the *Growing up in Ireland Survey* which surveyed the circumstances of around 8,500 children, found that African mothers of these children were better educated (54 per cent had third-level degrees) than Irish mothers (32 per cent had third-level degrees) and also had higher expectations that their children would attend third-level education (90 per cent compared to 70 per cent). Notwithstanding such expectations, African families were much more likely to experience economic disadvantage (27 per cent compared to 8 per cent of Irish families) to go to a disadvantaged school (25 per cent compared to 9 per cent) and their children were far more likely to have limited knowledge of English (24 per cent compared to 2 per cent).[102] It seems likely that children from such African families were the ones most likely to find themselves living in poverty in disadvantaged areas, and attending disadvantaged schools, whereas well-educated Africans, fluent in English and better off were less likely to be living in marginal areas or attending marginal schools.

Much of the focus of this chapter has been on Nigerians who comprise the largest African community in the Republic of Ireland. Africans from other countries, less well educated and/or non English-speaking, experience far greater barriers. Few of those interviewed in Elena Moreo and Ronit Lentin's 2010 study *From Catastrophe to Marginalisation: The Experiences of*

Somali Refugees in Ireland had found employment. Poor English-language fluency, education and training gaps and long periods of enforced unemployment whilst living in direct provision made it difficult for many to benefit from the Celtic Tiger. Amongst children, language barriers and gaps in schooling created obstacles to education in Ireland. The problems encountered by Somalis in Ireland recalled those of the Vietnamese: having to live in deprived areas; finding it hard to access employment because of language barriers and low levels of education; children finding the education system difficult and problems with family reunification. Clear information on how Somalis in Ireland have since fared is lacking but if their experiences of 'entrenched disadvantage' elsewhere – in the United Kingdom, Denmark, Norway, Australia and Canada – is anything to go by, many are likely to remain marginal.[103]

ELEVEN

IMMIGRATIONS

The experiences of migrants who came to work in the Republic of Ireland during the Celtic Tiger era were affected considerably by whether or not they came from other European member states. In 1992, the EU Maastricht Treaty extended existing agreements that allowed for the free movement of workers across member states, creating a right to free movement and residence in any member state. The so-called Celtic Tiger period is now generally understood by economists to constitute two distinct phases. From the mid-1990s to 2002, high levels of economic growth resulted from US investment in pharmaceuticals and information technology, among others, as a result of which, Irish exports rose. A second phase resulted from a boom in the service sector and consumption. An immigration-driven population increase partly fuelled this second growth phase. Between 1995 and 2000, 248,100 people moved to the Republic of Ireland. The majority were Irish citizens, but 18 per cent (45,600) were British subjects, many of whom were married to Irish citizens. 13 per cent (33,400) came from other EU countries and seven per cent (16,600) came from the United States. Twelve per cent (29,400) came from elsewhere in the world.[1]

A two-tiered work permit system emerged from 2000 onwards which fast-tracked applications for certain categories of skilled workers from non-EU countries, and was, in theory, more restrictive in other cases. In practice, a laissez-faire system operated until April 2003 when a new Employment Permits Act was introduced, which granted free access to the Irish job market to people from the new EU member states (from 1 May 2004) and restricted the granting of work permits to migrants from outside the EU. Until this point, the bar for demonstrating that jobs could not be filled in the Republic of Ireland had been set low. Migrants were recruited to fill low-paid jobs such as agricultural and restaurant work; jobs in areas such as construction where they were sometimes paid a lot less than Irish workers; and jobs requiring in-demand skills such in as nursing and information technology. Similar kinds of migrants were permitted to do similar kinds of work in Northern Ireland. This period saw the establishment of immigrant communities from the Philippines, India, Brazil and China as well as from a number of European countries.

The numbers of migrants from new EU countries grew hugely, while numbers from several non-EU countries also continued to expand after 2003 as a result of chain migration, family reunification and ongoing recruitment of skilled migrants in areas such as nursing. Deals between the Irish state and China and with Brazil resulted in significant numbers arriving on student visas, in addition to smaller numbers of labour migrants from both these countries.

From April 2003 it became considerably more difficult for employers to recruit workers from outside the EU to fill low-paid and low-skilled jobs. Whilst non-EU migrants continued to arrive, especially those qualified in areas such as nursing, the main era of non-European labour migration into Ireland was between 1999 and 2004. Yet after 2004, more Filipinos and Indians continued to arrive and some other existing migrant communities continued to grow. 18,006 work permits were granted to migrants from non-EU countries in 2000, a further 36,436 in 2001, 40,321 in 2002, 47,551 in 2003 and 34,067 in 2004. Many of these permits were for jobs that Irish people appeared to be unwilling to do or in areas such as construction which had expanded during the boom. Around 110,000 of these were granted between 2000 and 2004, some to migrants whose countries of origin became EU member states from 1 May 2004. A huge majority (approximately 100,000) were for low-skilled jobs, and permits in such cases were issued to employers rather than migrants themselves, thereby preventing migrants from changing jobs or remaining legally in the country unless sponsored by another employer.[2]

In February 2007 a 'Green Card' system was introduced that that allowed qualifying non-EU migrants, in areas such as healthcare, IT and finance and who received salaries above €30,000, permission to remain in Ireland for two years and to apply immediately for family reunification. They could then apply for long-term residency status, which would allow them to remain in the country for a further five years. Migrants in occupations not on this list were eligible if they earned above €60,000 per annum. As to the rest of the immigrant community, in both the Republic and the North, poorly paid non-EU migrants were prevented from bringing dependent family members with them or for obtaining long-term residency status. For example, in Northern Ireland in 2011, the minimum salary threshold that migrants needed to earn in order to be eligible to apply for indefinite leave to remain was £7.80 per hour. The average pay of senior care assistants at the time was £6.70 per hour.[3]

The overall number of immigrants in the Republic peaked in 2008 at 575,000 at the beginning of the economic crisis, and stood at 544,357 by

2011. By 2014, total numbers had risen to 564,300. Many had become successfully put down roots, believed that they were still comparatively better off in Ireland or felt that they had no choice but to remain there. Migrants from several countries examined in this chapter increased in number during the economic crisis period. Between the 2006 census and 2011 census the number of Filipinos increased from 9,548 to 12,791, a rise of 34 per cent. Between 2006 and 2011, the number of Indians doubled from 8,480 to 16,642 and the number of Brazilians rose 98.4 per cent by 4,316.

Northern Ireland also experienced similar kinds of immigration although on a scale that was less than in the Republic. The 2001 Census recorded 26,659 people born outside the United Kingdom or Ireland as living in the six counties, of whom 6,455 were from elsewhere in the EU; just 515 were non-EU citizens, which at the time included people from Poland and the Baltic states. The North's immigrant population in 2001 also included 3,116 Africans and 7,004 Asians, most of whom were Chinese. In addition, the UK Immigration Service estimated that there were around 2,000 undocumented migrants living in Northern Ireland.[4]

A few years into the twenty-first century, both the Republic and Northern Ireland contained some new non-European immigrant communities that were bigger than any of the handful of immigrant-descended communities that had arrived since the seventeenth century – the Huguenots, the Palatines or the Lithuanian Jews. While it is possible to consider how such earlier groups fared over several decades, all that can be done, as of yet, in the case of a number of early twenty-first-century immigrant communities, is to examine the initial experiences of some of these newcomers. As in earlier chapters, the approach is to focus on wider patterns (as revealed mostly by census and other quantitative data) hand-in-hand with the first-hand experiences of selected individuals and families.

LITHUANIANS AND LATVIANS

By 2004 about 3,000 migrants, recruited mostly from Lithuania and Latvia, worked for about 120 mushroom-growers in the Republic. Research by NGOs like the Migrants Rights Centre Ireland provides glimpses into the lives of some of these. Many appear to have been paid substantially less than the minimum wage, and some were made to work up to 16 hours per day in difficult conditions. Once the two countries acceded to the EU in May 2004, their citizens no longer needed to obtain work permits but some continued to be exploited, particularly those who did not speak English.[5]

Between 2002 and 2006, the number of Lithuanians living in the Republic grew twelve-fold from 2,104 to 24,628 and rose to 36,683 by 2011. Just over half lived in Dublin and other cities, the rest in smaller towns and villages. By 2006 Lithuanians made up 3 per cent of the population of County Monaghan, where many had come to work on mushroom farms and in food-processing plants; of the major towns in the county, Lithuanians counted for nine per cent of the population of Monaghan Town; seven per cent of Carrickmacross; and six per cent of Clones. Although noticeably concentrated in County Monaghan, almost every town in the Republic with a population of more than 1,500 had some Lithuanian residents by 2006.

EU and non-EU mushroom pickers described being recruited by a Northern Ireland agency only to be moved across the border to work on farms in the Republic.[6] Lydia was recruited in the Ukraine to work on a farm in the Republic where conditions were poor. Her employer then sent her North of the border to work on another mushroom farm. Conditions were better there, and she received £160 per week with £40 deduced to pay for accommodation in a house she shared with ten other people. Lydia's employer said he was applying for a work permit on her behalf, but it seems that he did not do so; he told her the permit had been refused. The practice of sending migrants like Lydia back and forth across the border gave employers leverage over their employees and reinforced a sense of isolation.[7]

Many of those recruited as mushroom-pickers in the North had quali-fications and skills beyond what they needed for this job. Pickers interviewed there by researchers included a chemical engineer, a welder, two accountants and some skilled textile workers. They were drawn by the prospect of higher wages than they could earn at home. Some had followed relatives and family members to Ireland. They had paid between £300 and £1,300 to recruit-ment agencies who arranged their jobs and promised to organise work permits in Ireland plus flight costs. They expected to earn between £180 and £220 a week. Some then found themselves having to work up to 75 hours a week, and were paid piece rates for the number of baskets they picked. Some never received work permits; some even received forged payslips. In other cases, employers deducted money from their wages, supposedly to cover tax and national insurance, but kept this money for themselves. Some who lost their jobs found themselves undocumented and not entitled to benefits because their employers had withheld tax and social insurance contributions.[8]

Migrants from the Baltic States also worked in other areas of agriculture on both sides of the border. Again, they were exploited by employers and could do little about it because they could not speak English. Vladis, a farm worker from Latvia, worked in a chicken factory in Northern Ireland from May to December 2008 before moving to another job on a farm. In his farm job, he never received payslips and was told that some of his salary was being lodged into a bank account. However, this did not happen. In October 2009 he was involved in an accident at work involving chemicals; his employer dropped him off at a hospital and had no further contact with him. Because Vladis had not been registered as employed on the farm he was not entitled to disability benefits. Social Services paid for his flight back to Latvia.[9]

The kinds of grievous exploitation documented in some cases appear to have been temporary, and some migrants from the Baltic States clearly fared well. A 2012 RTÉ television programme on Lithuanians in Ireland interviewed Ziggy Mandras, a young teenager who, after four years living in Ireland, spoke with a broad Tipperary accent. His parents could afford to bring Ziggy from Tipperary to a Lithuanian school in Cork city for four hours every Sunday where the curriculum focused on Lithuanian language, culture and history. The school was one of nine such weekend or afternoon schools in the Republic and had 50 pupils of various ages.[10] One of these was set up in 2007 in Mullaghmett, County Monaghan to teach Lithuanian language, history and geography. From 2009 on, pupils participated in choir festivals held in Vilnius, as well as summer camps held in various countries. By 2013 pupils, included children attending secondary school, were being preparing to sit Lithuanian as a Leaving Certificate higher-level exam subject. The school's motto (translated into English) read: 'I am going to Lithuanian School to learn to love Lithuania in (the) Lithuanian way. We welcome you.'[11]

Many Lithuanians who settled in the Republic and in the North as part of extended families joined in Ireland by siblings, parents and other relatives. It appears that chain migration has resulted in some migrants settling in Ireland alongside former neighbours and classmates as well as members of their extended family. For example, a study of Lithuanians in Northern Ireland found that a concentration of migrants from the same Silute region had settled in Dungannon.[12]

Some arrivals from the Baltic countries, in particular from Latvia, were Russian-speakers who, following the collapse of the Soviet Union, faced citizenship restrictions and other obstacles. After the Soviet Union annexed the Baltic countries during the Second World War, it settled hundreds of thousands of Russian migrants in these. When the Baltic countries became independent, the Russian Federation established a right of return for ethnic Russians born in the newly independent Baltic countries, but only some returned to Russia. Many remained on as resented ethnic minorities. Linguistic and citizenship restrictions imposed on Russian-speakers were most severe in Estonia, and least so in Lithuania, either 'ethnic tensions' or economic marginalisation experienced by Russian-speakers in all three countries provided an impetus for migration by some of these to Ireland.

Some Russian-speakers interviewed by researchers in 2006 had arrived in Ireland as early as 2000. Most had previously held low-paid white-collar jobs, or had worked in construction, in service industries as waiters or cleaners, or in manufacturing. Those who came before 2004 had been bought over by recruitment agencies, while more recent arrivals had been helped to find work and settle in Ireland by informal networks.[13] In addition to ethnic Russians, some 4,495 Russian citizens were resident in Ireland according to the 2006 census, most were members of the Russian Orthodox Church. The 2006 census recorded some 20,798 Orthodox Christians in the Republic of Ireland. Most of these were members of the Russian Orthodox Church whilst just under a quarter (4,234) belonged to the Romanian Orthodox Church. By 2011, the Orthodox Christian population had risen to 45,223 reflecting the rise in numbers of immigrants from Latvia, Lithuania, and Romania.

ROMANIANS

Romanians started to migrate to Ireland during the 1990s after, in many cases, having previously worked in Italy. Strong linguistic similarities between Romanian and Italian made Italy an attractive destination, but this was outweighed by the promise of far higher wages in Celtic-Tiger Ireland. A year before Romania joined the EU in 2007, census data identified 7,700 Romanians already living in the Republic most working in the informal economy.[14] The overall number of Romanian migrants (2.7 million scattered around Europe by 2014) was second only to the number of Poles.[15] In 2006 the net average monthly salary in Romania was €200 per month.[16]

The Republic's Romanian population reached 28,702 according to the 2016 census and it has been suggested that, as with other groups, official data has underestimated the actual number which should have included Moldovans who were ethnic Romanians and travelled to Ireland on Romanian passports. In Dublin signs on Romanian grocery shops variously describe these as either Moldovan or Transylvanian. The 2011 census identified 45,223 Orthodox Christians in the Republic, more than double the number (20,798) recorded in 2006. 26 per cent of these (11, 447) were of Romanian nationality. A Romanian Orthodox Church was established in Dublin in October 2000 in the Jesuit chapel in Belvedere College, in the north inner city. In 2005, it moved to a premises in Dublin leased from the Church of Ireland. Other Romanian Orthodox congregations were established in the city including two in Dublin 15 and in Cork, Galway and Belfast.

Victoria came to Ireland from Romania with her two daughters to join her husband in 2007. Although he did not have a work permit, he had been employed on Irish construction sites since 2001, as he had in Belgium, France and England. After 2007, when Romania joined the EU, it became easier for them to come and go even though work permit restrictions still applied. Although neither could obtain permits, it looked like the family could have a viable life in Ireland. Victoria found work cleaning houses, but her husband lost his job in the economic crash and returned to Romania in 2008 with the children. Victoria remained, and he subsequently returned. They lived as cheaply as possible in order to save money to renovate their house in Romania and invest in equipment for a timber processing business there.[17] Romanians like Victoria were able to travel back from Ireland several times a year thanks to cheap flights.

The Romanian diaspora, somewhat like the Irish one in earlier times, was stratified on the basis of ethnicity as well as social class. Romanian migrants differentiated themselves from Roma and Sinti (ethnic minorities sometimes known as gypsies) just as Protestant and Catholic Irish emigrants saw themselves as culturally different from one another during the nineteenth century. The vilification of Roma in Ireland by some other Romanians and some Irish people recalls too the experiences of Irish Travellers in recent decades. Both Travellers and Roma found themselves out of sync with modernising societies; they lived lives on the margins of these and were depicted, in a sense, as enemies of progress.[18] Under the Third Reich the Roma had been categorised as 'underserving of life'. Nazi propaganda depicted them as 'vermin'. The first Holocaust act of mass murder occurred in Buchenwald in January 1940 when 250 Roma children were gassed. An estimated 200,000 Roma died in Nazi concentration camps and around half-a-million perished in total during the Second World War.[19]

The majority of the estimated 5,000 Roma in Ireland came from Romania but some had also previously lived in a number of other new EU member states including Slovakia, Poland and Hungary.[20] It has been estimated that just 30 per cent of Roma children in Ireland attend school and that 95 per cent of Roma women in Ireland cannot read or write. The Roma in Ireland tend to live in multi-generational households in which parents, children, uncles, aunts and grandparents live together.[21] Stereotypes of the Roma as beggars and outcasts recall those of pre-Famine Irish migrants in England during the early nineteenth century examined in Chapter Five: the apparent disorder of their lives masked purposeful seasonable migration aimed at supporting their families at home. Many Roma migrated to Ireland in apparently well-organised extended family groups. As one ethnographer said of 'gypsies' in the US: 'stereotypes often show Gypsies to be demoralized, illiterates and thieves. To the contrary, I found them to be intelligent, flexible, and resourceful survivors.'[22]

Whilst Roma have most likely visited Ireland in small numbers for centuries, the first identifiable group of 40 migrants arrived in freight containers via the port of Rosslare in County Wexford. By August 1998, it was estimated that around 250 Romanians, most of whom were Roma, had arrived in Ireland by this same route. They applied for refugee status but their claims for asylum were rejected. From 2001, Roma groups settled in Monaghan, Dundalk and in a number of places near Dublin including Swords, Tallaght, Lucan and Leixlip.[23] In July 2007, the Irish government deported a community of Roma that had been living on a roundabout on the M50 motorway. Other members of this group lived in a nearby derelict house. The main assistance these received came from Pavee Point, a Traveller NGO affiliated with Roma organisations in international networks.[24] In response, the Minister of Justice, Brian Lenihan threatened to reduce funding to Pavee Point.[25] In October 2014, following an anti-Roma protest organised on Facebook, a mob of around 200 people attacked a house in Waterford inhabited by three Roma families who had been accused of committing robberies and burglaries.[26] More severe attacks on the homes of Roma have occurred in Northern Ireland; in June 2009, in one of a spate of attacks, two homes in east Belfast were attacked and vandalised by a gang who chanted slogans associated with the far-right group Combat 18 and made Nazi salutes. One hundred and fourteen people from 20 Roma families fled the area,[27] and all but two of them left Northern Ireland entirely, their flights paid for by the Northern Ireland Housing Executive.[28] The homes of non-Roma Romanians and other immigrant groups including Chinese and Poles in Belfast have also been the focus of racist attacks.[29]

In 2013, the two-year-old child of a Roma family in Athlone was taken into care following the receipt of an unsubstantiated allegation of child trafficking because the boy had blue eyes and blond hair. DNA samples were taken from the child as well as a Roma couple who proved to be his parents. Another blond and blue-eyed Roma child was similarly taken from her family in Tallaght by Gardaí and social workers and then returned to her parents when a DNA test disproved an anonymous claim that her family were child traffickers. The seven year-old had been born in Ireland. A report by the Ombudsman for Children described the actions of the Gardaí in these cases as 'racial profiling'.[30]

It is estimated that around 70 per cent of Roma in Ireland are Pentecostal Christians.[31] Roma Pentecostal congregations first developed in France during the 1950s and spread to Roma communities around the world. By 1995 there were around 70,000 Pentecostal Roma in France, about a quarter of the total. In 1969 the first Roma Pentecostal congregation was founded in Spain and by 2002 an estimated 15 per cent of Roma in Spain belonged to Pentecostal congregations. Pentecostalism spread rapidly in Bulgaria and Romania from the 1990s. By 2002 6.5% of Roma counted in the Romanian census were recorded as Pentecostals a making these both a small minority of the Roma in Romania and a small minority of Romanian

Pentecostals. Various estimates have calculated the total number of Romanian Pentecostals between 450,000 and 800,000 with somewhere in the region of 60,000 of these being Roma.[32] The evangelisation of the Roma seems to be due in no little part to the willingness of Pentecostal missionaries to preach in the Romani language and to incorporate Roma culture into religious services.

Ricardo, one of the participants in *I Am Immigrant,* a 2016 RTÉ documentary, was born in Romania and lived there with his Roma grandparents until 2007. When he was 11 years old, he joined his parents in Dublin where they had lived since 2000. His mother begged and worked as a flower seller; she spoke no English when she first arrived. His father became a pastor to an Evangelical Christian Roma congregation in Dublin. Ricardo joined the Gardaí, motivated to do so by hostility towards Roma he witnessed since arriving in Ireland.[33]

FILIPINOS

Filipinos who came to Ireland were part of a diaspora that extended around the world. Remittances to the Philippines in 2004 worldwide totalled US $8.55 billion, or 10.8 per cent of the GDP.[34] Filipinos typically migrated to provide financial support through remittances to family members and dependents at home. Large numbers of families came to depend on remittances to fund day-to-day life and the education of their children. Many such children grew up expecting that they too would migrate to support their families. Education and training in areas such as nursing was designed to prepare students to work abroad; by 2002 around 175 mostly private-sector nursing schools in the Philippines produced more than 5,000 qualified nurses per annum, most of these destined to work abroad.[35]

Studies of Filipino migrants have identified strong bonds of obligation towards extended families at home, and interviewees in one Irish study described pressures to increase the amount of money they remitted, which was difficult to do because of high living costs. Marisol, who worked as a nurse, described sending between €600 and €800 each month to family members out of a monthly salary of €2,300. Each month, she also saved €1,000, which meant that she had a very low standard of living in Ireland. At the time of her interview she had been working abroad for seven years while her children remained in the Philippines. Another interviewee who earned considerably less described the emotional pressure coming from her mother, who asked 'why are you sending us so little?' Decisions about who to send money to within extended families could also fuel conflicts and jealousies.[36] The dynamics within Filipino communities that depended on remittances from migrants like Marisol at times resembled those in Irish ones some generations earlier. The false impression that those who returned from abroad on visits to the Philippines were rich could put returnees under considerable social pressure. As in the case of early-twentieth-century migrants from Donegal to Scotland and the United States, as described by Peadar O'Donnell (see Chapter 8), the status of both returnees and family members at home was often linked to impressions of their financial success abroad.

Interviewees in another study identified three main reasons why they chose Ireland over other destinations. Firstly, Ireland was English-speaking, and many Filipinos spoke English. Secondly, Ireland was seen as a potential stepping-stone to other countries, particularly to the US, the UK and Canada, as experience gained from working in Irish hospitals helped to secure employment in such countries. Thirdly, Ireland, like the Philippines was predominantly Catholic.[37] Irish missionaries who traveled to the Philippines included Fr Shay Cullen who arrived in Olongapo City in 1969 and spent several decades working with impoverished women and children who were sold to brothels to serve a large American military base and sex tourists from abroad. Cullen led a campaign to close US military bases in the Philippines, ran projects to alleviate poverty through Fair Trade and was nominated three times for the Nobel Peace Prize.[38]

Since 2000, Catholic Filipino congregations in Dublin have celebrated the Santo Nino Novena, which includes a solemn outdoor procession, ceremonial masses and Filipino cultural events. However, some Filipinos are Pentecostal Christians. In March 2013 the Iglesia de Christo (Church of Christ) purchased a former Christian Science church near Queens University in Belfast to serve a congregation of several hundred Filipinos.[39]

Some Filipinos worked in Ireland as undocumented migrants on rates of pay far below the legal minimum wage as child-minders and carers, in the fishing industry and in fast-food restaurants. In one case, a group who worked on a mushroom farm were paid as little as £1 per hour. They were helped by a Catholic Priest to find employment elsewhere. When they sought to recover unpaid wages their old employer threatened to denounce them to the authorities. Eventually, they received financial compensation but not before they had left Northern Ireland. Some migrants working in fish processing and on trawlers experienced similar exploitation.[40] A 2009 estimate put the number of Filipinos working on Northern Irish trawlers at 160 and those working on vessels sailing from ports in the Republic at around 200. They were found to receive about £1.20 an hour, a small fraction of the legal minimum wage.[41] A 2015 investigation again uncovered widespread exploitation of migrants from the Philippines, Ghana and Egypt working on Irish trawlers. These typically received one quarter the wages of Irish citizen crew and were undocumented.[42]

In another study undertaken in the Republic, Filipino interviewees described their experiences working for a fast-food chain. The recruitment agency charged all of them the equivalent of €1,500, which included €500 – the actual cost of a work permit. The researchers calculated that, given living and accommodation costs in Ireland, it would take an average of 27 weeks working 45 hours per week to pay off these recruitment costs, and only then would they be in a position to save or remit money to their countries of origin.[43] To put this in historical context, this compares unfavourably to Matthew Carey's calculation from 1829 (see Chapter 6) that an unskilled Irish labourer could earn the price of his passage across the Atlantic to the United States in two months, over and above the cost of food and lodgings.

Georgio paid more than £800 to an agency in Manila to organise a job as a restaurant manager in Belfast. He borrowed money to pay this fee. His employer deducted £50 a week to pay for airfare. He brought his wife and children over to live with him in Belfast. After two-and-a-half years he was fired from his job soon after he tried unsuccessfully to convince his employer to provide sick pay for another migrant working in the restaurant. Georgio found alternative work in a fast-food restaurant, but his new employer was unwilling to sponsor a work permit or to pay him properly. He convinced the owner of a coffee shop to make such an application on his behalf but had to cover the cost of the permit and was forced to work for a time illegally whilst waiting for this permit to come through. He managed to remain in Belfast with his family.[44] Georgio fared well compared to many others whose stories are touched on here.

In 2000, the Philippines supplied about 90 per cent of the 557 non-EU overseas trained nurses working in the Republic of Ireland. In 2001, 95 per cent of working visas issued for registered nurses in 2001 were issued to nurses from the Philippines and Filipinos accounted for 69 per cent of all work visas issued in that year. By 2002 Ireland was the third-largest recruiter of Filipino nurses, after Saudi Arabia and the UK. Sixty per cent of them were employed in hospitals, and the rest worked as care assistants in residential nursing homes.[45] By 2006 there were some 3,831 nurses from the Philippines working in the Republic of Ireland.

By 2003 some 560 overseas nurses were employed by Northern Ireland's Health and Social Services Boards. Nurses employed in the North reported being typically charged approximately £300 each by the agency that recruited them in the Philippines.[46] However, one interviewee in the same study who worked in a nursing home said that she had been charged £2,000; he got his job without having to sit an exam or go through an interview.[47] Filipino nurses interviewed in a 2011 study of racism recalled experiences of hostility during their early years working in Ireland. One recalled how 'patients preferred to be cared by white Irish staff'. Whilst this became less of a problem over time she felt that hostility towards Filipinos had increased during the post-2008 economic crisis period.[48]

Many Filipino and other migrant nurses seem to have intended to stay in Ireland for a few years and move elsewhere or move home. Eighty-seven per cent of participants in a 2009 survey of 336 mostly Filipino and Indian nurses in the Republic revealed that they remitted large proportions of their salaries to family members back home on a regular basis. Almost a quarter remitted more than 40 per cent of what they earned. Those with children in Ireland tended to send less money home, and almost half of those with children had decided to settle in Ireland for the foreseeable future.[49] Many of these had purchased houses, settled with their families and were unwilling to disrupt the lives of their children by moving again.[50]

Some Filipino nurses interviewed in 2011 as part of a study of racism described experiences of harassment in neighbourhoods where they lived. Dexter had been living in South West Dublin for several years with his family when they became the focus of ongoing harassment by a gang of teenagers. On one occasion he witnessed the gang throwing stones at his three-year-old child. On another, his car was struck by a stone when he was driving home from church with his family. Dexter's friend Daphne, who was also a nurse from the Philippines, described how she was harassed by the gang in 2010 when she visited him at his home. The gang shouted racist abuse and threw stones at her; she was pregnant at the time. Dexter claimed that several other Filipinos had experienced similar racist harassment in West Dublin but had received limited support from the police.

Research suggests that almost half Filipinos employed in Northern Ireland have also experienced harassment and discrimination in the work-place, mostly from co-workers but also from managers and customers. Incidents recorded in a 2012 study include the case of a chef who was twice locked in a freezer by co-workers as well as less-favourable treatment when it came to breaks, work rotas and annual leave. Many Filipinos appear to have been unwilling to report such abuse in case it harmed their chances of staying in Northern Ireland.[51]

INDIANS

By 2006, a total of 8,460 Indians lived in the Republic. These included some 3,215 nurses who had been recruited from hospitals in countries such as Bahrain, Saudi Arabia, and Singapore. Together with nurses from the Philippines, these made up around 11 per cent of the total working in Irish hospitals.[52] By 2006 just over 1,000 Indians lived in Northern Ireland. Many of those who settled in both parts of Ireland had middle-class backgrounds and, unlike many well-educated migrants from other countries, found employment in the professions or established themselves in business. For example, by 2006 some 83 per cent of Indian householders in Northern Ireland were homeowners.[53]

By 2011, 4,854 of the 18,798 registered doctors in the Republic came from outside the EU. Of these, 511 were from India and 125 of these Indian doctors were specialists.[54] Indian medical professionals generally bought their families with them. The 2011 census identified 16.986 Indians in the Republic of Ireland of whom 3,922 were children under 15 years old. 10,688 of these were Hindus, whilst some Indians were Catholics and others were Sikh.

Ashock Varadkar, a Hindu doctor from Borivali, a suburb of Mumbai, met his Irish-born wife Miriam Howell in England where she had migrated to work as a nurse. The Varadkar family moved to India in 1973 before settling in Dublin in 1979. All three of their children became medical professionals. Sonia trained as a midwife and Sophie and Leo studied medicine at Trinity College Dublin.[55] By 2011 some 20.3 per cent of Hindus had become Irish citizens. Whilst the majority worked in some capacity in health care the 2011 census recorded significant numbers in a range of other occupations including 1,075 in food services, 580 in informational technology and 408 in manufacturing.

A small percentage of Indians who settled on both sides of the border were Sikh. Most arrived since the 1990s, but a trickle of Sikh settlement in Northern Ireland dates back to the 1930s. Census records identified 219 Sikhs in Northern Ireland by 2001 with around 1,500 living in the Republic after several waves of migration. During the 1920s and 1930s some businessmen, peddlers and students reached Ireland. The manner in which first-wave Sikh peddlers, sometimes with poor spoken English, sold clothes purchased from wholesalers in Glasgow in towns like such as Newry, Bangor, Antrim and Ballymena recalled some Litvaks decades earlier selling door-to-door. Like the Litvaks, some of the Indians subsequently set up family businesses, and many present-day members of the small Derry/Londonderry Sikh community were descended from these traders.[56] After the Partition of India there was a second wave of immigrants to the United Kingdom, and a few of these settled in Northern Ireland. A third wave consisted of relatives of this second wave who arrived during the 1960s both from India and from the United Kingdom. Again, they mostly settled in Northern Ireland.

A fourth group arrived from former British colonies after these became independent. Sikhs who arrived in Ireland during the 1970s did so as part of a larger migration of people from India and descendants of Indians who had settled in Uganda and Kenya and in other parts of the British Empire.

Unlike earlier waves, these Sikh migrants tended to be well educated, and came to Ireland as dentists, engineers and the like.

Early Sikh settlers in the Republic included some of a group of ten Punjabi immigrants hired in 1972 to work as chefs in restaurants owned by Mohinder Singh Gill who had arrived a few years earlier from Britain. Photographs of these men show that, like earlier Sikh arrivals in Ireland, they had cut their hair and did not wear turbans. Their reason for doing so was to avoid discrimination. Some of the first Sikhs to settle in Dublin relocated from the United Kingdom alongside a small number of Indian and Pakistani wholesalers. Many of these worked alongside and lived in proximity to Hindu migrants from India. Like earlier Sikh arrivals these men had little formal education.[57]

A fifth wave to the United Kingdom, some of whom reached Ireland, had fled the 1984 anti-Sikh riots in New Delhi and other parts of India. Some, including doctors, nurses, restaurant workers, IT professionals and business-men, were drawn to the Republic of Ireland by its 'Celtic Tiger' prosperity.[58]

Sikh *gurdawra* (temples) were established in Dublin, Derry/Londonderry and Belfast. By 2013, up to 300 people participated in a weekly religious service and communal meal at the Serpentine Avenue Gurdawra Guru Nahak Adrbar in the Ballsbridge area of Dublin.[59] This religious community traces its origin to weekly prayer sessions held from 1984 in a restaurant owed by an early Sikh immigrant. Efforts to establish a Dublin *gurdwara* gained momentum the following year when an Air India Flight 182 crashed off the Irish coast, killing all 329 passengers on board. Many of the victims were Sikhs, and the Indian Embassy found it difficult to organise funeral rites for them in Dublin. In December 1986, a premises was purchased with the help of the Sikh community in London.

In the aftermath of both the Twin Towers attacks in 2001 and the 2005 London bombings (perpetrated by radicalised Muslims) some assaults on turban-wearing Sikhs in Ireland were reported. In 2007 a Sikh who applied to join the Garda Reserve was turned down because he insisted on being allowed to wear a turban on duty.[60] The following year, a Sikh youth playing for a soccer team in Lucan (where a number of Sikh families had settled) was sent off by the referee for wearing headgear.[61] Interviews with Sikh parents (as part of the study cited extensively here) revealed similar problems in schools in the Republic of Ireland regarding turban-wearing.[62]

Amataya, interviewed in a 2011 study of experiences of racism in greater Dublin, had moved to Ireland from India in 2004 and worked in accountancy and the financial services sector. In August 2009, he was assaulted and badly beaten by a gang of teenagers and young adults whilst waiting at a bus stop near his home in west Dublin. Details of this incident appeared in an

Immigrant Council of Ireland report, which highlighted the poor response of the Gardaí to racist incidents. Following the assault Amataya moved away from the area, as he no longer felt safe there, and some time later moved to the United States. Amataya said that he had previously lived in the United Kingdom, Holland and Sweden and had never felt as unsafe as he felt in Dublin.[63]

By the time of the 2016 census some 20,969 Indian-born people were living in the Republic of Ireland. Between 2013 and 2015 alone some 4,461 of these became Irish citizens. A slightly-larger number (4,838) of Filipinos naturalised during the same period.[64]

Savita Andanappa Yalagi was born in the southwest Indian state of Karnataka in 1981. She grew up in the city of Belgaum where she also studied dentistry. She met Praveen Halappanavar, who had also grown up in Karnataka, through a matrimonial website. Savita had not planned to emigrate, but Praveen, who was an engineer, moved to Galway to work for Boston Scientific, a company that manufactured medical devices. Savita moved to Galway in 2008 after their wedding and became very involved in the city's Indian community, becoming one of the organisers of the annual Galway Diwali festival. In 2012 she sat the Irish Dental Council exams and became qualified to work as a dentist. In October 2012, when she was 17 weeks pregnant, she was admitted to hospital in Galway. She died from septic shock after miscarrying and from having contracted an E Coli infection after having been refused an abortion.[65] In 2014 following an inquiry into causes of the death of his wife, Praveen Halappanavar moved to the United States. They were typical Indian professionals but the circumstances of her death made her an iconic figure.

CHINESE

There have been two main waves of Chinese migration to Ireland. The first, dating to the mid-twentieth century, was made up mostly of Hong Kong Chinese who had previous settled in the United Kingdom and who moved to Ireland to establish restaurant businesses. These originated mostly from rural villages in the New Territories region which since the 1950s had experienced large-scale emigration for very much as why emigration from Ireland was also mostly from rural areas. As Commonwealth citizens, they were entitled to settle in the UK, and were then able to come to Ireland without work permits because of reciprocal agreements between the Republic of Ireland and the UK. Hong Kong Chinese also settled in Northern Ireland, mostly in Belfast though also in towns including Craigavon, Lisburn, Newtownabbey, North Down and Ballymena. Many of these, like first-wavers in the Republic came originally from the New Territories, the rural area of Hong Kong where Hakka and Cantonese are spoken.

The first Chinese restaurant in Belfast, the Peacock, opened in 1962; by 2006 there were more than 500 Chinese food businesses in the province. According to Anna Lo, who moved to Belfast in 1974, Chinese living in British cities set up takeaways in Northern Ireland because there was less competition there. During the Troubles these takeaways flourished because people were scared to eat out in restaurants. As Lo put it, 'You couldn't get food anywhere after the pubs closed and the only place was a Chinese carry-out.'[66]

A second wave arrived mostly from mainland China from the mid-1990s onwards when the PRC lifted travel restrictions on its citizens. Many were English-language students encouraged to come to Ireland as a result of agreements between the Irish and Chinese governments, most of whom attended poorly regulated English language schools in Dublin, while others attended Irish universities. Although they were admitted on student visas, they were permitted to work. Other Chinese mainlanders also migrated to Ireland because of the economic boom. Over time the numbers, who were 'privately sponsored', that is, those who reached Ireland though personal contacts with those already in Ireland and who had applied for work permits on their behalf, also rose.[67]

Li, whose case was taken up by the Migrant Rights Centre Ireland, was among them. In 2001, Li arrived in Wexford from the Fujian province in China to work as a chef. He had been promised £250 per week plus food and accommodation by a broker who charged 380,000 Yuan (€30,000) Li borrowed the sum from relatives, friends and a moneylender. When he arrived in Ireland, he was paid just £150 per week in cash. Li's English was very poor. There were eight other employees in the same situation, and all were dependent on the Chinese agent who had brought them to Ireland in their dealings with their Irish employer. When Li tried to leave, his employer threatened to call the police and have him deported. In January 2003, he was told that there was no longer a job for him. Yet as explained by Li: 'The truth is that in order to make another €30,000 the person who brought me to Ireland is the one who organised my dismissal, so that he could arrange for another person to replace me in the restaurant.[68]

Many Chinese living in the Republic of Ireland, various analyses suggest, do not appear on census records.[69] 5,842 were identified as resident in the 2002 census; by 2006 this number had almost doubled to 11,161.[70] Yet other estimates (also from 2006) which used work permit and student visa data put the Chinese population at about 60,000, which seems more accurate as 15,933 student visas were issued to students from China during 2004 alone. The 2006 report suggested that there were between 60,000 and 100,000 Chinese in Ireland.[71] In 2008, the Chinese ambassador claimed that about

80,000 Chinese lived in the Republic of Ireland.[72] The Chinese identified in the Republic's 2006 census were predominately second-wavers. Most were young adults in their twenties, 71 per cent were single and 43 per cent were on student visas. Ninety-five per cent lived in either towns or cities and half lived in Dublin. Twenty eight per cent were educated to at least degree level; a further 59 per cent had completed upper secondary education or no degree third level courses; the remaining 13 per cent were poorly educated. Over half of those in employment worked in hotels or restaurants. The proportion of equivalent second-wavers amongst the Chinese in Northern Ireland remained smaller. At least seventy per cent originated in Hong Kong, and between 80 and 90 per cent spoke Cantonese. Only a small percentage spoke Mandarin, the main language of the Chinese mainland.[73]

Community organisations emerged in both the Republic and in Northern Ireland. The Hau Shang Hui (Chinese Chamber of Commerce) was established in 1983 by a number of first-wave entrepreneurs. It later expanded its remit and changed its name to the Chinese Society of Ireland, and established a weekend school for Irish-born Hong Kong Chinese children. Two Dublin-based Chinese newspapers were established, the *Sun Emerald Chinese News* in 2003, and *Ireland Chinese News* in 2005; a Chinese Students' Association was established in 2003. Different voluntary organisations emerged to cater to Cantonese speakers from Hong Kong; Mandarin speakers from Northern China (the Association of Chinese Businesses in Ireland); and those from the Fujian province (the Irish Fujian Association), who spoke a regional dialect. A number of different informal professional associations and groups were also established, most of which were run on a voluntary basis, while a few others were funded by the Chinese government; none were run by the Irish state. These were variously concerned with maintaining a shared sense of Chinese solidarity and identity, with an ongoing emphasis on promoting Chinese culture, for example, through Chinese New Year events. They were similar to organisations in other countries that were part of the Chinese diaspora. They did not by and large engage in activism aimed at influencing the Irish state.[74]

Affirmations of Chinese identity in Ireland have focused primarily on loyalty to and concerns about China. Perhaps even more so than in the case of the Irish post-1820s diaspora, the 'motherland' has remained the focal point of Chinese communities around the world. The low profile of Chinese immigrants in Ireland appears to be in keeping with Chinese emigrants elsewhere. Some community campaigns in Ireland focused on funding schools in poor areas in China or on earthquake relief there. The Irish Chinese Sichuan Earthquake Appeal Committee was established on 14 May 2008, bought together Chinese organisations in Ireland who became involved in fundraising. A candlelight vigil organised by the Committee was attended by some 5,000 mostly Chinese people.[75]

Although there are far fewer Chinese in Northern Ireland than in the Republic, the former have had a higher political profile and have engaged with the state to a greater extent. Chinese immigrants in the North, mostly first-wavers, kept out of the sectarian conflicts which dominated politics and life in the province. However, they established an organisation, the Chinese Welfare Association, which worked to improve access to mainstream social, health, welfare, educational and legal services for Chinese immigrants and their families. Anna Lo, a former chairperson of the Chinese Welfare Association, was elected to the Northern Ireland Assembly for Belfast South in 2007, the first East-Asian-born politician to be elected to any legislative body in Northern Ireland.

Anna Lo was educated in Hong Kong, where she worked as a secretary. She moved to London in her early twenties, and married a journalist who worked for the *Belfast Telegraph*. In Belfast, she first worked as a secretary for a newspaper and then for the BBC World Service on current affairs broadcasts in Cantonese. She subsequently worked as a part-time police interpreter in cases involving the Chinese community, 'mostly racist incidents or car accidents'. From 1986 she worked for the Chinese Welfare Association as a part-time English teacher and trained as a social worker. In 1997 she became the first full-time director of the Chinese Welfare Association, and during her ten years in the post, funding was obtained for a purpose-built Chinese Community Centre and a sheltered housing scheme for elderly Chinese was established. In 1999 she was awarded an MBE for her work on behalf of the Chinese community.[76]

Anna Lo campaigned to have the 1976 UK Race Relations Act extended to Northern Ireland, which occurred in 1997. She became a member of the Alliance Party, and in 2006 stood successfully to become a member of the legislative assembly. In 2014 she was attacked by a Loyalist mob and became the focus of online abuse.[77] In an interview with the *Hong Kong Post* she said she was quitting politics because a rise in racism in Northern Ireland had left her feeling more vulnerable than previously, despite having lived through some of the province's worst sectarian violence.[78] In another 2014 interview she stated that during her 40 years in Northern Ireland there had 'always been low-level racist harassment of the Chinese community'.[79]

BRAZILIANS

In 1998, a meat processing plant-owner from Gort in County Galway recruited some workers from the small town of Vila Fabril, a suburb of Anápolis in the Brazilian state of Goiás. Vila Fabril had been built in the 1950s to accommodate the employees of nearby meat-processing plant. The plant closed during the late-1990s, but in 1998, an Irishman who had worked in Vila Favil as a plant manager arranged for 25 former employees to work in similar factories in Ireland. Various meat factories owners began to recruit Brazilians from Vila Fabril. Among them was Sean Duffy Meat Exports in Gort, which recruited six Brazilians 1999. Gort subsequently became to Vila Fabril what Springfield, Massachusetts was to the Blasket Islands. The chain migration that followed linked the two localities. Lucimeire Trindale, one of the first to arrive explained, 'Everyone who went brought another person. My friend who went first, she brought myself, her two sisters and her cousin. I brought my brothers and then my uncles. One brought another, and another, and another.'[80] Over time, Brazilians in Gort branched out into the retail, catering, construction and transport sectors.[81]

The arrival of the Brazilians in Gort reversed generations of population decline and injected, according to several newspaper articles, a new vibrancy into the social life of the town. One from 2004 described how each year hundreds of Brazilians gathered in the town's square to celebrate the carnival season. The article noted that Western Union had set up a new branch in Gort because the Brazilians sent so much money back home each week. The principal of the Convent of Mercy primary school reported that more than 30 children from Brazil had enrolled, and the school had recruited two language-support teachers to help the newcomers with English. The children, she said, fitted in well. The Brazilians were 'lovely people and very polite and refined'.[82] A 2008 interview quoted another teacher saying that the Brazilians brought 'a ray of light into a dark Irish town'. It also emphasised how many Irish residents people from Gort benefited from the arrival of Brazilian migrants. Some of the locals owned second houses, which they let to the newcomers; many hired Brazilian women as cleaners. Many apparently viewed the Brazilians as hardworking, responsible, well-organised and law-abiding. Broadly speaking, they were willing to turn a blind eye to the immigration status of some of the new arrivals;[83] 29 of 44 Brazilian interviewees who participated in a 2008 study were undocumented. They were worried about deportation, were wary of interacting with public services, and were afraid to return to visit Brazil in case they would not be allowed back in to Ireland.[84] However, during the post-2008 economic downturn, many were squeezed out.

A 2007 article by a journalist who visited both Vila Fabril and Gort described how most Brazilians expected to spend a few years in Ireland, save as much as possible, and then return home to a better life. However, some decided to settle permanently in Ireland. Darcy Gomes, who was interviewed in Vila Fabril, had spent five years in Ireland and had returned to Brazil for a few months. His wife and two adult sons had remained in Gort. Using money they had saved from his work as a panel-beater and his wife's job as a cook in Ireland his family now owned two other houses, which were rented out. One of their sons was engaged to an Irish woman, and both sons spoke good English and had what they regarded as good jobs; they wanted to remain permanently in Ireland.[85]Anderson Gomes went home in 2010 but came back in 2014 to work in a garage in Gort.[86]

By 2007 there were 1,600 Brazilians in Gort. By 2010, the total dropped back to around 500 as the economic crisis bit and unemployment levels rose. By 2010 five separate Pentecostal congregations were operating in Gort. These offered similar kinds of support to congregation members as churches serving Africans around the country described in Chapter 10. An interview with a member of the Assembléia de Deus congregation gave the example of how the church helped the family of a man who was unable to work because of serious health problems. The church helped pay the rent, provided some financial support for groceries, assisted with childcare and tried to help his wife to get a job.[87]

Some degree of segregation existed between Brazilians and other Gort residents, insofar as many of the former were members of Pentecostal churches, whereas the locals largely were not. However, the wider community shopped in businesses run by Brazilians and Irish-run shops carried products such as beans, rice and limes, that appealed to Brazilian customers. From 2002, Catholic Brazilians in Gort were ministered to by a Portuguese-speaking priest based in Limerick, who offered Mass every Sunday in the local Catholic Church. However, after a number of years the number of masses in Portuguese dropped to just one a month in an effort, according to a Catholic priest in Gort, to encourage integration of the Brazilians into the local Irish congregation.[88] Yet most interviewees (both Irish and Brazilian) already considered Brazilians to be well-integrated into daily life in the town. Brazilian shops and businesses included a grocery, an internet café in which the computers were default-set to Portuguese, a clothing store and a hairdresser.[89]

A smaller Brazilian community of 300 became established in Roscommon Town, which also had meat-rendering factories. Their religious needs were served by three Pentecostal churches including a branch of Assembléia de Deus, and a Portuguese-speaking Catholic priest.[90] Yet Brazilians in both towns made up but a small minority of Ireland's Brazilian population. The 2002 census identified a total of 1,087 rising to 4,388 by 2006 and to 8,704 by 2011. More than half (4,377) of those counted in 2011 lived in the Dublin area, More than 90 per cent of those who arrived in 2010 were aged between 15 and 34. Many arrived, like many second-wave Chinese migrants, on student visas to attend English-language schools and worked in the service industry. Again like the Chinese, this was facilitated by an agreement between the two governments, which permitted up to 4,000 Brazilian undergraduate students to come to Ireland between 2013 and 2016. A part of Brazil's multinational Science Without Borders scheme, 537 STEM undergraduates applied to study in Irish institutions in 2013, and a further 646 were redirected to Ireland that year because places in Portugal were oversubscribed.[91] In 2014, almost a quarter (7,263) of a total of 32,780 first-time migrant permits were granted to Brazilians.[92] Unlike their compatriots in Gort who had by then become the focus of a number of research projects, doctoral studies and newspaper features, the new arrivals live increasingly integrated lives in cities like Dublin. Visible signs of Brazilian culture in Dublin include a number of bodega restaurants, Brazilian DJs and night-club events.[93]

Whilst clearly many Brazilians envisaged temporary stays in Ireland, many have settled, with 459 Brazilians becoming Irish citizens in 2014, and 393 in 2015.[94] The 2016 census identified 15,798 Brazilians as residing in the Republic of Ireland.

INVISIBLE MINORITIES

Like the *gastarbeiter* who arrived in West Germany from the 1950s during its first post-war 'economic miracle' period, many 'guest workers' invited to Celtic Tiger Ireland became settlers. The experiences of many labour migrants who came to Ireland to fill low-skilled service industry and construction jobs recalled those of the Irish who took the boat train to England in the decades after Independence. Many of these found it impossible to return permanently to Ireland, instead many travelled home for holidays, kept up links with their home towns and helped others from there to find employment in England.

Many migrants from outside the EU came to Ireland to take up low-paid jobs that did not entitle them to permanent residency nor to bring their families with them. Yet some of these temporary residents remained in Ireland for many years as part of growing Filipino, Chinese, Romanian and other immigrant communities. Many of these sent remittances to families in their countries of origin. Those from outside the EU who were able help family members follow in their footsteps, and those who brought families with them were often in higher-skilled or better-paid jobs that were entitled to Green Cards.

Immigrants experienced higher levels of unemployment during the economic crisis, and whilst unemployment levels decreased as the economy improved, the percentage of immigrants who were still out of work remained higher. For example, unemployment levels for Irish nationals decreased from 11.7 per cent in 2014 and to 9.6 per cent in 2015. The unemployment rate was considerably higher among non-Irish nationals, running at 15.5 per cent in 2014. This also decreased but at 13 per cent in 2015 remained considerably higher than the rate amongst Irish nationals. Immigrants, especially those from non-EU countries were far more likely to be on low incomes than Irish nationals.[95]

Perhaps the most striking characteristic of many new immigrant communities has been their near-invisibility within Irish media and political debates. Compared to many other European countries immigration stayed off the political radar, and political emphasis upon the integration of immigrants, which tends to be driven by host community anxieties about immigration, has been half-hearted at best. In other words seen but not heard. Many immigrant communities established some degree of infrastructure in the form of places of worship, shops and community organisations. Whilst some Africans and Poles joined political parties in the Republic and have contested local government elections there since 2004 (see Chapter 10 and Chapter 12), none from Chinese, Brazilian or a number of other non-European immigrant communities did so. No political figure equivalent to Anna Lo emerged within Chinese community in the Republic for all that this became much larger than the one in Northern Ireland. Yet, Ashock Varadkar's son, Leo Varadkar became Taoiseach in 2017 following a heave within Fine Gael, the largest political party in the then-minority government.[96] From 2011, following a decision by the then-Minister of Justice, Alan Shatter, to remove administrative restrictions, immigrants from non-EU countries began to become Irish citizens in large numbers. Shatter, who is Jewish, was also the son of immigrants. By 2016 the number who had naturalised exceeded 120,000.

This chapter can but offer a glimmer of the complexity of several immigrant communities, each larger than some of the more long-established groups addressed earlier in this book. As of yet relatively little research has been undertaken on their experiences. Mostly, this chapter has drawn on research that has captured fragments of some people's lives. However, it is clear that, amongst these, immigrants from outside the European Union, like the Africans described in Chapter 10, have quickly embraced the opportunity to become Irish citizens and collectively these have complicated what is to be Irish in ways in which Irish politics, Irish literature, the media and academia have yet to come to terms with. Those who have not become Irish citizens have also complicated the Irish narrative. These have become part of Irish society if not, technically speaking, part of the Irish nation.

TWELVE

POLES

In 2004, when the European Union enlarged, the Republic of Ireland decided to immediately permit migrants from the new East European member states to live and work in the country without visas, and in doing so suddenly accelerated the pace of immigration. All pre-2004 EU states except Sweden, the Republic of Ireland and the United Kingdom held back introducing free movement for several years. Most post-2004 Polish migrants went to Britain, but Ireland received the highest proportion as a percentage of the overall population. Between 1 May 2004 and 30 April 2005 some 85,114 workers from the new EU member states were issued with Irish National Insurance numbers, which amounted to more than 10 times the number of new work permits given to migrants from those countries in the preceding 12 months.

The 2006 census identified 63,276 Poles as living in the Republic of Ireland, working mainly in construction (22 per cent), manufacturing (22 per cent), retail (17 per cent), and in hospitality (16 per cent). By 2011, the population of Poles had risen to 122,585, and Polish had overtaken Irish as the second-most commonly spoken language in the country.[1] Although some Poles left Ireland during the post-2008 economic crisis, most stayed, and these were joined by some additional migrants from Poland. The overall number of resident Polish nationals barely changed between 2011 (122,585) and 2016 (122,515), though these numbers do not count a very small proportion who became Irish citizens during this period.

Poland and other Eastern European countries have long histories of migration both within Europe and to the United States. During the Communist era before 1989, these included political refugees. Around 100,000 Poles were granted political asylum or temporary protection in various western countries during the 1980s, just as in previous decades some 194,000 refugees left Hungary following the 1956 Uprising and some 82,000 persons fled Czechoslovakia in 1967–8. Restrictions impeding emigration from their home countries affected some Eastern Europeans during this period, yet the lifting of the Iron Curtain did not result in permanent mass migration. Instead what developed were patterns of seasonal migration to some EU member states, particularly to Germany, and some labour migration between former-Soviet-bloc Eastern European countries.[2]

Seasonal migration occurred for many of the reasons it did from Ireland to Britain; it offered migrants a chance to supplement their family incomes without having to uproot their dependents. It also predominated due to difficulties in acquiring permanent residency visas, particularly in the case of Germany. During the 1990s, some Western European countries granted Poles tourist visas, which enabled these to engage in seasonal work. In 1993, some 143,861 Poles worked seasonally in Germany, and by 2004 this number had risen to 286,623. During this period, communities of undocumented workers from Poland who had outstayed their visas mushroomed in cities such as Berlin, Brussels, Rome, Vienna and London. Surveys conducted in Poland during the 1990s identified many areas in poorer parts of that country where between one-third and more than half of all households lived on remittances from such migrants.[3]

In 2004 unemployment rates in Poland were around 20 per cent, and unemployment levels amongst young Polish adults, who made up most of those who came to Ireland, were around 40 per cent. Unlike the seasonal workers who had travelled to Germany for the previous 15 years or so, the Poles who came to Ireland were comparatively well-educated. Those who went seasonally to Germany kept going there after 2004 even though they still needed visas to do so; they stuck to what they knew and continued to work in the same places. Those who flocked to Ireland, the United Kingdom and, to a lesser extent, Sweden after 2004 tended to be first-time migrants. Friends and relatives followed quickly in their wake.[4] Some of these had jobs in Poland and migrated in search of better-paid ones.

Most migrants from Poland and from other New Member States arrived between 2004 and 2008, and most were young adults. One analysis likened them to the immigrants who flocked to gold rush towns like Melbourne during the 1850s.[5] Those who arrived in the four years after EU enlargement found themselves able walk into certain kinds of employment without difficultly. Many seem to have expected to remain in Ireland temporarily, but became long-term settlers. By 2011 there were 81,318 migrants in Northern Ireland who were not from Britain or the Republic. Just under a quarter (19,658) of these were Polish. Lithuanians (7,241) comprised the next largest group.[6] Other than English Polish became the most commonly spoken language among immigrants (17,731 people) followed by Lithuanian (6,250).[7]

EARLY ARRIVALS

A small amount of Polish settlement in Ireland occurred in the aftermath of the Second World War following on from the arrival of Polish refugees and World War II veterans in Britain. Professor Jan Łukasiewicz, logician, philosopher and former President of Warsaw University, was received by Éamon de Valera who before the war had also helped the Austrian scientist Erwin Schrödinger. Łukasiewicz was appointed Professor of Mathematical Logic at the Royal Irish Academy in 1946 and he lectured at UCD. He died in Dublin in 1956.[8]

Some veterans and refugees used scholarships provided by the British government and Catholic organisations to attend Irish universities after the war. Most seem to have reached Ireland with the help of international Catholic networks. In 1945, Alfred O'Rahilly, President of University College Cork, offered to admit 12 Polish students, and similar invitations followed from other Catholic universities. In 1946, the first cohort of Polish students arrived. By the 1960s, several hundred had come to study medicine, economics and other subjects. Some remained on after they graduated. These included Josef Oslizlok, an economist who became a lecturer at University College Cork and who subsequently worked in the Central Bank; Andrzej Zakrzewski who studied architecture at UCD and later established his own architectural practice; and Jan Kaminski who studied Economics and Political Science at Trinity College and, with Zakrzewski, became a founding member of the Irish Polish Society in 1979.

Jan Kaminski was born in 1932 in Bilgoraj in eastern Poland, where he lived with his Jewish parents, brother and two sisters. Jan was seven years old when his family was rounded up and sent to a concentration camp. He ran away and escaped. None of his family survived. He told nobody that he was Jewish, and was later deported with a group of Polish children to a transit camp at Zwierzyniec. He was put on a train to Germany but again escaped with the help of the Polish resistance. He was taken in by a family in 1941, but had to run away when it was discovered that he was Jewish. He wandered from farm to farm, somehow surviving until 1944, when he was adopted as a mascot by a unit of Polish soldiers attached to the Russian army. By the end of the war, Jan had made his way to a refugee camp in Murnau in south-eastern Germany, where he attended school for the first time. He subsequently made his way to England via Italy with a group of Polish soldiers. In England, he continued his education, and in 1954 obtained a scholarship from the Catholic charity Veritas to study at University College Cork. Once in Ireland, he transferred to Trinity College in Dublin. He became an Irish citizen, worked in the embryonic computer industry and became a successful businessman. The businesses he ran included a restaurant, a nightclub, a travel business and hotels in Ireland, Poland and Spain.[9]

From the 1960s on, a small number of refugees from communist Poland settled in Ireland. These included Andrzej Wejchert, an architect who designed University College Dublin's Belfield campus. Wejchert taught architecture at UCD and established a practice that designed many prominent buildings and retail projects. Michal Ozmin, a graduate of Warsaw Academy of Fine Arts, worked for Andrzej Zakrzewski's architectural practice, before becoming a head of faculty the National Institute of Art and Design in Dublin. Maciej Smolenski who moved to England from Poland as a refugee when he was child in 1940 became a professor in the Royal Irish Academy of Music in 1974.

The impetus for the establishment of the Irish Polish Society was the visit to Ireland in 1989 of the Polish-born Pope, John Paul II. The Society purchased a large Georgian building on Fitzwilliam Place in Dublin, which came to be named Polish House, and has since been used by more recently established Polish community organisations.[10]

THE BIG BANG

This first wave was tiny compared to the post-2004 wave of Poles who came to the Republic and Northern Ireland. Like the Lithuanians, but on a far larger scale, Poles settled all around the island and mostly did jobs that the host population were unwilling to do. Most were young adults who initially saw themselves as temporary migrants.[11] A study by the anthropologist Marta Kempny interviewed 50 young Poles who settled in Belfast,[12] of whom many intended to remain in Ireland for less than five years. Some discussed plans to return to Poland after they had saved up money for a house there. Many apparently had no clear long-term plans for the future; most were in their twenties, and though many were in relationships with other Polish migrants, most did not have children at the time. Most lived in predominantly Protestant areas of Belfast where housing was available. Many were practicing Catholics and members of Polish congregations. They spoke Polish, kept up Polish customs and ate Polish food. Singletons mostly lived with other young Polish migrants, as did Basia, who arrived in Belfast in 2007 and lived in North Belfast with friends from Poland. She had worked as a sales assistant in Poland and found employment, like a number of other Poles, in a call centre that worked with customers in Poland. She spent her working day speaking Polish, and much of her spare time on Polish social media websites.

A Polish chaplaincy was established in Belfast in 2007 when Fr Mariusz Dabrowski arrived in Northern Ireland.[13] Polish Catholic priests similarly arrived to minister to migrants in the Republic, including Fr Marek who was 53 years old when he moved to Dublin from Krakow. The aims and objectives of the Polish chaplaincy resembled the one set up during the 1950s to minister to Irish Catholic emigrants in England. The Polish chaplaincy set up a wide range of facilities and networks to support migrants during their stay in Ireland. These included free English classes, information boards, support groups, legal advice centres, counselling services and Alcoholics Anonymous groups. Fr Marek and other migrants interviewed in a study of Polish religiosity argued that their Catholicism was distinct from Irish Catholicism because it was integral to Polish cultural and ethnic identity. As in the Irish case Catholicism in Poland became the basis of a distinct national ethnic identity. Churches used by the Polish chaplaincy were decorated to look like ones in Poland, and Masses were held in Polish.[14]

Most of the 41 devout interviewees who took part in a study of Polish Catholicism were either unmarried adults in their twenties, or migrants with families in their thirties. What they shared was that they turned to the Polish chaplaincy for support when they arrived in the Republic. Most were well-educated, like Beata, who arrived in Dublin aged 28 with a Master's in Psychology. She had lived with her mother in Krakow, did not earn enough in a local restaurant where she worked to move out of the family home. She was put in touch with Luckasz, a friend of a friend who worked in security in Dublin and met him for the first time at the spire on O'Connell Street, and he put her up for a while. She then established a social network of church-going friends. Like Beata and Luckasz these friends were devout Polish Catholics who attended services organised by a Polish chaplaincy. Luckasz had been a member of this congregation from the time of his arrival in 2005. Beata, who planned to stay in Ireland for just a few years, saw no particular need to assimilate into Irish society. She worked as a secretary and otherwise lived her life as part of a Polish Catholic congregation. She spoke to her mother every day on Skype.[15]

Except for access to the Internet, aspects of Beata's life in Ireland resembled that of the protagonist in Colm Tóibín's novel *Brooklyn* about a young educated Catholic Irishwoman who was helped to settle in New York during the 1950s by a friendly priest. And again, very much like so many migrants anywhere, Beata became a link in a chain of migration that came to include other members of her family and friends:

> Someone brave goes first. My sister and her husband, my sister-in-law, and uncle, and five friends came because we were here, and we told them they could stay. We know other people that came because they had friends over here. It was always like a family going together, for most part it would be brothers and sisters going over bringing their partners and family.[16]

Nadia, a 34 year-old interviewee in the same study described how her husband, again with help from Luckcsz, managed within a few months to get a job and rent a house. She then followed with their two children. Luckasz knew an employer who needed a receptionist, and fixed Nadia up with a job. Luckasz's sister helped Nadia to get her children into the same day care as their cousins.[17]

Not all the migrants were young adults, however. Wojtek, a 39-year-old former farmer from Wegorzewo came to Belfast in 2006. He lived with his girlfriend Magdelena in South Belfast, and worked at the O'Kane chicken factory. Their plan was to live in Belfast for a few years whilst saving up money for a house back home. Magdelena had worked as a hairdresser in Poland and now worked as a cleaner in Belfast. They shared their apartment with Magdelena's niece, Marzena, who had worked previously for two years in southern Spain as a waitress. Magdelena helped Marzena get a job as a cleaner at the factory where she worked. Krzysztof, a 42-year-old man from Lipno in Western Poland, had worked as a psychiatric nurse in Poland but was made redundant. In Belfast he worked as a cleaner. He lived with his wife, Monika, and their two young daughters in Central Belfast. She had worked as a psychiatric nurse in the same hospital in Poland, and had also been made redundant.

New Mobilities in Europe, a study in the Republic interviewed 22 young, mostly well-educated Polish adults several times each between 2008 and 2010. Interviewees typically took starter jobs when they arrived in Ireland, but managed to progress to employment that reflected their skills; they were willing to accept pay cuts in order to do so. Most weathered the post-2008 economic downturn successfully. Some, like Karol, who had worked in customer services, had left better-paid jobs in Poland to move to Dublin some years earlier as a temporary move. Karol's plan had been to spend a year in Ireland with his girlfriend. He initially worked as a kitchen porter, then as a labourer on a building site, and then moved to an entry-level position in the banking sector, which did not pay as well. After six years in Ireland, he returned to Poland to open a business. Olga similarly came to Ireland for what she thought of as a gap year. Six years later she was still working as a waitress, but now lived in North America having also worked as one in the United Kingdom.[18]

Many well-educated Poles, especially those unable to speak fluent English, were unable to obtain jobs that made use of their qualifications, and it typically took graduates several years to move into white-collar employment. For example, Piotr Gawlik grew up in Krakow. Six months after completing a Master's degree in Forestry Science at the Agricultural University of Krakow, he was recruited to work in Naas through an agency by Abrakebabra, an Irish fast food chain. Initially he planned to work in Ireland for a year or so before returning to Krakow. His employer arranged accommodation in Newbridge, in a house rented by a group of Polish migrants. He quit after a disastrous first night when he was put operating the till even though his English was poor and he was not familiar with the menu. Within a few days he found another job as a kitchen porter, and after a time he was temporarily promoted to chef.

He undertook related work until March 2008, during which time his English improved and he applied for many other jobs. He was recruited by the Bank of Ireland in 2008, where he has worked since as a commercial loans administrator and as a financial crime investigator in the bank's anti-money laundering unit. From 2008 to 2015 he studied part-time, and obtained qualifications from the Institute of Banking. In 2013, he was joined by his younger sister who worked as a child minder and then as a hospital cleaner before marrying and settling in Waterford. Her husband, whom she met in Ireland, was also Polish.[19]

Not all Poles fared well in Ireland. By 2006 the Polish Embassy estimated that up to 600 were accessing services for homeless people,[20] having either failed to obtain work or having become unemployed, and were prohibited from claiming unemployment benefits. Under the 2004 Social Welfare (Miscellaneous Provisions) Act all migrants to Ireland – including Irish citizens returning from a period living abroad – became ineligible for benefits for a two-year period. The Act was introduced at the same time that the Republic opened its borders to migrants from new EU member states. During the post-2008 economic crisis large numbers of Poles and other migrants working in the construction sector and elsewhere became unemployed. Many had been living in Ireland long enough to become entitled to unemployment benefits. By 2011 some 23,905 Poles were in receipt of some form of jobseekers allowance or unemployment benefit. During the recession, unemployment rates amongst Poles who remained in Ireland were disproportionately high. In 2012 Poles constituted some 3.3 per cent of the adult population and 4.39 per cent of claimants of unemployment schemes that were open to the working-age population.[21] Many of those Irish citizens who emigrated during the economic crisis (see Chapter 8) were under-employed rather than unemployed and had the resources to move elsewhere; most of those who were unemployed remained in Ireland. Likewise, many Poles who had become unemployed weathered the economic crisis in Ireland, in the absence of opportunities to do better elsewhere. For many, returning to Poland, where unemployment remained high, was not an option. If many Poles seemed to be sojourners before the economic crisis, some appeared by its end to have put down roots.

SETTLEMENT

Teresa Buczkowska arrived in Naas, County Kildare, in June 2005, having being encouraged to come to Ireland by her best friend who put her up when she arrived. She had completed four out of a five-year combined undergraduate and Master's degree programme in Social Anthropology at Jagiellonian University in Krakow and planned to spend the summer working in Ireland before returning to complete her studies. She had been pushed to go to Ireland by her mother, who had similarly encouraged her older brother and sister and two younger brothers to find jobs abroad. Her mother had raised five children as a lone parent in Nowa Sanzyna, a small town in south-eastern Poland near the Ukrainian border. By the time Teresa arrived in Ireland, all her siblings and her mother were working several different countries. Her older sister, who had trained as a baker, became an undocumented seasonal worker in Italy. Her mother also went to Italy. Both worked as carers sharing the same job on three-month rotas. Her mother subsequently settled in Liverpool, where her eldest brother was working in a warehouse. He had graduated as a chemical engineer, and eventually got a job in this same field in London. Previously he had worked as a seasonal fruit-picker in Sweden. Her two younger brothers then aged 18 and 19 went to work in construction in Spain.

Teresa envisaged working in Ireland for the summer before resuming her studies. However, it took her four weeks to find a job as a packer in a warehouse, and she deferred returning to college. She found a better-paid, similar job where she worked for a few months, then in a pizza takeaway restaurant for almost a year, and then in a butcher's shop for several years. Within eight weeks of getting her first job, her two younger brothers moved from Spain to stay with her in Naas. In Ireland, construction work was better paid and, because Spain had not yet removed visa requirements from migrants from new EU member states, conditions of employment were better. She subsequently put one of her brothers through college. He studied three-dimensional animation at Ballyfermot College and subsequently moved back to Poland to a town near Nowa Sanzyna where he set up a business. Teresa's sister also joined her, but returned to Poland after six months as a lack of fluency in English proved to be an insurmountable barrier. She became the sole member of the family to move back to Nowa Sanzyna. Her other brother moved to Liverpool, where their mother lived, and later followed his elder brother to London, where he settled.

Teresa resumed her studies on a part-time basis. She took social science courses at Maynooth University and travelled back and forth to Krakow to complete her Master's degree; she wrote a thesis about Polish migrants living in Naas and Newbridge. Between 2008 and 2010 she interviewed around 30 fellow migrants aged between 18 and 45 who had typically arrived in Ireland after EU Enlargement. Many experienced very poor living and housing conditions: 'They could not grasp that they did not have to accept such conditions.' Some had left families behind in Poland, lived very frugally and sent most of their wages back home, resulting sometimes in isolation. Interviewees described counting out how many slices of bread they could have for breakfast. Many of the Poles who came over to Ireland after EU enlargement believed that their stays in Ireland would be temporary and avoided commitments such as mortgages that suggested otherwise, and so left Ireland during the economic crisis, particularly if they were working in construction. Those with families returned to Poland or brought them to settle in Ireland which meant that they no longer had to send money back to home, and the number living in cheap and crowded accomodation dropped over time. Yet most Poles continued to behave as if they were going to return to Poland. Some, who thought they had saved enough to buy a house in Poland found themselves returning to Ireland when, because of poor economic conditions there, they could not afford to remain in Poland.[22]

Only a minority of Polish migrants left Ireland during the post-2008 economic crisis, and most of these were men who had worked in construction and related industries which declined hugely as a result of the crisis. This development restored somewhat the gender balance amongst Poles in Ireland, but most had been sufficiently long in Ireland to meet the two-year habitual residency criteria for entitlements to social security benefits. Polish women were less badly affected by the economic crisis because they worked in areas that survived the recession. Even if combined family incomes fell during the economic crisis in Ireland, they were often significantly higher than might be possible in Poland.[23]

Interviewees in a study completed in 2014 had mostly been living in Ireland for a decade, during which time their circumstances had changed. Most were in their 20s when they arrived and were now in their thirties; some had married, had children who spoke English fluently, and had purchased houses. Many continued to believe that their quality of life was better in Ireland than in Poland.[24] Many believed that their children would have better opportunities if they remained in Ireland.[25]

However, most Polish adults continued to speak Polish in their homes and to one another. Poor English-language fluency appears to be a reason why many Poles interacted predominantly with fellow Polish-speakers, relied on Polish acquaintances and family members. The large size of the Polish community meant that Polish was a viable community language; the total number who spoke Polish daily was at least twice the number who regularly spoke Irish. Whilst Poles did not live in geographical enclaves within Ireland, some worked in jobs in which fluent English was unnecessary such as in Lidl and Aldi supermarkets. Those uncomfortable with speaking in English or with no particular desire to integrate could go to Polish food shops, buy brands they knew from home, and purchase Polish newspapers and magazines. By 2009, there were at least 15 Polish shops in Cork City, with many more in Dublin, and Polish supermarkets opened in many Irish towns.[26]

Various studies of Poles in the Republic and Northern Ireland tell similar stories of how temporary stays became longer ones, how single migrants connected with family members or started new families of their own, set up community organisations, Polish scout troops, Polish schools and shops that sold Polish food. The grandmothers of some Polish children whose parents were working moved to Ireland. In both Northern Ireland and in the Republic, a system of Polish Saturday schools was quickly established.

By 2014, some 30 Polish complementary schools, offering classes to children in Polish on Saturdays and Sundays, had been established in the Republic. These followed Poland's school curriculum in Polish language studies, history, geography and, in some cases, maths. Their purpose was not just to help migrant parents pass on their language and culture to their children, but to prepare the children for re-entry into the Polish education and exam system should they return there. Agnieszka Grochola, the founder of one such school in Galway, had been a secondary school teacher in Poland. Her husband Tomasz was a manager in the Polish forestry service but still they could not make a living out of their two salaries. Agnieszka came to Ireland in 2007. Within a week of arriving, with very little English, she found a part-time job in a factory canteen. Even though this paid just the minimum wage she managed to send some money back to her family in Poland, and three months later, Tomasz came over with their children. He got as job as a tree surgeon with the Electricity Supply Board, and they settled in Tuam. The children attended a local school, which provided some English-language support. Agnieszka subsequently became concerned about one of the children's fluency in Polish, even though this is the spoken language at home. Agnieszka realised that others of her compatriots in Ireland had similar problems, so she decided to set up a Polish school. By 2015, the school had 350 pupils attending every Saturday and was one of the biggest in the country.[27]

The Irish State, for its part, recognised Polish as a leaving certificate exam subject and by 2013 some 1,470 children had sat leaving certificate examinations in the subject.[28] Five Szholny Punkt Konsultacyjny (SPK) schools were funded by the Polish Ministry of Education in Cavan, Cork, Dublin, Limerick and Waterford and catered to 2,641 pupils. In addition,

24 community schools were run and financed by Polish immigrants with financial assistance from the Polish Ministry of Foreign Affairs. Five of these community schools were located in County Dublin, three in County Galway, four in Mayo, two in Carlow, and one each in Donegal, Kerry, Kildare, Kilkenny, Laois, Limerick, Louth, Meath, Sligo, Tipperary, and Wexford. These catered for around 1,500 Polish children, a small minority of the total number.[29] Of the 122,585 Poles identified in the 2011 census, 25,291 were children or teenagers.[30]

A 2014 study of Poles who had settled in Northern Ireland almost a decade earlier described interviewees as simultaneously assimilated yet also leading transnational lives made possible by social media and cheap flights. These were parents of children who spoke English outside the home and either Polish or both languages at home. Some parents in Belfast were concerned that their children learn the Polish language and about Polish culture, so some sent their children to Polish-language Saturday schools in an effort to ensure that their children be taught both cultures.[31] The hope of returning someday to Poland lay behind the efforts of several interviewees to ensure that their children grew up speaking Polish.

The same study identified other parents who had made little or no effort to ensure that their children grew up Polish. Whilst their lives remained bound up with other Poles – family at home and fellow immigrants in Ireland – they did not insist on this for their children.[32] Whilst a sizeable minority sent their children to complementary Polish-language schools, the majority did not. Kasia, who was involved in the running of a Polish-language school in Belfast, spoke Polish at home and had Polish cable TV. Yet, her children didn't want her to speak Polish when their friends were around; they even asked her to send them text messages in English. Not everybody knew they were Polish, and after several years in Ireland they had the same accents as their classmates.[33]

POLSKA ÉIRE

Like most emigrants from EU countries, Poles in Ireland have tended not to become Irish citizens, as unlike immigrants from non-EU countries, they already have the right to move freely within the Union. As the largest immigrant group the Poles nevertheless attracted the interest of Irish political parties, for non-citizen residents are entitled to vote in local government elections only in the Republic. In the run-up to the 2009 election, the two then-largest political parties Fianna Fáil and Fine Gael each recruited a Polish integration officer to attract Polish voters. Crucially, both parties also selected a handful of Polish candidates.

For example, Katarzyna Gaborec stood as a Fianna Fáil candidate in Mullingar. She studied law in Wroclaw University and worked in Poland in a solicitor's office before deciding to move to Ireland for one year to improve her English. She arrived in Mullingar in 2007. To begin with, she worked in a hotel before being offered a job in the office of a construction company that was seeking investment opportunities in Poland; she ran one office in Mullingar and the company's branch in Poland. With the help of her employer, she set up the Mullingar Polish Association. Its aim was to support integration of the immigrants and to provide a range of free services including legal advice, document translation, and other advocacy services. Her employer was a member of Fianna Fáil in Mullingar. He knew she was active in the local community, and he encouraged her to stand as a candidate for election to the Mullingar Town Council. She encouraged Poles and Lithuanians in the town to register to vote, and printed election materials in Polish, Lithuanian, and Russian. However, like other Polish candidates she found that only a small proportion of her compatriots were interested in voting. She was one of nine candidates standing in a constituency in which 5,256 votes were cast and received 254 first-preference votes. After the election she withdrew from politics and had a child. Because she had to commute to work in Dublin she became less politically active in her local community over time.[34]

About 20 Eastern European candidates stood in the 2009 local government elections. Most were Polish, had children living with them in Ireland, were practising Catholics and none had been members of political parties in Poland. All referred to a general antipathy amongst Polish immigrants in Ireland to becoming involved in politics or even registering to vote, which they saw as a legacy of mistrust of government in Poland. Some explained their involvement in politics as an effort to promote such interaction.[35]

No Polish candidates were elected in 2009, nor did they bring significant numbers of immigrant votes that could be transferred from unelected candidates under the proportional representation voting system to other candidates in the same party. A smaller number of Polish candidates stood for election in 2014, none of whom were members of a political party. Some of these independent candidates emphasised the need to promote the integration of immigrants, yet most of their campaigning was directed at fellow Poles rather the wider community, suggesting that their main aim was to achieve prominence within the Polish community.[36]

Forum Polonia emerged as the main representative organisation of the post-2004 wave of Poles in the Republic. Its membership included most of the Polish candidates who stood in the 2009 and 2014 local government elections. Branches of Forum Polonia were set up to advocate on behalf of Polish migrants in the United Kingdom and the United States as well as in the Republic of Ireland. In 2008 and 2009 Forum Polonia ran an information and mobilisation campaign 'Give a voice', which aimed to increase the number of Poles registering and voting in Irish local elections, and to project a positive image of Poles to the host community. Active citizenship volunteers received training and organised a number of registration events. The training received drew on the support of organisations in Poland like the Warsaw-based School for Leaders Association, which has provided training and support for Polish organisations in more than 40 countries.

A larger and more ambitious civic participation campaign was launched in advance of the 2014 local government elections under the slogan 'Vote! You are at home.' This was based on 'Your vote, Your choice', a project funded by the Polish Ministry of Foreign Affairs aimed at encouraging migrants living in Italy, Spain, France, the Netherlands, the United Kingdom, Belgium, Hungary and Ireland to participate in the 2014 European Parliamentary elections. The project also encouraged Poles to register to vote in the Irish and British 2014 local government elections.[37] The 'Vote! You are at home' campaign had two elements: firstly, it encouraged voter registration; and secondly, it sought to build a network of Polish community leaders and volunteers in Ireland and mentor potential candidates. Forum Polonia became the chief co-ordinating body for the campaign in Ireland. It organised the distribution of around 10,000 voter registration forms, provided training on the Irish political system, and secured the support of 20 Polish (Catholic) Parishes, community organisations such as The Irish Polish Society in Dublin and the Together-Razem Centre in Cork, radio stations like Dublin City FM (which broadcast polish language programmess), newspapers and magazines including *Polska Gazeta* and social media platforms like polskiexpress.ie.

The 'Vote! You are at home' campaign exhorted Ireland's Polish community to engage with Irish politics, yet the networks that sought to promote integration in Ireland were politically and institutionally orientated towards Poland. Not only was the 2014 campaign financially supported by the Polish Embassy in Dublin, but the meetings and seminars in which the campaign developed and was publicised were almost exclusively Polish affairs where Poles networked with one another and with embassy officials. In summary, therefore, political activism seemed to be strongly orientated towards Polish communities rather than outwardly towards the wider electorate. This is in keeping with the political focus of Polish emigrants since the nineteenth century, especially in the United States where Polish organisations focused on second-generation retention of Polish language and culture there, and on Polish domestic politics.[38]

The 'Vote! You are at home' campaign and other 2014 efforts to encourage political participation were based on the presumption that Poles in Ireland were very reluctant to participate. Forum Polonia went so far as to prepare responses to typical statements from Poles unwilling to vote: 'It does not look good that we poke our nose in the matters of the Irish!'; 'I am better off here than in Poland, so I shouldn't be complaining about anything.'; 'We should sit quiet and be happy that they don't want to get rid of us'; 'The Irish might not like that we feel "at home". This is their country, not mine!'[39]

The tone of the 'Vote! You are at Home' campaign organised in the United Kingdom was somewhat different. The 2014 British local government elections took place in a context where, unlike the Irish case, anti-immigrant populism found ongoing expression in mainstream politics. In 2013, police officers arrested 585 people for hate crimes against Poles.[40] Polish organisations were openly critical of anti-Polish racism and of the British political establishment. Witold Sobków, the Polish Ambassador to the United Kingdom, publicly condemned prejudice against Poles in the British media.[41] In January 2014, the Polish Minister for Foreign Affairs did likewise following comments by David Cameron about child benefit payments for the children of Polish migrants.[42] Representatives of Polish organisations in the UK signed an open letter demanding that the Prime Minister 'state unequivocally that Poles should be treated equally to others'.[43] In February 2014, Polish activists organised a rally opposite Downing Street in London to protest discrimination against Polish people living in the UK. In April 2015, the Polish government expressed concern about what it described as an upsurge of racist attacks against Poles living in Northern Ireland: 88 out of some 476 hate crimes recorded there in 2014 were directed at Poles. Some of these involved Loyalist paramilitaries who targeted Catholic Poles that lived in Protestant areas.[44] In 2016, the majority referendum vote to leave the European Union (Brexit) was generally interpreted as one in support of restrictions on immigration by Poles (by then numbering more than 1 million) to the UK. Anti-immigrant political populism during the Brexit campaign apparently resulted in a rise in hate crime and racist abuse directed towards Poles amongst others that continued after the referendum was held.[45]

In 2014, the Polish Embassy in the Republic released 'Thank You Ireland' a comic video clip marking the tenth anniversary unrestricted travel in which a Polish narrator (speaking in Irish with English subtitles) says: 'On behalf of all the Poles in Ireland, we thank the Irish people for your welcome.' After a few droll scenes in which bemused Poles attempted to play Irish sports, read James Joyce's *Ulysses*, eat an Irish fried breakfast, and toast one another with pints of Guinness the video ended with a group shot of embassy staff holding balloons and the line, 'But most of all thank you for being so open, making us feel like at home for the last ten years.'

Research from 2011, which interviewed thousands of immigrants across a number of European countries, found that 15 per cent of the 1,056 Polish participants in Ireland believed that Poles were often or very often discriminated against there. When these were re-surveyed a year and a half later, the percentage had fallen to just over ten per cent. By comparison, almost 20 per cent of Polish interviewees in the United Kingdom believed that Poles living there often or very often experienced discrimination. When re-interviewed a year and a half later the percentage believing so had risen to almost 30 per cent.[46] Far higher proportions of Polish respondents in the Netherlands and Germany believed that discrimination against Poles occurred often or very often. For all that, Poles in Ireland may have felt that they had to keep their heads down they were apparently believed that they more welcome in the Republic of Ireland than in these other countries.

In 2015 the first of what has since become an annual Polska Éire festival was jointly organised by the Polish Embassy and Department of Justice officials, and included sporting events with Polish and Irish teams, concerts, art exhibitions, and social events 'to celebrate the diversity that Polish people bring to Ireland', 'strengthen integration between Irish and Polish communities', and to 'promote and strengthen Polish–Irish bilateral relations, both at national and community levels'.[47] Taken together with the slow inclusion of Polish as a secondary school exam subject, and the absence of initiatives by the Irish state to encourage the Poles to learn English, the Republic's response to its largest immigrant community might be described as the kind of weak multiculturalism that is no longer fashionable elsewhere in Europe. Simply put, the response of the Republic to its largest immigrant community has been one of benign neglect.

Whilst Polish organisations have focused on promoting the Polish language and culture, there has also been emphasis on engaging positively with wider Irish society. Small numbers of Poles have joined political parties. Others became active members of trades unions. The latter include Barnaba Dorda, a lawyer from Tychy in southern Poland employed by the SIPTU, who was also a leading member of Forum Polonia. Some Poles have become activists in organisations not focused exclusively on Polish issues. Piotr Gawlik in 2012 became the first Polish board member of the National LGBT Federation, and also became an active member of Forum Polonia where he sought to promote LGBT rights. He became the project manager of a 2014 Forum Polonia photography competition on the theme of Polish–Irish connections and exhibition aimed at marking the tenth anniversary of free Polish migration to Ireland. The winning entry was a black and white image of a father feeding his baby. The runner up was a photograph of a gay Polish couple.

As part of the first 2015 Polska-Éire Festival, Piotr Gawlik organised a screening of *I Still Believe*, a documentary about Ewa Holuszko, a transgender *Solidarno* (Solidarity trade union) activist who was imprisoned during the 1980s. The screening was followed by an interview with Anna Grodzka, a Polish MP, filmed during her visit to Ireland as Grand Marshal of the

Dublin Pride Parade. Piotr Gawlik found it difficult to pursue LGBT rights campaigns, in particular the campaign for same-sex marriage equality, within the confines of Forum Polonia. In 2014 he founded Dialogue and Diversity a campaign group focused on immigrant rights and integration, which has held several events involving African, Muslim and South American migrant organisations, trades unions and Polish organisations.[48]

For several years Teresa Buczkowska worked a volunteer for the Polish Information and Cultural Centre on a part-time basis in Dublin after which she did similar voluntary work with groups working with other immigrants. She moved into this field permanently when, following an internship with the Immigrant Council of Ireland, she was employed as a policy officer. In a 2014 essay, based on her research in Newbridge and Naas, Teresa recalled being asked by a customer at the butcher's shop where she worked, 'Why won't you all just go home?' The answer, she concluded, was 'because for the vast majority of us, this is home'.[49]

THIRTEEN

MUSLIMS

From the eighteenth century, small numbers of Muslims and Hindus from India visited and settled in Britain and Ireland – far fewer than travelled in the other direction as colonial administrators or soldiers. From the 1840s, Muslim students came to England, Scotland and Wales to attend boarding schools to qualify in the professions, particularly medicine. These included Mir Aulad Ali (1832–98), born in northern India, in what was in essence a vassal state of the British East India Company, where his father was a Superintendent of Public Works. Mir Aulud Ali became a Professor of Arabic, Hindustani and Persian at Trinity College Dublin after having previously been at University College London. He became involved in the Gaelic Revival as an early member of the Society for the Preservation of the Irish Language, which predated the Gaelic League. He was directly involved in setting up the first certification scheme for Irish-language teachers.[1]

At the end of the nineteenth century, a Muslim family that had previously worked for the East India Company opened a business and settled near Ballymena, County Antrim.[2] A handful of others who settled in Ireland can be identified from census records and registers of aliens. These included a few Egyptian sailors and their families found to be living in Dublin in 1918. Six Egyptian doctors arrived in 1919 from medical schools in England to take up further training in Dublin maternity hospitals. A 1931 *Irish Times* article estimated that 30 or 40 Muslim men worked as silk merchants, though some of these may well have been Hindu.[3]

Ireland's Muslim communities in the North and in the Republic were founded and came to be led by medical students, some of whom became permanent residents or established the first mosques. The first wave came from South Africa; these were the sons of well-to-do South Asians who fled apartheid. They were sympathetic to the political struggles of Arabic-speaking Muslims in Algeria and Egypt and North Africa and were joined by students and some other migrants from these countries. The Muslim Brother-hood, an Arab nationalist and religious Islamic movement that began in

Egypt during the 1920s, became an influential organisation amongst émigrés across Europe and particularly amongst Muslims in Ireland.[4] A loose analogy might be drawn between the Muslim Brotherhood and the Fenian movement that developed in the United States as part of the political mobilisation of Catholic immigrants there after the Famine. Fenianism came to influence nationalist politics in Ireland, and the political mobilisation of Irish Catholic emigrants in a number of countries. Its founders included émigré Young Irelanders, an educated elite. The Muslim Brotherhood became an important focal point for educated Muslims in Ireland and Irish-based members sought to lead the wider Muslim community as this expanded.

The Republic's 1991 census recorded 3,873 Muslims. By the mid-1990s there were more Muslims living in the Republic of Ireland and Northern Ireland than there were Jews, whose numbers on the island had peaked at 5,381 in 1946 and then slowly declined. Since 1991 the number of Muslims increased considerably after the arrival of refugees from Bosnia, the Middle East, and Sub-Saharan Africa, in addition to migrant workers from various Islamic countries. By 2002 the Republic's Muslim population stood at 19,147,[5] of whom around 2,000 were medical doctors.[6] For several decades the Republic's Muslim community had been decidedly middle-class, different in profile from the Muslim communities in a number of other European countries, which attracted many poorly educated post-colonial settlers, like France, or guest workers, like Germany.

By the turn of the century this profile had begun to shift. The 2002 census had identified 5,472 Muslims who were citizens of African countries, most of whom were asylum seekers. This number rose to 6,909 by 2006 and to 15,376 by 2011. Growing numbers also came to Ireland as migrant workers. Some of these were, like the earliest arrivals, medical students, doctors, nurses and other middle-class professionals. However, others arrived to fill comparatively poorly paid jobs in service industries. More than 20,000 work permits were issued to migrants from Muslim-majority countries between 1993 and 2015.[7]

The 2006 census identified a total of 32,539 Muslims; most were Sunni, about 2,000 were Shi'a, and they had arrived from 42 countries: 7,693 were citizens of African countries; 4,853 were Pakistani; 1,284 were Malaysian; 304 were from India; and 4,076 were from other Asian countries. About 10 per cent of the total population had arrived as asylum seekers or refugees; twenty-one per cent were educated to degree level or higher; 8.5 per cent were identified as 'employers or managers'; and 17.4 per cent as higher professionals. Muslims from Asian countries – in particular from Bangladesh and Pakistan – worked, like many other immigrants, in service industries (restaurants, the food sector, wholesale and retail) and some of these were badly paid and experienced the kinds of exploitation encountered by other migrant workers from non-European Union countries. A 2011 study found that most Muslim entrepreneurs in the Republic of Ireland employed ten or fewer employees.[8] Most lived in Dublin, but by then other smaller communities had become established and by 2011 there were there at least 16 small mosques around the country. The 2011 census counted a total of 49,204. By then, Muslims constituted just over one per cent of the Republic's total population, and were the country's third-largest religion, after Catholics and the Church of Ireland. Between 2011 and 2016 the Muslim population of the Republic grew by 28.9 per cent to 63,400.

In the Republic, as in other countries with significant Muslim immigrant populations, some there are cultural, linguistic and factional differences across the group. Consequently, it may not make sense to refer to Ireland's Muslim community as a distinct cohesive entity, as Muslims from different backgrounds – Arabic- or Urdu-speaking, Sunni or Shi'a – have bonded together in parts of Ireland where members of each linguistic or religious sub-set are too few to organise separate mosques or prayer rooms. The Islamic concept of *al-umma-al-islamiyya* (or *umma*) in the Qur'an refers to a universal community of believers. The concept is a symbolic, utopian one, but it finds expression in the use of Arabic, the language in which the Qur'an was written. But not all Muslims speak or read Arabic; Urdu, Farsi and, especially in Northern Ireland, English have emerged as languages spoken in the mosques on the island.[9]

EDUCATION AND TRADE

Small numbers of Muslim students from South Africa arrived to study medicine in Dublin from the late 1940s. These were the descendants of South Asians who had migrated within the British Empire. In 1946 Éamon de Valera met with Soqbjee Rustomjee, a prominent South African political activist in New York. de Valera, who was Chancellor of the National University of Ireland, secured six places per year for South Africans to study medicine at University College Dublin. From 1952, the Royal College of Surgeons in Dublin admitted a set quota of students descended from Indian immigrants to South Africa who found it difficult to study medicine there following the introduction of apartheid.[10] Many of the first group shared the same Gujarati ethnic heritage.[11] By the 1960s, South African students constituted one of the largest contingents of foreign students at the Royal College of Surgeons, which also attracted foreign students from Nigeria.[12] In 1963, some 200 out of a total of 280 foreign students who sat the entrance exam for the College were from South Africa. A number of these students stayed on in Ireland after graduation to work as doctors and some married into Irish families.[13]

The most prominent of these, Moosajee Bhamjee, who became the Republic of Ireland's first Muslim TD, was born in Pietermaritzburg in South Africa in 1947. He was the son of a Muslim Indian immigrant who opened a hardware shop there. From 1965 he studied medicine at the Royal College of Surgeons, after which he returned to South Africa to work as a GP. Two of his brothers also studied medicine in Dublin. He returned to Ireland in 1975, and after some time working in Galway and Cork, where he trained as a psychiatrist, he settled in County Clare where his wife came from. He became a member of the Labour Party in 1991, and a parliamentary candidate in 1992. He was elected to the Dáil and served one term as a backbencher whilst continuing to practice psychiatry.[14]

The main commercial relationship between the Republic and Muslim countries during the 1980s concerned the export of beef. One exporter, Goodman International, had an annual turnover of about £500 million during the 1980s, about 4 per cent of Ireland's GDP. [15] In September 1987 Charles Haughey's government agreed to indemnify Goodman for the sum of US $134.5 million for a beef sale deal with Iraq that depended on the Irish government providing credit insurance. Goodman's contract with Iraq was to supply high-grade, halal Irish beef that had been slaughtered no more than 100 days. Investigations in controversies surrounding this deal revealed that much of the beef labelled as halal was anything but.[16] The beef sold by Goodman was often years old, and invariably not halal. In any case, then leader of Iraq, Saddam Hussein, never paid for it, and the Irish State became liable for Goodman's financial losses.[17]

The international market for halal beef brought Sher Mohammad Rafique, a Pakistani entrepreneur, to Ballyhaunis, County Mayo, where he opened a meat-processing plant. His company, Halal Meats, expanded as United Meat Packers Limited to incorporate four other plants in counties Cork, Roscommon, Sligo, Cork, and Wexford. Sher Rafique recruited halal butchers, who settled with their families in Ballyhaunis and sponsored the construction of Ireland's first purpose-built mosque in the town. By the late 1980s, the halal meat industry came to employ more than 250 Muslims, most of whom lived in Ballyhaunis. By 1991 United Meat Packers accounted for 14.5 per cent of cattle and 24.5 per cent of sheep slaughtered for export in Irish meat plants; the company's Irish revenues for 1991 were estimated at £250 million. Following this peak, as result of sanctions that affected exports to Iraq, the company went into decline and the Rafique family moved abroad but many Muslim families stayed on in Ballyhaunis.

ARABIC MOSQUES AND INSTITUTIONS

The Dublin Islamic Society was founded at a time when thousands of members of the Muslim Brotherhood had been imprisoned by the Nasser regime in Egypt. Towards the end of the 1950s, many Muslim Brotherhood members sought political asylum abroad; most went to other countries in the Middle East, some to the United States and to European countries, and a few came to Ireland. Ahmed Elkadi, a member of the Brotherhood, came to Dublin as a medical student during the early 1960s. In Dublin he organised a prayer group for Arabic-speakers and promoted ideas associated with the Egyptian Islamic scholar Said Ramadan, a leader of the Muslim Brotherhood who had completed a doctorate in Switzerland in 1959 and settled there. Ramadam had established the Islamic Centre in Geneva, which became a model for other such combinations of mosque, school and community facilities. Elkadi subsequently settled in the United States where he worked as a cardiologist.[18]

Efforts to establish the first mosque date from 1969, by which time the Dublin Islamic Society had around 100 members. An ongoing fundraising campaign targeted the prosperous parents of students who could afford to send their children to study in Ireland. Donations were also sought from Muslim organisations in Kuwait, Libya, Saudi Arabia, Algeria, the UAE, Jordan and the United Kingdom. In 1972, members of the Dublin Islamic Society began contacting the embassies of these majority Muslim nations in London – none had diplomats in Dublin at the time – seeking funds. In 1973 a Muslim delegation from Ireland attended an international conference of Islamic Cultural Centres in Europe held in London. They were helped in particular by Salem Azzam, an Egyptian who worked as a diplomat at the Saudi embassy. He was a leading figure in European Muslim Brotherhood circles and a founder of the Islamic Council of Europe, an umbrella group of Muslim groups in various countries. [19] Substantial funds were received via the London Embassy of Saudi Arabia from King Faisal.[20] This enabled the Society to purchase in 1974 a four-story building at 7 Harrington Street, Dublin 8 on the South Circular Road to be used as a mosque.[21] Planning permission and works to convert the building into a mosque took three years. In 1977 the first mosque and Islamic Centre in Ireland was formally opened in a ceremony that included in attendance former President Cearbhall Ó Dálaigh.

Salem Azzam was appointed as a lifetime trustee of the mosque and during the years until a full-time imam was appointed the Islamic Council of Europe sent religious speakers to Dublin on a monthly basis.[22] The Society approached various embassies of Muslim countries appealing for funding to pay the salary of a full-time imam. In 1981, the Ministry of Endowment and Islamic Affairs in Kuwait agreed to provide some funding.

In 1981 a Sudanese student, was appointed as the first imam but he did not remain long in Ireland following his graduation. In 1983, Sheikh Yahya al-Hussein, also Sudanese and casually appointed, replaced Idris Ibrahim. At the time of writing, more than three decades later, he was still imam.[23]

By 1983 plans were already in train to establish a larger mosque to replace the one at Harrington Street. The Dublin Islamic Society purchased a former Presbyterian Church at 163 South Circular Road, and a primary school was established on the same site. From 1990 the school became formally recognised and funded by the Irish Department of Education. The opening of the school coincided with a change of name from the Dublin Islamic Society to the Islamic Foundation of Ireland. By then the Muslim community in Dublin had expanded well beyond the core of South African students to include some Muslims from Arabic-speaking countries.[24] Like its predecessor the Islamic Foundation of Ireland continued to be dominated by visiting university students and some graduates who had settled in Ireland. In 1992, Sheikh Hamdan Ben Rashid al-Maktoum, Deputy Governor of Dubai and Minister of Finance and Industry in the United Arab Emirates, agreed to finance the purchase of land for the construction of a Muslim primary school in Clonskeagh, adjacent to University College Dublin. The al-Maktoum family had substantial investments in the Irish bloodstock industry. Subsequently, it also funded the construction of a purpose-built mosque and Islamic centre on the same site, which was completed in 1996.

Sheikh Hussein Halawa was appointed imam of the Clonskeagh mosque in 1998. Originally from Egypt, he had been the general secretary of the European Council for Fatwa and Research (ECFR), a European network of Middle Eastern religious scholars who provided religious rulings to Muslims in accordance with Sunni Islamic jurisprudence that is associated with the Muslim Brotherhood. The ECFR came to be based in the Islamic Cultural Centre of Ireland following Halawa's appointment. The al-Maktoum Foundation funded the salaries of around 20 administrative staff, whilst the mosque and school were managed by the Islamic Foundation of Ireland.[25]

The Clonskeagh school, like other denominational primary schools in the Republic (most of which are Catholic) was funded by the Department of Education. It was formally opened in 1996 by President Mary Robinson. A second, state-funded Muslim primary school was opened on the north side of Dublin on the Navan Road in 2001, which was also administered by the Islamic Foundation of Ireland.[26] These have remained the only two Muslim primary schools in the Republic.

An estimated 5,000 Shi'a Muslims had settled in the Republic by 2011 with about half of these in the Dublin area. Most came from Pakistan or from Gulf Arab countries including Kuwait, Bahrain or the United Arab Emirates. Dr Ali Al-Saheh, the founder of the Shi'a Ahlul-Bayt Centre, was born in Iraq but arrived in Ireland from Saudi Arabia in 1985 to complete his medical studies. After qualifying as a doctor he completed his religious studies in Iran before returning to Dublin in 1987. Before then Shi'a medical students in Dublin had rented a house in Portobello and then one in Rathgar to meet for prayers.[27] According to a 2006 account about 50 or 60 families regularly attended the Shi'a Ahlul-Bayt Centre, of whom half the men worked as doctors. Several of these doctors were general practitioners in South Dublin. Shi'as living in other parts of Ireland often attended Sunni mosques. Some children of Sunni Muslims living in Dublin attended the primary school in Clonskeagh.[28]

In 1984, a Cork Muslim Society was established that operated independently of the Dublin Islamic Society for many years. It had a similar initial impetus. Muslim university students, mostly from Malaysia, began to congregate for prayers, and formed a Cork Malaysian Islamic Student Society (later the Cork Muslim Society) and many of its members worked in the field of medicine and in hospitals affiliated to University College Cork. These were joined by further Muslim immigrants from the 1990s. Initially the Society used a rented house for prayers and in 1994 it purchased a house for this purpose. After failing to obtain planning permission the Society relocated to a warehouse on an industrial estate. The purchase of this building for €1.3 million was supported by a private donor from Qatar. The opening of this mosque in 2000 coincided with the arrival of a full-time imam, Sheikh Salem Faituri Muftah, a refugee from Libya and a member of the Muslim Brotherhood. Salem Faituri remained on as imam until 2013.

As in Dublin and Cork, mosques in other Irish cities were founded by medical students or by doctors working in local hospitals. In 1978, a Galway Islamic Society was established. In 1981 it purchased a house for use as a mosque. By 2004 there were around 1,000 Muslims in Galway.[29] Efforts by the Society to purchase a site for a larger, purpose-built mosque were opposed by some city councilors on planning grounds. Galway Muslims continued to pray in a number of temporary facilities including converted warehouses.[30] In 2007 the Galway Islamic Society was renamed the Galway Islamic Cultural Centre. Similarly in Limerick, early arrivals included doctors who, during the 1990s, established the Limerick Islamic Centre in a converted house in the Raheen area. As in Galway, a number of other prayer rooms opened as the Muslim population grew.[31]

Masjid Maryam (The Mosque of Mary), Galway's first purpose-built mosque, was established by members of Ireland's small Ahmadiyya community, a minority within Islam that has been subject to persecution in Pakistan. Up to one-third of the Masjid Maryam community of around 200 people were former asylum seekers. Its imam, Ibrahim Noonan was an Irish convert from Waterford, who had become a Muslim in London.[32]

The influence of the Islamic Cultural Centre on mosques outside Dublin was fostered by financial support for a number of these provided by the al-Maktoum Foundation and channeled through Clonskeagh. For example, the al-Maktoum Foundation gave funding to a mosque established by the Cork Muslim Society, two mosques set up by the Galway Islamic Cultural Centre and one run by the Islamic Cultural Centre of Cavan. Several of the imams appointed to these were Muslim Brotherhood political refugees. These included Sheikh Ali Sallabi who left Libya during the mid-1990s, after his brother Sheikh Khalid Sallabi a prominent religious scholar imprisoned by Gaddafi. Another brother became a military leader of the 2011 Arab Spring Revolution against Gaddafi's regime. Ali Sallabi had studied mathematics and computing in Benghazi before leaving Libya in 1996 when he was 21 years old.[33] He travelled to a number of countries before settling in Ireland a few years later. He became a full-time imam in 2001.[34] Imams appointed to a number of other mosques funded by the al-Maktoum Foundation – in Tallaght, Cork and Galway – have also been Libyans.[35]

The appointment of imams in a number of Irish mosques came to be directed by the Sheik Halawa's European Centre for Fatwa and Research. Many of many these, including Sheik Halawa, were not fluent English speakers.[36] The al-Maktoum mosque network, as Adil Hussain Kahn described it, enabled Islam in Ireland to present a unified front to Irish society. When journalists wanted an 'Islamic point of view' or the Irish government wanted to include a Muslim in a public event they have tended to approach the ICCI at Clonskeagh. For example, Sheikh Halawa was invited the read from the Qur'an at the inauguration of President Mary McAleese in 2004.

An Irish Council of Imams chaired by Sheikh Halawa and Sheikh Yahya Al-Hussein of the Islamic Foundation of Ireland was established in 1996.[37] The apparently close relationship to the Islamic Foundation of Ireland and the Islamic Cultural Centre Ireland, influenced in turn by the Muslim Brotherhood and funded by the al-Maktoum Foundation infer a top-down authority structure. However, over time the number of warehouse mosques and prayer rooms around the country has grown. Most of these are independent of the al-Maktoum Foundation. The Irish Council of Imams now includes more than thirty members. It has projected a mostly symbolic unity. The ability of the Council to agree on substantial matters has been limited.[38]

OTHER MUSLIM COMMUNITIES

Mosques and institutions funded by the al-Maktoum network have been mostly orientated towards Muslims from Arabic-speaking countries and have reflected the Middle Eastern and North African background of the imams that established these.[39] Yet, since the establishment of the al-Maktoum network from the early 90s the number of Muslims in Ireland has risen by several hundred per cent and a number of additional mosques were established. Many of these were, in effect, prayer rooms established in converted warehouses on industrial estates, some of these alongside Pentecostal Churches also set up in such places for similar reasons: affordability, and the absence of a requirement to obtain planning permission. Some of these catered particularly to Urdu-speaking Muslims; from the 1970s, some Muslim businessmen and traders from the United Kingdom settled in the Republic and, to a lesser extent, in Northern Ireland. Many of these and their employees were from Urdu-speaking Muslims from Pakistan.

In Ballyhaunis Sher Rafique employed mainly Syrian and Pakistani workers and founded the first purpose-built mosque in 1986.[40] The Muslim population of the town grew through the birth of Irish-born children, the arrival of some further migrants from the same countries and, more recently, by asylum seekers. A 250-person direct provision centre was established in the town centre in 2001 resulting in a steady trickle of Muslim settlers into the town. Many of these were from the Middle-East, Asia and Africa.[41]

The 2002 census recorded 317 Muslims in the town out of a population of 1,381 within the electoral district that included Ballyhaunis. In 2004 planning permission was granted for a Muslim mortuary and graveyard. According to 2006 census, Muslims comprised 20 per cent (out of 1,700) of those living in the electoral district in which the town was located and 34 per cent of the population of the town centre (out of a population of 1,000 or so). They variously spoke Urdu, Punjabi and Arabic in their homes. The 2011 Census identified 44.6 per cent of the population of the town as non-Irish citizens. Some of these were migrants from Eastern Europe. This percentage did not include long-standing Muslim residents who had become Irish citizens.

In Dublin, a few new mosques and prayer rooms were opened by Pakistani immigrants. [42] The first mosque for Urdu-speakers in Dublin was founded in a warehouse on Blackpitts Road, which was close to the original Irish Islamic Foundation mosque on the South Circular Road. It was sponsored by Mian Ghulam Bari, a Pakistani entrepreneur who first arrived in Ireland during the 1970s and established successful clothing importation business. Bari opened a chain of shops around the country, and by the 1990s, employed a number of Muslims at his Blackpitts Road business premises. For a number of years during Ramadan, prior to the establishment of the Blackpitts Mosque, Bari had invited Urdu-speaking imams to his home in Dublin at which local South Asian Muslims would meet for prayers. This eventually turned into a full-time appointment and planning permission was obtained to convert the warehouse into a mosque in 2011. Bari, who became an Irish citizen, has been a leading figure in Dublin's Urdu-speaking community as a philanthropist. He also played a role in lobbying the government of Pakistan to open an embassy in Ireland.[43] Along the same lines Abdul Hameed, another Pakistani entrepreneur and restaurant owner supported the establishment of the Anwar-e Madina mosque on Talbot Street in the city centre, which opened in 2008 and which has come to be associated with the Sufi tradition of Islam. The Hameed and Bari families became related through marriage.[44] Both prayer rooms quickly attracted large numbers of students and migrant workers, most from Pakistan and Bangladesh, many with connections to the United Kingdom. Some Muslims migrated to Ireland from the UK for much the same reasons as did some British-based Chinese formally from Hong Kong and the New Territories. Ireland offered opportunities to expand businesses in areas that where there was much competition between immigrants in British cities.

A mosque was established in Clondalkin in West Dublin to serve a mostly South Asian community in a warehouse on an industrial state in a building that also contained an Asian grocery store.[45] Another, the Al-Mustafa Islamic Centre, was established in 2004 a few miles north in Blanchardstown, again on an industrial estate, to serve an Urdu-speaking Sufi Muslim community.

Umar Al-Quadri, the founder of the Al-Mustafa Islamic Centre, grew up in the Netherlands. His father arrived there from Lahore in 1980 to serve as imam and a Sufi teacher at a mosque in the Hague for a community mostly from Pakistan, India, and Surinam. In 1984 Umar Al-Quadri came to live in the Netherlands aged two with his mother. His three younger brothers were born in the Netherlands. He went to a secular school, but by the time he was 13 years old, had memorised the Qur'an. He returned to Lahore where he spent seven years in a boarding school. During this time his mother died. His brothers settled in the Netherlands. Two trained as physical education teachers and one set up a business in this area in which both worked. The third brother set up a media company. He got married in Pakistan 2002 at a time when the Netherlands had become more hostile to Muslim immigrants. Some Dutch Muslims he knew had moved to other European countries where it proved easier to arrange family reunification. He weighed up his options and decided to move to Ireland, where he worked in an accounts office. He had not yet decided to become an imam, but was approached by a few Pakistani Muslims in Lucan where he lived to tutor their children in the Qur'an. These were doctors and professionals who were long settled in

Ireland and had become Irish citizens. After a short time, some 25 children had enrolled in classes which he held in his home. He founded the mosque in 2004, and for the first 18 months he conducted services in Urdu, but thereafter switched to English as the congregation grew to include Muslim immigrants from a number of countries including Nigeria, Somalia, Iran and a number of Asian countries. By 2016, the Al-Mustafa Islamic Centre served a congregation of about 600.[46]

Small mosques in residential areas and prayer rooms on industrial estates proliferated in Dublin, Cork, and Limerick. In 2010 a second Shi'a Mosque was opened in the Stadium Business Park in Blanchardstown.[47] Another Shi'a prayer room was set up in Cork city centre to serve immigrants from Iraq. Some other Sunni mosques came to be established in Cork, including one in a suburban house, which was attended by Urdu-speaking Pakistanis. Another, led by a Sudanese imam, Sheikh Ihab Ahmed, was established in an economically deprived area in the north of the city. This initially served Nigerian Muslims in the area but has since attracted migrants from many other countries of origin.[48]

The Belfast Islamic Centre was established in 1978, and the first mosque opened in 1980 in Belfast near the Queen's University. The Belfast Islamic Centre is affiliated with the Muslim Council of Great Britain. In 1984, it moved to its present building, a converted house in a residential area at 38 Wellington Park in South Belfast, where no more than 200 people, crammed into every room, could simultaneously attend Friday prayers. The 2001 Northern Irish census, the first to identify Muslims, identified 1,943 rising to 3,832 by 2011. Most Muslims in Northern Ireland live in Belfast, with small numbers in Craigavon, Derry, Ballymena, and Coleraine. The majority of Muslims in Northern Ireland come from Pakistan, with the remainder coming from other Asian and North African countries. Some had previously lived in England, Scotland or the Republic of Ireland.[49]

In 2013, Mahammad Saleem Tareen, a Consultant Psychiatrist, was elected as chairman of the Belfast Islamic Centre. Five of the six elected members of the Belfast Islamic Centre board were either medical doctors or held doctorates.[50] A 2014 profile in the *Economist* described Islam in Northern Ireland as a world away from the Midlands and northern English cities where poor Pakistanis arrived half a century ago. Many of the estimated 4,000 or so Muslims who lived in Ulster according to the *Economist*, were doctors, academics, entrepreneurs or property developers. The article interviewed Raied al-Wazzan, another member of the Belfast Islamic Centre board who came to Northern Ireland 25 years earlier from Iraq to complete a doctorate in physics. He became a founding member of Andor, a high-tech photography company based in Belfast that was purchased by a British firm for £175 million.[51]

In 2016 the Centre was preparing to move again to a larger purpose-built premises on the University Road.[52] Leaders of the Belfast Islamic Centre have proactively encouraged the use of English. Classes for adults and children at the Belfast Islamic Centre use English-language translations of the Qur'an prepared by the Centre as part of a project involving Belfast Muslims that took several years to complete.[53] The reasons for this, given by Northern Irish Muslims in interviews, are that not all Muslims speak Arabic; secondly the 'community' isn't big enough to function except through English; thirdly, the community was anxious about being treated with suspicion if overhead by non-Muslims, as explained by A'ishah, a 58-year-old woman originally from Syria:

> We don't have a Muslim neighborhood, or a Pakistani, Arab neighborhood and so on. We spend our life within the local society, so we use and have to use English. There are already problems with languages in this city, so why add a new one. We can teach Arabic to our children, and we do, yet they have to live here, their life is here.[54]

The deliberately low profile of Muslims in Northern Ireland owed much to the sectarian tensions in the Province. Like those Hong Kong Chinese who settled in Ulster, they kept their heads down.[55]

UMMA IN IRELAND

A number of studies of in the Republic have identified both religious and socio-economic differences between a well-to-do and well-educated Muslim middle class on one hand and some very marginal and sometimes poorly educated refugees, asylum seekers, and migrant workers on the other. One such analysis suggested that some Muslims who had arrived as asylum seekers were more conservative in their religious practices and dress and who were less willing or able to integrate into Irish society than members of the Arabic-speaking middle class. As described by Tuula Sakaranaho in 2006:

> In the view of the present Islamic establishment, some refugees from north Africa and Nigeria are so strict and narrow in their interpretation of Islam that their religiosity becomes destructive for the Muslim community at large. For some time in recent years, these Muslims provoked open conflict within the Muslim community by challenging the knowledge and authority of the Sheikh and distributing leaflets against the Islamic cultural centre. For instance, they opposed any interaction with the Westerners.[56]

The basis of such conflicts is illustrated by another study which interviewed 18 Algerian, Arabic-speaking women living in Cork and Dublin in 2009/10. Ten women identified with a Salafi understanding of Islam, and eight were Akhwawat, as female members of the Muslim Brotherhood are called. The Salafi believe that only Muslims following a Salafi interpretation of the Qur'an are true Muslims; any other interpretations – *bid'a* (innovations) – constituted heresy and are forbidden. The Salafi women were concerned with protecting themselves and their families from *bid'a* associated with other Muslims as well as non-Muslim influences in Ireland. They saw themselves as belonging to an idealised global Islamic community, *al-ummah al-aslamiyya* in keeping with their strict interpretations of Islam rather than an Irish Muslim community or to Irish society. Berber Arabs, they had arrived as refugees and been associated with the *Front Islamique du Salut* (FIS, trans. Islamic Salvation Front). Most arrived in Ireland during the 1990s, and came from a lower-middle-class background. None had third-level education. None engaged in paid employment. FIS activists and sympathisers were jailed or sought asylum in European countries such as Ireland. They saw themselves as living in exile, and sought to isolate themselves and their children from heretical Muslim influences and *Kafir* (infidels) and to ensure that their children could speak Arabic. Most Salafi interviewees did not send their children to either of the two Muslim schools in Dublin. Partly, this was because they believed the Islamic ethos of these schools and of some Muslim pupils was *bid'a*. Some considered it to be easier to protect their children from heretical versions of Islam by sending them to Catholic school, while others worried about the possible influence of Catholicism on their children.

By contrast, Akhawat interviewees identified a lot of similarities between Irish and Arab culture in terms of family values, social solidarity and considered that the acceptance of Catholicism in Irish society benefited them as Muslims. They supported engagement by Muslims with Irish society. As one interviewee put it: 'We came here to study and to educate ourselves further.' All eight had obtained a college degree in nursing or midwifery back in Algeria. Unlike the Salafi women, they had not believe in *al-ummah al-islamiyya* but acknowledged diversity in the interpretation and practice of Islam. Salafi women covered their faces as well as their heads outside the home, as did many other kinds Muslim women in Algeria; styles of Muslim dress are often regional more than religious traditions per se. One Akhawat interviewee decided to no longer cover her face when she came to Ireland once she realised that this would be interpreted as a symbol of Salafism.[57]

A 2012 article in the *Mayo News* proclaimed Ballyhaunis as Ireland's most 'cosmopolitan' town. By 2015, according to a feature article in the *Irish Examiner*, 'White Irish' people accounted for just 40 per cent of the town's population and for just 29 per cent of the 322 pupils enrolled in the local national school, Scoil Íosa. The article exemplified a generally positive portrayal of Muslims in the town in the local and national press: 'Pakistani names have featured on Ballyhaunis hurling teams for over two decades. There are Eastern European and Syrian names on the Ballyhaunis soccer team whilst the recently established Ballyhaunis Cricket Club is a strong outlet for members of the Muslim community.'[58]

The same article described how Manar Cherbatji, a Syrian Muslim from Aleppo, arrived in Ballyhaunis in 1988 after she married her husband. By then her brothers had already established a successful meat processing plant, Iman Casings, in the town, for which her husband worked. The couple had four sons who grew up in Ballyhaunis, attending local schools and playing Gaelic games until they went to college in Galway. When Manar arrived, she could not speak English, but she enrolled in English-language and parenting classes, knowing that her children would grow up in Ireland where life would be different than what she had known in Syria. Manar would regularly attend Sunday Mass in the Catholic Church as well as the Mosque on Fridays. She became involved in a number of community groups, including the Family Resource Centre, the Community Council and the Parents' Associations of the Catholic primary and secondary schools her sons attended. Whilst her older sons had typical Muslim names – Mohammed, Nadeem and Mouhanad – she named the youngest, Niall.[59]

Manar's family was, however, atypical; a doctoral study which interviewed 33 Muslim teenagers in Ballyhaunis in 2010/11 depicted a community that was, to some extent, divided between long-established Pakistani and Syrian inhabitants and more recently-arrived asylum seekers from a range of countries. To some extent these differences appear to have been socio-economic – many asylum seekers lived a direct provision hostel and were prevented from seeking employment – but cultural variances were also identified. Nine out of the 17 teenage girls (three of them Irish-born) interviewed in a study in Ballyhaunis wore headscarves to school. The Ballyhaunis mosque had long been associated in particular with the town's Pakistani community, and since it opened in 1986 prayers had been conducted in Urdu. Following the arrival of asylum seekers from across the Muslim world, prayers were led on alternate Fridays by an Arabic-speaking imam. Newcomer and long-time residents interacted at the mosque, yet interviewees who arrived in the town as asylum seekers described feeling alienated and excluded by the more established Muslim community.[60]

Similar divisions were outlined in another study by Wasim, whose Pakistani family had arrived in Ireland from the United Kingdom during the 1970s. Wasim's father had set up a business in a West of Ireland, where he employed other Pakistanis who had settled there with their families. Wasim was educated in a Catholic boarding school. He considered that other

Muslims who had settled in the town had integrated well, but that many Pakistanis tended to keep to themselves, particularly those who originally came from small rural communities. Wasim described some of these as lost and insecure in their new surroundings. Some, in his view, had integrated poorly:

> You have kids that are born here that leave school and come home and their first language is Urdu or Punjabi. Their mothers have been here for 25 years and they still don't speak English. Their fathers still don't speak English. They still go home and do exactly what they would do as if they were in Pakistan or if they were wherever they came from.[61]

Another interviewee Wahab first came to Ireland during the 1970s on holiday. He had been living in England for some time by then. He became a successful businessman. He and his wife sent both of their children to a Catholic school because he believed they would get the best education there. His children were the only Muslim pupils, but the school supported their practice of their faith. Wahab described how he encouraged his children, and now his grandchild, to become involved in the wider Irish community through sports like hurling, soccer, and swimming.[62]

Some other respondents practiced versions of Islam that brought them into very little contact with non-Muslims. Akifah, a university student in her twenties from Pakistan recalled passing through London on her way to Ireland and being horrified by the behavior and dress of people she saw ('I was thinking, oh my God where am I. People were hugging and kissing – boys and girls. I thought I was in hell.'). In Ireland, she restricted her social interaction as much as possible to other Muslims. Every evening she taught the Qur'an to children at a mosque.[63]

Others came to feel rejected by Irish society. Nazeer, a man in his thirties, described becoming more devout since arriving in Ireland. In Pakistan he had not been very religious. When he arrived in Ireland he had been clean shaven and passed unnoticed. Once he grew a beard, he encountered the kinds of harassment experienced by some women who wore headscarves. He stopped taking the bus to work because people refused to sit beside him even when the bus was standing-room only.[64]

Wasim recalled birthday parties at the house he grew up in, which were full of Irish non-Muslim children, and social events where he and his sister had been the only non-white children. However, during the early 1990s, this began to change when other Pakistani Muslims arrived in the town. His family began to socialise solely with these other Muslim families, and had very little interaction with their Irish Catholic neighbours thereafter. The Muslim community in the town expanded to include Muslims from different countries of origin and these, too, tended to stick to their own, except at the mosque:

> On Friday's it's great, you say hello to everybody and there's all different languages and different ethnic groups. But there's one thing for sure. This is in the prayer time. But when people go home the Arabs stick with the Arabs, the Pakistanis stick with the Pakistanis and the Punjabis stick with and the Punjabis and the Afghanis stick with the Afghanis and the Africans stick with the Africans. Oh of course they all greet each other but are they actually friends? I've never seen it.[65]

Muslim interviewees in a number of studies suggest that because of differences in religious practice, social class, language or ethnicity, there is no single Irish Muslim community. Many see themselves as belonging to the *umma*, or worldwide Islamic community, but what this means is differently understood by various groups. In Ireland, as elsewhere, some do not practice their religion at all, whilst others define their lives entirely according the precepts of their faith. Efforts to define what it is to be Muslim in Ireland by imams and bodies such as the Clonskeagh-based European Council for Fatwa and Research now compete with fatwas issued by religious leaders in other countries that can be easily accessed via social media. Islam has become for many Muslims a kind of transnational virtual community within which, religious leaders compete for the attention of the *umma*.[66] At the same time, mosques in Ireland, as elsewhere, have been important focal points for Muslim immigrants. In effect, Muslim communities in Ireland were founded upon efforts by immigrants to establish mosques and places in which to pray.

In both Northern Ireland and in the Republic Muslims have experienced racism and what has been termed Islamophobia. For example, in November 2015, the home of a family who had lived for almost two decades in Ballymena, County Antrim was firebombed soon after terrorist attacks in Paris that were widely reported in the Irish media.[67] A 2016 study in the Republic reported first-hand experiences of specifically anti-Muslim verbal abuse, physical assault, and harassment on public transport. Stereotypes of Muslims as terrorists were frequently invoked by the perpetrators of assaults and harassment. Much of this hostility was aimed at women on public transport and in public spaces who wore headscarves. Some respondents described discrimination when trying to obtain places for their children in schools, when applying for jobs and going about their daily lives. Two prayer rooms and the homes of some respondents were vandalised with graffiti telling Muslims they were not welcome in the area.[68]

Yet, the visible presence of Muslims in the Republic of Ireland has not become politicised to the extent that it has in several other European countries. There are perhaps several reasons for this. Until recently the Republic's Muslim community has been small and middle class at a time when countries like France, the Netherlands and the United Kingdom included significant populations of poorly educated and economically marginalised Muslims from former colonies. Secondly, the Republic of Ireland appears to have been less hostile to expressions of religion in public spaces than countries such as France, in which women and girls were prohibited from wearing the hijab in schools. In contrast to the principle of *la laïcité*, which is invoked to insist upon secularism in France, the Irish Republic's 1937 Constitution explicitly provides for denominational education. Most schools are Catholic, a smaller number are Protestant and a few are Jewish. More recently, some multi-denominational schools have been established. The two Muslim schools – which like other denominational schools follow the national curriculum and employ qualified teachers funded by the Department of Education – fit readily into this landscape.

The syllabus of both Dublin's Muslim national schools is the same as in other national schools in Ireland. There is also instruction in the Arabic language and Islamic religion which is taught by Muslim teachers funded by the al-Maktoum Foundation. The time spent on religious education during the school day corresponds with practices in Catholic and other denominational schools. Female pupils in senior classes in both schools are required to wear the hijab.[69] Yet, most Muslim children in the Republic attend Catholic denominational schools. Unlike in some other European countries there has been little official opposition to girls wearing the hijab within the Irish school system. For example, the Joint Management Body for Secondary Schools and the management association of Catholic secondary schools advise schools not to make an issue of school uniform rules where these conflict with a child's religion.[70] Constitutional provisions initially designed to ensure the autonomy of Catholic education, have resulted in an effectively multicultural school system that allows state-funded schools with a Muslim ethos to exist alongside Catholic and Protestant ones.[71]

Like the Irish in the United Kingdom from the 1970s to the 1990s, but to a far greater extent, Muslims in Western countries have come to be treated as a suspect population. This has occurred to far less an extent in the Republic of Ireland than some other countries in the absence of prominent anti-Islamic political movements and of terrorist incidents. Yet, there are concerns that some Irish Muslims have become influenced by radical Islamic movements, as expressed by a few imams, most prominently Sheikh Umar Al-Quardi, that Muslim leaders had not done enough to combat the radicalisation of some youth by extremist speakers who had visit Ireland, and by others whose teachings were accessed online. In 2007, another Blanchardstown-based imam, Sheikh Shaheed Satardien, who arrived as an asylum seeker from South Africa after his brother had been killed by Islamic extremists, claimed that Wahhabi extremism had some influence at the Clonskeagh mosque.[72] In 2015 Sheikh Al-Quadri criticised the Irish Council of Imams for not discussing extremism at its meetings, and called for less tolerance of extremism in mosques, warning that young Muslims were at risk of being radicalised on social media.[73] During 2016 and 2017, in interviews following Islamic-State-inspired terrorist attacks in Paris, Brussels and London, Al-Quadri reiterated such warnings.

In November 2016 an Islamic State suicide bomber who died in Mosul in Iraq was identified as Terry 'Kahid' Kelly, a Dublin-born convert to Islam. Kelly apparently became radicalised while serving a jail sentence in Saudi Arabia, and had lived in London before returning to Ireland in 2003. Rachid Redouane, of Moroccan-Libyan origin, was one of the three perpetrators of the June 2017 Tower Bridge attack in London. A pastry chef, he had lived in Rathmines in Dublin, and had married an Irish woman. Redouane's Irish connection was widely reported in the media.[74] On 5 June 2017, during evening prayers, rocks were thrown through the windows of the Ahmadiyyi mosque in Galway in what was described by the media as a reprisal for the Tower Bridge attack. The mosque's imam, Ibrahim Noonan, had been one of the most vocal Irish Muslim opponents of Islamic extremism.[75]

Some Muslims in Ireland have remained politically engaged with the countries they or their families migrated from. Housam 'Sam' Najjair was born in Dublin in 1989. He attended a Christian Brothers' School and the Harrington Street mosque. His father had arrived in Ireland from Libya as a student, stayed on to work in the beef export business and married his Irish-born wife who converted to Islam. When Sam was nine years old, he moved with his family to Tripoli, and returned with them to Dublin when he was 14 years old. After he left school when he was 16, he worked in restaurants and on market stalls. At 19, he briefly became the manager of a small restaurant. He returned to Libya for two years, where he worked in a jewellery business and as a tour guide. He returned to Ireland again at the age of 21 and worked in construction in Dublin for several years. His experience of growing up between Ireland and Libya in many respects echoed the experiences of some English-born children of Irish emigrants who returned to meet relatives during the summers.

However, some of the Libyan families Sam Najjair had known in Dublin had fled persecution in Libya or had relatives who were imprisoned there. In 2011 Sam Najjair returned in Libya to enlist as a combatant in the NATO-supported revolution against Gaddafi's regime, and subsequently wrote a book about his experiences that was published in Ireland.[76] He served under his uncle, Mahdi al-Harati, also an Irish citizen, who was commander of the Tripoli Brigade. Al-Harati was sent abroad by his family to Egypt for safety when he was 16 years old after an uncle was imprisoned for 10 years by Gaddafi. He settled in Dublin with his Irish-born convert wife and worked as an Arabic teacher.

To date much of the identifiable political focus of Muslims in Ireland has been upon their countries of origin. The Muslim Brotherhood, which has had some members who have settled to Ireland, became internationally prominent during the Arab Spring in 2011. In Egypt, the Muslim Brotherhood leader, Mohamed Morsi was elected President and was later deposed by military coup. In August 2013, during the protests which followed, Ibrahim Halawa, the 17-year-old son of Sheikh Halawa was arrested with his three older sisters. With the assistance of the Irish Department of Foreign Affairs, the women were released after three months. However, Ibrahim Halawa remained in prison without trial for several years. Amnesty International declared him a prisoner of conscience. Media coverage in the Republic has consistently emphasized that Halawa is an Irish citizen. In 2016, he was visited in prison by a cross party delegation of Irish members of parliament who campaigned for his release. In July 2017 the Taoiseach Leo Varadkar met privately with members of the Halawa family and made public statements, along with other Irish political leaders, aimed at putting pressure on the Egyptian government to release Ibrahim. In September 2017 Ibrahim Halawa was found not guilty by the Egyptian courts and was freed a few weeks later and repatriated to Ireland.

FOURTEEN

UNSETTLEMENTS

According to the sociologist Robert Putnam, the most certain prediction that we can make about almost any modern society is that it will be more diverse a generation from now than it is today. However, large-scale immigration, like other kinds of dramatic social and economic change, is unsettling and can undermine social cohesion – temporarily at least.[1] Political agendas of restricting migration are nothing new. Present-day European political parties seeking to appeal to or exploit racism and xenophobia are hardly the first of their kind. Immigration was as intensely politicised in the United States during the nineteenth century, when the Irish settled there in large numbers, as it is during the early twenty-first century. The precursors of present-day anti-immigrant politics include the mid-nineteenth-century nativist 'Know-Nothings' in the United States, who won a series of electoral victories in Massachusetts, Pennsylvania, New Jersey, Delaware, Maryland, Kentucky, and California in 1854.[2] The 'Know-Nothings' were nativist groups hostile to the deluge of Catholic post-Famine Irish immigrants and to the abolition of slavery. Anti-immigrant political populism in the United States was fuelled by anti-Catholicism, but also by unsettling social change, with migrants being blamed for the latter.

Putnam has examined how early twenty-first century immigration has undermined social cohesion in the same American cities where the Irish settled more than a hundred years before. Putnam's 2006 article, 'E Pluribus Unum' (the motto of the United States, translated as 'Out of many, one') concluded that accelerated social diversity seemed to trigger anomie and reduce feelings of trust.[3] However disruptive, migration – whether by the Irish to American or English cities during the nineteenth century, or by others to the same places more recently – has proven that the pressure placed on social cohesion need not be permanent. Putnam's own concluding expectation was that any current phase of 'hunkering down', like all its predecessors, would be eventually superseded by new, shared senses of belonging. If anxieties about immigration have been something of a constant, so too have processes of social adaptation. Whilst the focus of much of this book has been on the experiences of migrants these have, to no little extent, been affected by the fears, anxieties and needs of host societies.

REGULATION

One of the cross-cutting themes that emerged in a number of previous chapters is the role of law – as it relates to freedom of movement, the right to work and citizenship entitlements – in influencing decisions as to where to migrate and in shaping experiences of migration. For example, Palatine migration to England and Ireland at the beginning of the eighteenth century was triggered by a law that permitted settlement by European Protestants. This decision was politically controversial at the time, supported by the Whigs, opposed by the Tories. More than half a century before then, Oliver Cromwell removed restrictions on Jews and made it possible for those living in England to openly practice their faith (after centuries of prohibition), and for new waves of Jewish migrants to settle there and in Ireland.

Large-scale migration from Poland, Lithuania, Latvia, and other new member states of the European Union was similarly enabled by the removal in 2004 of visa requirements from migrants from these countries by the Irish and British governments. A conscious decision was made to proactively attract migrants from the new member states. Many other EU countries held off removing visa restrictions at the time. Entitlement to free movement made migration to the Republic and Northern Ireland and access to employment easier, reduced the risk of exploitation and, in short, made the decision to come to the island of Ireland a far less risky one. As a result large, numbers of Poles, Lithuanians, and Latvians migrated to the Republic and the North. Poles became the biggest immigrant community in both parts of Ireland. This 2004 decision was perhaps the single greatest act of social engineering since the post-1608 Plantation of Ulster.

The scale of change resulting from several waves of land confiscations, from expulsions of defeated Gaelic leaders and from better-organised colonial settlements changed Ireland to an unprecedented extent. Nicholas Canny titled his history of the 1580-1650 period *Making Ireland British,* reflecting the goals of successive generations of servitors and settlers during this period.[4] In a 1655 pamphlet, *The Great Case of Transplantation Discussed,* Vincent Gookin, a colonial landowner and one-time Chief Surveyor of the Cromwellian Plantation, argued – over-optimistically – that the Irish had been subdued for all time and, more presciently, that the seeds of Anglicisation had been sown:

The Irish numbers (now abated by Famin, Pestilence, the Sword, and Forein Transportations) are not like to overgrow the English as formerly, and so no fear of their being obnoxious to them hereafter: but being mixed with, they are likelyer to be swallowed up by the English, and incorporated into them; so that a few Centuries will know no difference present, fear none to come, and scarce believe what were pas'd.[5]

Gookin contended that the balance of power had shifted sufficiently in Ireland to remove the factors that had led to the assimilation of previous waves of English setters into Irish ways of life, language and religion. English, Gookin argued in 1655, would come to replace Irish as the main language of commerce and the population would by necessity, become anglicised.[6] However, in pamphlets such as *The Political Anatomy of Ireland*, (1672) his contemporary William Petty was far more pessimistic arguing that the sheer numerical superiority of Catholics over Protestant settlers could not but determine Ireland's future.

Migration to and from Ireland has been at times engineered, organised and incentivised.[7] The Plantation of Ulster differed from earlier Elizabethan and Anglo-Norman colonial efforts insofar as the criteria for allocating lands included more stringent requirements to introduce settlers. Various earlier projects to introduce colonist settlers were mooted, and a few were implemented. For example, Thomas Shirley in 1607 and James Harrington in 1656 proposed fanciful schemes to settle European Jews in Ireland, neither of which found much support. A tiny number of Jews made their own way to Dublin during the seventeenth century, and when larger numbers arrived in the late nineteenth century, they did so as economic migrants rather than as part of an organised settlement programme.

Nothing seems at times to be so conducive to human misery as cack-handed attempts to regulate the admission of refugees, whether by corralling them in camps for years at a time or deliberately impeding efforts they might make under their own steam to integrate into reluctant host societies. Official and legal definitions of refugees tend to define these narrowly as people who are fleeing some kind of oppression. Refugees, unsurprisingly, want better lives for themselves and their families – to fulfil the usual range of human ambitions – as well as to be safe. Responses to those designated as refugees sometimes expect them to behave like patients in a hospital – passive and deferential – whilst treating them coercively like inmates in other kinds of institutions.

Efforts to distinguish refugees from other categories of migrant tend to presume that these are one or the other. Asylum seekers are often turned down on grounds that they are economic migrants, even though the reasons for forced migration often go beyond the narrow criteria acknowledged in assessing applications for asylum.[8] Where exactly specific migrants might be placed along a continuum between migration by choice and forced migration is often contested. Karl Marx used the term forced migrant to refer to the masses of Irish who migrated to the United States after the Famine.[9] Hardly any of these would meet criteria for admission derived from the UN Convention on the Rights of Refugees. The reasons why many people migrate today who have no easy legal right to travel (other than declaring themselves to be refugees) are no less compelling than the reasons why millions of post-Famine emigrants left Ireland. Freedom of movement, taken for granted by migrants from Ireland for centuries, is a prize denied to many millions of migrants in today's world.

The absence of legal permission to migrate has not stopped millions of people from doing so, but it does make life harder and more expensive, and can lead to the exploitation of migrants by traffickers and by middlemen. It is more difficult to integrate when you are living in fear of deportation and when you are literally disenfranchised. Emigrants from Ireland have, for the most part, migrated to places where they had an automatic right to do so. Mostly they settled in countries that have been part of the British Empire, where English was also spoken. Only a tiny minority of the millions who emigrated from Ireland have been what are variously called irregular, illegal or undocumented migrants.

Since independence, Irish emigrants have mostly travelled to countries where work visas were not required, the main exception being some of those when went to the United States during the 1980s. The larger number who migrated to Britain during the same period were not only allowed to work legally and to travel back and forth freely, but were allowed to vote in local and parliamentary elections. Irish people have taken unrestricted travel to the United Kingdom for granted, and it is likely that present day Irish society might be very different had this not been possible. At any given moment from 1851 to 1951 there was never less than half a million Irish-born people living in Britain. Although travel controls were introduced during the Second World War, more than 100,000 'guest workers' from Ireland were admitted on work permits followed by at least another 100,000, who arrived soon after the War when free travel was restored.

However, during the 1920s and 1930s sectarian hostility to Irish Catholic immigrants in Scotland led to intermittent campaigns to introduce immigration controls. For example, a work permit system was proposed to a Home Office committee in 1927. A scheme considered by the British Cabinet in 1928 proposed that migrants who had become unemployed should be repatriated to the Irish Free State and that a similar arrangement to repatriate

British subjects living in Ireland be simultaneously introduced. Unsurprisingly, the Irish government did not engage with proposals for reciprocal welfare restrictions, although a willingness to consider individual cases was offered in 1932. A further impediment to introducing restrictions at that time was Ireland's Dominion status. The issue of restricting Irish immigration was considered by the British Cabinet on a number of subsequent occasions in 1934, 1937 and in 1939 when an IRA bombing campaign resulted in five people dead and 70 injured in Coventry. Yet no restrictions were implemented. Wartime controls were lifted immediately afterwards.[10]

Again during the post-1969 conflict in Northern Ireland, when IRA terrorism included bombing campaigns in British cities where Irish immigrants lived, there was no restriction on migration from Ireland to Britain. Britain's Irish communities encountered the kinds of suspicion and, at times, harassment that has since been directed at Muslims in a number of Western countries. Anti-terrorism legislation which made it possible to deport migrants who were from Northern Ireland (which was part of the United Kingdom), alongside reports of police harassment and miscarriages of justice (the imprisonment of the patently innocent, to Irish eyes at least, Birmingham Six and Guildford Four) reflected a wider sense that the Irish were a 'suspect community'. By 1982 some 5,501 Irish in Britain had been detained under the Prevention of Terrorism Act. Of these only 96 were subsequently charged with offences, many of these for supposedly refusing to cooperate with the authorities at ports when they were arrested. Newspapers such as the *Daily* and *Sunday Express* 'appeared to be obsessed with the Irish' and published 'countless' anti-Irish cartoons and articles.[11]

Yet, immigration from Ireland was not restricted, and the perceptions of many Irish immigrants who had settled in London was that anti-Irish stereotypes and discrimination were more prevalent in the 1950s and '60s than during the post-1969 Troubles era; the kind of blatant 'No blacks, no Irish' racism characteristic of the earlier period appeared to be less widespread, as least in case of the Irish. Whilst some Irish immigrants and their descendents were politicised by the Northern Irish conflict it appears that most were not and that most did not support the IRA even if they saw themselves as Irish nationalists.[12] The post-1950s Irish in Britain were hitting middle age by the time the Northern Ireland conflict was in full swing, and interviewees in a study of these Irish in London 'almost unanimously expressed disgust at the violence emanating from Northern Ireland'. They displayed little of the kind of vicarious support for the IRA expressed by some Irish-Americans who were descended from immigrants.[13]

Prior to the 1990s only a few non-British groups had ever been encouraged to settle in Ireland. German Palatines were introduced as anchor tenants to Protestant landlords in mostly Catholic areas. Some years earlier, Huguenot soldiers were pensioned off in Ireland. Centuries before that, Anglo-Norman efforts to settle migrant tenants from England, Wales and Normandy resulted in small numbers of immigrants compared to the size of the local population. Many Anglo-Norman lords married the daughters of Irish nobles and relied mostly upon native tenants. The descendants of this immigrant elite came to speak Gaelic. In only a handful of places did immigrant languages take root, such as in Forth and Bargy in County Wexford where the proportion of commoners introduced by Anglo-Norman landholders was larger than elsewhere. Even the coastal towns founded by Northmen that passed into Anglo-Norman control drew much of their populations from Gaelic-speaking hinterlands. Not all of those who adopted the customs and languages of the invaders who controlled such enclaves were themselves migrants or descended from such. Most of the great changes that occurred in Ireland from pre-history to the seventeenth century owed much to a more general diffusion of culture, ideas, techniques and technologies than to the direct influence of conquering immigrants.

Present-day immigration to Ireland has been encouraged by laws and treaties and recruitment schemes not unlike the kinds of campaigns run by William Penn to encourage migrants from Ireland, Germany, and England to settle his Pennsylvania colony. The 1608 plantation required servitors to import Scottish or English tenants. Poorer migrants from Ireland sometimes funded their journeys by signing indenture contracts whilst some present-day migrants have to work of large debts to agents on arrival in Ireland. Armies of middlemen and the precursors of present-day recruitment agencies greased the wheels for past waves of emigration from and immigration to Ireland. Present-day examples of such arrangements include Filipino and Indian nurses recruited to work in Irish hospitals; crop-pickers brought over from Latvia and Lithuania to work on farms in the border counties, and Brazilians brought to small Irish towns to work in meat-packing plants. Arrangements whereby migrants pay legal brokers and recruitment agencies significant sums to organise employment, passage and work visas are still commonplace, as they were in previous centuries.

Systems of indentured servitude, through which migrants would work off the cost of their passage over several years, were commonplace before the nineteenth century and sometimes inaccurately equated with chattel slavery. The essential difference is that the period of service 'owed' by a migrant was time-limited whilst the children of slaves also became enslaved. The use of indenture contracts declined as the costs of ocean travel decreased. What has remained constant has been the persistence of efforts by some employers and agents to exploit vulnerable migrants not in a position to organise their own journeys or find employment without the help of a middleman. Modern-day illegal traffickers organise transportation, employment and accommodation for migrants not in a position to obtain visas or find work for themselves. Some have incurred huge debts that result in deductions from their wages for several years. Some twenty-first-century migrants have been heinously exploited. By the nineteenth century, when Catholic emigrants became the majority of those who sailed for North America for the first time, the cost of transatlantic travel was falling and travel to Britain was relatively cheap. Systems of indenture, as these had operated in earlier times, were no longer necessary. The poorest mostly travelled to Britain, and those with more resources went to North America. They were enabled to do so in many cases by remittances from earlier migrants, help from their families or savings obtained from working for a time in Ireland, or sometimes in England. Many may have been relatively fortunate compared to millions of twenty-first-century migrants. Millions of Irish migrated to countries that did not, at the time, impose visa restrictions, where they spoke the language and were granted citizenship rights on arrival. By constant, many non-European migrants to Ireland and other Fortress Europe countries encounter significant initial barriers.

ECONOMIC DRIVERS

That said millions of emigrants were squeezed out of Ireland by processes of social and economic modernisation. England's industrial revolution drew rural migrants from all parts of the United Kingdom into its cities, in addition to migrants from Ireland. In a pejorative sense people were presumed to migrate from backward to more advanced places, from rural peripheries to metropolitan economic cores, whilst at the same time resources and sometimes manpower flowed from the colonies to the colonial or industrial powers.[14] Colonial history since the Elizabethan plantation of Munster might be summarised as one of 'accumulation by dispossession',[15] and critics of economic liberalism understandably viewed economic progress as a new phase of colonial expropriation.

The Famine ushered in a new phase of dispossession in which the beneficiaries were mostly better-off Irish Catholics. In *The Last Conquest of Ireland (perhaps)*, John Mitchel described how in 1847 alone, some 24,147 small farms between five to fifteen acres, 27,379 farms between five and fifteen acres and 4,274 farms between fifteen and thirty acres vanished: 'In all seventy thousand occupiers, with their families, numbering about three hundred thousand, were rooted out of the land.[16] Between 1845 and 1855, as many as 2.1 million fled, out of fear of death or as a result of eviction. Around 800,000 – 10 per cent of the population – died from hunger and disease between 1845 and 1851. These were followed by 4 to 5 million others who had been born into a society acculturated to emigration.[17] According to Kerby Miller:

> Put bluntly, emigration became a societal imperative of post-famine Ireland: in reality less of a choice than a vital necessity both to secure the livelihoods of nearly all who left and most who stayed and to ensure the relative stability of a fundamentally 'sick' society.[18]

After the Famine inheritance patterns changed and this more so than the amalgamation of small holdings drove emigration from rural Ireland for more than a century. Many not due to inherit the use of land were pushed by their families to emigrate. Ireland's population plunged from eight million to less than half that number during the century after 1841. As claimed by Joseph Lee: 'Few people anywhere have been as prepared to scatter their children around the world in order to preserve their own living standards'.[19] The tides of emigration in the post-Famine era were integral to processes of Irish social modernisation. In the aftermath of the Famine Irish society changed considerably. Farms became bigger and more prosperous. Housing got better. Living standards rose for those who remained. Emigration consolidated the rise of a Catholic middle class and a property-owning peasantry.[20]

Legacies of colonialism and of the Famine perverted the trajectory of Irish modernisation. Irish society restructured in ways that squeezed extremely large numbers of people out. What occurred was not just a process of urbanisation, but the replacement of one social order with another. What is now understood as traditional Irish society was in fact a social order that emerged after the Famine. However, more than more than 50 million Europeans migrated to the New World between 1820 and 1913 for broadly similar reasons as did most Irish emigrants. About 30 million of these went to the United States, most of the rest to South America. As in the Irish case much of this emigration was also influenced by inheritance practices and, as such, was regulated within families. A classic study *The Polish Peasant* published in 1918 described similar practices whereby family farms were left to one son with the expectation that the others would emigrate. Other similarities included traditions of seasonal migration (mostly to Germany) alongside large-scale migration to the United States.[21] Emigration from any European country to the Americas required a level of resources that were not available to the poorest of the poor.[22]

Large numbers of southern Italians who migrated to the Americas during the late nineteenth century were able to return to their communities of origin. For example, some 308,900 did so between 1908 and 1910.[23] Many were able to re-join the communities they had left because the rural

south of Italy had not hugely changed in the meantime. Places that underwent catastrophic modernisation like parts of Ireland were more likely to
give rise to permanent emigration.[24] While many southern Italians went to
the United States many others during the late nineteenth century worked
seasonally in other European countries, which enabled their families at
home to stay on the land.[25]

After the Famine many Irish migrants to Britain no longer had this option.
Some seasonal migration persisted although many seasonal migrants went
on to become permanent emigrants. The structural pressures to emigrate –
be it as a result of modernisation processes that rationalised rural communities, or enticements that pulled people from underdeveloped areas to richer
places – can amount to immigrants making a calculation with little or no
choice. Ireland has been described as an 'emigrant nursery' which reared
generations of young people for export to wealthier economies.[26] Under-
development theory explains emigration in terms of inequalities within a
capitalist world economic system that leads to the expropriation of skilled
people as well as other resources to wealthy metropolitan centres or economic
cores.[27] From this perspective the modernisation trajectories of peripheral
countries are malignant insofar as these foster new chains of transnational
economic exploitation. Global inequalities continue to drive migration from
poorer to richer countries.

Ireland in the early twenty-first century is less plausibly an emigrant
nursery than hitherto. Like other rich countries, it has benefited from present-
day migrant nurseries like the Philippines, which educate large numbers of
people as nurses and carers who then must work abroad and remit much of
what they earn to support families at home. Rich Western countries, now
including Ireland, operate immigration systems that admit mostly well-
educated and skilled migrants. Doctors, nurses and other professionals
whose training was paid for in their countries of origin constitute what has
been called a 'brain drain.' Whilst suitably skilled migrants may have a choice
where to work their menu of options might not include the one of using their
skills in their home countries.[28]

ADAPTATIONS

Academic writing about present-day migration has come to place considerable emphasis on the role of modern communications systems and social
media in the lives of migrants[29] A number of studies of the lives of early
twenty-first-century immigrants in Ireland describe how they used social
media to contact friends and acquaintances to find jobs or accommodation,
and to keep in touch with family in their countries of origin. For instance, a

Pole living in Ireland might have found a place to live in Ireland via social media, watch Polish TV and keep in contact with family in Poland using Skype. Outside of the workplace, and perhaps even there, her interactions with non-Poles might be minimal. She might see herself as part of the Polish diaspora more so than a member of Irish society, initially at least.

Migrants sometimes appear to choose segregated lives, and this is generally perceived by host-community pundits to be a problem. Segregation, whether self-selected or not, can work against integration and foster inequalities that, in turn, undermine social cohesion. Yet, the kinds of transnational processes and relationships that some migrants appear to cling onto can also foster integration. Migration is enabled by transnational support systems and inter-dependencies that begin with information shared between friends and kin, by help and advice provided to newcomers by established migrants, by financial assistance and remittances and by sticking together with people from the old country.

Kerby Miller has argued, drawing on analysis of thousands of letters written by Irish emigrants to the United States, that emigrants generally imparted objective and carefully balanced information concerning the United States and its comparative advantages and disadvantages to potential migrants. Irishmen and women who were already established in America generally provided very cautious and even derogatory information about conditions there, especially during the economic depressions that occurred so frequently between the American Civil War and the First World War. Emigrants hardly painted idyllic pictures of their lives in the United States and sometimes made conscious efforts to shatter naïve expectations that, they believed, prevailed in rural Ireland, 'warning their correspondents that the remittances sent home were usually the products of great effort, hardship and sacrifice by the donors themselves'.[30] Migrants themselves depended on transnational support structures involving kin and friends, as outlined by Enda Delaney in his analysis of mid-twentieth century migration to Britain:

> These informal networks, in essence the product of personal relationships, enabled those with relatively little resources or indeed initiative to depart for Great Britain. Far from being displaced from a rural idyll and transferred to the faceless environment of urban Britain, Irish migrants actually possessed a remarkable degree of knowledge about what the move involved. This complex web of transnational relationships lessened the inherent dislocation involved in migration. Family and friends offered emotional and practical support driven by norms of obligation and duty towards prospective migrants and newcomers. These ties were centred on well-established conventions of reciprocity and co-operation that were a feature of Irish rural society.[31]

Pretty much the same could be said in the case of Ireland's own recently-established immigrant communities. However, it is important not to romanticise communal bonds and interdependencies too much. Migrants are sometimes exploited by more powerful or better-established members of their own communities, especially when newcomers do not have meaningful access to rights in the country where they have settled or cannot speak the host community language.

The canonical theory of assimilation as it developed in the case of the United States presumes a progression across three generations: a first generation that may not speak English experiences poverty and discrimination; a second generation advances economically, but retains some distinct 'ethnic' cultural and linguistic traits; a third generation becomes fully assimilated, and disconnected from the place of origin of their grandparents. Across these three generations, education levels rise and the second and third generations climb the ladder of social class. Most of the groups this 'theory' referred to were white emigrants from Europe: Italians, Poles and Irish. By comparison, some European countries that became emigrant destinations after the Second Word War admitted migrants from their own former empires. Migrants from colonies and ex-colonies experienced overt racism and discrimination that contributed to the marginalisation of subsequent generations.[32]

While earlier patterns of migrant assimilation took generations to effect, some twenty-first-century migration processes and host-society expectations about integration might be described as a kind of speed dating. Many migrants admitted to Ireland are better educated than all but the most recent generation of emigrants from Ireland. Many parts of the world are generically modern, with comparable education, health and administrative systems, similar supermarkets, brands and mass-produced foods and goods, all sharing a globalised mass media. Well-equipped immigrants may even fare better from the outset than marginal groups within a given host society. Economic rules of belonging, where those with marketable skills find favour, do not just apply to emigrants.

Cultural integration will always be a hot-button topic in politics, and for good reason. Nations and nationalisms have persisted into the twenty-first century as much due to as in spite of processes of economic globalisation. Twenty-first-century 'white nationalism' and anti-immigrant populism has earlier antecedents. These include not just Know-Nothing opposition to Irish immigrants arriving in the United States during the nineteenth century but, on a smaller scale, how Jews were depicted as enemies of the Irish nation in 1904 by Fr Creagh in Limerick and by some trades unions in Dublin. Immigration is often perceived in host countries as a symptom of wider disconcerting and threatening change, and seeking to harness the public mood, populist politicians often seek to demonise recent migrants and longer established ethnic and religious minorities.

Ideals of multiculturalism that supposedly countenance immigrant ethnic or religious groups living separately have been widely criticised in recent decades. Yet, different religions have provided broadly similar transnational support systems for emigrants from Ireland (Quakers, Presbyterians, Catholics and Jews) and amongst immigrants to Ireland (Jews, Pentecostals, Orthodox, Muslims and Catholics). Quakers and other Protestant dissenters who emigrated from Ireland to North America were assisted in doing so by their churches, while institutions such as Orange Lodges became focal points for Protestant Irish emigrants who settled in Canada, the United States and Britain. During the nineteenth and twentieth centuries, when most Irish emigrants were Catholic, the Catholic Church established missions in emigrant communities to help the vulnerable, schools and community infrastructure that greatly helped the Irish abroad to adapt.

Similar processes in twenty-first-century Ireland can be seen in relation to Brazilian and African Pentecostal churches, and Polish Catholic and Russian Orthodox ones. The most high-profile mosque in Ireland in Clonskeagh, with its imposing building, attached school and community facilities, resembles nothing so much as the architecture of a typical Irish Catholic parish – with a church, a rectory, a parish hall and perhaps a school – found in Ireland and in cities and towns wherever Irish Catholics have settled. However, the two primary schools established by the Islamic Cultural Centre in Dublin during the 1990s are exceptions.

The vast majority of immigrant children today attend mainstream (mostly Catholic-run) schools, while perhaps also attending Qu'ranic classes or Polish or Lithuanian schools in the evening or on the weekend. A tiny number of new primary schools came to have a majority of immigrant pupils because existing schools were 'oversubscribed' with children who met admissions criteria (such as Catholicism or having siblings already enrolled) that worked against the children of immigrants.[33] More generally, some immigrant children seem to have been shunted into schools in disadvantaged areas for similar reasons.[34] As in some other countries some of the main obstacles to integration are likely to be institutional barriers.[35]

Integration, as host communities might understand this, does not generally seem to be an immediate priority amongst immigrants, but it does tend to happen, eventually, in a range of ways – unless immigrants are deliberately excluded by residency and citizenship rules, or encounter debilitating levels of racism or discrimination. Elsewhere, I have used the term 'functional integration' to denote what migrants themselves might consider as viable lives in the host society, as distinct from the host society's expectation of integration.[36] Migrants might arrive in Ireland, or anywhere else, hoping to make a living or build better lives for their families at home. Some have clearly have experienced dysfunctional and damaging levels of exploitation. Others might be part of a supportive community that is somewhat detached from the host society, but where day-to-day life is nonetheless socially and economically viable.

Cultural bonds between immigrants are unlikely to impede integration where individuals have the capability to participate economically and socially in the wider community, and where the host society does not impose its own barriers to participation. By such criteria, most immigrants in early twenty-first-century Ireland are functionally integrated. Many are at least as well integrated as many Irish-born people. Ireland is a society where economic rules of belonging matter greatly and where cultural ones have never prevented emigration or other kinds of marginalisation.

One of the distinctive ways in which migration has shaped modern Ireland has been the influence of emigrants to the United States upon the development of Irish nationalism. The failed Young Irelander rebellion in 1848 saw the emigration of a nationalist intelligentsia alongside the huddled masses more preoccupied by the legacies of Famine and economic survival. Out of these grew the Fenian Brotherhood which proclaimed an Irish Republic, organised a failed rebellion in 1867 and inspired subsequent waves of radical and insurgent nationalism.

Irish immigrants in the Eastern cities of the United States appeared ghettoised and intent on clinging to a distinct Irish ethnic identity. Irish American newspapers such as the *New York Nation, The American Celt* and *The Irish World,* edited by Patrick Ford who emigrated from Galway to Boston in 1845 as an eight year old child, billed itself as a 'religious and national' weekly newspaper dedicated to 'the Irish Race throughout the World'.[37] Yet, alongside a fervent belief that there was such a thing as an Irish race Ford championed the notion of hyphenated identities: Irish-Americans, German-Americans, African-Americans and Anglo-Americans. Modern Irish nationalism is, in part, the creation of people who also saw themselves as Americans. So too can we expect that twenty-first-century conceptions of Irishness will be shaped in part by immigrants and their descendants who see themselves as having hyphenated Irish identities.

In both the Republic and Northern Ireland it is too early to tell how recent immigrants will integrate in the longer term. Much of the island's immigrant population arrived as twenty-somethings and are now thirty-somethings. In the Republic they arrived in a society that defined itself very much in mono-cultural terms. In the North, immigrants have experienced collateral fallout from the still-festering sectarian divides. A tired old joke recounts how a Belfast Jew was once asked whether he was a Protestant Jew or a Catholic Jew, but the point is clear. In the Republic, the issue of where even those immigrants who have become Irish citizens fit within the Irish nation state has yet to be addressed, and while religious identities may matter less and less to many people in the Republic, they matter a great deal to some immigrants.

The politics of immigration in Northern Ireland cannot be detached from the wider UK context, where political opposition to the free movement of migrants resulted in a decision in 2016 to leave the European Union. In the Republic, there has been little evidence of an equivalent anti-immigrant political populism, at least at the time of writing. In the 2004 Referendum on Citizenship, almost 80 per cent of those who voted agreed to remove an existing constitutional right to Irish citizenship for all children born on the island of Ireland.

The Republic of Ireland's response to immigration has been complex: open to labour migrants, often hostile to asylum seekers, not seeing the Irish-born children of immigrants as intrinsically Irish but willing to include migrants who naturalise their children, such as Ibrahim Halawa, within the Irish nation. Since 2014 many immigrants from non-EU countries have applied to become Irish citizens, and refusal rates for such applications have been very low. The empirical answer to the question 'who are the Irish?' has changed as people of every race, faith and tradition from around the world become Irish citizens. However, this has yet to be reflected in Irish institutions, politics, the media, or popular culture. Migrants from EU countries have tended not to apply for Irish citizenship but many will become permanent members of Irish society. The children of migrants grow up speaking with Irish accents. They will think of themselves, perhaps, as Polish-Irish, Filipino-Irish or African-Irish or maybe mostly as people from some particular Irish county or town.

The last several chapters have addressed relatively new immigrant communities who have been barely written about to date, let alone written into Irish history or into mainstream thinking about Irish society and identity. The great late Benedict Anderson once described nations as 'imagined communities'. Those that experience immigration to the extent that has occurred recently in the Irish case need to some extent to become reimagined communities.

NOTES

ONE: *Introduction*

1   Patrick Fitzgerald and Brian Lambkin, *Migration in Irish History, 1607–2007* (London: Palgrave, 2007).

2   Enda Delaney, 'Migration and diaspora', in Alvin Jackson (ed.) *The Oxford Handbook of Modern Irish History* (Oxford: Oxford University Press, 2014), p. 129.

3   Breda Gray, *Women and the Diaspora* (London: Routledge, 2004), p. 2.

4   Bryan Fanning, 'Racism, rules and rights', in Bryan Fanning (ed.), *Immigration and Social Change in the Republic of Ireland* (Manchester: Manchester University Press, 2007), p. 12.

5   Nicholas Canny, 'Ireland and Continental Europe, c1600–1700', in Alvin Jackson (ed.), *The Oxford Handbook of Modern Irish History* (Oxford: Oxford University Press, 2014), p. 335.

6   Warren R. Hofsta (ed.), *Ulster in America: The Scots-Irish Migration Experience, 1680–1830* (Knoxville: University of Tennessee Press, 2012), p. xxv.

TWO: *Invasions*

1   James Lydon, *The Making of Ireland: From Ancient Times to the Present* (London: Routledge, 1998), p. 27.

2   *Historica Brittonum* cited by J. P. Mallory, *The Origins of the Irish* (London: Thames and Hudson, 2013), p. 211.

3   Mallory, *Origins of the Irish,* p. 39.

4   Ibid., pp 37–41.

5   Ibid., pp 51–63.

6   Peter Woodman, 'The post-glacial colonisation of Ireland', in Daithí Ó'Corráin (ed.), *Irish Antiquity: Essays and Studies Presented to Professor M. J.* Kelly (Cork: Tower Books, 1981), p. 103.

7   Mallory, *Origins of the Irish,* p. 69.

8   Ibid., pp 73–103.

9   Peter Woodman, 'Prehistoric settlers', in Patrick Loughrey (ed.), *The People of Ireland* (Belfast: Appletree, 1988), p. 15.

10 Ibid., p. 22.

11 Ibid., p. 25.

12 Mallory, *Origins of the Irish*, p. 242.

13 Ibid., p. 131.

14 Ibid., p. 290.

15 Ibid., p. 264.

16 Norman Davies, *The Isles: A History* (London: Macmillan, 1999), p. 43.

17 Davies, *The Isles*, p. 101.

18 Ibid., p. 101.

19 Thomas Bartlett, *Ireland: A History* (Cambridge: Cambridge University Press, 2010), pp 2–4.

20 Davies, *The Isles*, p. 155.

21 Bartlett, *Ireland*, pp 26–7.

22 Davies, *The Isles*, p. 206.

23 Robert Ferguson, *The Vikings: A History* (London: Penguin, 2009), p. 78.

24 Brian McEvoy, Claire Brady, Louise T. Moore and Daniel G. Bradley, 'The scale and nature of Viking settlement in Ireland from Y-chromosome admixture analysis', *European Journal of Human Genetics*, 14 (2006), pp 1,288–94.

25 Ferguson, *The Vikings*, p. 95.

26 Claire Downham, 'The historical importance of Viking-age Waterford', in *Eighteenth Irish Conference of Medievalists*, 18:1 (2004), 71–95, p. 93.

27 Ferguson, *The Vikings*, p. 195.

28 Paul Holm, 'The slave trade of Dublin, ninth to twelfth centuries', in *Perita*, 5 (1980), pp 317–45.

29 Downham, 'Viking-age Waterford', pp 86–8.

30 Donncha Ó Corráin, *Ireland before the Normans* (Dublin: Gill and Macmillan, 1972), p. 857.

31 Bartlett, *Ireland*, p. 31.

32 Davis, *The Isles*, pp 233–4.

33 Bartlett, *Ireland*, p. 34.

34 Kevin Whelan (ed.) *Tintern Abbey County Wexford* (Wexford: Friends of Tintern Abbey, 1990).

35 John Watt, *The Church in Medieval Ireland* (Dublin: UCD Press, 1998), pp 29–30.

36 Ibid., pp 1–3.

37 Ó Corráin, *Ireland before the Normans*, pp 171–2.

38 Michael Dolley, *Anglo-Norman Ireland* (Dublin: Gill and Macmillan, 1972), p. 55.

39 Robert Frame, *Colonial Ireland: 1169–1369* (Dublin: Four Courts Press, 2012), p. 7.

40 Ibid., p. 84.

41 Ibid., p. 104.

42 Ibid., pp 106–7.

43 Watt, *The Church in Medieval Ireland*, p. 92.

44 Ibid., pp 116–23.

45 Frame, *Colonial Ireland 1168–1369*, p. 1.

46 Ó Corráin, *Ireland before the Normans*, pp 171–2.

47 Billy Colfer, 'Anglo-Norse settlement in County Wexford', in Kevin Whelan (ed.), *Wexford History and Society* (Dublin: Geography Publications, 1987), p. 93.

48 Richard Roche, 'Forth and Bargy – a place apart', in Kevin Whelan (ed.), *Wexford History and Society* (Dublin: Geography Publications, 1992), p. 114.

49 Billy Colfer, *Arrogant Trespass: Anglo-Norman Wexford 1169–1400* (Enniscorthy: Duffry Press, 2002), p. 124.

50 Colin Veach, *Lordship in Four Realms: The Lacy Family 1166–1241* (Manchester: Manchester University Press, 2004), p. 256.

51 Frame, *Colonial Ireland 1169–1369*, p. 95.

52 Lydon, *The Making of Ireland*, p. 64–5.

53 Watt, *The Church in Medieval Ireland*, p. 47.

54 Dolley, *Anglo-Norman Ireland*, p. 87.

55 Frame, *Colonial Ireland 1169–1369*, p. 36.

56 Ibid., p. 137.

57 James Lydon, *Ireland in the Later Middle Ages* (Dublin: Gill and Macmillan, 1973), pp 61–3.

58 Bartlett, *Ireland*, p. 65.

59 Dolley, *Anglo-Norman Ireland*, p. 94.

60 Frame, *Colonial Ireland 1169–1369*, p. 151.

61 John Davies, *A Discovery of the True Causes Why Ireland was Never Entirely Subdued, Nor Brought Under Obedience of the Crown Of England, until the Beginning of the Reign of his Majesties Happie Reign* (Shannon: Irish University Press, 1969 [1612 first edition facsimile]), pp 113–41.

THREE: *Plantations*

1 Michael MacCarthy-Morrough, *The Munster Plantation: English Migration to Southern Ireland 1583–1641* (Oxford: Clarendon Press, 1986), p. vii.

2 Roy Foster, *Modern Ireland: 1600–1972* (London: Allen Lane, 1988), p. 5.

3 Nicholas Canny, *Making Ireland British: 1580-1650* (Oxford: Oxford University Press, 2001), p. 194.

4 Ibid., p. 193.

5 Jane Ohlmeyer, *Civil War and Restoration in the Three Stuart Kingdoms: The Career of Ranald McDonnell, Marquis of Antrim 1609–1683* (Cambridge: Cambridge University Press, 1993), p. 210.

6 Raymond Gillespie, 'Material culture and social change in early modern Ireland', in James Lyttleton and Colin Rynne (eds), *Plantation Ireland: Settlement and Material Culture, c.1550–1700* (Dublin: Four Courts Press, 2009), p. 43.

7 Gillespie, *Material Culture and Social Change in Early Modern Ireland*, p. 46.

8 MacCarthy-Morrogh, *The Munster Plantation*, p. 285.

9 Thomas Bartlett, *Ireland: A History* (Cambridge: Cambridge University Press, 2010) p. 89.

10 Tadhg Ó Hannracháin, 'Plantation 1580–1641', in Alvin Jackson (ed.) *The Oxford Handbook of Modern Irish History* (Oxford: Oxford University Press, 2014), p. 293

11 David Dickson, *Old World Colony: Cork and South Munster 1630–1830* (Cork: Cork University Press, 2005), p. 10.

12 Canny, *Making Ireland British*, p. 130.

13 Ibid., p. 130.

14 Ibid., p. 132.

15 MacCarthy-Morrogh, *Muster Plantation*, pp 115–16.

16 Canny, *Making Ireland British*, pp 145–6.

17 MacCarthy-Morrogh, *Munster Plantation*, p. 25.

18 Dickson, *Old World Colony*, p. 25.

19 MacCarthy-Morrogh, *Munster Plantation*, p. 135.

20 MacCarthy-Morrogh, 'Credit and remittance: Monetary problems in early seventeenth-century Munster', *Irish Social and Economic History*, XIV (1987), 5–19, p. 10.

21 Dickson, *Old World Colony*, p. 20.

22 Ibid., p. 11.

23 MacCarthy-Morrogh, *Munster Plantation*, p. 247.

24 Jonathan Bardon, *The Plantation of Ulster* (Dublin: Gill and Macmillan, 2011), p. 21.

25 Jenny Wormald, 'The "British" crown, the earls and the plantation of Ulster', in Éamonn Ó Ciardha and Micheál Ó Siochrú (eds), *The Plantation of Ulster: Ideology and Practice* (Manchester: Manchester University Press, 2012), p. 21.

26 Jane Ohlmeyer, 'Civilizing of those rude parts': Colonization within Britain and Ireland, 1580s–1640s', in Nicholas Canny (ed.), *The Oxford History of the British Empire*, (Oxford: Oxford University Press, 1998), pp 124–47.

27 Wormald, 'The "British" crown, the earls and the plantation of Ulster', p. 27.

28 J. Micheal Hill, 'The origins of the Scottish Plantation in Ulster to 1625: A reinterpretation', in *Journal of British Studies*, 32 (1993), pp 24–43.

29 Ibid., p. 40.

30 Ibid., p. 25.

31 Philip Robinson, *The Plantation of Ulster* (Dublin: Gill and Macmillan, 1994), p. 44.

32 Hill, 'Origins of the Scottish Plantation of Ulster', p. 27.

33 Ibid., p. 29.

34 Robinson, *The Plantation of Ulster*, p. 51.

35 See G. Hill (ed.), *The Montgomery Manuscripts, 1603–1706, Compiled from Family Papers* (Belfast, 1877).

36 John Harrison, *The Scot in Ulster* (London: Blackwood and Sons, 1888), p. 7.

37 D. A. Chart, 'The break-up of the estate of Con O'Neill, Castlereagh, County Down', *Proceedings of the Royal Irish Academy. Section C: Archaeology, Celtic Studies, History, Linguistics, Literature*, 48 (1942/3), pp 119–51, p. 129.

38 P. Roebuck, 'The making of an Ulster great estate: The Chichesters, Barons of Belfast and Viscounts of Carrickfergus, 1599–1648', *Proceedings of the Royal Irish Academy*, 79, 1979, pp 1–25, p. 8.

39 Roebuck, 'The making of an Ulster great estate', p. 8.

40 Jean Agnew, *Belfast Merchant Families in the Seventeenth Century* (Dublin: Four Courts Press, 1996), pp 10–12.

41 Raymond Gillespie, *Colonial Ulster: The Settlement of East Ulster: 1600–1641* (Cork: Cork University Press, 1985), p. 150.

42 Ibid., pp 135–6.

43 Raymond Gillespie, 'Thomas Raven and the mapping of the Clandeboye estate c.1625', in *Bangor Historical Society Journal* vol. 1 (1981), 7–9, p. 7.

44 Gillespie, *Colonial Ulster*, p. 30.

45   Harold O'Sullivan, 'The Magennis Lordship of Iveagh in the Early Modern Period, 1534 to 1691', in Lindsay Proudfoot (ed.), *Down History and Society* (Dublin: Geography Publications, 1997), p. 168.

46   W. R. Hulchinson, *Tyrone Precinct: A History of the Plantation and Settlement of Dungannon and Mountjoy to Modern Times* (Belfast: W. E. Maine, 1951), p. 38.

47   Robinson, 'The Ulster Plantation in the Manor of Dunnalong', p. 267.

48   Marcus Tanner, *Ireland's Holy Wars: The Struggle for a Nation's Soul 1500–2000* (New Haven: Yale University Press, 2001), p. 124.

49   Jonathan Bardon, *The Plantation of Ulster* (Dublin: Gill and Macmillan, 2011), p. 19.

50   T. W. Moody, 'The treatment of the native population under the scheme for the Plantation of Ulster', *Irish Historical Studies*, March 1938, 1.1, pp 59–63, p. 61.

51   Ruth Dudley Edwards and Bridget Hourican, *An Atlas of Irish History: 3rd Edition* (Manchester: Manchester University Press, 2005), p. 159.

52   Canny, *Making Ireland British*, p. 192.

53   R. J. Hunter, 'The Fishmonger's Company of London and the Londonderry Plantation, 1609–41', in Gerald O'Brien (ed.), *Derry and Londonderry History and Society* (Dublin: Geography Publications, 1999), p. 208.

54   Brian Lacy, *Siege City: The Story of Derry and Londonderry* (Belfast: Blackstaff Press, 1990), pp 82–9.

55   Canny, *Making Ireland British*, p. 218.

56   Bardon, *Plantation of Ulster*, p. 94.

57   Robinson, *Plantation of Ulster*, pp 113–4.

58   Cited in Bardon, *Plantation of Ulster*, p. 144.

59   Ibid., p. 1.

60   Bartlett, *Ireland*, p. 94.

61   Quoted in W. Bailie, *The Six Mile Water Revival of 1625* (Belfast: Presbyterian Historical Society of Ireland, 1984), p. 2.

62   Hill, *Origins of the Scottish Plantations*, p. 4.

63   Revd James Barkley Woodburn, *The Ulster Scot: History and Religion* (London: H. R. Allenson, 1914), p. 69.

64   Patrick Fitzgerald, 'From the Flight of the Earls to the Famine: Tyrone's Migration history 1600 to 1845', in Charles Dillon and Henry A. Jefferies (eds), *Tyrone: History and Society* (Dublin: Geography Publications, 2000), p. 461.

65   Cited in Bardon, *Plantation of Ulster*, p. 40.

66   Nicholas Canny, 'Hugh O'Neill, earl of Tyrone, and the changing face of Gaelic Ulster', *Studia Hibernica*, 1970, 10, pp 27–35, p. 27.

67   Philip Robinson, 'The Ulster Plantation and its impact on the settlement pattern of Co. Tyrone', in Charles Dillon and Henry A. Jefferies (eds), *Tyrone: History and Society* (Dublin: Geography Publications, 2000), p. 249.

68   W. R. Hutchison, *Tyrone Precinct* (Belfast: Erskine Mayne, 1951), p. 41.

69   Robinson, *The Settlement Pattern of Co Tyrone*, p. 249.

70   Hill, *Origins of the Scottish Plantations*, p. 40–2.

71   Ibid., p. 34.

72   Ibid., p. 249.

73 Ibid., p. 249.

74 Bardon, *Plantation of Ulster*, p. 278.

75 Ibid., p. 215.

76 Ibid., p. 216.

77 Robinson, *The Settlement Pattern of Co Tyrone*, p. 254.

78 Ibid., p. 251.

79 Audrey J. Horning, 'Archaeological explorations of cultural identity and rural economy in the North of Ireland: Goodland, County Antrim', in *International Journal of Historical Archaeology*, 2004, Vol. 8, No.3, pp 119–225.

80 William Roulston, 'The Ulster Plantation in the Manor of Dunnalong, 1610–70', in Charles Dillon and Henry A. Jefferies (eds), *Tyrone: History and Society* (Dublin: Geography Publications, 2000), p. 286–7.

81 Bardon, *Plantation of Ulster*, p. 216.

82 Robinson, *Plantation of Ulster*, p. 124.

83 Tanner, *Ireland's Holy Wars*, p. 125.

84 Roebuck, *The Making of an Ulster Great Estate*, p. 16.

85 Hill, *Origins of the Scottish Plantations*, p. 36.

86 Ibid., p. 42.

87 Ibid., p. 37.

88 A. T. Q. Stewart, *The Narrow Ground: The Roots of Conflict in Ulster* (London: Faber and Faber, 1977), p. 40.

89 Canny, *Making Ireland British*, p. 211.

90 Robinson, *The Plantation of Ulster*, p. 105.

91 Ibid., p. 114.

92 William Mcaffe, 'The population of County Tyrone 1600–1991', in Charles Dillon and Henry A. Jefferies (eds), *Tyrone: History and Society* (Dublin: Geography Publications, 2000), p. 435.

93 Horning, *Archaeological Explorations of Cultural Identity*, p. 211.

94 Ibid., p. 209.

95 Hill, *Origins of the Scottish Plantation*, p. 28

96 Barkley Woodburn, *The Ulster Scot*, p. 88.

97 William J. Smyth, 'Towards a cultural geography of the 1641 rising/rebellion', in Micheál Ó Siochrú and Jane Ohlmeyer (eds), *Ireland 1641: Contexts and Reactions* (Manchester: Manchester University Press, 2013), p. 76.

98 Ibid., p. 77.

99 Stewart, *The Narrow Ground*, p. 46.

100 Robert Armstrong, 'Ireland's Puritan revolution? The emergence of Ulster Presbyterianism reconsidered', *English Historical Review*, 121.493 (2005), pp 1,048–72, pp 1,061–9.

101 Ibid., p. 1,073–4.

102 Charles Ivar McGrath, 'Securing the Protestant interest: the origins and purpose of the penal laws of 1695', *Irish Historical Studies*, 30.117 (1996), pp 22–46.

103 R. C. Burns, 'The Irish Penal Code and some of its historians', *The Review of Politics*, 21.1 (1959), 276–99, p. 276.

104 Smyth, 'Towards a cultural geography', p. 75.

Notes

105 John Harrison, *The Scot in Ulster* (London: William Blackwood and Sons, 1888), pp 53–4.
106 Darragh Curran, *A Society in Transition: The Protestant Community in Tyrone 1836–42* (PhD eprint: NUI Maynooth), p. 10.

FOUR: *Transplantation*

1   L. M. Cullen, *The Emergence of Modern Ireland 1600–1900* (London: Batsford Academic and Educational Ltd, 1981), p. 15.
2   Ibid., p. 87.
3   Cullen, 'Population trends in the seventeenth-century', *Economic and Social Review*, 1975, 6.2, pp 49–65, p. 150.
4   Ibid., p. 151; p. 160.
5   Cullen, *The Emergence of Modern Ireland 1600–1900*, p. 96.
6   Aubrey Gwynn SJ, 'Early Irish emigration to the West Indies', *Studies*, 1928, 18.72, pp 648–63, p. 661.
7   Frank D'arcy, *Wild Geese and Traveling Scholars* (Dublin: Mercier Press, 2001), pp 31–2.
8   Ibid., p. 69.
9   Youssef Courbage, 'The demographic factor in Ireland's movement towards partition (1607–1921)', *Population: An English Selection*, 1977, 9, pp 169–90, p. 172.
10   Harman Murtagh, 'Irish soldiers abroad, 1600–1800', in Thomas Bartlett and Keith Jeffery (eds), *A Military History of Ireland* (Cambridge, Cambridge University Press, 1996), p. 294.
11   Gráinne Henry, *The Irish Military Community in Spanish Flanders* (Dublin: Irish Academic Press, 1992), p. 19.
12   Terry Clavin, 'Stanley, Sir William', *Dictionary of Irish Biography* (Cambridge: Cambridge University Press). http://dib.cambridge.org
13   Henry, *The Irish Military Community*, p. 99.
14   Enrique Garcia Hernán, 'Irish clerics in Madrid, 1598–1665', in Thomas O'Connor and Mary Ann Lyons (eds), *Irish Communities in Early Modern Europe* (Dublin: Four Courts Press, 2006), pp 267–8.
15   Hernán, 'Irish Clerics in Madrid', pp 270–1.
16   Ciaran O'Scea, *Surviving Kinsale: Irish Emigration and Identity Formation in Early Modern Spain* (Manchester: Manchester University Press, 2015), p. 44.
17   Ibid., p. 46.
18   Ibid., p. 47.
19   Ibid., p. 48.
20   Ibid., p. 51.
21   Ibid., p. 81.
22   Michael Browne, 'Irish college in Salamanca – last days', *The Furrow*, 1971, 22.11, pp 697–702, p. 697.
23   Denis Murphy, 'The college of the Irish Franciscans at Louvain', *The Journal of the Royal Society of Antiquaries in Ireland, Fifth Series*, 1893, 3.3, pp 237–50, p. 239.
24   Bernadette Cunningham, *The Annals of the Four Masters: Irish History, Kingship and Society in the Early Seventeenth Century* (Dublin: Four Courts, 2014), p. 34.
25   Ibid., p. 35.

26 Murphy, 'The college of the Irish Franciscans at Louvain', p. 239.

27 Jerrold Casway, 'Henry O'Neill and the formation of the Irish regiment in the Netherlands, 1605', *Irish Historical Studies*, 1973, 18.72 , pp 481–8.

28 Henry, *The Irish Military Community in Spanish Flanders*, p. 145

29 Ibid., pp 76–80.

30 Ibid., p. 146.

31 Ibid., pp 79–85.

32 Ibid., p. 100.

33 Michael Browne, 'Irish college in Salamanca – last days', *The Furrow*, 1971, 22:11, pp 697–702, p. 697.

34 D'arcy, *Wild Geese and Traveling Scholars*, p. 16.

35 Ibid., p. 23.

36 Edmond Fitzmaurice, *The Life of Sir William Petty 1623–1687* (London: John Murray, 1895), p. 24.

37 Thomas Bartlett, *Ireland: A History* (Oxford: Oxford University Press, 2010), p. 113.

38 T. C. Barnard, 'Planters and polices in Cromwellian Ireland', *Past and Present*, 1973, 61, pp 31–69, p. 32.

39 Bartlett, *Ireland: A History*, p. 130.

40 Barnard, 'William Petty', *Oxford Dictionary of National Biography* (vol. 43), https://doi. org/10.1093/ref:odnb/22069.

41 Keith Lindley, 'Irish adventurers and godly militants in the 1640s', *Irish Historical Studies*, 1994, 29.113, pp 1–12, p. 2.

42 Ibid., pp 11–12.

43 Samuel R. Gardiner, 'The transplantation to Connaught', *The English Historical Review*, (1899), 14.56, pp 700–34, p. 701.

44 Harold O'Sullivan, 'The plantation of Cromwellian soldiers in the Barony of Ardee, 1652–1656', *County Louth Archaeological and History Society*, 1998, 21.4, pp 415–52.

45 Ibid., p. 420.

46 Ibid., p. 425–6.

47 T. C. Barnard, *Improving Ireland? Projectors, Prophets and Profiteers, 1641–1786* (Dublin: Four Courts, 2008), pp 55–8.

48 Barnard, 'Petty as Kerry iron master', p. 2.

49 Bartlett, *Ireland: A History*, p. 131.

50 Barnard, 'Planters and polices in Cromwelliam Ireland', p. 32.

51 Raymond Gillespie, *Seventeenth Century Ireland: Making Ireland Modern* (Dublin: Gill and McMillan, 2006), p. 241.

52 Bryan Fanning, *Histories of the Irish Future* (London: Bloomsbury, 2015), pp 23–5.

53 Donald Akenson, *If Ireland Ruled the World: Montserrat, 1630–1730* (Liverpool: Liverpool University Press, 1997), p. 93.

54 Ibid., p. 53.

55 Ibid., p. 45.

56 Kristen Black and Jenny Shaw, 'Subjects without an empire: The Irish in the early modern Caribbean', *Past and Present*, 2011, no. 210, 33–60, p. 38.

57 The Commissioners for the Administration of the Affairs of the Commonwealth of England in Ireland (1 July 1653), cited in Peter Berresford Ellis, *Hell or Connaught: The Cromwellian Colonisation of Ireland 1652–1660* (Belfast: Blackstaff Press, 1975), p. 85.

58 Ibid., p. 87.

59 Ibid., p. 95.

60 Ibid., p. 59.

61 Akenson, *If Ireland Ruled the World*, p. 8.

62 Liam Hogan, Laura McAtackney and Matthew C. Reilly, 'The Irish in the Caribbean: servants or slaves?: Why we need to confront the "Irish slave myth" and how terminology is not simply semantics', *History Ireland*, March 2016, pp 18–23.

63 Akenson, *If Ireland Ruled the World*, pp 49–50.

64 Ibid., p. 72.

65 Black and Shaw, 'Subjects without an empire', p. 34.

66 Ibid., p. 37.

67 Akenson, *If Ireland Ruled the World*, p. 194.

68 Ibid., p. 149.

69 Ibid., p. 153.

70 D'arcy, *Wild Geese and Traveling Scholars*, p. 30.

71 Nicholas Canny, 'Ireland and Continental Europe, *c.*1600–1700', in Alvin Jackson (ed.), *The Oxford Handbook of Modern Irish History* (Oxford: Oxford University Press, 2014), p. 347.

72 Walsh, *The Wild Goose Tradition*, p. 183.

73 O'Scea, *Surviving Kinsale*, p. 243.

74 R. A. Stradling, *The Spanish Monarchy and Irish Mercenaries: The Wild Geese in Spain 1618–68* (Dublin: Irish Academic Press, 1994), p. 163.

75 Ibid., p. 138.

76 Ibid., p. 142.

77 Cited in ibid., p. 96.

78 Ibid., p. 67.

79 Michelle Kearney Walsh, 'The wild goose tradition', in Harman Murtagh (ed.), *Irishmen in War from the Crusades to 1798: Essays from the Irish Sword, Volume I* (Dublin: Irish Academic Press, 2005), pp 189.

80 Eoghan O'hAnnracháin, 'Clogher veterans in the Hotel Royal des Invalides', *Clogher Record*, 2005, 18.3, pp 467–500, p. 468.

81 Ibid., p. 484.

82 Eoghan O'hAnnracháin, 'Louth wild geese veterans in the Hotel Royal Des Invalides', *Journal of the County Louth Archaeological and History Society*, 1999, 24.3, pp 380–90, p. 382.

83 T. P. Le Fanu, 'Huguenot veterans in Dublin', *The Journal of the Royal Society of Antiquaries of Ireland*, 1944, 12.2, pp 64–70, p. 70.

84 Janet G. Gray, 'The origin of the word Huguenot', *The Sixteenth Century Journal*, 1983, 14.3, pp 349–59.

85 Ruth Whelan, 'The Huguenots and the imaginative geography of Ireland: A planned immigration scheme in the 1680s', *Irish Historical Studies*, 2007, 35.140, pp 477–95, p. 478.

86 Ibid., p. 481.

87 Ibid., p. 482.

88 James McGuire, 'Government attitude to religious non-conformity in Ireland 1660–1719', in Eric Caldicot, Hugh Gough and Jean-Paul Pittion (eds), *The Huguenots and Ireland: Anatomy of an Emigration* (Dublin: Gelendale Press, 1987), p. 261.

89 David George Mullan, 'A hotter sort of Protestantism? Comparisons between French and Scottish Calvinisms', *The Seventeenth Century Journal*, 2008, 39.1, pp 45–69, 50–8.

Notes

90 Ibid., p. 57.
91 Pierre Drelincourt, *De l'etat present d'Irlande, et des avantages qu'y peuvent trouver les protestans francois: et une letter d'un des chapelains de monseineur le duc d'Ormond, viceroy d'Irlande, a un de ses amis en Angleterre* (Dublin 1688), p. 5, cited by Ruth Whelan, p. 483.
92 Ibid., p. 484.
93 Le Fanu, 'Huguenot veterans in Dublin', p. 66–9.
94 Patrick Kelly, 'Lord Galway and the Penal Laws', in Caldicott et al (eds), *The Huguenots and Ireland*, p. 243.
95 Raymond Pierre Hylton, 'Massue de Ruvigny, Henri', *Dictionary of Irish Biography*. (Cambridge University Press). http://dib.cambridge.org/viewReadPage.do?articleId=a5505
96 Louis Cullen, 'The Huguenots from the perspective of the merchant networks of W. Europe (1680–1790): the example of the brandy trade', in Caldicott et al (eds), *The Huguenots and Ireland*, pp 129–50.
97 Grace Lawless Lee, *The Huguenot Settlements in Ireland* (Massachusetts: Clearfield, 1936), p. 203.
98 John S. Powell, 'Languedoc in Laois: the Huguenots of Portarlington', *History Ireland*, 1995, 3.1, pp 29–32, p. 29.
99 John S. Powell, 'The Huguenots of Portarlington', *Studies*, 1972, 61.244, pp 343–53, p. 345.
100 Ibid., p. 345.
101 Jean-Paul Pittion, 'The question of religious conformity and non-conformity in the Irish refuge', in Caldicot et al (eds), *The Huguenots and Ireland*, p. 287.
102 Powell, *The Huguenots of Portarlington*, pp 343–53.
103 Ibid., p. 343.
104 Carolyn Lougee Chapell, '"The pains I took to save my/his family": Escape accounts by a Huguenot mother and daughter after the Revocation of the Edict of Nantes', *French Historical Studies*, 1999, 22.1, pp 1–64.
105 Lawless Lee, *Huguenot Settlements in Ireland*, p. 158.
106 Ibid., pp 158–9.
107 Hylton, Raymond The Huguenot settlement at Portarlingon 1672–1771', in Caldicott, Gough, Pittion (eds), *The Huguenots and Ireland*, p. 314.
108 Ibid., p. 315.
109 Lawless Lee, *Huguenot Settlements in Ireland*, p. 160.
110 Charles Nicholas de la Purdon, 'The French settlers in Ireland: The Huguenot colony at Lisburn, county of Antrim', in *Journal of Archaeology*, 1853, 1, pp 217–18.
111 Ibid., pp 209–20.
112 Lawless Lee, *Huguenot Settlements in Ireland*, p. 178.
113 Roy Sundstrum, 'French Huguenots and the civil list, 1696–1727: A study of alien assimilation in England', *Albion: A Quarterly Journal Concerned with British Studies*, 1976, 8.3, pp 219–35, p. 228.
114 Lawless Lee, *Huguenot Settlements in Ireland*, p. 196.
115 Philip Benedict, 'The Huguenot population of France, 1600–1685: The demographic fate and customs of a religious minority', in *Transactions of the American Philosophical Society*, 1991, 81.5, pp 1–164, p. 7.
116 Kenneth Ferguson, 'Rocque's map and the history of nonconformity in Dublin: a search for meeting houses', *Dublin Historical Record*, 2005, 58.2, pp 129–65, p. 143.

117 Powell, 'Languedoc in Laois', p. 31.

118 Powell, 'Huguenots of Portarlington', p. 349.

119 Black and Shaw, 'Subjects without an empire', pp 33–60, p. 35.

120 Thomas Bartlett and Keith Jeffery, 'An Irish military tradition?', in Thomas Bartlett and Keith Jeffery (eds), *A Military History of Ireland* (Cambridge, Cambridge University Press, 1996), pp 10–12.

FIVE : *Palatines*

1   W. E. H. Lecky, *A History of Ireland in the Eighteenth Century: vol. I* (London: Longman, Green and Co., 1913[1892]), pp 351–2.

2   Mr & Mrs S. C. Hall *Ireland: Its Scenery, Character, etc, vol. 1* (London: How and Parsons, 1861), p. 354.

3   Tom Dunne, *Rebellions: Memoir, Memory and 1798* (Dublin: Lilliput Press, 2010), p. 249.

4   H. T. Dickinson, 'The poor Palatines and the parties'. *The English Historical Review*, Jul., 1967, 82.324, pp 464–85, p. 464.

5   John Tribbeko, *A Funeral Sermon on the Death of H. R. H. Prince George of Denmark* (London, 1709), p. 17.

6   Cited in Walter A. Knittle, *Eighteenth Century Palatine Emigration* (Philadelphia, 1937), p. 29.

7   Ibid., p. 26.

8   Patrick J. O'Connor, *People Make Places: The Story of the Irish Palatines* (Newcastle West: Oireacht na Mumhan Books, 1989), p. 4.

9   Knittle, *Eighteenth Century Palatine Emigration*, p. 78.

10   Report of the [officers] of the Transport Office to the Lords of the Treasury, 20 February 1694, *Calendar of Treasury Papers, Volume 1: 1556–1696* (1868), pp 338–50. URL: http://www.british-history.ac.uk/report.aspx?compid=79472 Date accessed: 14 October 2014.

11   Ute Lotz-Heumann: Confessional Migration of the Reformed: The Huguenots, in: Europäische Geschichte Online (EGO), hg. vom Leibniz-Institut für Europäische Geschichte (IEG), Mainz European History Online (EGO), published by the Leibniz Institute of European History (IEG), Mainz 2012-07-04. URL: http://www.ieg-ego.eu/lotzheumannu-2012-en URN: urn:nbn:de:0159-2012070405

12   Dickinson, 'The poor Palatines and the parties', p. 466.

13   O'Connor, *People Make Places*, p. 7.

14   Dickinson, 'The Poor Palatines and the parties', p. 464.

15   Knittle, *Eighteenth Century Palatine Emigration*, p. 56.

16   Ibid., pp 59–61.

17   Dickinson, 'The Poor Palatines and the parties', p. 471.

28   Ibid., p. 469.

19   O'Connor, *People Make Places*, p. 11.

20   Knittle, *Eighteenth Century Palatine Emigration*, p. 78.

21   Ibid., p. 72.

22   Ibid., p. 80.

23   Daniel Defoe, *The Review*, 2 July 1709.

24   Defoe, *A Brief History of the Poor Palatine Refugees* (London, 1709).

25 Knittle, *Eighteenth Century Palatine Emigration*, p. 78.

26 Dickinson, 'The Poor Palatines and the parties', pp 478–9.

27 Knittle, *Eighteenth Century Palatine Emigration*, p. 83.

28 O'Connor, *People Make Places*, p. 22.

29 Ibid., p. 29.

30 Dickinson, 'The Poor Palatines and the Parties', p. 479.

31 O'Connor, *People Make Places*, p. 21.

32 Ibid., pp 37–8.

33 Ibid., pp 29–35.

34 Ibid., p. 53.

35 Ibid., p. 83.

36 Ibid., pp 60–4.

37 Ibid., p. 175.

38 Ibid., p. 96.

39 D. N. Hempton, 'The Methodist crusade in Ireland 1795–1845', in *Irish Historical Studies*, 1980, , 22.85, p. 36.

40 O'Connor, *People Make Places*, pp 69–79.

41 Walter C. Shier, 'The Shier family, 1709–1850: Pioneers of Brock Township and elsewhere in Ontario' (1961) wordpress.com/2010/05/waltercshierbook.pdf

42 Vivienne Hick, 'The Palatines: 1798 and its aftermath', in *The Journal of the Royal Society of Antiquaries of Ireland*, 1996, 126, p. 35.

43 Dunne, *Rebellions: Memoir, Memory and 1798*, p. 188.

44 Mark Codd, 'The sudden demise of an ancient parish', in *The Past: The Organ of the Ui Cinsealaigh Historical Society*, 2004, 25, pp 39–44, p. 41.

45 Daniel J. Gahan, 'New Ross, Scullabogue and the 1798 Rebellion in southwestern Wexford', in *The Past: The Organ of the Ui Cinsealaigh Historical* Society, 1998, 21, pp 3–33, p. 5.

46 Codd, 'The sudden demise of an ancient parish', p. 40.

47 Ibid., p. 41.

48 Kevin Whelan, 'The religious factor in the 1798 Rebellion', in P. O'Flannagan et al (eds), *Rural Ireland Modernisation and Change 1600–1900* (Cork, 1987), p. 75.

49 Dunne, *Rebellions: Memoir, Memory and 1798*, p. 190.

50 Gahan, 'New Ross, Scullabogue and the 1798 Rebellion', p. 10.

51 Dunne, *Rebellions: Memoir, Memory and 1798*, pp 251–4.

52 Ibid., p. 174.

53 O'Connor, *People Make Places*, p. 118.

54 Ibid., p. 134.

55 Hick, 'The Palatines: 1798 and its aftermath', pp 5–36, 6–7.

56 In what were termed 'Outrage Papers', 'State of the Country Reports' and 'Police report' see Hick, 'The Palatines', p. 8.

57 Ibid., pp 13–14.

58 Ibid., p. 22.

59 Ibid., pp 15–27.

60 Knittle, *Eighteenth Century Palatine Emigration*, p. 97.

61 Ibid., p. 97.

62 Arthur Young, *A Tour of Ireland*, vol 1 (London: Cassell and Company, 1897) , p. 379.

63 Gerald Griffin, *Tales of the Munster Festivals* (London, 1827) discussed in Vivien Hick, 'Images from folk tradition, novels and traveller's accounts', *Béaloideas* 1996/7, 64/5, pp 1–61.

64 Hick, *Images of Palatines*, pp 11–12.

65 Hick, *Images of Palatines*, p. 25.

66 Ibid., p. 33.

67 Ibid., p. 40.

68 Dr Richard Hayes, *The German Colony in County Limerick* (1937), cited in Ibid., p. 6.

SIX: *Emigration*

1 Kerby A. Miller, Arnold Schrier, Bruce D. Boling and David N. Doyle, *Irish Immigrants in the Land of Canaan: Letters and Memoirs from Colonial and Revolutionary America, 167–181* (Oxford: Oxford University Press, 2003), p. 35.

2 Donald Harman Akenson, *The Irish Diaspora: A Primer* (Belfast: Institute of Irish Studies, 1996), p. 56.

3 Ibid., p. 7.

4 Lawrence J. McCaffrey, *The Irish Catholic Diaspora in America* (Washington DC: Catholic University Press of America, 1997), pp 4–9.

5 Lawrence J. McCarthy, *The Irish Diaspora in America* (Indiana: Indiana University Press, 1976).

6 Ibid., p. ix.

7 William Macafee, 'The demographic history of Ulster', in H. Tyler Blethen and Curtis W. Wood Jr. (eds), *Ulster and North American Transatlantic Perspectives on the Scotch-Irish* (Tuscaloosa: University of Alabama Press, 1997), p. 42.

8 K. H. Connell, *The Populations of Ireland, 1750–1845* (Oxford: Oxford University Press, 1950).

9 Kerby Miller, *Emigration and Exiles, Ireland and the Irish Exodus to North America* (Oxford: Oxford University Press, 1995), p. 83

10 Youssef Courage, 'The demographic factor in Ireland's movement towards partition (1607–1921)', *Population: An English Selection*, 1997), 9, pp 169–90, 176–7.

11 Karl Marx, 'Forced emigration', *New York Daily Tribune*, 22 March 1853.

12 Kevin Kenny, 'Diaspora and comparison: The global Irish as a case study', in *Journal of American History* 90 (June 2003), pp 134–162, p. 143.

13 Kevin Kenny, *The American Irish: A History* (London: Pearson, 2000), p. 131.

14 Kenny, 'The global Irish as a case study', pp 135–7.

15 Kenny, *The American Irish*, p. 101.

16 Andy Bielenberg, *Irish Emigration to the British Empire*, in Andy Bielenberg (ed.), *The Irish Diaspora* (London: Longman, 2000) p. 219.

17 Cecil J. Houston and William J. Smyth, *Irish Emigration and Canadian Settlement: Patterns, Links and Letters* (Toronto: University of Toronto Press, 1990), pp 8–9.

18 Akenson, *Irish Diaspora*, pp 99–102.

19 David Fitzpatrick, 'Emigration, 1801–70', in W. E. Vaughan (ed.), *A New History of Ireland vol. V: Ireland Under the Union, Part 1, 1801–70* (Oxford: Clarendon Press, for the Royal Irish Academy, 1989), p. 613.

20 Barry Reay, *The Quakers and the English Revolution* (London: Temple Smith, 1985), p. 27.

21 Ibid., p. 50.

22 Ibid., p. 51.

23 T. C. Barnard, *Cromwellian Ireland* (Oxford: Oxford University Press, 1975), p. 133.

24 Albert Cook Myers, *Immigration of the Irish Quakers into Pennsylvania 1662–1750* (Baltimore: Genealogical Publishing, 1985), pp 12–18.

25 Ibid., p. 22.

26 Catherine Owens Peare, *William Penn: A Biography* (London: Dennis Dobson, 1956), p. 185.

27 Ibid., p. 209.

28 Cook Myers, *Immigration of the Irish Quakers*, pp 237–8.

29 Autobiography of James Logan cited in Cook Myers, *Immigration of the Irish Quakers*, pp 238–40.

30 Ibid., pp 246–56.

31 Ibid., p. 56.

32 Ibid., p. 57.

33 Maurice J. Wigham, *The Irish Quakers: A Short History of the Religious Society of Friends in Ireland* (Dublin: Historical Committee of the Religious Society of Friends in Ireland, 1992).

34 Cook Myers, *Immigration of the Irish Quakers*, pp 69–79.

35 Ibid., pp 100–01.

36 Cited in Graeme Kirkham, 'Ulster emigration to North America, 1680–1720', in H. Tyler Blethen and Curtis W. Wood Jr. (eds), *Ulster and North American Transatlantic Perspectives on the Scotch-Irish* (Tuscaloosa: University of Alabama Press, 1997), pp 77–9.

37 Ibid., pp 79–80.

38 Kerby A. Miller, Arnold Schrier, Bruce D. Boling and David N. Doyle, *Irish Immigrants in the Land of Canaan: Letters and Memoirs from Colonial and Revolutionary America, 167–181* (Oxford: Oxford University Press, 2003), p. 24.

39 Kenny, *The American Irish*, p. 14

40 Patrick Griffin, *The People with No Name: Ireland's Ulster Scots, America' Scot's Irish and the Creation of a British Atlantic World 1689–1764* (New Jersey: Princeton, 2001) p. 1.

41 Kenny, *The American Irish*, pp 15–18.

42 Kirkham, 'Ulster Emigration to North America', p. 87.

43 Cook Myers, *Immigration of the Irish Quakers*, p. 47.

44 R. I. Dickinson, *Ulster Emigration to Colonial America, 1718–1775* (Belfast: Ulster Historical Foundation, 1988), p. 98.

45 Kirkham, 'Ulster Emigration to North America', p. 84.

46 Archbishop King June 1719 cited in ibid., pp 87–8.

47 Timothy L. Smith, 'Religion and ethnicity in America', in *The American Historical* Review, 1978, 83.5, pp 1,155–85, p. 1,163.

48 Cited in Dickinson, *Ulster Emigration to Colonial America*, p. 109.

49 Ibid., pp 221–5.

50 Bielenberg, *Irish Emigration to the British Empire*, p. 217.

51 Kerby A. Miller, Arnold Schrier, Bruce D. Boling and David N. Doyle, *Irish Immigrants in the Land of Canaan: Letters and Memoirs from Colonial and Revolutionary America, 167–181* (Oxford: Oxford University Press, 2003), pp 135–43.

52 Albert Cook Myers, *Immigration of the Irish Quakers jnto Pennsylvania 1662–1750* (Baltimore: Genealogical Publishing, 1985), p. 101.

53 Dickinson, *Ulster Emigration to Colonial America*, pp 88–90.

54 Ibid., p. 92.

55 Maurice Bric, *Ireland, Philadelphia and the Re–invention of America, 1760–1800* (Dublin: Four Courts Press, 2008), p. 15.

56 Cook Myers, *Immigration of the Irish Quakers*, p. 100.

57 Dickinson, *Ulster Emigration to Colonial America*, pp 254–65.

58 Bric, *Ireland, Philadelphia and the Re–invention of* America, pp 36–7.

59 Houston and Smyth, *Irish Emigration and Canadian Settlement*, p. 4.

60 Bruce S. Elliott, *Irish Migrants in the Canadas: A New Approach* (Montreal: McGill, 1988), pp 15–16.

61 Donald McKay, *Flight From Famine: The Coming of the Irish to Canada* (Ontario: McClelland and Stewart, 1990), pp 29–33.

62 Elliott, *Irish Migrants in the* Canadas, pp 71–99.

63 Ibid., p. 214.

64 Cecil J. Houston and William J. Smyth, *The Sash Canada Wore: A Historical Geography of the Orange Order in Canada* (Toronto: University of Toronto Press, 1980), p. 5.

65 David Fitzpatrick, 'Exporting brotherhood: Orangism in south Australia', *Immigrants and Minorities: Historical Studies in Ethnicity, Migration and Diaspora*, 2005, 23.2–3, pp 277–310, p. 280.

66 Bielenberg, *Irish Emigration to the British Empire*, p. 288.

67 William Jenkins, '"Two Irelands beyond the sea": exploring long-distance loyalist networks in the 1880s', in Mary Gilmartin and Alan White (eds), *Migrations: Ireland in a Global World* (Manchester: Manchester University Press, 2013), p. 38.

68 Akenson, *The Irish* Diaspora, p. 6.

69 Kerby A. Miller, *Emigrants and Exiles: Ireland and the Irish Exodus to North America* (Oxford: Oxford University Press, 1985), pp 4–5.

70 Ibid., p. 105.

71 John Mitchel, *The Last Conquest of Ireland (Perhaps)* (Dublin; UCD Press, [1873] 2005).

72 Miller, *Emigrants and Exiles*, p. 107.

73 Kenny, 'Diaspora and Comparison', p. 139.

74 Friedrich Engels, *Schweizerischer Republikaner 51*, June 27, 1843.

75 T. R. Malthus, *Principles of Political Economy: Second Edition* (New York: Augustus M, Kelly, {1936} 1968), p. 346.

76 Ibid., p. 347.

77 Brian Conway and Michael R. Hill, 'Harriet Martineau and Ireland', in *Social Thought on Ireland in the Nineteenth Century*, (ed.) Séamus Ó Síocháin (Dublin: UCD Press, 2009), p. 62.

78 Harriet Martineau, *Letters from Ireland* (Dublin: Irish Academic Press, 2001), p 53.

79 Ibid., pp 109–14.

80 Horace Plunkett, *Ireland in the New Century* (Port Washington: Kennikat, 1970), pp 101–02.

81 Akenson, *Irish Diaspora*, p. 34.

82 Miller, *Emigrants and Exiles*, p. 39.

83 Arthur Herman, *The Scottish Enlightenment: The Scots' Invention of the Modern World* (London: Fourth Estate, 2001), pp 368–9.

84 McCarthy, *The Irish Catholic Diaspora*, pp 67–8.

85 Ruth-Ann M. Harris, *The Nearest Place that Wasn't Ireland: Early Nineteenth-Century Irish Labor Migration* (Ames?/Iowa: Iowa State University Press, 1994), p. 27.

86 Cited in Cormac Ó'Grada, *Ireland Before and After the Famine: Explorations in Economic History, 1800–1925* (Manchester: Manchester University Press, 1993), p. 17.

87 Harris, *The Nearest Place that Wasn't Ireland*, p. 13.

88 Ibid., p. 17.

89 Letter from Whatley to Nassau Senior (undated) August 1834, cited in E. Jane Whately, *Life and Correspondence of Richard Whately, DD Late Archbishop of Dublin: Vol. 1* (London: Longmans, Green and Co., 1866), p. 95.

90 Harris, *The Nearest Place that Wasn't Ireland*, p. 9.

91 Ibid., p. 25.

92 Houston and Smyth, *Irish Emigration and Canadian Settlement*, pp 16–17.

93 McKay, *Flight from Famine*, pp 56–65.

94 Ibid., pp 64–76.

95 Elliot, *Irish Migrants in the Canadas*, p. 129.

96 McKay, *Flight from Famine*, pp 93–8.

97 Houston and Smyth, *The Sash Canada Wore*, pp 31–7.

98 Elliot, *Irish Migrants in the Canadas*, pp 104–06.

99 Francis Evans, *Emigrant's Directory and Guide to Obtain Lands and Effect a Settlement in the Canadas* (1933), cited in Elliot, *Irish Migrants in the Canadas*, p. 69.

100 Bielenberg, *Irish Emigration to the British Empire*, pp 220–1.

101 Patrick O'Farrell, *The Irish in Australia* (Kensington: New South Wales University Press, 1987), p. 47.

102 Robert Hughes, *The Fatal Shore* (London: Pan, 1987), pp 161–2.

103 David Fitzpatrick, *Oceans of Consolation: Personal Accounts of Irish Migration to Australia* (Cork: Cork University Press, 1994), pp 162–9.

104 Ibid., pp 13–14.

105 Eric Richards, 'An Australian map of British and Irish literacy in 1841', in *Population Studies: A Journal of Demography*, 2010, 53.3, pp 345–59, 346–7.

106 Ibid., p. 348.

107 Ibid., pp 354–5.

108 Ibid., p. 356.

109 Akenson, *The Irish Diaspora*, p. 97.

110 Kenny, *The American Irish*, pp 138–9.

111 Fitzpatrick, *Oceans of Consolation*, pp 39–95.

112 Ibid., p. 19.

113 Donald Akenson, *Small Differences: Irish Catholics and Irish Protestants, 1815–1922: An International Perspective* (Montreal: McGill-Queens University Press, 1988), p. 58.

114 M. A. G. Ó Tuathaigh, 'The Irish in nineteenth-century Britain: Problems of integration', in *Transactions of the Royal Historical Society*, 1981, 31, pp 149–73, 149–52.

115 Ibid., pp 152–5.

116 Freidrich Engels, *Condition of the Working Class in England* (Cambridge: Cambridge University Press, 1892), pp 117–19.

117 Ibid., pp 94–5.

118 Ibid., p. 119.

119 Mary Hickman, *Religion, Class and Identity* (Aldershot: Avery, 1995), p. 103.

120 Ibid., pp 96–7.

121 Ibid., p. 109.

122 Gerard Moran, 'Faith, famine and fenianism: Paul Cullen and the Irish emigrant world', in Dáire Keogh and Albert McDonnell, *Cardinal Cullen and His World* (Dublin: Four Courts Press, 2011), pp 167–70.

123 CPSC Reports 1848 and 1849, cited by Hickman, *Religion, Class and Identity*, p. 163.

124 Cited in Hickman, *Religion, Class and Identity*, p. 174. Also see S. Fielding, 'The Labour Party and Catholics in Manchester: 1906–35', in G. Chapman (ed.), *Catholics and Their Church in Britain, Warwick Working Papers in Social History* (Warwick: University of Warwick: Coventry, 1988), p. 50.

125 Kenny, *The American Irish*, p. 171.

126 Lawrence J McCaffrey, *Textures of Irish America* (New York: Syracuse University Press, 1980), p. xii.

127 J. A. Murphy, 'The influence of America on Irish nationalism', in David Doyle andOwen Dudley Edwards (eds), *America and Ireland, 1776–1976* (Westport Conn: Greenwood Press, 1992), pp 110–11.

128 John Belchem, 'Nationalism, republicanism and exile: Irish emigrants and the revolutions of 1948', *Past and* Present, 1995, 146, pp 103–35, 103–04.

129 Noel Ignatiev, *How the Irish Became White* (London: Routledge, 1995), p. 65.

130 David A. Wilson, *United Irishmen, United States: Immigrant Radicals in the Early Republic* (Dublin: Four Courts Press,1998), p. 155.

131 Matthew Carey 'Emigration from Ireland, and immigration into the United States', in *Miscellaneous Essays: Volume 1* {1830} (New York: Burt Frankin, check year), pp 321–5.

132 Denis Clark, *The Irish in Philadelphia: Ten Generations of Urban Experience* (Philadephia: Temple University Press, 1973), pp 54–60.

133 Ibid., p. 48.

134 Kenny, *The American Irish*, p. 115

135 Mitchel, *Last Conquest of Ireland*, p. 207.

136 Ignatiev, *How the Irish Became White*, pp 66–7.

137 Ibid., p. 26.

138 Ibid., p. 31.

139 Ibid., p. 127.

140 Cited in ibid., p. 136.

141 For spreadsheets of Irish slave owners Irish surnames and analysis see Liam Hogan, *Kiss Me, My Slave Owners Were Irish*, 2016): www.medium.com/@Limerick1914

142 Kerby A. Miller, 'Emigration to North America in the era of the Great Famine, 1845–55', in John Crowley, William J. Smyh and Mike Murphy (eds), *Atlas of the Great Irish Famine* (Cork: Cork University Press, 2012), pp 215–19.

143 Clark, *The Irish in Philadelphia*, p. 87.

144 Tyler Anbinder, '"We will dirk every mother's son of you": Five points and the Irish conquest of New York politics', *Éire–Ireland*, 2001, 36.1, pp 29–46, p. 31.

145 Herbert Asbury, *The Gangs of New York* (New York: Alfred A. Knoph, 1927).

146 Donald MacRaild, 'Crossing migrant frontiers: Comparative reflections on Irish migrants in Britain and the United States during the nineteenth century', 1999, 18.2–3, pp 40–70, p. 56.

147 Fitzpatrick, 'Exporting Brotherhood', p. 291.

148 Clark, *The Irish in Philadelphia*, p. 132.

149 Kenny, *The American Irish*, p. 113.

150 Moran, 'Paul Cullen in the Irish emigrant world', p. 172.

151 James R. Barrett and David R. Roediger, 'The Irish and the "Americanization" of the "new immigrants" in the streets and in the churches of the urban United States, 1990–1930', *Journal of American Ethnic* History, 2005, 24.4, pp 3–33, p. 17.

152 Hickman, *Religion, Class and Identity*, p. 115.

153 Clark, *The Irish in Philadelphia*, p. 104.

154 Seamus P. Metress, *The American Irish and Irish Nationalisam: A Sociohistorical Introduction* (Maryland: Scarecrow Press, 1995), pp 21–2.

155 Victor A. Walsh, '"A fanatic heart": The cause of Irish American nationalism in Pittsburgh during the gilded age', *Journal of Social* History, 1981, , 15.2, pp 187–204, p. 199.

156 Mitchel, *The Last Conquest of* Ireland, p. 75

157 Kenny, *The American Irish*, p. 123.

158 N. Mulligan, 'Absence makes the heart grow fonder: Transatlantic Irish nationalism and 1867 Rising', *Social and Cultural* Geography, 2005, 6.3, pp 439–54, p. 447.

159 'The friends of Irish freedom: A case–study in Irish-American nationalism, 1916–1921', in *History Ireland*, 2008, 16.2, pp 3–11.

160 Donal Lowry, 'The crown, empire loyalism and the assimilation of non–British white subjects in the British world: An argument against ethnic determinism', in *The Journal of Imperial and Commonwealth History*, 2003, 1.2, pp 96–120, p. 111.

161 Bielenberg, *Irish Emigration to the British Empire*, p. 221.

162 Charles Gavan Duffy, *My Life in Two Hemispheres: Vol II* (Shannon: Irish University Press (1898), 1969), pp 133–9.

163 David Fitzpatrick, 'Irish emigration in the later nineteenth century', in *Irish Historical* Studies, 1980, 22.86, pp 126–43, p. 127.

164 Mitchel, *Last Conquest of Ireland*, p. 217.

SEVEN: *Jews*

1 John Toland, *Reasons for Naturalizing the Jews in Great Britain and Ireland on the Same Foot with all Other Nations. Containing Also a Defence of Jews Against All Vulgar Prejudices in All Countries* (London: J.Roberts, 1714).

2 J. G. Simms, 'John Toland (1670–1722): A Donegal heretic', in *Irish Historical Studies*, 1969, 16.63, pp 304–20, p. 305.

3 Thomas Duddy, *A History of Irish Thought* (London: Routledge, 2002), p. 85.

4 Toland, *Reasons for Naturalizing the Jews*, p. 18.

5 Ibid., pp 29–31.

6 Ibid., p. 36.

7   Don Patinkin, 'Mercantalism and the re-admission of the Jews to England', in *Jewish Social Studies*, 1946, 8.3, pp 161–78, p. 162.

8   David S. Katz, *Philo-Semitism and the Re-admission of the Jews to England 1603–1655* (Oxford: Clarendon Press, 1982), pp 1–2.

9   Ibid., p. 91.

10   Ibid., p. 211.

11   Nathan Osterman, 'The controversy over the proposed re-admission of the Jews to England', in *Jewish Social* Studies, 1941, 3.3, pp 310–28, p. 310.

12   Patinkin, 'Mercantalism and the re-admission of the Jews', p. 165.

13   Pierre Lurbe, 'John Toland and the naturalization of the Jews', in *Eighteenth-Century Ireland*, 1999, 14, pp 37–48, p. 42.

14   Patinkin, 'Mercantalism and the re-admission of the Jews', p. 177.

15   Toland, *Reasons for Naturalizing the Jews*, p. 5.

16   Ibid., p. 40.

17   Ibid., p. 6.

18   Ibid., p. 7.

19   Ibid.

20   John Toland (ed.), *The Commonwealth of Oceana and Other Works of James* Harrington (London, 1700).

21   James Harrington, *The Commonwealth of Oceana* (London, 1656) cited in Katz, *Philo–Semitism*, p. 240.

22   J. G. A. Pocock (ed.), *The Political Works of James Harrington* (Cambridge: Cambridge University Press, 1977), p. 159.

23   Katz, *Philo–Semitism*, p. 165.

24   Louis Hyman, *The Jews of Ireland from the Earliest Times to the Year 1910* (Shannon: Irish University Press, 1972), pp 3–4.

25   Ibid., p. 6.

26   Edmund Valentine Campos, 'Jews, Spaniards and Portingales: Ambiguous identities of Portuguese Marranos in Elizabethan England', in *EHL*, 2002, 69.3, pp 599–616, p. 607.

27   Hyman, *The Jews of Ireland*, p. 8.

28   Ibid., p. 12.

29   Ibid., p. 17.

30   Ibid., p. 19.

31   Ibid., p. 24.

32   Diarmuid G. Hiney, '5618 and all that: The Jewish cemetery Fairview strand', in *Dublin Historical* Record, 1997, 50.2, pp 119–29, p. 119, p. 124.

33   Dana Rabin, 'The Jew bill of 1793: Masculinity, virility and the nation', in *Eighteenth-Century Studies*, 2006, 39.2, pp 151–71, p. 151.

34   Robert Liberies, 'The Jews and their bill: Jewish motivations in the controversy of 1753', in *Jewish* History, 1987, 2.2, pp 29–36, 30–1.

35   Ibid., p. 34.

36   Hyman, *The Jews of Ireland*, p. 49.

37   Ibid., pp 62–3.

38   Ibid., p. 52.

39   Ibid., pp 89–90.

40   Ibid., pp 94–5.

41   Ibid., p. 143.

42   Ibid., pp 147–52.

43   Gillian McIntosh, 'Ireland's first Jewish Lord Mayor: Sir Otto Jaffé and Edwardian Belfast's civic sphere', in *Jewish Culture and History*, 2009, 11.3, pp 3–11.

44   Lithuania 1897 Census Database: www.jewishgen.org/databases/Lithcensus1897.html. For analysis see Cormac O'Grada, *Jewish Dublin in the Time of Joyce* (New Jersey: Princeton, 2006).

45   O'Grada, *Jewish Dublin*, p. 12.

46   Ibid., pp 12–18.

47   Ibid., p. 46.

48   Ibid., pp 13–15.

40   Ibid., p. 22.

50   The script of a television documentary published as Louis Lentin, 'Grandpa. . . speak to me in Russian', in Translocations, Spring, 2008, 3.1, pp 153–63, p. 158.

51   O'Grada, *Jewish Dublin*, pp 17–18.

52   Gerald Y. Goldberg, 'The lost soul of the world: The Cork Jewish community and the fiction of David Marcus', in *The Cork* Review, 1992, pp 19–23.

53   Enid Mescon, 'From County Cork to New York with the Jacksons', cited by Ray Rivlan, *Jewish Ireland: A Social History* (Dublin: History Press Ireland, 2003), p. 30.

54   Stanley Price, 'In search of Charles Beresford'. In *The Jewish Quarterly*, May 2013, 44.1, pp 41–4, p. 41.

55   Price, 'In search of Charles Beresford', p. 44.

56   Lentin, 'Grandpa. . . speak to me in Russian', p. 157.

57   Hannah Berman and Melisande Zlotover, *Zlotover Story: A Dublin Story with a Difference* (Dublin: Hely Thom, 1966), pp 30–1.

58   Ibid., p. 33.

59   O'Grada, *Jewish Dublin*, p. 409.

60   Lentin, 'Grandpa. . . speak to me in Russian', p. 158.

61   O'Grada, *Jewish Dublin*, p. 64.

62   Berman and Zlotover, *Zlotover Story*, pp 30–1.

63   Myer Joel Wigoder, *My Life*, Trans. Louis E. Widoger, (ed.) Samuel Abel (Leeds, 1935), p. 32.

64   Nick Harris, *Dublin's Little Jerusalem* (Dublin: Farmer, 2002), p. 3.

65   O'Grada, *Jewish Dublin*, p. 210.

66   Rivlin, *Jewish Ireland*, p. 35.

67   Ibid., p. 11.

68   Ibid., pp 9–11.

69   Fr Thomas Finlay, 'The Jew in Ireland', in *Lyceum*, 1873, 6.70, pp 215–18.

70   Rivlin, *Jewish Ireland*, p. 54.

71   O'Grada, *Jewish Dublin*, pp 111–12.

72   Dermot Keogh, *Jews in Twentieth-Century Ireland: Refugees, Anti–Semitism and the Holocaust* (Cork: Cork University Press, 1998), p. 9.

73   Rivlin, *Jewish Ireland*, p. 54.

74 Ibid.

75 Moore, *Socio-Economic Aspects of Anti–Semitism in Ireland*, p. 196.

76 Finlay, 'The Jew in Ireland', pp 215–18.

77 *United Irishman*, 13 Jan. 1904.

78 *The Leader*, 16 July 1904.

79 Dermot Keogh and Andrew McCarthy, *Limerick Boycott 1904: Anti–Semitism in Ireland* (Cork: Mercier Press, 2005), p. 106.

80 Goldberg, 'The lost soul of the world', p. 19.

81 McIntosh, 'Ireland's first Jewish Lord Mayor', p. 14.

82 Census records of Jews in Ireland (1926) and Lithuania (1923) taken from the *American Jewish Yearbook* (1926).

83 Keogh, *Jews in Twentieth-Century Ireland*, p. 72.

84 Chaim Herzog, *Living History: A Memoir* (New York: Pantheon, 1996), p. 12.

85 Goldberg, 'The lost soul of the world', p. 20.

86 Harris, *Dublin's Little Jerusalem*, p. 3.

87 Ibid., p. 80.

88 Keogh, *Jews in Twentieth-Century Ireland*, p. 82.

89 Harris, *Dublin's Little Jerusalem*, p. 55.

90 Ibid., p. 97.

91 Ibid., p. 86.

92 Bethel Solomons, *One Doctor in his Time* (London: Christopher Johnson, 1956), pp 12–13.

93 O'Grada, *Jewish Dublin*, p. 213.

94 'Anti-Jew move in Dublin', *Irish Times*, 30 Nov. 1937.

95 Keogh, *Jews in Twentieth-Century Ireland*, p. 147.

96 Harris, *Dublin's Little Jerusalem*, p. 178.

97 O'Grada, *Jewish Dublin*, pp 75–83.

98 Harris, *Dublin's Little Jerusalem*, p. 33.

99 Rivlin, *Jewish Ireland*, p. 128.

100 Harris, *Dublin's Little Jerusalem*, p. 16.

101 David Marcus, *Oughtobiography: Leaves from the Diary of a Hyphenated Jew* (Dublin: Gill and Macmillan, 2001).

102 David Marcus, *To Next Year in Jerusalem* (London: St Martins' Press, 1954), p. 27.

103 David Taub, 'Jewish education in Dublin: organizational development and conflicts', in *Irish Educational* Studies, September 2005, 24.2–3, pp 145–57, p. 146.

104 A. J. Leventhal, 'What it means to be a Jew', *The Bell*, 1945, 10.3, pp 207–16.

105 Catherine Hezser, 'Are you Protestant Jews or Roman Catholic Jews? Literary representations of being Jewish in Ireland', in *Modern Judaism*, May 2005, 25.2, pp 159–88, p. 162.

106 Price, ;In search of Charles Beresford', p. 143.

107 www.belfastjewishcommunty.org

108 David Landy, 'Zionism, multiculturalism and the construction of Irish-Jewish identity', in *Irish Journal of* Sociology, 2007, 16.1, pp 62–79, p. 64.

109 Katrina Goldstone, 'Now you see us, now you don't: reflections on Jews, historical amnesia and the histories of a multi-ethnic Dublin', in Translocations, Winter, 2008, 4.1, pp 102–09, p. 103.

110 Rivlin, *Jewish Ireland*, p. 237.

111 Ibid., p. 238.

112 Goldstone, 'Now you see us, now you don't', p. 103.

113 Rivlin, *Jewish Ireland*, p. 237.

114 Landy, 'Zionism, multiculturalism and the construction of Irish-Jewish identity', p. 65.

115 Ibid., p. 66.

116 Gerald Davis, 'A Jew from Kimmage', *The Irish Times*, 23 June 1998.

117 Landy, 'Zionism, multiculturalism and the construction of Irish-Jewish identity', pp 66–7.

118 Rivlin, *Jewish Ireland*, p. 236.

119 Declan McSweeney, 'Embracing the multiculturalism of Manchester', *Irish Times*, 9 Apr. 2014.

EIGHT: *Expatriates*

1 Jack White, *Minority Report: The Protestant Community in the Irish Republic* (Dublin, Gill and Macmillan, 1975).

2 Mo Moulton, *Ireland and the Irish in Interwar England* (Cambridge: Cambridge University Press, 2014), pp 217–24.

3 Diarmuid Ferriter, *The Transformation of Ireland 1900–2000* (London: Profile Books, 2004), p. 210.

4 Damien Courtney, 'A quantification of Irish migration', in Andy Bilenberg, *The Irish Diaspora* (Dublin: Longman, 2000), p. 294.

5 Central Statistics Office, www.cso.ie

6 Kevin Kenny, *The American Irish: A History* (Harlow: Pearson, 2000), pp 181–2.

7 Ibid., p. 194.

8 Ibid., p. 184.

9 Ibid., pp 221–3.

10 Irial Glynn, Tomás Kelly and Piaras Mac Éinrí, *The Re–Emergence of Emigration from Ireland: New Trends in an Old Story* (Washington: Migration Policy Institute, 2015), p. 3.

11 2001 Census analysis cited from Kevin Howard, 'Constructing the Irish in Britain: Ethnic recognition an the 2001 UK Censuses', in *Ethnic and Racial Studies*, 2001, 29.1 , pp 104–23.

12 Bronwen Walter, '"From flood to trickle": Irish migration to Britain 1987–2006', in *Irish Geography*, 2008, 41.2, pp 181–94, p. 182.

13 Glynn, Kelly and Mac Éinrí, *The Re–Emergence of Emigration from Ireland*, p. 8.

14 Ibid., p. 11.

15 Liam Kennedy, Madeleine Lyes and Martin Russell, *Supporting the Next Generation of the Irish Diaspora* (Dublin: Clinton Institute, 2014), p. 10.

16 J. J. Lee, *Ireland 1912–1985: Politics and Society* (Cambridge: Cambridge University Press, 1989), p. 71.

17 From interviews with this author 2015.

18 Frank McCourt, *Angela's Ashes* (London: Harper Collins, 1997).

19 Mícheál de Mórdha, *An Island Community: The Ebb and Flow of the Great Blasket Island* (Dublin: Liberties Press, 2015), p. 246.

20 Ibid., pp 340–50.

21 Ibid., p. 357.

22 Ibid., pp 352–6.

23 Translated and cited in ibid., p. 359.

24 Translated and cited in ibid.

25 Translated ant cited in ibid., p. 365.

26 Ibid., p. 366.

27 George Thompson, *Island Home: The Blasket Heritage* (Dingle: Brandon Press, 1988), p. 20.

28 Peadar O'Donnell, 'The Irish in Britain', *The Bell*, 1943, 6.3, pp 361–70.

29 Friedrich Engels, *The Condition of the Working Class in England* (London, 1892 [1845]).

30 Mary J. Hickman, 'Incorporating and de-nationalising the Irish in England: The role of the Catholic Church', in Patrick O'Sullivan (ed.), *The Irish Worldwide: History, Heritage, Identity: Religion and Identity* (ed.) Patrick O'Sullivan (London: Leicester University Press, 1996), p. 272.

31 Paul Blanshard, *American Freedom and Catholic Power* (Boston MA: Beacon Press, 1959), p. 30.

32 Hickman, 'Incorporating and de-nationalising the Irish in Britain', pp 258–232

33 Enda Delaney, '"Almost a class of helots in an alien land": The British State and Irish immigration 1921–45', *Immigrants and Minorities*, 1999, 18.2–3, pp 240–65.

34 Clair Wills, *That Neutral Island: A Cultural History of Ireland during the Second World War* (London: Faber and Faber, 2007), p. 355.

35 H. L. Morrow cited in ibid., p. 318.

36 James Deeny, *To Cure and To Care: Memoirs of a Chief Medical Officer* (Dublin: Glendale Press, 1989), p. 79.

37 See Wills, *That Neutral Island*, pp 313–14.

38 Peadar O'Donnell cited by Flann O'Brien, 'The dance halls, *The Bell*, 1941, 1.5, pp 44–53.

39 Seán Ó Faoláin, 'The Gaelic League', *The Bell*, 1942, 4.2, pp 77–86.

40 Lee, *Ireland 1912–1986*, pp 226–7.

41 1942 Department of External Affairs correspondence cited by ibid., pp 226–8.

42 Brian Girvin, 'The forgotten volunteers of World War II', in *History Ireland*, 1998, 6.1, pp 46–51.

43 Commission on Emigration and Other Population Problems (Dublin, 1956).

44 Damien Hannan, Rural Exodus: A Study of the Forces Influencing Large-Scale Emigration of Irish Rural Youth (London, 1965).

45 Cormac O'Grada, 'Determinants of Irish emigration: A note', in *International Migration Review,* 1986, 20.1, pp 650–6.

46 Mary E. Daly, 'Foreword' to A. E. C. W. Spencer, *Arrangements for the Integration of Irish Immigrants in England and Wales* (Dublin: Irish Manuscripts Commission, 2012), p. x.

47 Fr Eamon Gaynor, 'The Irish in Britain', *The Furrow*, 1954, 5.4, pp 235–40, p. 236.

48 Frank Duff, 'Emigration and providence', *The Furrow*, 1957, 8.9, pp 564–8, p. 566.

49 Oliver Reilly, 'A worker in Birmingham', *The Furrow*, 1958, 9.4, pp 230–6, p. 231.

50 Patrick Brophy, 'Letter to an English priest', *The Furrow*, 1958, 9.4, pp 260–3, p. 261.

51 Spenser, *Arrangements for the Integration of Irish Immigrants in England and Wales*, p. 21.

52 Ibid., p. 22.

53 Ibid., pp 24–5.

54 Patricia Kennedy, *Welcoming the Stranger: Irish Migrant Welfare in Britain Since 1957* (Dublin: Irish Academic Press, 2015), p. 69.

55 Ibid., p. 30.

56 Ibid., p. 71.

57 Ibid., pp 114–17.

58 Nessa Winston, *The Return of Older Irish Migrants: An Assessment of Needs and Issues* (Dublin: Irish Episcopal Commission for Emigrants, 2002), p. 1.

59 Mary Corcoran, *Transients between Two Societies* (Westport CT: Greenwood Press, 1993), p. 90.

60 Ibid., p. 99.

61 Ibid., p. 140.

62 Ibid., p. 63.

63 Ibid., p. 86.

64 Ibid., p. 39.

65 Ibid., p. 47.

66 Ibid., p. 134.

67 Ibid., pp 40–1.

68 Unless otherwise stated figures cited are from the Central Statistics Office www.cso.ie

69 Glynn, Kelly and Mac Éinrí, *The Re-Emergence of Emigration from Ireland*, p. 15.

70 Irial Glynn, Tomas Kelly and Piaras MacÉinrí, *Irish Emigration in an Age of Austerity* (Cork: Department of Geography, 2013), p. 11.

71 Ibid., p. 40.

72 Glynn, Kelly and Mac Éinrí, *The Re-Emergence of Emigration from Ireland*, p. 10.

73 Ciara Kenny, 'The embedded emigrant', *Irish Times*, 2 July 2016.

74 Ibid.

75 Kennedy, Lyes and Russell, *Supporting the Next Generation of the Irish Diaspora*, p. 61.

76 Ibid., p. 17.

77 Ibid., p. 67.

78 David Monahan, 'Beyond leaving', National Photographic Archive, Dec. 2016.

NINE: *Refugees*

1 Keith Lowe, *Savage Continent: Europe in the Aftermath of World War II* (London: Penguin, 2012), p. 211.

2 *Dail Éireann*, 14 Feb. 1979 cited in Mark Maguire, *Differently Irish: A Cultural History Exploring 25 Years of Vietnamese-Irish Identity* (Portadown: Woodfield Press, 2004), p. 19.

3 National Archives of Ireland, Dublin (hereafter NAI), Department of An Taoiseach (hereafter DT), 16 Nov. 1938.

4 NAI, DT, 16 Nov. 1938.

5 Dermot Keogh, *Jews in Twentieth-Century Ireland: Refugees, Anti–Semitism and the Holocaust* (Cork: Cork University Press, 1998), p. 142.

6 NAI, DT, 69/8027, 24 Sept. 1945.

7 NAI, DT, S11007, 23 Sept. 1953.

8 Andreas Roth, *Mr Bewley in Berlin: Aspects of the Career of an Irish Diplomat, 1933–1939* (Dublin: Four Courts Press, 2000), p. 28.

9   Robert Briscoe, *For the Life of Me* (London: Longmans, 1958), pp 260–70.

10 Keogh, *Jews in Twentieth-Century Ireland*, p. 143.

11 Ben Briscoe described the visits of Peter Berry to his father Robert Briscoe's house at a lecture given by this author in 2002 about Ireland and the Holocaust at the Reform Synagogue in Rathfarnham in Dublin. He stated that his parents had no idea of Berry's persistent efforts to prevent Jewish refugees from being admitted to Ireland.

12 Andreas Roth, *Mr Bewley in Berlin: Aspects of the Career of an Irish Diplomat, 193–1939* (Dublin: Four Courts Press, 2000), p. 4.

13 George Clare, *Last Waltz in Vienna: The Destruction of a Family, 1842–1942* (London: Mcmillan, 1981), p. 205.

14 Ibid., p. 204.

15 Keogh, *Jews in Twentieth-Century Ireland*, p. 136.

16 Ibid., p. 239.

17 Keogh, *Jews in Twentieth-Century Ireland*, p. 141.

18 Walter Moore, *A Life of Erwin Schrödinger* (Cambridge: Cambridge University Press, 1994), pp 243–7.

19 Ben Maier, 'The farm at Millisle', *Irish Pages*, 2011, 6.1, pp 123–33.

20 Barbara Barnett (ed.), *The Hide and Seek Children: Recollections of Jewish Survivors from Slovakia* (Glasgow: Mansion Field, 2012).

21 Albert Leicht, 'Memoir', cited in ibid., pp 260–72.

22 Zoltan Zinn-Collis, *Final Witness: My Journey from the Holocaust to Ireland* (Dunshaughlin: Maverick House, 2006).

23 Tomi Reichental, *I Was a Boy In Belsen* (Dublin: O'Brien Press, 2011).

24 Helen Lewis, *A Time to Speak* (Belfast: Blackstaff Press, 1992).

25 Daniel Leach, *Fugitive Ireland: European Minority Nationalists And Irish Political Asylum, 1937–2008* (Dublin: Four Courts Press, 2009), p. 222.

26 Ibid., pp 105–16.

27 Ibid., p. 266.

28 Ibid., p. 169.

29 Ibid., p. 173.

30 Ibid., p. 178.

31 Bettina Stangneth, *Eichmann before Jerusalem: The Unexamined Life of a Mass Murderer* (New York: Penguin Random House, 2014).

32 Leach, *Fugitive Ireland*, p. 140.

33 Mirjana Cupek Hamell, 'Irska godina' (trans. 'The Irish year of Andrije Artukovica'), in *Journal of Contemporary History*, 2014, 2, pp 265–75, p. 275.

34 Hubert Butler, 'The Artukovich file', *Independent Spirit: Essays* (New York: Farrar, Straus and Giroux, 1996), pp 465–87.

35 Leach, *Fugitive Ireland*, p. 135.

36 Eilis Ward, '"A big show-off to show what we could do": Ireland and the Hungarian Refugee Crisis of 1956', in *Irish Studies in International Affairs*, 1996, 8, pp 131–41, p. 135.

37 NAI, Department of Justice, D/T S 11007 B (2), 16 Feb. 1953.

38 *Irish Independent*, 30 Nov. 1956.

39 Ward 'A big show-off to show what we could do', pp 131–41.

40 *Clare Champion*, 10 Nov. 1956.

41 *Irish Times*, 18 Jan. 1957.

42 NAI, DT, S11007, 10 Dec. 1956.

43 NAI, DT, S11007, 19 Jan. 1957.

44 Ibid.

45 *Irish Independent*, 17 Jan. 1957.

46 Ibid.

47 NAI, DT, S11007, 21 Jan. 1957.

48 Ibid.

49 *Irish Independent*, 11 Jan. 1957.

50 NAI, DT, S11007, 10 Jan. 1957.

51 A memorandum from Department of Defence to Department of an Taoiseach. NAI, DT, S11007, 4 Dec. 1956.

52 Ibid, 19 Jan. 1957.

53 *Irish Times*, 30 Apr. 1957.

54 A memorandum from the UNHCR to the Department of External Affairs confirms that some refugees who agreed to Ireland on the expectation that they would later be relocated to the United States. NAI, DT, S11007, 13 May 1957.

55 *Irish Press*, 3 Jan. 1959.

56 *Irish Times*, 14 Jan. 1957.

57 Ibid.

58 Pauline Conroy, Tommy McKearney and Quintin Oliver, *All Over the Place: People Displaced To and From the Southern Border Counties as a Result of the Conflict 1969–1994* (Dublin: Ralaheen Ltd, 2005), p. 10.

59 Ibid., pp 30–1.

60 Ibid., pp 46–64.

61 Ibid., pp 26–8.

62 Drogheda Community Forum, '"Dispelling the myths": Research on displacement from Northern Ireland to Drogheda at the onset of the Troubles and the subsequent lessons learned from this experience' (Drogheda, 2004), p. 12.

63 January 1973 memorandum contained in a 1984 file in the 1984 State Papers. 2014/2/2058 See Aoife Barry, 'Thousands of Northern refugees streamed over the border in the 1970s – some were called ungrateful', *Journal.ie*, 27 Dec. 2014.

64 Maguire, *Differently Irish*, p. 27.

65 Chris McIvor, 'From Vietnam to Coolock', *Magill Annual*, 1987, p. 42.

66 Frieda McGovern, 'Vietnamese refugees in Ireland, 1979–1989', unpublished M.Ed Thesis (Trinity College Dublin, 1990).

67 McGovern, 'Vietnamese refugees', pp 92–5.

68 Mark Maguire, *Differently Irish: A cultural history exploring 25 years of Vietnamese–Irish identity* (Dublin: Woodford Press, 2004), p. 34.

69 Michael Pelly, 'Interim report' (Irish Episcopal Commission for Emigrants, 1982 Unpublished, 1982) cited in ibid., pp 38–40.

70 Irish Red Cross *Vietnamese Refugee Report*, cited by McGovern, 'Vietnamese refugees', chp 4.

71 McIvor, 'From Vietnam to Coolock', p. 43.

72 Ronit Lentin, 'five years of trial for Vietnamese boat People', *Irish Times*, 25 Apr. 1984.

73 McIvor, 'From Vietnam to Coolock', p. 43.

74 Ibid., p. 44.
75 Maguire, *Differently Irish*, p. 54.
76 Ibid., p. 99.
77 Vera Sheridan, 'Tuyen Pham: Caught betwenn two cultures', in Bryan Fanning (ed.), *Immigration and Social Change in the Republic of Ireland* (Manchester: Manchester University Press, 2006), pp 129–52.
78 Maguire, *Differently Irish*, pp 142–6.
79 J. O'Neill, Integration of Refugees in Ireland: Experience with Programme Refugees 1994–2000, (2000) www.democraticdialogue.org/report14/r14oneill.htm
80 Frieda McGovern, 'Vietnamese refugees', chp 4.
81 Cited in Maja Halilovic-Pastuovic, 'The "Bosnian project" in Ireland: A "vision of divisions"', in Fanning (ed.), *Immigration and Social Change in the Republic of Ireland*, p. 161.
82 Halilovic-Pastuovic, 'The "Bosnian project" in Ireland', p. 156.
83 Cited in ibid., p. 161.
84 Halilovic-Pastuovic, '"Settled in mobility" as a "space of possibility": Bosnian post-refugee transnationalism as a response to the bio-politics of Irish interculturalism', in *Translocations*, 2009, 2.1, pp 1–20, p. 18,
85 Halilovic-Pastuovic, 'Bosnian post-refugee transnationalism', p. 10.
86 Cathal O'Regan, 'Report of a survey of the Vietnamese and Bosnian refugee communities living in Ireland' (Dublin: Refugee Agency, 1998), p. 82.
87 Ibid., p. 123. S. Bradley, *From Bosnia to Ireland's Private Sector* (Dublin: Clann Housing Association, 1999) p. 26.
88 Bairbre Ní Chiosáin, 'Ireland and its European refugees: The case of the Kosovars', in *Nordic Irish Studies*, 2005, 4.1, pp 89–97, p. 90.
89 Ibid., p. 93.

TEN: *Africans*

1 Unless otherwise stated figures are cited from the Central Statistics Office: www.cso.ie
2 Dirk Kohnert, *African Migration to Europe: Obscured Responsibilities and Common Misconceptions*, German Global and Areas Studies (GIGA) Research Programme: Working Paper 49 (Hamburg: GIGA, 2007), p. 7.
3 Theophilus Ejorh, 'African, immigrant experiences of racism, adaptation and belonging', in Bryan Fanning and Ronaldo Munck (eds), *Globalization, Migration and Social Transformation: Ireland in Europe and the World* (London: Ashgate, 2011), p. 149.
4 Cited in Dianna J. Shandy, 'Irish babies, African mothers: Rites of passage and rights of citizenship in post-millennial Ireland', *Anthropological Quarterly*, 2008, 81.4, pp 803–31, p. 815.
5 Ibid., p. 816.
6 Kohnert, *African Migration to Europe*, p. 9.
7 Figure for number of citizens arrived at by subtracting number of Nigerian nationals (16,300) from number of Nigerian born (16,667) living in the Republic of Ireland as identified in the 2006 Census.
8 Ejorh, 'African, immigrant experiences of racism, adaptation and belonging', p. 146.
9 Enda Staunton, 'The forgotten war', in *History Ireland*, 2000, 8.1, pp 44–49

10 Dáil Debates, 23 Oct. 1968m at www.oireachtas.ie

11 Diarmuid Ferriter, *The Transformation of Ireland: 1900 to 2000* (London: Profile Books, 2004), pp 579–81.

12 Kevin O'Sullivan, *Ireland, Africa and the End of Empire* (Manchester: Manchester University Press, 2012), p. 96.

13 Robert Collis, 'What end in Nigeria', *Irish Times*, 29 July 1969.

14 O'Sullivan, *Ireland, Africa and the End of Empire*, p. 97.

15 Ibid., p. 92.

16 'Attacks on Nigerians to be investigated?', *Irish Times*, 20 Aug. 1964.

17 'List of attacks on Nigerians given: Police negligence alleged', *Irish Times*, 21 Aug. 1964.

18 'Nigerian reports annoy government: Concern at charges of racialism', *Irish Times*, 22 Aug. 1964.

19 'US child specialists discuss young negros' problems', *Irish Times*, 22 Aug. 1964.

20 'Assault charges struck out', *Irish Times*, 17 Nov. 1964.

21 'Human relations', *Irish Times*, 22 Aug. 1964.

22 'Group to advise coloured student: Will investigate attacks', *Irish Times*, 21 Aug. 1964.

23 Obituary of Christine Buckley (1946–2014), *Irish Times*, 15 Mar. 2014.

24 Paul McGrath, *Back from the Brink* (London: Arrow Books, 2007).

25 Kitty Holland, 'Mixed race Irish: We were the dust to be swept away', *Irish Times*, 18 July 2015.

26 Correspondence with author Sept. 2016.

27 Association of Mixed Race Irish. See mixedraceblogspot.ie

28 Julius Komolafe, 'Nigerian migration to Ireland: Movements, motivations and experiences', in *Irish Geography*, 2008, 41.2, pp 225–41, p. 229.

29 Ibid., pp 230–1.

30 Elisa Joy While, 'Forging African diaspora places in Dublin's retro-global spaces', *City*, 2002, 6.2, pp 251–70, 263–6.

31 Abel Ugba, *Dear Mama* (London: Minerva Press, 1999).

32 Komolafe, 'Nigerian migration to Ireland', pp 225–1.

33 For non-fictionalised case studies of migrant experiences see Kirsten Kastner, 'Moving relationships: Family ties of Nigerian migrants on their way to Europe', in *African and Black Diaspora: An International Journal*, 2010, 3.1, pp 17–34.

34 Caroline H. Bledsoe, 'Reproduction at the margins: Migration and legitimacy in the new Europe', in *Demographic Research*, 2004, 3.4, pp 87–116, 98–9.

35 Komolafe, 'Searching for fortune: The geographical process of Nigerian migration to Dublin, Ireland', in *Ininkerindo: A Journal of African Migration*, 2002, 1.1: www.africamigration.com

36 Jo Murphy-Lawless and Patricia Kennedy, *The Maternity Care Needs of Refugee and Asylum Seeking Women* (Dublin: East Coast Health Board, 2000), p. 8.

37 Ibid., pp 44–7.

38 A. Klemm and L. McManus, *The Experiences of Women Asylum Seekers in Ireland* (Dublin: Joint Oireachtas Committee on Justice, Equality and Women's Rights, 1999).

39 Shandy, 'Irish babies, African mothers: Rites of passage and rights of citizenship', pp 810–12.

40 Komolafe, 'Searching for fortune': http://www.africanmigration.com

41 *Eurstat* asylum applications and first instance decisions in third quarter 2000.

42 Komolafe, 'Nigerian migration to Ireland', p. 235.

43 Office of the Refugee Applications Commissioner, at www.orac.ie

44 Kennedy and Lawless, *The Maternity Care Needs of Refugee and Asylum Seeking Women*, p. 62.

45 Bryan Fanning, Angela Veale and Dawn O'Connor, *Beyond the Pale: Asylum-Seeking Children and Social Exclusion in Ireland* (Dublin: Irish Refugee Council, 2001), p. 39.

46 Sean O'Riordan, 'Heartbroken parents hit out over death', *Irish Examiner*, 5 Dec. 2001.

47 Nogugo Mafu, 'Seeking asylum in Ireland', *Irish Journal of Applied Social Studies*, 2006, 7.2, pp 27–34, 20–30.

48 M. Begley et al, Asylum in Ireland: A Public Health Prespective *Needs of Migrants, Refugees and Asylum Seekers in County Clare* (Dublin: Dept of Public Health Medicine, UCD, 1999), p. 49.

49 '200 asylum seekers on hunger strike over living conditions', *Irish Times*, 30 Jan. 2007.

50 Éidín Ní Shé, Tom Lodge and Maura Adshead, *Getting to Know You: A Local Study of the Needs of Migrants, Refugees and Asylum Seekers in County Clare* (Limerick: Centre for Development and Peace Studies, 2007), p. 49.

51 AkiDwA, *No Place to Call Home: Safety and Security Issues of Women Seeking Asylum in Ireland* (Dublin: Akina Dada Wa Africa, 2012).

52 Elena Moreo and Ronit Lentin, 'From catastrophe to marginalisation: The experiences of Somali refugees in Ireland (Dublin: Trinity Immigration Initiative/Horn of Africa People's Aid (HAPA), 2010).

53 D. O'Connell and C. Smith, 'Citizenship and the Irish Constitution', in (eds) U. Fraser and C. Harvey, *Sanctuary in Ireland: Perspectives on Asylum Law and Policy* (Dublin: Institute of Public Administration, 2003) p. 265.

54 Siobhan Mullally, 'Children, citizenship and constitutional change', in Bryan Fanning (ed.), *Immigration and Social Change in the Republic of Ireland* (Manchester: Manchester University Press, 2007), p. 28.

55 Michael McDowell, *Sunday Independent*, 14 Mar. 2004.

56 'Two of the masters have contested the Minister's claims that they pressed for measures to stem the arrival of non-national women as distinct from asking for more resources', *Irish Times*, 13 Mar. 2004.

57 Ronit Lentin, 'Remember the citizenship referendum?', *Free Radikal*, 24 May 2014: www.ronitlentin.net

58 Irish nationalisation and immigration service procedure and forms for applications for Irish born child renewals of residency status and conditions of renewal, IBC 2013: www.inis.gov.ie/en

59 'Citizen processes in need of overhaul', Press Release, Immigrant Council of Ireland, 7 May 2009. www.ici.ie

60 'Citizenship processes', 2009, 111: www.ici.ie

61 'Citizenship stats show 14,000 refusals in 4 years', *Metro Éireann*, 1 July 2013.

62 Alan Barret, Frances McGinnity and Emma Quinn, *Annual Monitoring Report of Integration: 2016* (Dublin: Economic and Social Research Institute, 2017).

63 Nicole Antoine, 'New citizens express their delight at Ireland's largest oath ceremony', *Metro Éireann*, 15 July 2013.

64 Chinedu Onyejelem, 'Immigration: Welcomes and goodbyes – Enda praises new citizens', *Metro Éireann*, 15 Feb. 2012.

65 'New African churches arrive here with vibrating ovations', *Metro Éireann*, June 2000.

66 Abel Ugba, 'African pentecostals in twenty-first century Ireland: Identity and integration', in Fanning (ed.), *Immigration and Social Change in the Republic of Ireland*, p. 173.

67 Abel Ugba, *Shades of Belonging: African Pentecostals in Twenty-First Century Ireland* (Trenton: African World Press, 2009), p. 98.

68 Ibid., p. 110.

69 Ibid., p. 111.

70 Ibid., p. 134.

71 Ibid., pp 185–7.

72 Ibid., p. 147.

73 From a group interview this author conducted with midwives in Ennis in 1999.

74 Ní Shé, Lodge and Adshead, *Getting to Know* You, p. 34.

75 Ibid., pp 83–4.

76 Mark Maguire and Fiona Murphy, *Integration in Ireland: The Everyday Lives of African Migrants* (Manchester: Manchester University Press, 2012), p. 44.

77 Bryan Fanning and Neil O'Boyle, 'Immigrants in Irish politics: African and East European candidates in the 2009 local government elections', in *Irish Political* Studies, 2010, 25.3, pp 417–35.

78 Bryan Fanning, Fidele Mutwarasibo and Neltah Chadmayo, *Positive Politics: Participation of Immigrants and Ethnic Minorities in the Electoral Process* (Dublin: Africa Solidarity Centre, 2003); Theo Ejorh, *Inclusive Citizenship in 21st Century Ireland: What Prospects for the African Community?* (Dublin: Africa Centre, 2006).

79 Fidele Mutwarasibo, *(New) Migrant Political Entrepreneurs: Overcoming Isolation and Exclusion through Creative Resistance in Ireland* (Dublin: University College Dublin, 2011: unpublished PhD).

80 Salome Mbungua, 'Opinion: equality and social justice for women is my life's work', *The Journal.ie*, 23 May 2014.

81 Fanning and O'Boyle 'Immigrants in Irish Politics, p. 428.

82 AkiDwA, *Understanding Gender-Based Violence: An African Perspective* (Dublin: Akina Dada Wa Africa, 2008).

83 Ebun Akpoveta, *Trapped: Prison Without Walls* (Bloomington: Authorhouse, 2013).

84 Asier Altuna-García de Slaazar, '"Migrant women are always added": In conversation with Ebun Joseph Akpoveta', in *Esudios Irlandeses*, 2017, 12.1, pp 158–66.

85 www.Sicklecellsocietyireland.org

86 Esther Onolememen, 'African parents' experiences of living and coping with children living with sickle cell disease (SCD) in Ireland' (Dublin: M.Soc. Thesis, School of Social Work and Social Policy Trinity College, 2008).

87 'Ill Nigrerian girl spared deportation', www.Breakingnews.ie, 3 Feb. 2010.

88 D. Kelly, 'Dublin's spatial narrative – the transition from essentially monocultural place to polycultural spaces', *Irish Geography*, 2005, 28.2, pp 209–24, 212–13.

89 Trutz Hasse and Jonathan Pratsche, *New Measures of Deprivation for the Republic of Ireland* (Dublin: Pobal, 2008).

90 Neil O'Boyle and Bryan Fanning, 'Immigration, integration and the risks of social exclusion: The social policy case for disaggregated data in the Republic of Ireland', *Irish Geography*, 2009, 42.2, pp 145–62, p. 150.

91 E. McGorman and C. Sugure, *Intercultural Education: Primary Challenges in Dublin 15* (Dublin: Department of Education and Science, 2007).

92 Census 2006 Vol. 8 – Occupations, Table 11A, p. 47.

93 F McGinnity, P. J. O'Connell, E. Quinn and J. Williams, 'migrants experience or racism and discrimination in Ireland: Results of a survey conducted by the Economic and Social Research Institute for the European Union monitoring centre on racism and xenophobia' (Dublin: ESRI, 2006), in G. Kingston, P. O'Connell and E. Kelly, *Ethnicity and Nationality in the Irish Labour Market* (Dublin: The Equality Authority/ESRI, 2013).

94 On taxis See, Mark McGuire and Fiona Murphy, *Integration in Ireland: The everyday lives of African Migrants* (Manchester: Manchester University Press, 2012), pp 31–4.

95 V. Jaichand, 'Riding along with racism? Research on the Galway taxi industry: Employment opportunities, patterns of public use and user perceptions' (Galway: Irish Centre for Human Rights, 2010), presents the experiences of taxi drivers in Galway.

96 Lorna Siggins, '"Shocking racism towards African drivers," says study', *Irish Times*, 10 Nov. 2010.

97 Ugba, *Shades of Belonging*, p. 45.

98 Barret, McGinnity and Quinn, *Annual Monitoring Report of Integration: 2016*.

99 McGinnity et al, Migrants experiences of racism and discrimination, p. 40.

100 European Union Minorities and Discrimination Survey, Fundamental Rights Agency (2009): http:///fra.europa.eu/eu–midis/

101 Bryan Fanning, Brian Kiloran and Saorlaith Ni Bhroin, 'Taking racism seriously: Migrants experience of violence, harassment and anti-social behaviour in the Dublin area' (Dublin: Immigrant Council of Ireland, 2011), in Lucy Michaels, *Afrophobia* (ENAR, 2015).

102 Frances McGinnity, Merike Darmody and Aisling Murray, 'Academic achievement amongs immigrant children in Irish primary schools', in *Economic and Scacial Research Institute*, Working paper no. 512, Sept. 2015, p. 8.

103 Moreo and Lentin, 'From catastrophe to marginalisation', p. 25.

ELEVEN: *Immigrations*

1   Unless otherwise stated figures cited are from the Central Statistics Office: www.cso.ie

2   Martin Ruhs, *Managing the Immigration and Employment of Non-EU Nationals in Ireland* (Dublin: The Policy Institute, 2005), pp xi–xiii.

3   Northern Ireland Council for Ethnic Minorities, *Bayanihan: The Filipino Community in Northern Ireland* (Belfast: NICEM, 2012), p. 13.

4   Kathryn Bell, Neil Jarman and Thomas Lefebvre, *Migrant Workers in Northern Ireland* (Belfast: Institute for Conflict Research, 2004), pp 27–8.

5   Mushroom Workers Support Group, *Harvesting Justice: Mushroom Workers Call for Change* (Dublin: MRCI, 2006), pp 5–6.

6   Ibid., p. 17.

7   Allamby et al., *Forced Labour in Northern Ireland*, p. 21.

8   Ibid., pp 26–8.

9   Ibid., pp 19–20.

10   'Lithuanians in Ireland', *Nationwide*, www.rte.ie

11   Monaghan Lithuanian School website: www.monaghanlt.com

12   Neringa Liubinine, *Lithuanians in Northern Ireland: New Home, New Homeland, Irish*

Journal of Anthropology, 2008, 11.1, pp 9–13, p. 12.

13 Sofya Aptekar, 'Contexts of exit in the migration of Russian speaker from the Baltic countries to Ireland', in *Ethnicities*, 2009, 9.4, pp 507–26.

14 Sabina Stan, 'Transnational healthcare practices of Romanian migrants in Ireland: Inequalityies of access and privatisation of healthcare services in Europe' in *Social Science and Medicine*, 2015, 124.C, pp 346–55, p. 348.

15 Sabina Stan and Roland Erne, 'Explaining Romanian labour migration: From development gaps to development trajectories', in *Labour History*, 2014, 55.1, pp 21–46, p. 23.

16 Ibid., p. 34.

17 Stan, 'Transnational healthcare practices of Romanian migrants in Ireland', p. 349.

18 Bryan Fanning, *Irish Adventures in Nation-Building* (Manchester: Manchester University Press, 2016), pp 112–18.

19 Miroslav Atanasov Atanasov, 'Gypsy pentecostals: The growth of the pentecostal movement amongst the Roma in Bulgaria and its revitalization of their communities' (Orlando: Asbury Theological College, 2008), p. 47.

20 Ronnie Fay, 'Irish travellers and Roma: Shadow report a response to Ireland's Third and Fourth Report on the International Convention of the Elimination of all forms of racism' (CERD) (Dublin: Pavee Point), p. 36.

21 Louise Lesovitch, 'Roma educational needs in Ireland: Context and challenges' (Dublin: City of Dublin Vocational Educational Committee, 2005), p. 23.

22 Anne Sutherland, *Gypsies; The Hidden Americans* (Prospect Heights: Waveleigh Press, 1975), p. ix.

23 Lesovitch, 'Roma educational needs in Ireland', p. 33.

24 See www.paveepoint.ie

25 *Irish Times*, 27 July 2007.

26 Wayne O'Connor and Geraldine Gittens, 'Three Roma families evacuated from home as 200-strong protests outside', *Irish Independent*, 26 Oct. 2014.

27 'Northern Ireland: Further racist attack against Romanians in Belfast', *Telegraph*, 18 June 2009.

28 Emily Moulon, 'Only to Roma from 114 remain after Northern Ireland race shame', *Belfast Telegraph*, 27 June 2009.

29 Allan Preston, 'Romanian family's car torched in Belfast race hate attack', *Belfast Telegraph*, 27 Jan. 2014; Chris Fitzpatrick, 'Two racist attacks every day in Northern Ireland's race-hate crime surge', *Belfast Telegraph*, 21 Apr. 2014.

30 Henry McDonald, 'Irish police return blond girl to Roma family', *The Guardian*, 24 Oct. 2013.

31 Fay, 'Irish travellers and Roma', p. 36.

32 Atanasov Atanasov, 'Gypsy Pentecostals', pp 133–7.

33 'I am immigrant', broadcast by RTE, 31 Mar. 2016.

34 Diane Nititham, 'Filipino articulations of community', in Fanning and Ronaldo Munck, *Globalization, Migration and Social Transformation: Ireland, Europe and the World* (London: Ashgate, 2011), p. 53.

35 Donna S. Kline, 'Push and pull factors in international nurse migration', in *Journal of Nursing Scholarship*, 2003, 35.2, pp 107–11, p. 109.

36 Nititham, *Making Home in Diasporic Communities: Transnational Belonging amongst Filipina Migrants* (London: Routledge, 2017), pp 64–5.

37 Nititham, 'Filipino articulations of community', p. 56.

38 Shay Cullen, *Passion and Power: An Irish Missionary's Fight against Child Sex Slavery* (Mullingar: Killynon House Books, 2006).

39 Alf McCreary, 'Filipino church buys Belfast landmark building', *Belfast Telegraph*, 8 Mar. 2013.

40 Lee Allemby, John Bell, Jennifer Hamilton, Ulf Hansson, Neil Jarman, Michael Potter and Sorina Toma, *Forced Labour in Northern Ireland: Exploiting Vulnerability* (York: Joseph Rowntree Foundation, 2011), p. 37.

41 Ibid., p. 36.

42 Ronan Duffy, 'Major investigation by *The Guardian* lays bare "modern slavery" on Irish fishing trawlers', *The Journal.ie*, 2 Nov. 2015.

43 Tony Dundon, Maria-Alejandra Gonsález-Pérez and Terrence McDonough, 'Bitten by the Celtic Tiger: Immigrant workers and industrial relations in the new "glocalized" Ireland, in *Economic and Industrial Democracy*, 2007, 20.4, pp 501–22, 509–10.

44 Allemby et al, *Forced Labour in Northern Ireland*, p. 41.

45 Nicola Yeates, 'Ireland's contribution to the global healthcare crisis' community' in Fanning and Munck, *Globalization, Migration and Social Transformation: Ireland, Europe and the World*, p. 43.

46 Kathryn Bell, Neil Jarman and Thomas Lefebvre, *Migrant Workers in Northern Ireland* (Belfast:Institute for Conflict Research, 2004), p. 12.

47 Ibid., p. 56.

48 Bryan Fanning, Brian Killoran, Saorlaith Ní Bhroin, *Taking Racism Seriously: Migrants' Experiences of Violence, Harassment and Anti–Social Behaviour in the Dublin Area* (Dublin: Immigrant Council of Ireland, 2011).

49 Niamh Humphries, Ruarai Brugha and Hannah McGee, 'Sending money home: a mixed-Methods study of remittances by migrant nurses in Ireland, in *Human Resources for Health*, 2009, 7.66, pp 1–12.

50 Humphries, Brugha and McGee, '"I won't be staying here long": A qualitative study on the retention of migrant nurses in Ireland', in *Human Resources for Health*, 2009, 7.68, pp 1–19.

51 Northern Ireland Council for Ethnic Minorities, *Bayanihan: The Filipino Community in Northern Ireland*, p. 23.

52 Yeates, 'Ireland's contribution to the global healthcare crisis' community', p. 44.

53 Fiona Meredith, *The Indian Community in Northern* Ireland; northernireland.org, 2006

54 Conor Talbot, *Highly-Skilled Indian Migrants in Ireland* (Florence: European Union Institute, 2013), p. 6.

55 'Leo Varadkar's Indian relatives express pride at his election', *Irish Times*, 29 June 2017.

56 Satwinder Singh, 'Formations of the Sikh community in Ireland' (Dublin: Dublin Institute of Technology thesis, 2013), pp 48–50.

57 Ibid., pp 50–1.

58 Ibid., pp 44–51.

59 Ibid., p. 20.

60 '"No turban", Gardaí tell Sikh recruits', *Metro Éireann*, 7 June, 2007.

61 'Referee told Sikh boy to remove turban', *The Observer*, 14 Dec. 2008.

62 Singh, 'Formations of the Sikh community in Ireland', p. 91.

63 Bryan, Killoran, and Ní Bhroin, *Taking Racism Seriously* (Dublin: Immigrant Council of Ireland, 2011), p. 25.

64 Data received from the Irish Naturalisation and Immigration Service, Aug. 2016.

65 Kitty Holland, *Savita: The Tragedy that Shook a Nation* (Dublin: Transworld Ireland, 2013)

66 Fiona Meridith, *The Chinese Community of Northern Ireland*: Culturenothernireland.org, 31 Jan. 2006.

67 Yin Yung Wang, 'Chinese-led migrant activism beyond invisibility: The Irish Chinese Sichuan earthquake appeal committee', in Ronit Lentin and Elena Moreo (eds), *Migrant Activism and Integration from Below in Ireland* (London: Palgrave Macmillan, 2012), pp 119–21.

68 Migrant Rights Centre Ireland, 'Exploitation in Ireland's restaurant industry' (Dublin: MCRI, 2008).

69 A. Feldman, M. Gilmartin, S. Loyal and B. Migge, 'Getting on: From migration to integration: Chinese, Indian, Lithuanian and Nigerian migrants' experiences in Ireland' (Dublin: Immigrant Council of Ireland, 2008), p. 126.

70 Ibid.

71 See, for example; Y. Y. Wang and R. Chiyoko King, 'Chinese students in Ireland' (Dublin: NCCRI, 2006), p. 18.

72 'Building a bridge to the East', *Metro Éireann*, 7 Aug. 2008.

73 Chinese Welfare Association website, assessed 2 Feb. 2016.

74 Wang, 'Chinese-led migrant activism beyond invisibility', pp 122–3.

75 Ibid., p, 128.

76 Anna Lo, *The Place I Call Home* (Belfast: Blackstaff Press, 2016).

77 Henry McDonald, 'Only Chinese-born parliamentarian in UK to quit politics over racist abuse', *The Guardian*, 19 May 2014.

78 'Growing hostility to foreigners drives Hong Kong-born Anna Lo out of Northern Ireland', *Hong Kong Post*, 30 May 2014.

79 Rebecca Black, 'Anna Lo: "It was horrible, I had people ringing saying how dare you"', *Belfast Telegraph*, 10 Mar. 2014.

80 David McKechnie, 'Gort still reverberating to the samba beat', *The Irish Times*, 5 July 2014.

81 Claire Healy, 'Carnaval do Galway: The Brazilian Community in Gort, 1999–2006, *Irish Migration Studies in Latin America*, 2006, 4.3, pp 150–3.

82 *Independent on Sunday*, 10 Oct. 2004.

83 Olivia Sheringham, 'White identity and integration amongst Brazilians in Gort, Ireland', in *Irish Migration Studies in Latin America*, 2009, 7.1, pp 93–104, p. 99.

84 Ibid., pp 100–01.

85 Rudhan MacCormac, 'Faraway fields give Gort a new gloss', *Irish Times*, 11 Apr. 2007.

86 McKechnie, 'Gort still reverberating to the samba beat', 5 July 2014

87 Brian McGrath and Frank Murray, 'Brazilian migrant networks and social capital', in Fanning and Munck (eds), *Globalization, Migration and Social Transformation*, p. 190.

88 '"I like it here, it's quiet, better for the children" – Integration in Ireland's "little Brazil"', 23 Nov. 2014.

89 The scheme, funded in Dublin by the Department of Justice and the International Organisation for Migration, offers asylum seekers and undocumented migrants a flight to their country of origin and 'reintegration assistance' to the value of €600 for each person or up to €1,200 a family: www.iomdublin.org

90 G. Maher, 'Transnational religions: The Brazilians in Ireland' Irish Migration Studies in Latin America 7.4(2011), 1–5, p. 3.

91 Tom Hennigan, 'A second home: the Brazilian influx to Irish universities', *Irish Times*, 9 Feb. 2016.

92 'There were loads more Brazilians in Ireland last year. . . and here's why', *The Journal.ie*, 22 Oct. 2014.

93 Fergal Browne, 'The boys (and the girls) from Brazil', *Evening Herald*, 16 Mar. 2012.

94 Data received from the Irish Naturalisation Service, Aug. 2016.

95 Alan Barret, Frances McGinnity and Emma Quinn, 'Annual Monitoring Report of Integration: 2016' (Dublin: Economic and Social Research Institute, 2017).

96 'Leo Varadkar's Indian relatives express pride at his election', *Irish Times*, 29 June 2017.

TWELVE: *Poles*

1 Figures cited from the Central Statistics Office unless otherwise stated: www.cso.ie

2 Agnieszka Fihel, Pawel Kaczmar and Marek Okólski, 'Labour mobility in the enlarged European Union: Internatioanl migration from the EU8 countries' (Warsaw: Centre of Migration Research, 2006).

3 Ibid., pp 24–5.

4 Ibid., pp 68–76.

5 James Wickham, Elaine Moriarty, Alicja Bobek and Justyna Salamónska, 'Working in the gold rush: Polish migrants' careers and the Irish hospitality sector', in Sharon Bolton and Maeve Houlihan (eds), *Work Matters: Critical Reflections on Contemporary Work* (London: Palgrave Macmillan, 2009), pp 81–96.

6 Kathryn Bell, Neil Jarman and Thomas Lefebvre, 'Migrant workers in Northern Ireland' (Belfast: Belfast Institute for Conflict Research, 2004), pp 27–8.

7 Anna Krausova and Carlos Vargas-Silva, 'Northern Ireland census profile' (2011): www.nisra.gov.uk

8 Hanna Dowling, 'Poles in Ireland: Their contribution to Irish life and the beginnings of the Irish Polish society', in (ed.) Jaroslaw Plachechi, *The Irish Polish Society Yearbook*, vol. 2 (Dublin: Irish Polish Society, 2015), p. 26.

9 For a brief biography of Jan Kaminiski see the website of the Holocaust Education Trust Ireland: www.heti.ie

10 Jaroslaw Plachechi, 'Retaining the national identity: 35 years of the Irish Polish society', in (ed.) Plachechi, *The Irish Polish Society Yearbook*, p. xx.

11 A. Nolka and M. Nowoesielski, 'Poles living in Ireland and their quality of life', in *Journal of Identity and Migrations Studies*, 2009, 3.1, pp 28–46.

12 Martha Kempny, *Polish Migrants in Belfast* (Cambridge: Cambridge Scholars Press, 2010).

13 Ibid., p. 176.

14 Kerry Gallagher, 'Mediating Catholicism: Religious identities, Polish migrants and the Catholic Church in Ireland (National University of Ireland Maynooth: PhD, 2014).

15 Ibid., pp 184–9.

16 Cited in ibid., p. 131.

17 Ibid., p. 139.

18 Torbens Krings, Elaine Moriarty, James Wickham, Alicija Bobek and Jutyna Salamónska, *New Mobilities in Europe: Polish Migration to Ireland post 2004* (Manchester: Manchester University Press, 2013), p. 127.

19 Interview with this author Aug. 2016.

20 Carl O'Brien, '600 Poles may be homeless in Ireland, Embassy finds', *Irish Times*, 29 July 2006.

21 John Drennan, 'One in four Polish workers in country claiming dole', *Irish Independent*, 5 Aug. 2012.

22 Interview with this author, Aug. 2016.

23 P. Muhlau, M. Kaliszewska and A. Roder (2011), Polonia in Dublin: Preliminary report of survey findings, report no 1: Demographic overview (Dublin: Trinity Migration Initiative, 2011), pp 15.

24 John Simon, 'Ireland from boom to bust: To what extent has the downfall in the Irish economy impacted on Polish migrants living and working in Ireland?' (Leicester: Unpublished PhD thesis, University of Leicester, 2004), p. 15.

25 Ibid., pp 134–8.

26 Liam Coakley, 'Exploring the significance of Polish shops within the Irish foodscape', in *Irish Geography*, 2010, 43.2, pp 105–17, p. 108.

27 Sheila Wayman, 'Polish mothers happy to be rearing their children into Irish family life', *Irish Times*, 17 Mar. 2015.

28 Niamh Nestor, 'The Polish complementary schools and Irish mainstream education', in *The Irish Polish Society Yearbook, 1* (Dublin: Irish Polish Social Society, 2014), p. 41.

29 Ibid., p. 37.

30 Ibid., p. 31.

31 Marta Kempny-Mazur, 'Between transnationalism and assimilation: Polish parents' upbringing approaches in Belfast, Northern Ireland', in *Social Identities*, published online 23 May 2016, p. 7.

32 Ibid., pp 10–11.

33 Ibid., p. 12.

34 'Parties flock to the Poles in late push for votes', *Irish Independent*, 26 May 2009.

35 Bryan Fanning, Kevin Howard and Neil O'Boyle, 'Immigrants in Irish politics: African and East European candidates in the 2009 local government elections', in *Irish Political Studies*, 2011, 25.3, pp 417–20.

36 Neil O'Boyle, Bryan Fanning and Viola Di Bucchianico, 'Polish immigrants and the challenges of political incorporation in Ireland', in *Irish Political Studies*, 2015, 21.2, pp 204–22, 217–18.

37 O'Boyle, Fanning and Di Bucchianico, 'Polish immigrants and the challenges of political incorporation in Ireland', p. 212.

38 Robert C. Smith, 'Diasporic members in historical perspective: Comparative insights from the Mexican, Italian and Polish cases', in *International Migration Review*, 2003, 37.3, pp 724–59, p. 743.

39 O'Boyle, Fanning and Di Bucchianico, 'Polish immigrants and the challenges of political incorporation in Ireland', p. 11.

40 *The Guardian*, 11 June 2014.

41 *The Times*, 6 Feb. 2013.

42 BBC (2014) Polish minister attacks David Cameron's child benefit plan, published on 6 Jan. 2014, available at: www.bbc.com/news/uk–politics–25628791

43 An open letter to the Rt Hon Mr David Cameron about the demonstration on the 24 Feb. 2014 to stop discrimination of Poles in the United Kingdom, available at: http://www. aarbd.org/open–letter.html

44 'Polish concern over rise in racist attacks in Northern Ireland', *The Irish Times*, 14 Apr. 2015.

45 '"No more Polish vermin": Wave of hate crime and racial abuse reported after Brexit', *Irish Independent*, 27 June 2016.

46 Frances McGinnity and Merove Gijsberts, 'Perceived group discrimination among Polish migrants to Western Europe: Comparing Germany, The Netherlands, the UK and Ireland: ESRI working paper no 502' (Dublin: Economic and Social Research Institute, 2015), pp 13–15.

47 www.polskaeire.org

48 Sara Bojarczuk and Bashir Otukoya, '*Integration roadmap: A synopsis of migrant issues and recommendations* (Dublin: Dialogue and Diversity, 2016).

49 Teresa Buczkowska, '"Why won't you all just go back home?" Patterns of migration and settlement of Polish diaspora in Ireland in the presence of economic downturn', in Jasroslaw Plachecki (ed.), *The Irish Polish Society Yearbook* (Dublin: Irish Polish Society, 2014), p. 75.

THIRTEEN: *Muslims*

1   Vivian Ibrahim, 'Salors, merchants and migrants: From the sack of Baltimore to World War II', in Oliver Scharbrodt, Tuula Sakaranaho, Adil Hussain Kahn, Yafa Shanneik and Vivian Ibrahim, *Muslims in Ireland: Past and Present* (Edinburgh: Edinburgh University Press, 2015), pp 32–4.

2   Gabriele Marranci, '"We speak English": Language and identity processes in Northern Ireland's Muslim community', in Ethnologies, 2003, 25.2, pp 59–75, p. 61.

3   'Islam in Dublin: Dublin's Muslim population', *The Irish Times*, 13 Feb. 1931.

4   Adil Hussain Kahn, 'Political Islam in Ireland and the role of Muslim Brotherhood Networks', in Scharbrodt et al., *Muslims in Ireland*, p. 91.

5   All statistics from the Central Statistics Office unless otherwise stated: www.cso.ie

6   Kieran Flynn, 'Understanding Islam in Ireland', *Islam and Christian-Muslim Relations*, 2006, 17.2, pp 223–38, p. 228.

7   Oliver Scharbrodt, 'Muslim immigration to Ireland after World War II', in Scharbrodt et al., *Muslims in Ireland*, p. 96.

8   Thomas Cooney, Jennifer Manning and Amr Arisha, 'Muslim entrepreneurship in Ireland' (Dublin: Institute for Minority Entrepreneurship, 2011).

9   Marranci, 'We speak English', pp 64–5.

10 Scharbrodt, 'Muslim immigration to Ireland after World War II', p. 51.

11 Kahn, 'Early Muslim organisations and mosques in Ireland', in Scharbrodt et al. (eds), *Muslims in Ireland*, p. 77,

12 'Africans biggest Foreign , *Irish Times*, 7 May 1970.

13 Oliver Scharbrodt, 'Muslim immigration to Ireland after World War II' in Scharbrodt et al., *Muslims in Ireland*, p. 51.

14 'The newsmakers: Where are they now', *Irish Times*, 2 Aug. 2010.
15 Fintan O'Toole, *Meanwhile Back the Ranch: The Politics of Irish Beef* (London: Vintage, 1995). p. 35.
16 Ibid., p. 25.
17 Elaine A. Byrne, *Political Corruption in Ireland 1922–2010* (Manchester: Manchester University Press, 2012), p. 125.
18 Kahn, 'Political Islam in Ireland and the role of Muslim Brotherhood Networks', pp 92–3.
19 Ibid., pp 94–5.
20 Kahn, 'Early Muslim organisations and mosques in Ireland', p. 82.
21 Islamic Foundation of Ireland, *History of Muslims in Ireland*: www.islaminIreland.com
22 Kahn, 'Political Islam in Ireland and the Role of Muslim Brotherhood Networks', p. 95.
23 Kahn, 'Early Muslim organisations and mosques in Ireland', p. 84.
24 Ibid., p. 85.
25 Kahn, 'Political Islam in Ireland and the Role of Muslim Brotherhood Networks', pp 98–9.
26 Oliver Scharbrodt and Tuula Sakaranaho, *Islam and Muslims in the Republic of Ireland An Introduction*, Journal of Muslim Minority Affairs, 31.4 (2011), 469–85, p. 478.
27 Kahn, Scharbrodt and Sakaranaho, 'Mosque communities and Muslim organisations in Dublin and other cities', in Schabrodt et al., *Muslims in Ireland*, p. 120.
28 Sakaranaho, *Religious Freedom, Multi-culturalism, Islam: Cross-reading Finland and Ireland* (Leinden: Brill, 2006), pp 287–90.
29 'Galway Muslims seek to build first Islamic centre', *Galway Advertiser*, 1 June 2004.
30 Kahn, Scharbrodt and Sakaranaho, 'Mosque communities and Muslim organisations in Dublin and other cities', pp 129–30.
31 Flynn, 'Understanding Islam in Ireland', p. 228.
32 'Galway Muslim group "heartened" by support after mosque damaged', *Irish Times*, 6 June 2017.
33 Lorna Siggins, 'Muslim cleric welcomes Irish support for Libyan council', *Irish Times*, 10 Sept. 2011.
34 Kahn, 'Political Islam in Ireland and the role of Muslim Brotherhood Networks', p. 105.
35 Ibid.
36 Ibid., p. 103.
37 Ibid., pp 100–02,
38 Ibid., pp 106–07.
39 Flynn, 'Understanding Islam in Ireland', pp 226–7.
40 Ibid., p. 228.
41 Orla McGarry, 'Identity formation among teenaged members of the Muslim population of Ballyhaunis, Co. Mayo' (PhD, National University of Ireland, Galway, 2012).
42 Sakaranaho, *Religious Freedom, Multiculturalism, Islam*, p. 275.
43 Kahn, Scharbrodt and Sakaranaho, 'Mosque communities and Muslim organisations in Dublin and other cities', pp 114–15.
44 Ibid., pp 115–16.
45 Ibid., p. 117.
46 Interview with this author, Feb. 2016.
47 Kahn, Oliver Scharbrodt and Sakaranaho, 'Mosque communities and Muslim organisations in Dublin and other cities', p. 120.

48 Ibid., pp 127–9.

49 Marranci, 'We speak English', p. 61.

50 According to the website of the Belfast Islamic Centre: www.belfastislamiccentre.org.uk

51 'Muslims in Ulster', *The Economist*, 14 June 2014.

52 David Young, 'Belfast Islamic Centre on to move to bigger and better premises as Muslim community grows', *Belfast Telegraph*, 21 Jan. 2016.

53 See 'Quran translation' at www.belfastislamicentre.org.uk

54 Marranci, 'We speak English', p. 67.

55 Ibid., p. 73.

56 Saharanaho, *Religious Freedom, Multiculturalism, Islam*, pp 311–13.

57 Yafa Shanneik, 'Religion and diasporic dwelling: Algerian Muslim women in Ireland', in *Religion and Gender*, 2012, 2.1, pp 80–100.

58 Edwin McGreal, 'Ballyhaunis Ireland's most "cosmopolitan" town', *Mayo News*, 8 Oct. 2012.

59 'Life in Ballyhaunis: Ireland's most culturally diverse town', *Irish Examiner*, 2 Dec. 2015.

60 McGarry, 'Identity formation', pp 174–7.

61 Colette Colfer, *Muslims in Ireland* (Waterford: Waterford Institute of Technology, 2009), p. 170.

62 Ibid., p. 178.

63 Ibid., p. 156.

64 Ibid., p. 215.

65 Ibid., p. 168.

66 Peter Mandaville, 'Reimaging Islam in diaspora: The politics of mediated community', *International Communication Gazette*, 2001, 63.2–3, pp 169–86.

67 'Ballymena home petrol bombed in "anti–Islam" attack', 17 Nov. 2015.

68 James Carr, 'Islamophobia in Dublin: Experiences and how to respond' (Dublin: Immigrant Council of Ireland, 2016), p. 6.

69 Shcharbrodt and Sakaranaho, *Islam and Muslims in the Republic of Ireland*, p. 478.

70 Kieran Flynn, 'Understanding Islam in Ireland', p. 231.

71 Ibid.

72 Henry McDonald, 'Dublin Imam takes on the fanatics', *The Guardian*, 14 Jan. 2007.

73 Maeve Sheehan, 'Imams split over fears Irish Muslims are being radicalised in Mosques', *Irish Independent*, 22 Nov. 2015.

74 'London terror attack: Who was attacker Rachid Redouane', *Irish Times*, 6 June 2017.

75 Galway Imam tells of his jihad rows with Isil's Irish suicide bomber', *Irish Independent*, 7 Nov. 2017.

76 Sam Najjair, *Soldier for a Summer: One Man's Journey from Dublin to the Frontline of the Libyan Uprising* (Castleknock: Hachette Ireland, 2015).

FOURTEEN: *Unsettlements*

1 Robert D. Putnam, '"E pluribus unum": Diversity and community in the twenty-first century', in *Scandinavian Political Studies*, 2006, 30.2, pp 137–74, p. 137.

2 Kevin Kenny, *The American Irish: A History* (New York: Pearson, 2000), pp 116–17.

3 Putnam, 'E pluribus unum', pp 149–51.

4 Nicholas Canny, *Making Ireland British 1580–1650* (Oxford: Oxford University Press), p. 551.

5 Vincent Gookin, *The Great Case of Transplantation in Ireland Discussed* (London: John Cook, [1655]1955).

6 William Petty, *The Political Anatomy of Ireland* (Shannon: Irish University Press, [1672]1970).

7 Patrick J. Duffy (ed.), *To and From Ireland: Planned Migration Schemes c.1600–2000* (Dublin: Geography Publications, 2004).

8 Oliver Bakewell, 'Some reflections on structure and agency in migration theory', in *Journal of Ethnic and Migration Studies*, 2010, 36.10, pp 1,189–1,708, p. 1,690.

9 Karl Marx, 'Forced migration', *New York Daily Tribune*, 4 Mar. 1953.

10 Enda Delaney, '"Almost a class of helots in an alien land": The British State and Irish immigration', in *Immigrants and Minorities*, 1999, 18.2–3, pp 240–65.

11 Seán Sorohan, *Irish London during the Troubles* (Dublin: Irish Academic Press, 2012), pp 82–7.

12 Ibid., pp 97–8.

13 Ibid., p. 75.

14 Michael Kearney, 'From the invisible hand to visible feet: Anthropological Studies of migration development', in *Review of Anthropology*, 1986, 15.1, pp 331–61, p. 333.

15 Kerby Miller, *Ireland and Irish America* (Cork: Field Day, 2008), p. 1.

16 Ibid., p. 219.

17 Ibid., p. 10.

18 Kerby Miller, *Emigrants and Exiles* (New York: Oxford University Press, 1971), p. 4.

19 J. J. Lee, *Ireland 1912–1986* (Cambridge: Cambridge University Press, 1989), p. 522.

20 Jim MacLaughlin, *Ireland: The Emigrant Nursery and the World Economy* (Cork: Cork University Press, 1994), p. 3.

21 William I. Thomas and Florian Znaniecki, *The Polish Peasant* (Chicago: University of Illinois Press, [1918]1958), pp 71–7.

22 Timothy Hatton and Jeffrey Williamson, *What Fundamentals Drive World Migration?* (Canberra: Austrian National University Centre for Economic Policy Research, 2002), p. 10.

23 Dino Cinel, *The National Integration of Italian Return Migration 1870–1929* (Cambridge: Cambridge University Press, 1991), pp 104–05.

24 Ibid., p. 114.

25 J. D. Gould, 'European inter-continental emigration 1815–1914: Patterns and causes', in *Journal of European Economic History*, 1989, 8.3, pp 593–679.

26 MacLaughlin, *Ireland: The Emigrant Nursery*, p. 73.

27 Immanuel Wallerstein, *The Modern World System: Capitalist Agriculture and the Origins of the European World Economy in the Sixteenth Century* (New York: Academic Press, 1974).

28 Mohammad A Chaichian, 'The new phase of globalization and brain drain: Migration of educated and skilled Iranians to the United States', in *International Journal of Social Economics*, 2012, 39.1/2, pp 18–38.

29 Mary Gilmartin, *Ireland and Migration in the Twenty-First Century* (Manchester: Manchester University Press, 2015), pp 141–2.

30 Miller, *Ireland and Irish America*, p. 103.

31 Enda Delaney, 'Transnationalism, networks and emigration from post-war Ireland', in *Immigrants and Minorities*, 2005, 23.2–3, pp 425–46, p. 437.

32 Alejandro Portes, 'Immigration theory for a new century: Some problems and opportunities', in *The International Migration Review*, 1997, 31.4, pp 799–825, 814–15.

33 Rosita Boland, 'Faith before fairness', *Irish Times*, 8 Sept. 2007.

34 E. Smith, M. Darmody, F. McGinnity and D. Byrne, 'What do we know about large scale immigration and Irish schools?: ESRI Research Bulletin 2009/2/6 (Dublin: Economic and Social Research Institute, 2009), p. 67.

35 Bryan Fanning, *Immigration and Social Cohesion in the Republic of Ireland* (Manchester: Manchester University Press, 2011), p. 122.

36 Ibid., p. 90.

37 Cian T. MacMahon, The *Global Dimensions of Irish Ireland: Race, Nation and the Popular Press 1840–1880* (Chapel Hill: University of North Carolina Press, 2015), p. 171.

SELECT BIBLIOGRAPHY

NEWSPAPER ARTICLES, CORRESPONDENCE AND ARCHIVAL MATERIAL
ARE CITED IN CHAPTER ENDNOTES

Agnew, Jean, *Belfast Merchant Families in the Seventeenth* Century (Dublin: Four Courts Press, 1996)

Akenson, Donald, H., *Small Differences: Irish Catholics and Irish Protestants, 1815–1922 An International Perspective* (Montreal: McGill-Queens University Press, 1988)

———, *The Irish Diaspora: A Primer* (Belfast: Institute of Irish Studies, 1996)

———, *If Ireland Ruled the World: Montserrat, 1630–1730* (Liverpool: Liverpool University Press, 1997)

Akpoveta, Ebun, *Trapped: Prison Without Walls* (Bloomington: Authorhouse, 2013)

Allemby, Lee, Bell, John, Hamilton, Jennifer, Hansson, Ulf, Jarman, Neil, Potter Michael and Toma, Sorina, *Forced Labour in Northern Ireland: Exploiting Vulnerability* (York: Joseph Rowntree Foundation, 2011)

Anbinder, Tyler, 'We will dirk every mother's son of you': Five points and the Irish conquest of New York politics', *Éire-Ireland*, 2001, 36.1, pp 29–46

Aptekar, Sofya, 'Contexts of exit in the migration of Russian speakers from the Baltic countries to Ireland', *Ethnicities*, 2009, 9.4, pp 507–26

Armstrong, Robert, 'Ireland's Puritan revolution? The emergence of Ulster Presbyterianism reconsidered', *English Historical Review*, 2005, 121.493, pp 1,048–72

Asbury, Herbert, *The Gangs of New York* (New York: Alfred A. Knoph, 1927)

Bakewell, Oliver, 'Some reflections on structure and agency in migration theory', *Journal of Ethnic and Migration Studies*, 2010, 36.10, pp 1,189–708

Bardon, Jonathan, *The Plantation of Ulster* (Dublin: Gill and Macmillan, 2011)

Barkley Woodburn, James, *The Ulster Scot: His Religion and his History and Religion* (London: H. R. Allenson, 1914)

Barnard, T. C., 'Planters and polices in Cromwellian Ireland', *Past and Present*, 1973, 61, 31–69

———, *Cromwellian Ireland* (Oxford, 1975)

———, *Improving Ireland? Projectors, Prophets and Profiteers, 1641–1786* (Dublin: Four Courts Press, 2008)

Barnett, Barbara (ed.), *The Hide and Seek Children: Recollections of Jewish Survivors from Slovakia* (Glasgow: Mansion Field, 2012)

Barrett, James R. and Roediger, David R., 'The Irish and the "Americanization" of the "new immigrants" in the streets and in the churches of the urban United States, 1990–1930', *Journal of American Ethnic History*, 2005, 24.4, pp 3–33

Bartlett, Thomas, *Ireland: A History* (Cambridge: Cambridge University Press, 2010)

Bartlett, Thomas and Keith Jeffery, Keith (eds), *A Military History of Ireland* (Cambridge, Cambridge University Press, 1996)

Belchem, John, 'Nationalism, republicanism and exile: Irish emigrants and the revolutions of 1848', *Past and Present*, 1995, 146, pp 103–35

Bell, Kathryn, Jarman, Neil and Lefebvre, Thomas, *Migrant Workers in Northern Ireland* (Belfast: Institute for Conflict Research, 2004)

Berman, Hannah and Zlotover, Melisande, *Zlotover Story: A Dublin Story with a Difference* (Dublin: Hely Thom, 1966)

Berresford Ellis, Peter, *To Hell or Connaught: The Cromwellian Colonisation of Ireland 1652–1660* (Belfast: Blackstaff Press, 1975)

Belchem, John, 'Nationalism, Republicanism and Exile: Irish Emigrants and the Revolutions of 1848', *Past and Present*, 1995, 146, pp 103–35

Bielenberg, Andy (ed.), *The Irish Diaspora* (Dublin: Longman, 2000)

Black, Kirsten and Shaw, Jenny, 'Subjects without an empire: the Irish in the early modern Caribbean', *Past and Present*, 2011, 210, pp 33–60

Blethen, H. Tyler and Wood Jr. Curtis W. (eds), *Ulster and North American Transatlantic Perspectives on the Scotch-Irish* (Tuscaloosa: University of Alabama Press, 1997)

Bojarczuk, Sara and Otukoya, Bashir, 'Integration roadmap: A synopsis of migrant issues and recommendations' (Dublin: Dialogue and Diversity, 2016)

Bric, Maurice, *Ireland, Philadelphia and the Re-invention of America, 1760–1800* (Dublin: Four Courts Press, 2008)

Briscoe, Robert, *For the Life of Me* (London: Longmans, 1958)

Butler, Hubert, *Independent Spirit: Essays* (New York: Farrar, Straus and Giroux, 1996)

Caldicot, Eric, Hugh Gough and Pittion, Jean-Paul (eds), *The Huguenots and Ireland: Anatomy of an Emigration* (Dublin: Gelendale Press, 1987)

Canny, Nicholas, *Making Ireland British: 1580–1650* (Oxford: Oxford University Press, 2001)

Carr, James, *Islamophobia in Dublin: Experiences and How to Respond* (Dublin: Immigrant Council of Ireland, 2016)

Casway, Jerrold, 'Henry O'Neill and the formation of the Irish regiment in the Netherlands, 1605', *Irish Historical Studies*, 1973, 18.72, pp 481–8

Clare George, *Last Waltz in Vienna: The Destruction of a Family, 1842–1942* (London: Macmillan, 1981)

Clark, Denis, *The Irish in Philadelphia: Ten Generations of Urban Experience* (Philadephia: Temple University Press, 1973)

Coakley, Liam, 'Exploring the significance of Polish shops within the Irish foodscape', *Irish Geography*, 2014, 43.2, pp 105–17

Colfer, Billy, Anglo-Norse Settlement in County Wexford', in Kevin Whelan (ed.), *Wexford History and Society* (Dublin: Geography Publications, 1987)

Connell, K. H., *The Populations of Ireland, 1750–1845* (Oxford: Oxford University Press, 1950)

Conroy, Pauline, McKearney, Tommy, and Quintin Oliver, *All Over the Place: People Displaced to and from the Southern Border Counties as a Result of the Conflict 1969–1994* (Dublin: Ralaheen Ltd, 2005)

Cook Myers, Albert, *Immigration of the Irish Quakers into Pennsylvania 1662 1750* (Baltimore: Genealogical Publishing, 1985)

Corcoran, Mary, *Transients between Two Societies* (Westport CT: Greenwood Press, 1993)

Crowley, John, Smyth, William J. and Murphy, Mike (eds), *Atlas of the Great Irish Famine* (Cork: Cork University Press, 2012)

Cullen, L. M., 'Population trends in the seventeenth-century', *Economic and Social Review*, 1975, 6.2, pp 149–65

——, *The Emergence of Modern Ireland 1600–1900* (London: Batsford Academic and Educational Ltd, 1981)

Cullen, Shay, *Passion and Power: An Irish Missionary's Fight against Child Sex Slavery* (Mullingar: Killynon House Books, 2006)

Cunningham, Bernadette, *The Annals of the Four Masters: Irish History, Kingship And Society in the Early Seventeenth Century* (Dublin: Four Courts Press, 2014)

D'arcy, Frank, *Wild Geese and Traveling Scholars* (Dublin: Mercier Press, 2001)

Davies, Norman, *The Isles: A History* (London: Macmillan, 1999)

de la Purdon, Charles Nicholas, 'The French settlers in Ireland , no.1: The Huguenot Colony at Lisburn, county of Antrim' *Journal of Archaeology, First Series*, 1853, 1, pp 209–20

de Mórdha, Mícheál, *An Island Community: The Ebb and Flow of the Great Blasket Island* (Dublin: Liberties Press, 2015)

Defoe, Daniel, *A Brief History of the Poor Palatine Refugees* (London, 1709)

Delaney, Enda, '"Almost a class of helots in an alien land": The British state and Irish immigration 1921–45', *Immigrants and Minorities*, 1999, 18.2–3, pp 240–65

——, 'Transnationalism, networks and emigration from post-war Ireland', *Immigrants and Minorities*, 2005, 23.2–3, pp 425–46

Dickinson, H. T., 'The poor Palatines and the parties', *The English Historical Review*, 1967, 82.324, pp 464–85

Dickinson, R. I., *Ulster Emigration to Colonial America, 1718–1775* (Belfast: Ulster Historical Foundation, 1988)

Dickson, David, *Old World Colony: Cork and South Munster 1630–1830* (Cork: Cork University Press, 2005)

Dillon, Charles and Jefferies, Henry A., *Tyrone: History and Society* (Dublin: Geography Publications, 2000)

Dolley, Michael, *Anglo-Norman Ireland* (Dublin: Gill and Macmillan, 1972)

Downham, Clare, 'The historical importance of Viking-age Waterford', *Eighteenth Irish Conference of Medievalists*, 2004, 18.1, pp 71–95

Dunne, Tom, *Rebellions: Memoir, Memory and 1798* (Dublin: Lilliput Press, 2010)

Ejorh, Theo, *Inclusive Citizenship in 21st-Century Ireland: What Prospects for the African Community?* (Dublin: Africa Centre, 2006)

Elliott, Bruce S., *Irish Migrants in the Canadas: A New Approach* (Montreal: McGill, 1988)

Engels, Friedrich, *The Condition of the Working Class in England* (London, 1892 [1845])

Fanning, Bryan, *Immigration and Social Cohesion in the Republic of Ireland* (Manchester: Manchester University Press, 2011)

———, *Histories of the Irish Future* (London: Bloomsbury, 2015)

———, *Irish Adventures in Nation-Building* (Manchester: Manchester University Press, 2016)

Fanning, Bryan, Kiloran, Brian, and Ni Bhroin, Saorlaith, *Taking Racism Seriously: Migrants Experience of Violence, Harassment and Anti-Social Behaviour in the Dublin Area* (Dublin: Immigrant Council of Ireland, 2011)

Fanning, Bryan, Howard, Kevin, and O'Boyle, Neil, (2010) 'Immigrant Candidates and Politics in the Republic of Ireland: Racialization, Ethnic Nepotism, or Localism?', Nationalism and Etnic Politics, 16:3–4, 420–442

Fanning, Bryan and Munck, Ronaldo (eds), *Globalization, Migration and Social Transformation: Ireland in Europe and the World* (London: Ashgate, 2011)

Fanning, Bryan, and O'Boyle, Neil, 'Immigrants in Irish politics: African and East European candidates in the 2009 local government elections', *Irish Political Studies*, 2010, 25.3, pp 417–35

Ferguson, Robert, *The Vikings: A History* (London: Penguin, 2009)

Fitzgerald, Patrick and Lambkin, Brian, *Migration in Irish History, 1607–2007* (London: Palgrave, 2007)

Fitzpatrick, David, 'Irish emigration in the later nineteenth century', *Irish Historical Studies*, 22.86 (1980), pp 126–43

———, *Oceans of Consolation: Personal Accounts of Irish Migration to Australia* (Cork: Cork University Press, 1994)

———, 'Exporting brotherhood: Orangeism in South Australia', *Immigrants and Minorities: Historical Studies in Ethnicity, Migration and Diaspora*, 2005, 23.2–3, pp 277–310

Flynn, Kieran, 'Understanding Islam in Ireland', *Islam and Christian-Muslim Relations*, 2006, 17.2, pp 223–38

Foster, Roy, *Modern Ireland: 1600–1972* (London: Allen Lane, 1988)

Frame, Robert, *Colonial Ireland: 1169–1369* (Dublin: Four Courts Press, 2012)

Gallagher, Kerry, 'Mediating Catholicism – Religious identities, Polish migrants and the Catholic Church in Ireland' (Maynooth: National University of Ireland Maynooth PhD, 2014)

Gardiner, Samuel R., 'The transplantation to Connaught', *The English Historical Review*, 1899, 14.56, pp 700–34

Gavan Duffy, Charles, *My Life in Two Hemispheres: Vol II* (Shannon: Irish University Press [1898], 1969)

Gillespie, Raymond, *Colonial Ulster: The Settlement of East Ulster: 1600–1641* (Cork: Cork University Press, 1985)

Gilmartin, Mary, *Ireland and Migration in the Twenty-First Century* (Manchester: Manchester University Press, 2015)

Gilmartin, Mary, and White, Alan (eds), *Migrations: Ireland in a Global World* (Manchester: Manchester University Press, 2013)

Glynn, Irial, Kelly Tomás and MacÉinrí, Piaras, *Irish Emigration in an Age of Austerity* (Cork: Department of Geography, 2013)

———, *The Re-Emergence of Emigration from Ireland: New Trends in an Old Story* (Washington: Migration Policy Institute, 2015)

Goldstone, Katrina, 'Now you see us, now you don't: Reflections on Jews, historical amnesia and the histories of a multi-ethnic Dublin', *Translocations*, 2008, 4.1, pp 102–09

Gould, J. D., European inter-continental emigration 1815–1914: Patterns and causes', *Journal of European Economic History*, 1989, 8.3, pp 593–679

Gray, Breda, *Women and the Diaspora* (London: Routledge, 2004)

Griffin, Patrick, *The People with No Name: Ireland's Ulster Scots, America's Scot's Irish and the Creation of a British Atlantic World 1689–1764* (New Jersey: Princeton University Press, 2001)

Halilovic-Pastuovic, Maja, '"Settled in mobility" as a "space of possibility": Bosnian post-refugee transnationalism as a response to the bio-politics of Irish interculturalism', *Translocations*, 2009, 2.1, pp 1–20

Harris, Nick, *Dublin's Little Jerusalem* (Dublin: A. & A. Farmer, 2002)

Harris, Ruth-Ann M., *The Nearest Place that Wasn't Ireland: Early Nineteenth-Century Irish Labor Migration* (Ames: Iowa State University Press, 1994)

Harrison, John, *The Scot in Ulster* (London: Blackwood and Sons, 1888)

Hatton, Timothy and Williamson, Jeffrey, *What Fundamentals Drive World Migration?* (Canberra: Australian National University Centre for Economic Policy Research, 2002)

Hempton, D. N., 'The Methodist crusade in Ireland 1795–1845', *Irish Historical Studies*, 1980, 22.85, pp 33–48

Henry, Gráinne, *The Irish Military Community in Spanish Flanders* (Dublin: Irish Academic Press, 1992)

Hick, Vivien, 'The Palatines: 1798 and its aftermath', *The Journal of the Royal Society of Antiquaries of Ireland*, 1996, 126, pp 5–36

Hickman, Mary, *Religion, Class and Identity* (Aldershot: Avery, 1995)

Hill, J. Michael 'The origins of the Scottish Plantation in Ulster to 1625: A reinterpretation', *Journal of British Studies,* 1993, 32, 24–43

Hofsta, Warren R. (ed.), *Ulster in America: The Scots-Irish Migration Experience, 1680–1830* (Knoxville: University of Tennessee Press, 2012)

Hogan, Liam, McAtackney, Laura and Reilly, Matthew Conor, 'The Irish in the Caribbean: servants or slaves?: Why we need to confront the 'Irish slave myth' and how terminology is not simply semantics', *History Ireland*, March 2016, pp 18–23

Holm, Paul, 'The slave trade of Dublin, ninth to twelfth centuries', *Perita*, 1980, 5, pp 317–45

Horning, Audrey J., 'Archaeological explorations of cultural identity and rural economy in the north of Ireland: Goodland, County Antrim', *International Journal of Historical Archaeology*, 2004, 8.3, pp 119–225

Houston, Cecil J. and Smyth, William J., *The Sash Canada Wore: A Historical Geography of the Orange Order in Canada* (Toronto: University of Toronto Press, 1980)

———, *Irish Emigration and Canadian Settlement: Patterns, Links and Letters* (Toronto: University of Toronto Press, 1990)

Howard, Kevin, 'Constructing the Irish in Britain: Ethnic recognition and the 2001 UK censuses', *Ethnic and Racial Studies*, 2001, 29.1, pp 104–23

Hughes, Robert, *The Fatal Shore* (London: Pan Books, 1987)

Humphries, Niamh, Brugha, Ruairí and McGee, Hannah, 'Sending money home: a mixed-Methods study of remittances by migrant nurses in Ireland, *Human Resources for Health*, 2009, 7.66, pp 1–12

———, '"I won't be staying here long"; A qualitative study on the retention of migrant nurses in Ireland', *Human Resources for Health*, 2009, 7.68, pp 1–19

Hutchinson, W. R., *Tyrone Precinct: A History of the Plantation and Settlement of Dungannon and Mountjoy to Modern Times* (Belfast: W. E. Maine, 1951)

Hyman, Louis, *The Jews of Ireland from the Earliest Times to the Year 1910* (Shannon: Irish University Press, 1972)

Ignatiev, Noel, *How the Irish Became White* (London: Routledge, 1995)

Jackson, Alvin (ed.), *The Oxford Handbook of Modern Irish History* (Oxford: Oxford University Press, 2014)

Kempny, Martha, *Polish Migrants in Belfast* (Cambridge: Cambridge Scholars Press, 2010)

Kennedy, Liam, Lyes, Madeleine and Russell, Martin, *Supporting the Next Generation of the Irish Diaspora* (Dublin: Clinton Institute, 2014)

Kenny, Kevin, *The American Irish: A History* (London: Pearson, 2000)

———, 'Diaspora and comparison: The global Irish as a case study', *Journal of American History*, 2003, 90, pp 134–62

Keogh, Dáire and McDonnell, Albert (eds), *Cardinal Cullen and his World* (Dublin: Four Courts Press, 2011)

Keogh, Dermot, *Jews in Twentieth Century Ireland: Refugees, Anti-Semitism and the Holocaust* (Cork: Cork University Press, 1998)

Keogh, Dermot and McCarthy, Andrew, *Limerick Boycott 1904: Anti-Semitism in Ireland* (Cork: Mercier Press, 2005)

Knittle, Walter A., *Eighteenth Century Palatine Emigration* (Philadelphia, 1937)

Komolafe, Julius, 'Nigerian Migration to Ireland: Movements, motivations and experiences', *Irish Geography*, 2008, 41.2, pp 225–41

———, 'Searching for fortune: The geographical process of Nigerian migration to Dublin, Ireland', *Ininkerindo: A Journal of African Migration*, 2002, 1.1, www.africamigration.com

Krings, Torbens, Moriarty, Elaine, Wickham, James, Bobek, Alicija and Salamónska, Jutyna, *New Mobilities in Europe: Polish Migration to Ireland Post-2004* (Manchester: Manchester University Press, 2013)

Lacy, Brian, *Siege City: The Story of Derry and* Londonderry (Belfast: Blackstaff Press, 1990)

Landy, David, 'Zionism, multiculturalism and the construction of Irish-Jewish identity, *Irish Journal of Sociology*, 2007, 16.1, pp 62–79

Lawless Lee, Grace, *The Huguenot Settlements in Ireland* (Massachusetts: Clearfield, 1936),

Leach, Daniel, *Fugitive Ireland: European Minority Nationalists and Irish Political Asylum, 1937–2008* (Dublin: Four Courts Press, 2009)

Lecky, W. E. H., *A History of Ireland in the Eighteenth Century: Vol. I* (London: Longman, Green and Co, 1913, originally published in 1892)

Lee, J. J., *Ireland 1912–1986* (Cambridge: Cambridge University Press, 1989), p. 522

Le Fanu, T. P., 'Huguenot veterans in Dublin', *The Journal of the Royal Society of Antiquaries of Ireland*, 1942, 12.2, pp 64–70

Lentin, Louis, 'Grandpa… speak to me in Russian', *Translocations*, 2008, 3.1, pp 153–63

Lentin, Ronit, and Moreo, Elena (eds), *Migrant Activism and Integration from Below in Ireland* (Basingstoke: Palgrave Macmillan, 2012)

Leventhal, A. J., 'What it means to be a Jew', *The Bell*, 1945, 10.3, pp 206–16

Lewis, Helen, *A Time to Speak* (Belfast: Blackstaff Press, 1992)

Lindley, Keith, 'Irish adventurers and godly militants in the 1640s', *Irish Historical Studies*, 1994, 29.113, pp 1–12

Liubinine, Neringa, 'Lithuanians in Northern Ireland: New home, new homeland', *Irish Journal of Anthropology*, 2008, 11.1, pp 9–13

Loughrey, Patrick (ed.), *The People of Ireland* (Belfast: Appletree Press, 1988)

Lowe Keith, *Savage Continent: Europe in the Aftermath of World War II* (London: Penguin, 2012)

Lurbe, Pierre, 'John Toland and the naturalization of the Jews', *Eighteenth-Century Ireland*, 1999, 14, pp 37–48.

Lydon, James, *Ireland in the Later Middle Ages* (Dublin: Gill and Macmillan, 1973)

———, *The Making of Ireland: From Ancient Times to the Present* (London: Routledge, 1998)

MacCarthy-Morrough, Michael, *The Munster Plantation: English Migration to Southern Ireland 1583–1641* (Oxford: Clarendon Press, 1986)

MacLaughlin, Jim, *Ireland: The Emigrant Nursery and the World Economy* (Cork: Cork University Press, 1994)

MacMahon, Cian T., *The Global Dimensions of Irish Ireland: Race, Nation and the Popular Press 1840–1880* (Chapel Hill: University of North Carolina Press, 2015)

MacRaild, Donald, 'Crossing migrant frontiers: Comparative reflections on Irish migrants in Britain and the United States during the nineteenth century', *Immigrants and Minorities*, 1999, 18. 2–3, pp 40–70

Maguire, Mark, *Differently Irish: A Cultural History Exploring 25 Years of Vietnamese-Irish Identity* (Portadown: Woodfield Press, 2004)

Maguire, Mark and Murphy, Fiona, *Integration in Ireland: The Everyday Lives of African Migrants* (Manchester: Manchester University Press, 2012)

Mallory, J. P. *The Origins of the Irish* (London: Thames and Hudson, 2013)

Marcus, David, *Autobiography: Leaves from the Diary of a Hyphenated Jew* (Dublin: Gill and Macmillan, 2001)

Marranci, Gabriele, '"We speak English": Language and identity processes in Northern Ireland's Muslim community', *Ethnologies*, 2003, 25.2, pp 59–75

McCaffrey, Lawrence J, *The Irish Diaspora in America* (Indiana: Indiana University Press, 1976)

———, *Textures of Irish America* (New York: Syracuse University Press, 1992)

———, *The Irish Catholic Diaspora in America* (Catholic University Press of America, 1997)

McCourt, Frank, *Angela's Ashes* (London: Harper Collins, 1997)

McEvoy, Brian, Brady, Claire, Moore, Laoise T. and Bradley, Daniel G., 'The scale and nature of Viking settlement in Ireland from Y-chromosome admixture analysis', *European Journal of Human Genetics*, 2006, 14, pp 1,288–94

McGarry, Orla, 'Identity formation among teenaged members of the Muslim population of Ballyhaunis, Co. Mayo (Galway: PhD, National University Galway, 2014)

McGinnity, Frances and Gijsberts, Merove, *'Perceived Group Discrimination among Polish Migrants to Western Europe: Comparing Germany, the Netherlands, the UK and Ireland: ESRI Working Paper No.502* (Dublin: Economic and Social Research Institute, 2015)

McGinnity, Frances, O'Connell, Philip J., Quinn, Emma and Williams, James, *Migrants Experience or Racism and Discrimination in Ireland: Results of a Survey Conducted by the Economic and Social Research Institute for the European Union Monitoring Centre on Racism and Xenophobia* (Dublin: ESRI, 2006)

McGovern, Frieda, 'Vietnamese refugees in Ireland, 1979–1989', unpublished Med thesis (Dublin: Trinity College Dublin, 1990)

McGrath, Charles Ivar, 'Securing the Protestant interest: The origins and purpose of the penal laws of 1695', *Irish Historical Studies*, 1996, 30.117, pp 22–46

McGrath, Paul, *Back from the Brink* (London: Arrow Books, 2007)

McIntosh, Gillian, 'Ireland's first Jewish Lord Mayor: Sir Otto Jaffé and Edwardian Belfast's civic sphere', *Jewish Culture and History*, 2009, 11.3, pp 3–11

McKay, Donald, *Flight from Famine: The Coming of the Irish to Canada* (Ontario: McClelland and Stewart, 1990)

Metress, Seamus P., *The American Irish and Irish Nationalism: A Socio-Historical* Introduction (Maryland: Scarecrow Press, 1995)

Michael, Lucy, *Afrophobia* (Dublin: ENAR, 2015)

Miller, Kerby A., *Emigrants and Exiles* (Oxford: Oxford University Press, 1971)

——, *Ireland and Irish America* (Cork: Field Day, 2008)

——, Kerby A., *Emigrants and Exiles: Ireland and the Irish Exodus to North America* (Oxford: Oxford University Press, 1985)

Miller, Kerby A., Schrier, Arnold, Boling, Bruce D. and Doyle, David N., *Irish Immigrants in the Land of Canaan: Letters and Memoirs from Colonial and Revolutionary America* (Oxford: Oxford University Press, 2003), pp 167–81

Miller, Rory, 'The politics of trade and diplomacy: Ireland's evolving relationship with the Muslim Middle East', *Irish Studies in International Affairs*, 2004, 15.1, pp 123–45

Mitchel, John, *The Last Conquest of Ireland (Perhaps)* (Dublin; UCD Press, [1873] 2005)

Moody, T. W., 'The treatment of the native population under the scheme for the plantation of Ulster', *Irish Historical Studies*, 1938, 1.1, pp 59–63

Moore, Walter, *A Life of Erwin* Schrödinger (Cambridge: Cambridge University Press, 1994)

Moreo, Elena, and Ronit Lentin, 'From catastrophe to marginalisation: The experiences of Somali refugees in Ireland (Dublin: Trinity Immigration Initiative/Horn of Africa People's Aid (HAPA), 2010)

Moulton, Mo, *Ireland and the Irish in Interwar England* (Cambridge: Cambridge University Press, 2014)

Mullan, David George, 'A hotter sort of Protestantism? Comparisons between French and Scottish Calvinisms', *The Seventeenth Century Journal*, 2008, 39.1, pp 45–69

Mulligan, Adrian N., 'Absence makes the heart grow fonder: Transatlantic Irish nationalism and 1867 Rising', *Social and Cultural Geography*, 2005, 6.3, pp 439–54

Murtagh, Harman (ed.), *Irishmen in War from the Crusades to 1798: Essays from the Irish Sword, Volume I* (Dublin: Irish Academic Press, 2005)

Mushroom Workers Support Group, *Harvesting Justice: Mushroom Workers Call for Change* (Dublin: Migrants Rights Centre Ireland, 2006)

Najjair, Sam, *Soldier for a Summer: One Man's Journey from Dublin to the Frontline of the Libyan Uprising* (Castleknock: Hachette Ireland, 2015)

Ní Chiosáin, Bairbre, 'Ireland and its European refugees: The case of the Kosovars', *Nordic Irish Studies*, 2005, pp 89–97

Nolka, A. and Nowoesielski, M., 'Poles living in Ireland and their quality of life' *Journal of Identity and Migrations Studies*, 2009, 3.1, pp 28–46

Northern Ireland Council for Ethnic Minorities, *Bayanihan: The Filipino Community in Northern Ireland* (Belfast: NICEM, 2012)

O'Boyle, Neil, Fanning, Bryan, and Di Bucchianico, Viola, 'Polish immigrants and the challenges of political incorporation in Ireland', *Irish Political Studies*, 2015, 21.2, pp 204–22

O'Brien, Flann, 'The Dance Halls', *The Bell*, 1941, 1.5, pp 44–53

O'Brien, Gerald (ed.), *Derry and Londonderry History and Society* (Dublin: Geography Publications, 1999)

Ó Ciardha, Éamonn and Ó Siochrú, Micheál (eds), *The Plantation of Ulster: Ideology and Practice* (Manchester: Manchester University Press, 2012)

O'Connor, Patrick, *People Make Places: The Story of the Irish Palatines* (Newcastle West: Oireacht na Mumhan Books, 1989)

O'Connor, Thomas and Lyons, Mary Ann (eds), *Irish Communities in Early Modern Europe* (Dublin: Four Courts Press, 2006)

Ó Corráin, Donncha, *Ireland before the Normans* (Dublin: Gill and Macmillan, 1972)

O'Donnell, Peadar, 'The Irish in Britain', *The Bell*, 1943, 6.3, pp 361–70

O'Faolain, Sean, 'The Gaelic League', *The Bell*, 1942, 4.2, pp 77–86

O'Farrell, Patrick, *The Irish in Australia* (Kensington: New South Wales University Press, 1987)

Ó'Grada, Cormac, 'Determinants of Irish emigration: A note', *International Migration Review*, 1986, 20.1, pp 650–6

——, *Ireland Before and After the Famine: Explorations in Economic History, 1800–1925* (Manchester: Manchester University Press, 1993)

——, *Jewish Dublin in the Time of Joyce* (New Jersey: Princeton University Press, 2006)

O'hAnnracháin, Eoghan, 'Louth wild geese veterans in the *Hotel Royal des Invalides*', *Journal of the County Louth Archaeological and History Society*, 1999, 24.3, pp 380–90

——, 'Clogher veterans in the *Hotel Royal des Invalides*', *Clogher Record*, 2005, 18.3, pp 467–500

Ohlmeyer, Jane, *Civil War and Restoration in the Three Stuart Kingdoms: The Career of Ranald McDonnell, Marquis of Antrim 1609–1683* (Cambridge: Cambridge University Press, 1993)

O'Regan, Cathal, 'Report of a survey of the Vietnamese and Bosnian refugee communities in Ireland' (Dublin: Refugee Agency, 1998)

O'Scea, Ciaran, *Surviving Kinsale: Irish Emigration and Identity Formation in Early Modern Spain* (Manchester: Manchester University Press, 2015)

Ó Siochrú, Micheál and Ohlmeyer, Jane, *Ireland 1641: Contexts and Reactions* (Manchester: Manchester University Press, 2013)

O'Sullivan, Harold, 'The plantation of Cromwellian soldiers in the Barony of Ardee, 1652–1656', *County Louth Archaeological and History Society*, 1998, 21.4, pp 415–52

O'Sullivan, Kevin, *Ireland, Africa and the End of Empire* (Manchester: Manchester University Press, 2012)

O'Sullivan, Patrick (ed.), *The Irish Worldwide: History, Heritage, Identity: Religion and Identity* (Leicester: Leicester University Press, 1996)

Ó Tuathaigh, M. A. G., 'The Irish in nineteenth-century Britain: Problems of integration', *Transactions of the Royal Historical Society*, 1981, 31, pp 149–73

Owens Peare, Catherine, *William Penn: A Biography* (London: Dennis Dobson, 1956)

Patinkin, Don, 'Mercantilism and the readmission of the Jews to England', *Jewish Social Studies*, 1946, 8.3, pp 161–78

Petty, William, *The Political Anatomy of Ireland* (Shannon: Irish University Press, [1672]1970)

Plachecki, Jaroslaw (ed.), *The Irish Polish Society Yearbook, vol. 1* (Dublin: Irish Polish Society, 2014)

———, *The Irish Polish Society Yearbook, vol. 2* (Dubln: Irish Polish Society, 2015)

Portes, Alejandro, 'Immigration theory for a new century: Some problems and opportunities', *The International Migration Review*, 1997, 31.4, pp 799–825

Proudfoot, Lindsay (ed.), *Down History and Society* (Dublin: Geography Publications, 1997)

Putnam, Robert D., '"E pluribus unum": Diversity and community in the twenty-first century', *Scandinavian Political Studies*, 2006, 30.2, pp 137–74

Ravenstein, Ernst George, 'The laws of migration', *Journal of the Royal Statistical Society*, 1885, 52.2, pp 167–235

Reichental, Tomi, *I Was a Boy in Belsen* (Dublin: O'Brien Press, 2011)

Richards, Eric, 'An Australian map of British and Irish literacy in 1841', *Population Studies: A Journal of Demography*, 2010, 53.3, pp 345–59

Robinson, Phillip, *The Plantation of Ulster* (Dublin: Gill and Macmillan, 1994)

Roth, Andreas, *Mr Bewley in Berlin: Aspects of the Career of an Irish Diplomat, 1933–1939* (Dublin: Four Courts Press, 2000)

Ruhs, Martin, *Managing the Immigration and Employment of Non-EU Nationals in Ireland* (Dublin: The Policy Institute, 2005)

Sabenacio Nititham, Diane, *Making Home in Diasporic Communities: Transnational Belonging amongst Filipina Migrants* (London: Routledge, 2017)

Sakaranaho, Tuula, *Religious Freedom, Multiculturalism, Islam: Cross-Reading Finland and Ireland* (Leinden: Brill, 2006)

Scharbrodt, Oliver, Sakaranaho, Tuula, Hussain Kahn, Adil, Shanneik, Yafa and Ibrahim, Vivian, *Muslims in Ireland: Past and Present* (Edinburgh: Edinburgh University Press, 2015)

Shandy, Dianna J., 'Irish babies, African mothers: Rites of passage and rights of citizenship in post-millennial Ireland', *Anthropological Quarterly*, 2008, 81.4, pp 803–31

Simms, J. G., 'John Toland (1670–1722): A Donegal heretic', *Irish Historical Studies*, 1969, 16.63, pp 304–20

Simon, John, 'Ireland from boom to bust: To what extent has the downfall in the Irish economy impacted on Polish migrants living and working in Ireland?' (Leicester: Unpublished PhD thesis, University of Leicester, 2014)

Solomons, Bethel, *One Doctor in his Time* (London: Christopher Johnson, 1956)

Sorohan, Seán, *Irish London during the Troubles* (Dublin: Irish Academic Press, 2012)

———, *Irish London during the Troubles* (Dublin: Irish Academic Press, 2012)

Spencer, A. E. C. W., *Arrangements for the Integration of Irish Immigrants in England and Wales* (Dublin: Irish Manuscripts Commission, 2012)

Stan, Sabina, 'Transnational healthcare practices of Romanian migrants in Ireland: Inequalities of access and privatisation of healthcare services in Europe', *Social Science and Medicine*, 2015, 124.C, pp 346–55

Stan, Sabina and Erne, Roland, 'Explaining Romanian labour migration: From development gaps to development trajectories', *Labour History*, 2014, 55.1, pp 21–46

Stewart, A. T. Q., *The Narrow Ground: The Roots of Conflict in Ulster* (London: Faber and Faber, 1977)

Stradling, R. A., *The Spanish Monarchy and Irish Mercenaries: The Wild Geese in Spain 1618–68* (Dublin: Irish Academic Press, 1994)

Tanner, Marcus, *Ireland's Holy Wars: The Struggle for a Nation's Soul 1500–2000* (New Haven: Yale University Press, 2001)

Thomas, William I. and Znaniecki, Florian, *The Polish Peasant* (Chicago: University of Illinois Press, [1918] 1958)

Thompson, George, *Island Home: The Blasket Heritage* (Dingle: Brandon Press, 1988)

Toland, John, *Reasons for Naturalizing the Jews in Great Britain and Ireland on the Same Foot with all other Nations. Containing also a Defence of Jews against All Vulgar Prejudices in all Countries* (London: J. Roberts, 1714)

Tqaub, David, 'Jewish education in Dublin: Organizational development and conflicts', *Irish Educational Studies*, 2005, 24.2–3, pp 145–57

Ugba, Abel, *Dear Mama* (London: Minerva Press, 1999)

—————, *Shades of Belonging: African Pentecostals in Twenty-First Century Ireland* (Trenton: African World Press, 2009)

Veach, Colin, *Lordship in Four Realms: The Lacy Family 1166–1241* (Manchester: Manchester University Press, 2004)

Wallerstein, Immanuel, *The Modern World System: Capitalist Agriculture and the Origins of the European World Economy in the Sixteenth Century* (New York: Academic Press, 1974)

Walsh, Victor A., '"A fanatic heart": The cause of Irish American nationalism in Pittsburgh during the Gilded Age', *Journal of Social History*, 1981, 15.2, pp 187–204

Walter, Bronwen, 'From "flood" to "trickle": Irish migration to Britain 1987–2006', *Irish Geography*, 2008, 41.2, pp 181–94

Ward, Eilis, '"A big show-off to show what we could do": Ireland and the Hungarian refugee crisis of 1956', *Irish Studies in International Affairs*, 1996, 8, pp 131–41

Whelan, Ruth, 'The Huguenots and the imaginative geography of Ireland: A planned immigration scheme in the 1680s', *Irish Historical Studies*, 2007, 35.140, pp 477–95

White, Elisa Joy 'Forging African diaspora places in Dublin's retro-global spaces', *City*, 2002, 6.2, pp 251–70

White, Jack, *Minority Report: The Protestant Community in the Irish Republic* (Dublin, Gill and Macmillan, 1975)

Wills, Clair, *That Neutral Island: A Cultural History of Ireland During the Second World War* (London: Faber and Faber, 2007)

Wilson, David A., *United Irishmen, United States: Immigrant Radicals in the Early Republic* (Dublin: Four Courts Press, 1998)

Wokeck, Marianne S., *The Beginnings of Mass Migration to North America* (Pennsylvania: Pen State University Press, 1999)

Zinn-Collis, Zoltan, *Final Witness: My Journey from the Holocaust to Ireland* (Meath: Maverick House, 2006)

Index

Bhamjee, Moosajee 241
Biafra 180–1
Black Death 16–17
Blair, Robert 36
Blennerhasset, Thomas 30
Bnei Akivah 132
Board of Guardians 130
Boland, F. H. 143–4
Bonneval, Pasteur 57
Book of Invasions 7
Bosnian Community Project 176
Bosnian refugees *see* refugees, Bosnian
Boston 108, 142
Boyd, Sir Thomas 32
Boyle, Richard 23
Boyne, Battle of the 37
Boyne Valley 9
Brexit 235, 269–70
Briscoe, Ben 127–8
Briscoe, Lily 159–60
Briscoe, Robert 127–8, 159–60, 167
Broder, Rabbi 132
Bronze Age 10
Browne, Vincent 182
Bruce, Edward 16
Bruce, King Robert 24
Buckley, Christine 182–3
Buczkowska, Teresa 229, 237
Burton, Benjamin 72
Butler, Hubert 161
Butler, James, Duke of Ormond 54–5
Butler, James 55
Byrne, Tony 180

Calvinism 54–5, 64
camp followers 45
Canada, Dominion of 110
Canny, Nicholas 20, 22, 258
Carey, Matthew 106
Carlebach, Rabbi Alexander 131
Carlyle, Thomas 103
Carrickfergus 24–6
Casey, Bishop Eamon 147–8
Catholic Educational Council 104
Catholic emancipation 94, 118

Catholic Housing Aid Society (CHAS) 148
Catholic Poor School Committee 104
Catholic Social Welfare Bureau (CSWB) 144–6
Catholics *see also* emigrants, from Ireland; planters; Roman Catholic Church
    American 109
    English 104
Cavan, County 23
Celestine I, Pope 11
Celtic languages 10
Celtic Tiger 149, 152, 200, 205
Celts 10–11
Chachanoff family 124
Chachanoff, Bernard 124, 128
Chamberlin, Robert 44
Champagné, Arthur 58
Champagné, Josias 58
Charles I, King 46
Charles II, King 65, 85–6
Cheroy (de la Cherois) family 58–9
Chichester, Arthur 26, 28–9, 32, 34
Chinese societies 216–17
Chinese Society of Ireland 216
Chinese Students' Association 216
Church of England 65
Church of Ireland 36, 55, 57, 60, 240
Church of Scotland 35
Cistercian foundations 13
Citizen, The 110
citizenship
    British 113
    Irish 189
Citizenship Referendum (2004) 189, 270
civil wars
    American 110
    English 32–3, 46
    Irish 134
Clan na Gael 110
Clandeboye, Lord 36
Clandeboye O'Neills 24–6
Clare (Klarr), George 160–1

Index

Index

Huguenots 4, 41, 65–6, 261–2
  refugees *see* refugees, Huguenot
  settlement in Ireland 54–60
Hundred Years' War 16
Hungarian refugees *see* refugees,
  Hungarian
hunter-gatherers 7–8
Hyman, Louis 118

ice age 7
Ignatiev, Noel 107
imams 242–5
Immigrant Council of Ireland 190
immigrants in Ireland 200–2 *see also*
  African immigrants, Jewish
  immigrants, Muslims in Ireland,
  Polish immigrants
  Bangladeshi 239
  Brazilian 217–20, 262
  British 200
  Chinese 214–17
  EU 200–1
  Filipino 201, 208–11, 262
  Indian 201, 211–14, 239, 262
  Latvian 202–5, 258, 265
  Lithuanian 202–5, 223, 258, 262
  Malaysian 239
  non-EU 200–1
  occupations 200–5, 209–20, 239–40
  Pakistani 239, 246, 251–2
  Romanian 205–8
  South African 240–1
  Syrian 251
  undocumented 149–50
  US 200
immigration
  control 153
  effects of 257–8
  policies 64, 135, 257
  regulation 257–63
Immigration Act (1924) (US) 135
Immigration and Naturalization Service
  (US) (INES) 135
indenture 2–3, 49–51, 61, 90, 106, 262

Independence, American War of 74
Independence, Irish War of 110, 134
internment 161, 168, 170
IRA 134, 261
  Dublin branch 127
Ireland
  colonisation of 14–15
  population of 15, 39, 81, 200
  Ireland Chinese News 216
Irish *see also* emigration
  clergy 42
  colleges 44–5
  diaspora 82–4
  language 139
  refugees, in Spain 42–3 *see also*
    Galicia
  soldiers/regiments: 39–45, 52–3, 61;
    Mountcashel Brigade 53; O'Neill
    44–6; Wild Geese 41, 53
Irish, Protector of the 43
Irish-Americans 83, 105, 109, 135
  newspapers 269
Irish Citizenship Nationality Act (1956)
  190
Irish Council of Imams 245
Irish Emigrant Chaplaincy Scheme 147
Irish Episcopal Commission for
  Emigrants (IECE) 173
Irish Farmers' Gazette 97
Irish Independent 167–8
Irish News 110
Irish Party 111
Irish Polish Society 224–5
Irish Press 143
Irish Race Conference 110
Irish Refugee Council 193
Irish Revolutionary Brotherhood (IRB)
  110
Irish Times 169, 181–2
Iron Age 10
Islam, in Ireland 5, 240 *see also* Muslims
  in Ireland
Islamophobia 5
Islamic Foundation of Ireland 243

Scots Gaelic 24, 35
Scottish
 Calvinists 55
 'Pale' 25
 settlers 3, 19–21, 23, 26, 34 *see also*
  planters
Scottish Covenanter Army 36–7
Second World War 142–4
sectarianism 98–9, 107, 158, 170, 260
segregation 266
Selleck, David 50
servitors 28, 32
settlement in Ireland, early 7–8
Shatter, Alan 191, 220
Shaw, John 27
Sheehan, Jasper 51
Sheehy Skeffington, Hanna 110
Shelter 148
Shier (Scheier, Shire) family 74
Shirley, Sir Thomas 116, 259
shtetls 120–2, 124
sickle cell anaemia 195–6
Sickle Cell Society Ireland 195
Sidney, Sir Henry 19
Sikhs 212–13
Sinti 206
Skinner, Thomas 52
slave(s)/slavery 50, 262 *see also* West
  Indies
 owners 50–1, 90, 107–8
 trade 47
slums
 Manchester 141
 US 106, 108–9
Smith, Sir Thomas 25
Smolenski, Maciej 225
Smyth, William J. 36–7
Social Welfare (Miscellaneous
  Provisions) Act (2004) 228
Solom (Solome), David 117
Solomans, Bethel 129
Somali refugees *see* refugees, Somali
South Carolina 66, 90–1
Southern Citizen 110
Southwell, Edmund 71

Southwell, Sir Thomas 71
Spanish
 army 42
 court, Irish at 42–3
Spanish Armada 41, 44
Spanish Inquisition 113
Spanish Succession, War of 53, 67
Sparling, Christopher 77
Spencer, Anthony 145–7, 151
Spenser, Edmund 71
Stanley, Sir William 41–2
Stephens, James 110
Stewart, A. T. Q. 34, 36
Stewart, Andrew 31
Strongbow (Richard Fitzgilbert) 13
Struntz, Erwin 161
subinfeudation 16
Succession, Act of (1701) 65
Sudanese refugees *see* refugees,
  Sudanese
Sun Emerald Chinese News 216
Sweet, Stephen 70
Switzer, George 77
synagogues, in Ireland 117–20, 123–5,
  127, 131–2

Talbot, Richard 92
Talbot group 92, 99
Tanner, Marcus 33
Thirty Years' War 52, 54, 64
Thompson, Maurice 47
Tintern de Voto 13
Tóibín, Colm 226
Toland, John 113–15
towns, walled 16
Trade, Board of 69
trade, early 10
transportation
  to Australia 100–1
  to New England 50
  to Virginia 50
  to the West Indies 3, 47–50
Trant, Sir Patrick 56
traffickers 2, 185–6, 189, 260, 262–3
Travellers 206